Business Law

CW01590540

putyourknowledgeintopractice

Business Law
J. Scott Slorach and Jason G. Ellis

Foundations for the LPC
George Miles *et al.*

Lawyers' Skills
Julian Webb *et al.*

Criminal Litigation Handbook
Martin Hannibal and Lisa Mountford

Civil Litigation Handbook
Susan Cunningham-Hill and Karen Elder

Property Law Handbook
Robert Abbey and Mark Richards

A Practical Approach to Civil Procedure
Stuart Sime

A Practical Approach to Conveyancing
Robert Abbey and Mark Richards

A Practical Approach to ADR
Susan Blake *et al.*

Commercial Law
Robert Bradgate and Fidelma White

Employment Law
James Holland and Stuart Burnett

Family Law Handbook
Jane Sendall

Writing and Drafting in Legal Practice
Paul Rylance

Interactive online resources
www.oxfordinteract.com

LPC Skills Online
Liz Polding and Jill Cripps

For more vocational law titles please visit www.oxfordtextbooks.co.uk

Business Law

Professor J. Scott Slorach MA (Oxon), Solicitor
Vice President (Education), University of Law;
Visiting Professor at Strathclyde University

Jason G. Ellis MA (Oxon), LLM, Solicitor
Head of Instructional Media Design, University of Law

OXFORD
UNIVERSITY PRESS

OXFORD
UNIVERSITY PRESS

Great Clarendon Street, Oxford, OX2 6DP,
United Kingdom

Oxford University Press is a department of the University of Oxford.
It furthers the University's objective of excellence in research, scholarship, and education by publishing worldwide. Oxford is a registered trade mark of Oxford University Press in the UK and in certain other countries

© J. S. Slorach and J. Ellis 2013

The moral rights of the authors have been asserted

Eighteenth edition 2010
Nineteenth edition 2011
Twentieth edition 2012

Impression: 1

All rights reserved. No part of this publication may be reproduced, stored in a retrieval system, or transmitted, in any form or by any means, without the prior permission in writing of Oxford University Press, or as expressly permitted by law, by licence or under terms agreed with the appropriate reprographics rights organization. Enquiries concerning reproduction outside the scope of the above should be sent to the Rights Department, Oxford University Press, at the address above

You must not circulate this work in any other form
and you must impose this same condition on any acquirer

Public sector information reproduced under Open Government Licence v1.0
(http://www.nationalarchives.gov.uk/doc/open-government-licence/open-government-licence.htm)

Crown Copyright material reproduced with the permission of the
Controller, HMSO (under the terms of the Click Use licence)

Published in the United States of America by Oxford University Press
198 Madison Avenue, New York, NY 10016, United States of America

British Library Cataloguing in Publication Data
Data available

ISBN 978–0–19–968147–1

Printed in Great Britain by
Ashford Colour Press Ltd, Gosport, Hampshire

Links to third party websites are provided by Oxford in good faith and for information only. Oxford disclaims any responsibility for the materials contained in any third party website referenced in this work.

OUTLINE CONTENTS

DETAILED CONTENTS

PREFACE

With some amazement we have now come to the 21st edition of this book. Business Law is a somewhat protean entity but, over the years, we hope that the text has focused on its important elements and has responded appropriately to legislative changes. Feedback that we have received has assisted us in this task and we are grateful to those people who have taken the time to provide the same.

We should also thank the staff at OUP, whose assistance makes this annual process as efficient as possible.

Scott Slorach
Jason Ellis

June 2013

ONLINE RESOURCES TO ACCOMPANY THIS BOOK . . .

Online Resource Centres are developed to provide students and lecturers with ready-to-use teaching and learning resources. They are free of charge, designed to complement the textbook and offer additional materials that are suited to electronic delivery. The Online Resource Centre to accompany this book can be found at:

www.oxfordtextbooks.co.uk/orc/business13_14/

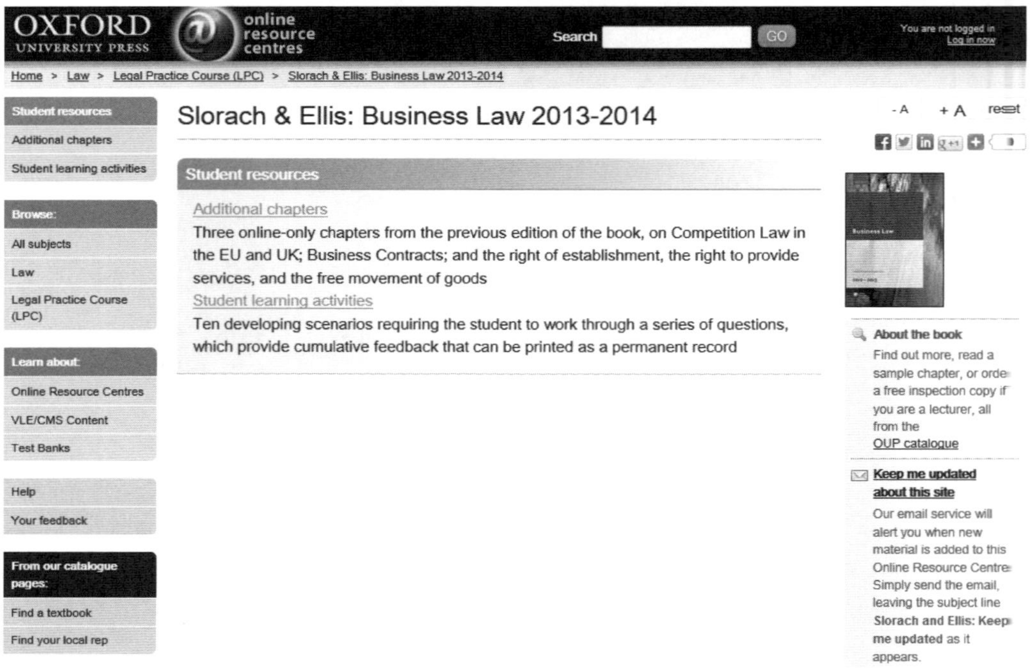

Student resources

Student learning activities

Freely accessible with no need for a password, this book is accompanied by student learning activities designed to help students to test their knowledge and understanding of the practical application of business law. Made up of several developing scenarios, the activities require the student to work through a series of questions which provide cumulative feedback that can be printed out as a permanent record.

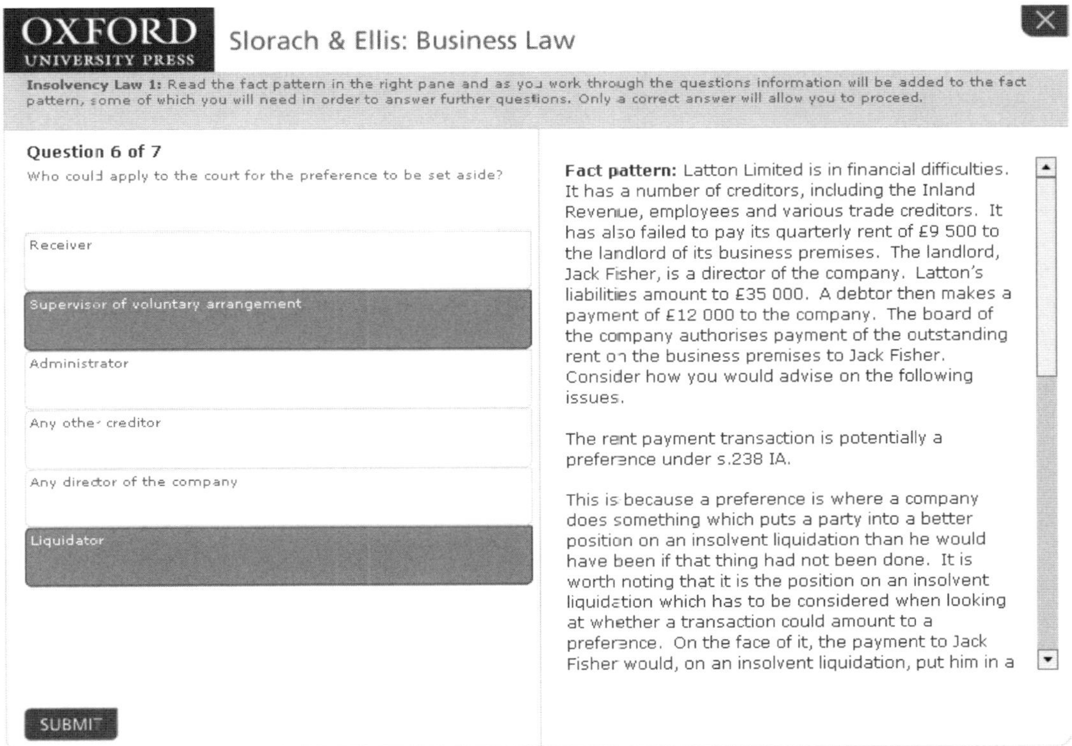

Additional chapters

Three additional chapters from the 2011–2012 edition of the book are provided as a useful reference for students wishing to expand their knowledge of the relevant topics:

- Web chapter A: *Competition law in the European Union and the United Kingdom*
- Web chapter B: *The right of establishment, the right to provide services, and the free movement of goods*
- Web chapter C: *Business contracts—agency or distributorship agreements*

TABLE OF CASES

TABLE OF STATUTES

TABLE OF SECONDARY LEGISLATION

European secondary legislation

Partnerships

1

Characteristics of partnerships

This chapter covers the following topics:

1.1 Introduction

1.1.1 Types of business medium

The established business media in the United Kingdom (UK) are sole traders, partnerships and companies. Sole traders by definition tend to be relatively small concerns, as do partnerships, although a number of professional partnerships overturn this assumption. Companies cover the full spectrum of business sizes.

Chapters 1 to **6** of this book cover partnerships; **Chapters 7** to **16** cover companies. Since 6 April 2001, a new business medium has been in existence, known as the 'limited liability partnership'. This is discussed in **Chapter 29**. As limited liability partnerships are a hybrid of company and partnership law concepts, it is recommended that they are not studied until partnerships and companies have been covered.

In this chapter, we will look at the rules for determining whether a partnership has come into existence as well as the formalities with which businesses which will be run through partnerships must comply. (This book will not consider the rules relating to limited partnerships created under the Limited Partnership Act 1907.)

We will not look separately in this chapter, or in the ones which follow, at sole proprietorships. However, many of the formalities to which partnerships are subject (for example, in relation to the choice of a business name) apply equally to sole proprietors.

1.2 Relevant law

Much of the law relating to partnership is to be found in the Partnership Act (PA) 1890. The Act was mainly declaratory of the law of partnership as it had developed up to 1890. The Act does not provide a complete code of partnership law, and indeed s. 46 specifically provides that: 'The rules of equity and of common law applicable to partnership shall continue in force except so far as they are inconsistent with the express provisions of this Act.'

1.3 Definition of partnership

The definition of a partnership is to be found in s. 1(1) PA 1890 which states: 'Partnership is the relation which subsists between persons carrying on a business in common with a view of profit.' (A registered company is specifically excluded from the definition by s. 1(2).) To satisfy the definition, two or more persons must be carrying on a business. It follows from this that an agreement to run a business in the future does not constitute an immediate partnership, nor does the taking of preliminary steps to enable a business to be run. 'Business' is defined by s. 45 PA 1890 as including 'every trade, occupation or profession'.

Section 2 PA 1890 lays down certain 'rules for determining the existence of a partnership'. These provide that:

(a) Joint or common ownership of property 'does not of itself create a partnership' even where profits from the property are shared (s. 2(1)).

(b) The sharing of *gross* returns does not of itself create a partnership (s. 2(2)). A person is not, therefore, a partner in a business merely because he receives commission on sales which he has introduced.

(c) The receipt of a share of *profits* is prima facie evidence of partnership (s. 2(3)). This topic is dealt with in **2.6**.

It should be noted that a written partnership agreement is *not* a prerequisite for the existence of a partnership. The existence of a partnership is *always* a question of fact.

1.4 Nature of partnership and terminology

A partnership is, in law, a very different type of institution from a company. The most significant difference is that partners have unlimited liability for the debts of the partnership, whereas the liability of shareholders for a company's debts is limited. (The liability of partners to creditors is considered in **Chapter 3**.) Partnerships, unlike companies, are not required to go through any registration process when they are formed and, again unlike companies, they are under no obligation to make their accounts public.

A partnership is not a separate legal entity from its partners (in contrast to companies, which are legally distinct from their shareholders). However, to a limited extent in relation to litigation (see **Chapter 3**) and taxation (see **Chapter 17**), the existence of the partnership is recognised as being independent of the individual members.

As a means of recognising the differences which exist between a partnership and a company, the former is commonly referred to as a *firm*.

1.5 Number of partners

Historically, the maximum number of persons who could be members of a particular partnership was usually 20 (s. 716 Companies Act (CA) 1985). Numerous exemptions to this limit existed, in particular for certain professions, including solicitors and accountants. This rule was abolished completely in late 2002, so that no limits apply in any circumstances.

1.6 Capacity

Generally speaking, any person including a minor (person under 18) is legally capable of forming a partnership with any other person. Companies as well as individuals can, provided their objects clause gives them the power to do so, enter into a partnership with other companies or with individuals. (This book will not consider any rules applicable where one or more companies are members of a partnership.)

1.7 Duration of partnership

Most partnerships are partnerships 'at will'. This means that no particular period is agreed upon as being the time during which the partnership is to last. A partnership at will can be dissolved by notice by any partner unless there is an agreement to the contrary (see ss. 26(1) and 32(c) PA 1890).

A partnership for a fixed term or for a term defined by reference to some event (e.g., the completion of some particular job) is also possible. Such a partnership cannot generally be dissolved by notice.

There may sometimes be difficulty in deciding when a partnership begins. Because of the way a partnership is defined, this is essentially a question of fact. The terms of a partnership agreement as to commencement may be evidence (though not conclusive) of when a partnership begins.

1.8 Partnership name and publicity of information

A partnership is entitled (subject to what is said below) to choose any name which it wishes. There is nothing in partnership law corresponding with the requirement that a company should have a corporate name which is registered with the Registrar of Companies (see **8.6.3.1**).

The law relating to partnership names is contained in Pt 41 of the Companies Act (CA) 2006. The Act permits the free use of certain names and requires approval for others. In addition it contains rules requiring publicity as to the membership of partnerships in certain circumstances.

1.8.1 Automatically permitted names

If the business of a partnership is carried on under a name which consists of the surnames of all the partners, no restrictions apply (s.1192 CA 2006). This is also the case where the name consists of the partners' surnames together with 'permitted additions' and nothing else. The permitted additions are:

(a) the forenames or initials of the partners;

(b) the addition of an 's' to a surname to signify that there is more than one partner with that name; and/or

(c) a statement that the business is being carried on in succession to the business of a former owner.

Where the name of the partnership does not consist solely of the surnames of the partners, or of the surnames of the partners together with permitted additions, then the disclosure requirements of s.1200 CA 2006 will apply and in some cases approval of the name may be required under either s. 1193 or s. 1194.

1.8.2 Disclosure requirements of s.1200 CA 2006

Any partnership which uses a business name (other than one comprising only the surnames of the partners, as explained above) is required to state the name of each partner (together with an address for service in the UK) on every:

(a) business letter;

(b) order for goods or services;

(c) invoice;

(d) receipt; and

(e) written demand for payment of a debt (s. 1202(1) CA 2006).

The same information must also be given by a notice in a prominent position at each place of business of the partnership (s. 1204(1) CA 2006). The same information must also be given (in writing) to anyone with whom the partnership has had business dealings and who asks for the information (s. 1202(2) CA 2006).

The requirement of including names and addresses in letters, etc., does not apply to a partnership with more than 20 members (s. 1203(1) CA 2006) provided that, instead of the partners' names, the letter states the address of the principal place of business and that the names and addresses of the partners can be inspected there (s. 1203(2) CA 2006).

1.8.3 Approval under ss. 1193 and 1194 CA 2006

Section 1193 CA 2006 makes it an offence to carry on business (without the approval of the Secretary of State) under a name which suggests a connection with the Government or a local or public authority. Furthermore, s. 1194 CA 2006 also requires the approval of the Secretary of State for inclusion in a business name of a word specified in regulations made under the Act, namely the Company, Limited Liability Partnership and Business Names (Sensitive Words and Expressions) Regulations 2009 (SI 2009/2615). The list of sensitive names contained in the Regulations is extensive and should be consulted for the complete picture. However, by way of a general understanding of the sort of words regarded as 'sensitive', the following are a few examples:

(a) adjudicator;

(b) banking;

(c) charitable;

(d) dental;

(e) institute;

(f) police;

(g) registered;

(h) royal;

(i) tribunal; and

(j) trust.

Partners who are starting a business and who wish to use a business name should consult the Regulations. If they find that their name includes a word covered by the Regulations they should first write to the government department or other body (as specified in the Regulations) which is to be consulted in relation to that word asking it whether it objects. They should then apply to the Secretary of State for approval stating that they have made such a request and enclosing a copy of any reply that they have received from the government department or other body that they have consulted.

online resource centre

For further resources and online chapters please visit the Online Resource Centre at www.oxfordtextbooks.co.uk/orc/business13_14/.

2

Partnership management and finance

This chapter covers the following topics:

2.1 Introduction

In this chapter we will look at:

(a) the ways a partnership can be managed;

(b) the relationship of the partners to each other and the obligations which partners owe to each other; and

(c) how the finances of a partnership can be handled, both in terms of raising capital to finance the business and distribution of profits the business makes.

2.2 The legal relationship between the partners (s. 24)

Section 24 PA 1890 lays down a number of rules which regulate the relationship between partners and the management of their business. These rules '. . . may be varied by the consent of all the partners, and such consent may be express or inferred from a course of conduct'. The most common way in which the rules in s. 24 are varied is where the partners enter into a partnership agreement (see **Chapter 6**).

If partners do not wish specific provisions of s. 24 to apply to their business then, for certainty, contrary provisions should be incorporated in their partnership agreement.

Several of the subsections of s. 24 deal with the relationship of the partners in respect of the distribution of profits and losses made by the partnership; these subsections are dealt with in **2.6**.

2.2.1 Management of the business

Section 24(5) provides that (subject to contrary agreement, express or implied): 'Every partner may take part in the management of the partnership business.'

If the management structure of a particular partnership is to be different from the equality of partners presumed by s. 24(5), then express agreement should be made. For example, a large partnership may have different grades of partners, major decisions being taken only by the senior grade. Similarly, some partners may be 'sleeping partners', that is, partners who have contributed capital but who do not take an active part in management or decision-making.

2.2.2 Decisions of the partners

Section 24(8) says that (subject to contrary agreement, express or implied):

> Any differences arising as to ordinary matters connected with the partnership business may be decided by a majority of the partners, but no change may be made in the nature of the partnership business without the consent of all the partners.

In most circumstances, therefore, a simple majority of the partners is required to take a decision. If there is an equality of votes a decision has not been taken and the status quo is preserved.

2.2.3 Restrictions on majority rule

There are three main limitations imposed on the ability of the majority of the partners to bind the whole firm. First, partners are under a fiduciary duty to each other and so must exercise their powers for the benefit of the firm as a whole. For example, in *Blisset v Daniel* (1853) 10 Hare 493, a power was given (by the partnership agreement) to the majority of the partners permitting them to expel a partner. The majority exercised this power with a view to obtaining cheaply the expelled partner's shares in the partnership. This was held to be an illegal use of the power to expel as it amounted to a breach of the duty of good faith required of a fiduciary.

Secondly, the majority may not impose their views on the minority without first consulting them (*Const v Harris* (1824) T & R 496). However, there is no requirement that consultation should take the form of a meeting (unless the partnership agreement so provides).

Thirdly, the following provisions of the Partnership Act limit majority rule:

(a) Section 24(8) requires unanimity for a change in the partnership business. This is so that a partner who has decided to invest in one particular type of business will not be forced to invest in something else against his wishes.

(b) Section 24(7) provides that: 'No person may be introduced as a partner without the consent of all the existing partners.' Such a rule is vital to the running of a small partnership where each partner will wish to ensure that his fellow partners cannot force him to go into partnership with someone of whom he disapproves. In a large partnership it may be considered appropriate that s. 24(7) should not apply (so that, for example, the senior partners may be given power to decide who to take on as junior partners and who to promote to senior partnership), in which case the partnership agreement must exclude the requirement of unanimity in this respect.

(c) Unanimity is required by s. 19 for an alteration to the partnership agreement. The agreement of the partners to an alteration can be inferred from a course of dealings.

(d) Section 25 prevents expulsion of a partner by a majority of the partners unless all the partners have *expressly* agreed to such a power being conferred.

2.2.4 Other provisions

Other provisions of s. 24 which affect the relationship between the partners are as follows:

(a) Section 24(2) gives a partner a right to be indemnified by the firm in respect of payments made and personal liabilities incurred 'in the ordinary and proper conduct of the business of the firm or in or about anything necessarily done for the preservation of the business or property of the firm'.

(b) Section 24(9) gives all the partners a right to inspect and copy the partnership accounts.

2.3 The duty of good faith

2.3.1 Equitable provisions

The contract of partnership is a contract *uberrimae fidei* (of the utmost good faith), so that a partner is required to disclose all relevant information in his possession to his partners. If he fails to do so his partners may set aside transactions which they have entered into with him as a result of the non-disclosure.

Similarly, a partner owes a fiduciary duty to his fellow partners; that is, he owes the duty of good faith to his partners in his dealings with them which a trustee owes to a beneficiary.

2.3.2 Statutory provisions

The requirement of good faith in dealings between partners is of general application, but three particular aspects of the duty are dealt with in ss. 28–30 PA 1890.

2.3.2.1 Duty to disclose information

Section 28 provides that: 'Partners are bound to render true accounts and full information of all things affecting the partnership to any partner or his legal representative.' This is really just a formulation in statutory language of the duty of disclosure imposed by equity. A good illustration of the working of the rule is given by *Law v Law* [1905] 1 Ch 140. In that case one partner offered to buy the share of another at a price which seemed fair to the vendor who was not actively engaged in running the business. The purchaser, however, knew of facts which made the vendor's share more valuable than the vendor realised. When the vendor discovered this it was held that he was entitled to rescind the contract of sale on the ground of non-disclosure.

2.3.2.2 Duty to account for secret profits

Section 29 states that:

> (1) Every partner must account to the firm for any benefit derived by him without the consent of the other partners from any transaction concerning the partnership, or from any use by him of the partnership property, name or business connection.
>
> (2) This section applies also to transactions undertaken after a partnership has been dissolved by the death of a partner, and before the affairs thereof have been completely wound up, either by any surviving partner or by the representative of the deceased partner.

This section imposes similar restrictions and duties on partners as apply to company directors (see **9.10**). Any profit made in breach of the section is held on trust for the benefit of the partnership as a whole. The rule applies to transactions entered into by a partner where the opportunity came to him as a result of the partnership, to commissions received on contracts introduced to the partnership, to sales of property to the partnership by a partner and to profits derived from sales of partnership property. A partner may retain any such profit if his partners consent following full disclosure of the circumstances.

2.3.2.3 Duty to account for profits from competing business

Section 30 PA 1890 provides that:

> If a partner, without the consent of the other partners, carries on any business of the same nature as and competing with that of the firm, he must account for and pay over to the firm all profits made by him in that business.

The provisions of s. 30 are quite narrow. In order to succeed under this section the partners must show that the businesses are of the same nature and that they are in fact competing for the same customers. Thus in *Aas v Benham* [1891] 2 Ch 244, a partner in a firm of shipbrokers was held not to be accountable for profits he had made from shipbuilding. However, in

Glassington v Thwaites (1823) 1 Sim & St 124, a partner in a morning newspaper who set up an evening newspaper was held to be accountable. It should be noted that there is overlap between s. 30 and s. 29(1) (see **2.3.2.2** above)—a partner may be held accountable because he is competing with his partners or because he is using 'the partnership property name or business connection'; often a partner who sets up a new business will be doing both these things.

2.3.2.4 Preventing a partner from setting up a non-competing business

A partner who sets up a non-competing business and who does not use the partnership property, name or business connection is not liable to his partners in any way under the Act. Many partnership agreements, therefore, provide that the partners are to devote their whole time to the partnership and specify that the partners are not to start any other businesses. With such an agreement the partners may be able to obtain an injunction, damages or dissolution of the partnership against the partner who sets up a new business, even though it does not compete with the firm's business. They will not, however, have any right to make him contribute his profits in the other business to the partnership.

2.4 The partnership's finances

2.4.1 Sources of finance

The sources of finance for a partnership are basically the same as those available to any business. A partnership will need assets and cash in order to run its business. Money (or in some cases assets) may be contributed in the form of a permanent investment by the partners or it may be borrowed from either the partners or outside sources. Once the business of the partnership has started further finance may also be provided by retention of profits.

2.4.2 Partners' capital

The permanent investment of a partner is described as his 'capital'. The capital of a partner may be contributed by him in the form of cash or property (including, for example, business premises or the goodwill of an existing business). The term 'capital' is somewhat ambiguous. It refers to the actual cash or other assets contributed to the partnership by a partner and the indebtedness of the partnership as a whole to the partner resulting from this investment. A partner's capital in this latter sense should be contrasted with other debts which the firm owes to the partner, as repayment of the capital cannot normally be claimed from the firm until dissolution (see **5.2.2.3**). Other indebtedness to a partner (for example, a loan) may be repaid before dissolution.

2.5 The distinction between a partner and a lender

As we saw in **Chapter 1**, the essential nature of a partnership is that two or more people are sharing profits of a business. A person who merely lends to a partnership is not a partner. The distinction between a partner and a lender is extremely important as a partner bears unlimited liability for the debts of the partnership whereas the lender only stands to lose the money invested if the business fails (if he has taken security for his loan, his risk of losing even that much may be small). However, if a business is successful a partner stands to earn a great deal of profit whereas a lender will receive only interest on his loan.

Many investors would like to have the best of both worlds, i.e., limited liability and a share of profits. This can be achieved by investing in a company. However, in the case of partnerships, s. 2(3) PA 1890 effectively restricts this type of investment. It provides that: 'The receipt by a person of a share of profits . . . is prima facie evidence that he is a partner . . . but does not of itself make him a partner . . . '. The subsection then sets out some particular rules which provide that:

(a) A person does not become a partner merely because a debt or other liquidated sum is paid to him by instalments out of profits.

(b) A servant or agent does not become a partner merely because his remuneration varies with profits.

(c) A widow or child of a partner is not a partner merely because a proportion of profits is paid to that person as an annuity.

(d) A lender whose interest varies with profits is not automatically a partner if the contract is in writing and signed by all the parties.

(e) A vendor who receives payment for his business in the form of an annuity varying with profits is not automatically a partner.

Sharing of profits is only prima facie evidence of partnership and particular types of contract are covered by the five rules mentioned above. However, there remains a risk that anyone who receives a share of profits *may* be held to be a partner and therefore personally liable for debts. Anyone entering into such an arrangement who does not wish to take on the risk of unlimited liability should take steps to ensure that he or she does not become a partner, e.g., by avoiding any suggestion that he has a right to take part in management and by having a written agreement setting out the terms of his involvement with the firm.

2.6 Division of profits and sharing of losses between partners

Section 24 PA 1890 lays down a number of rules as to division of profits. These rules may be varied by an express or implied agreement of the partners, and for the avoidance of doubt it is preferable to state in a partnership agreement how both profits and losses are to be shared even if the agreement follows some or all of the statutory presumptions. Section 24 deals with the division of both income and capital profits.

2.6.1 Share of profits and losses (s. 24(1))

Section 24(1) states:

> All the partners are entitled to share equally in the capital and profits of the business, and must contribute equally towards the losses whether of capital or otherwise sustained by the firm.

This rule may be broken down into three parts which will be examined in turn.

2.6.1.1 Sharing of capital

The first part of the rule states that 'all the partners are entitled to share equally in the capital'. On the face of it this means that when a partner leaves the firm or when the firm is dissolved he is entitled to take out a part of the capital corresponding with the total amount of capital divided by the number of partners. However, in practice this is unlikely to be so. All the rules in s. 24 are subject to contrary agreement express or implied. Where the partners have contributed unequally to the capital, there is an *implied* agreement that they are entitled to withdraw capital unequally. For example, if A contributes £10,000, B £20,000, and C £30,000, those are the sums which each can withdraw on leaving in the absence of any express agreement to the contrary.

2.6.1.2 Sharing of profits

The second part of the rule in s. 24(1) states that 'all the partners are entitled to share equally in the profits of the business'. The provision of capital in unequal shares *does not* give rise to the implication that this part of the rule has been displaced. Thus in the example given above if the profits of the firm were £9,000, A, B, and C would each be entitled to £3,000. If a partner is to receive more than an equal share of profits because of his capital contribution or the work he does, this must be specifically agreed to and should be expressly stated in the partnership agreement.

The rule as to share of profits applies to capital as well as income profits. 'Capital profits' is the term for amounts remaining following the payment of all creditors and repayment of capital contributions to partners on the dissolution of a partnership. When the firm in our example is dissolved, any capital profit will be shared equally even though the capital was not contributed equally. Thus after A has received £10,000, B £20,000, and C £30,000, any surplus will be divided equally. The partners are, of course, free to agree to the contrary. It may well be decided that capital profits should be divided in the same ratio as capital was provided. The ratio in which capital profits are divided (sometimes called the 'asset surplus ratio') is often different from the income profit-sharing ratio.

2.6.1.3 Sharing of losses

The third part of the rule in s. 24(1) states that losses of capital and income are prima facie to be shared equally. However, if the partners share profits unequally (because of an express or implied agreement to do so), then s. 44 PA 1890 says that losses will also be shared unequally unless there is an agreement to the contrary.

2.6.2 Interest on capital

Section 24(4) provides that: 'A partner is not entitled . . . to interest on capital.' Where capital is contributed unequally, it may be considered appropriate to make provision in the partnership agreement for interest on capital to compensate the partner who has contributed more. The agreement should specify the rate of interest or the method by which the rate is to be determined. Interest on capital is *not* a deductible expense of the business in determining its net profits (see **17.5.2**). It is merely a preferential appropriation of profits. This means that once the net profit of the partnership has been ascertained the partners' first entitlement will be to interest and then the remaining net profit will be allocated in accordance with the agreed profit-sharing ratio.

2.6.3 Interest on loans

In the absence of contrary agreement a loan by a partner to the partnership carries only 5% interest (s. 24(3)). It should be noted that this rate of interest is paid only on 'actual payments or advances'. Interest is not payable under s. 24(3) on a share of profits which is simply left in the business. The partners are, of course, free to agree that interest will be paid on undrawn profits if they wish.

2.6.4 Remuneration of partners

Section 24(6) provides that: 'No partner shall be entitled to remuneration for acting in the partnership business.' In many partnerships the division of work between the partners is unequal, and therefore it will have to be expressly agreed that some of the partners be paid a salary to compensate them for the extra work which they have done. As with interest on capital, a salary payable to a partner is *not* a deductible expense but is merely a preferential appropriation of profit.

EXAMPLE In a partnership with three members it might be agreed that:

(a) the profit-sharing ratio will be D 20%, E 40%, F 40%;

(b) interest on capital will be paid at a rate of 10% p.a. (D's capital is £10,000, E's £20,000, and F's £30,000); and

(c) D is to have a salary of £20,000 p.a.

If profits of £100,000 are made they will be divided as follows:

		£	£
Profit			100,000
Interest:	D	1,000	
	E	2,000	
	F	3,000	
			6,000
Salary:	D		20,000
Share of profits:	D (20%)	14,800	
	E (40%)	29,600	
	F (40%)	29,600	
			74,000
			100,000

In some partnerships (particularly professional partnerships) there may be relatively junior partners who are entitled to a salary to the exclusion of any other share of profits. At first sight it is hard to see how such 'salaried partners' can be regarded as partners at all, as partnership requires that the partners are 'carrying on business in common with a view of profit' (s. 1(1) PA 1890). Nevertheless, in *Stekel v Ellice* [1973] 1 WLR 191, it was held that a salaried partner could be, in law, a full partner with all the rights and duties which that entails.

2.6.5 Drawings

The amount to which a partner is entitled from the profits in a firm (as salary and interest, if agreed to, and share of profits) will not be known until the profit and loss account has been drawn up after the end of the partnership's financial year. The partnership agreement will, therefore, usually provide that a partner is to have the right to take a specified amount of money on account of his expected profits during the course of the year. Sums taken on account in this way are called 'drawings'. If at the end of the year the partner has taken less than he was entitled to he can draw the balance; if he has taken more than it turns out he was entitled to then the partnership agreement will probably require him to pay back the excess and/or pay interest on it. The partnership agreement may provide that each partner is to leave undrawn in the business a proportion of his entitlement to profit. This is because businesses normally need to retain funds to meet increased costs of trading and to fund any future expansion.

2.7 Payment of interest

A payment of interest by a partnership to a creditor will usually be a business expense. This is because the interest payment will satisfy the test for deduction of expenses, that is, that the payment is incurred 'wholly and exclusively for the purposes of the trade'. (As mentioned above, payment of interest on capital to a partner is *not* a business expense, it is an allocation of profits to the partner.)

Where a partnership *receives* interest this is treated as income of the partners.

2.8 Partnership property

2.8.1 Introduction

There is a major reason why it may be important to decide what property is and what is not partnership property. When the firm is dissolved each partner is entitled to retain any property which is his own personal property; property which is partnership property is used first to pay creditors of the firm and then any surplus is distributed among the partners in accordance with the terms of the partnership agreement (equally in the absence of contrary agreement). This is so, once it is decided that an asset is partnership property, even though the asset was introduced by one particular partner and the asset has risen in value thus creating a capital profit for the partnership.

2.8.2 Definition

Partnership property is partly defined by s. 20(1) PA 1890 as:

> All property and rights and interests in property originally brought into the partnership stock or acquired, whether by purchase or otherwise, on account of the firm, or for the purposes and in the course of the partnership business . . .

Section 21 deals with a slightly different situation and states:

> Unless the contrary intention appears, property bought with money belonging to the firm is deemed to have been bought on account of the firm.

2.8.3 The test

Whether property is partnership property or remains the separate property of a partner depends on the intention of the partners, express or implied. Property is not partnership property merely because it is used by the firm. The court does not readily assume, therefore, that property introduced by a partner thereby becomes partnership property.

This is illustrated by the leading case of *Miles v Clarke* [1953] 1 All ER 779. Clarke carried on a photographic business in premises of which he owned the lease. He and Miles went into partnership and for a time the business was successful. However, eventually a petition for dissolution was presented as the partners were unable to agree. The question arose as to which assets were partnership property and which belonged to the partners individually. Harman J held that in the absence of express agreement he would hold property to be partnership property to the extent necessary to give business efficacy to the agreement. Therefore, the lease of the business premises belonged on dissolution to Clarke alone, each partner was entitled to his own business connections which he had brought into the firm, and only the stock-in-trade (unused films, chemicals, etc.) could be regarded as partnership property.

online resource centre

For further resources and online chapters please visit the Online Resource Centre at www.oxfordtextbooks.co.uk/orc/business13_14/.

3 Liability of partners to outsiders

This chapter covers the following topics:

3.1 Introduction

In the course of carrying on the partnership's business, the partners will incur debts and other obligations. In this chapter, we look at the nature of the partners' liabilities in these circumstances as well as the extent to which an individual partner can bind the partnership as a whole. We will then go on to look at whether it is possible for individuals who are not partners at the time the debt or obligation was incurred (whether because they have been held out as partners or because they are admitted to the partnership subsequently) to be liable for that debt or obligation.

3.2 Nature of liability

Partners are liable for the debts and obligations of the partnership without limit (s. 9 PA 1890). Their liability is joint in the case of contractual obligations and joint and several in the case of tortious obligations (see **3.6**). The significance of this distinction was much reduced by the Civil Liability (Contribution) Act 1978 which allows proceedings to be brought successively against persons jointly liable despite an earlier judgment against others.

Where a partnership is unable to pay its debts out of partnership property, the creditor is entitled to obtain payment from the private estates of the partners. Special rules apply in such cases, so as to attempt to do justice both to the creditors of the firm and to the creditors of the individual partners. It is not our intention to deal with these rules in detail. However, they may be summarised as follows:

(a) In the first instance, the partnership property is used to pay partnership creditors in priority to private creditors and the private property of each partner is used to pay his private creditors in priority to partnership creditors.

(b) If the private creditors of a particular partner are paid in full from private property, then partnership creditors may resort to the balance of that partner's private property.

(c) If the partnership creditors are paid in full from partnership property then the private creditors of a partner may resort to the balance of his share of the partnership assets.

3.3 Partnership and agency

3.3.1 Introduction

The relationship between partnership law and agency is very close. Indeed, most of the rules regulating the relationship between a partnership and the outside world can be explained purely in terms of particular applications of agency principles.

3.3.2 Types of authority of a partner

The partnership as a whole is bound by a partner acting within the scope of his authority. The authority of a partner may arise in three ways:

(a) First, the authority of the partners (or of a particular partner) may be specifically agreed upon by the partners—authority of this type is called 'express actual' authority.

(b) Secondly, authority may be implied either from a course of dealings between the partners (which amounts to an actual agreement) or because the authority is a natural consequence of an authority actually given to the partner—this is normally called 'implied actual' authority.

(c) Thirdly, authority may arise from the fact that a person dealing with a partner is, in certain circumstances, entitled to assume that the partner has authority to bind the firm—this type of authority is generally called 'apparent' or 'ostensible' authority, although terminology in agency law is far from consistent.

3.3.3 Express and implied actual authority

The scope of express and implied actual authority depends on the agreement between the parties. The partnership agreement may specify what powers the partners individually are to have and may specify that some are to have greater powers than others. The extent of actual authority, whether express or implied, is not, in practical terms, of great significance to a person dealing with a partner. This is because, whether or not there is actual authority, he will be able to rely on apparent authority in most circumstances in relation to most normal types of transaction. The outsider need only rely on actual authority where the partner has done something which the law does not consider to be within the apparent authority of a partner.

A partnership is bound by decisions and actions of its employees acting within the scope of their authority. An outsider seeking to rely on a decision or action of an employee would have to show that the employee had actual authority, had been held out (by the partners) as having actual authority or had been held out (by the partners) to be a partner. An individual partner cannot delegate authority to the employees (this is an application of the well-known maxim of agency law *delegatus non potest delegare*).

The Partnership Act 1890 has little to say about a partner's actual authority. However, s. 6 recognises that the firm is bound by 'the acts or instruments' entered into with the authority of the firm.

3.3.4 Apparent authority

3.3.4.1 General principles

The scope of apparent (or ostensible) authority is not always easy to establish or describe. Such authority is sometimes said to result from a type of estoppel whereby the principal (in this case the partnership as a whole) represents, by words or conduct, that the agent (that is the partner who is negotiating with the outsider) has authority to bind the firm. Once such a representation is made and acted upon by the outsider the partnership cannot deny the authority of the individual partner to bind the firm. Alternatively, apparent authority may be said to arise simply from the fact that the partner who is negotiating *appears* to have authority to bind the firm and it is, therefore, reasonable for the outsider to assume such authority.

In fact nothing really turns on this distinction, since application of either test is likely to produce the same result in most circumstances.

3.3.4.2 Section 5 PA 1890

It is clear that the liability of the firm may result from the actual holding out of an agent (not necessarily a partner) as having a particular authority. However, in most cases the outsider seeks to rely on an apparent authority resulting from the fact that a person is known to be a partner in a firm. The outsider is then entitled to assume that the partner has the usual authority of a partner to bind his firm. This principle is laid down in s. 5 PA 1890 which says:

> Every partner is an agent for the firm and his other partners for the purpose of the business of the partnership; and the acts of every partner who does any act for carrying on in the usual way the business of the kind carried on by the firm of which he is a member bind the firm and his partners, unless the partner so acting has in fact no authority to act for the firm in the particular matter, and the person with whom he is dealing either knows that he has no authority, or does not know or believe him to be a partner.

The easiest way to understand the scope of the section (and thus of that part of the partner's authority which derives from the usual authority given to partners generally), is to examine each of the qualifications on a partner's authority which the section recognises.

(a) *Partner can only bind the firm 'for the purposes of the business of the partnership'*

The first qualification is that the partner can only bind the firm 'for the purposes of the business of the partnership'. The section does not say, therefore, that *anything* which a partner does binds the firm. The partnership agreement may be of some assistance in deciding what is the scope of the partnership business. However, it is not conclusive. In *Mercantile Credit Co Ltd v Garrod* [1962] 3 All ER 1103, Mocatta J held that the test as to whether a type of business is within the scope of the partnership depends on what is apparent to the outside world in general. Consequently a sleeping partner in a garage business whose agreement specifically excluded dealing in cars was held liable on a contract for the sale of a car as this was within the scope of what outsiders would expect the business to include.

(b) *Partner must do act 'for carrying on in the usual way the business of the firm'*

The second qualification in s. 5 is that the partnership is only bound if a partner does an act 'for carrying on in the usual way the business of the firm'. This restriction excludes the liability of the firm where the transaction is for the purposes of the business but is itself of an unusual type. For example, in *Niemann v Niemann* (1890) 43 ChD 198, a debt was owed to a partnership; one of the partners intended to accept payment of the debt in the form of shares in a company. This was held not to be binding on the other partner in the absence of a specific agreement. Similarly, *Powell v Brodhurst* [1901] 2 Ch 160 decided that a partner does not have ostensible authority to accept payment of a debt due to another partner personally rather than to the firm.

(c) *No actual authority and outsider knows this or does not know or believe that person is a partner*

The third qualification to s. 5 is that the firm is not bound if the partner has no actual authority and the outsider either knows this or does not know or believe the person with whom he is dealing to be a partner. Clearly in such cases the firm is not bound whether one takes the view that apparent authority depends on estoppel or on appearance of authority. The outsider cannot say that he has relied on any misrepresentation nor can he claim that there appeared to be authority when he knows this to be untrue or does not think he is dealing with an agent at all.

A partner who makes a contract with an outsider without authority will be personally liable to the outsider for breach of warranty of authority where the partnership as a whole is not made liable on the contract. However, where a contract made without authority is ratified by the partnership, it becomes binding on them as well as on the outsider.

Section 8 PA 1890 provides that an outsider is not prejudiced by any restriction placed on the powers of a partner unless he has notice of it.

3.3.5 Examples of apparent authority

The question of what apparent authority a partner has in a particular case is determined by the application of s. 5 to that particular case. This is at least in part a question of fact. However, over the years the courts have decided upon examples of powers which will be assumed to be covered by apparent authority in the case of all partners in the absence of some special circumstance. The court has also recognised certain powers which it will be assumed all partners in a trading partnership have in the absence of some special circumstance. The powers of partners in a trading partnership are more extensive than the powers of partners in general. This is because the court recognises the need of the partners and the persons dealing with them to rely on normal trading practices.

Examples of powers assumed to be available to partners generally include:

(a) power to buy and sell goods (not just stock) used in the business;
(b) power to hire employees;
(c) power to receive payment of debts due to the partnership;
(d) power to pay debts owed by the partnership including a power to draw cheques for this purpose;
(e) power to engage a solicitor to represent the firm.

A partner in a trading partnership will be assumed to have all the above powers and also:

(a) power to grant security for borrowings (this does not, however, include a power to create a legal mortgage);
(b) a wider power than is given to a non-trading partner to deal with cheques and bills of exchange.

3.4 Persons held out as partners

So far we have only considered the liability of actual partners to outsiders. A person who holds himself out as a partner or who 'suffers himself to be represented as a partner' is liable to anyone who 'on the faith of such representation' gives credit to the firm as if he were a partner (s. 14 PA 1890). The commonest example of the application of this rule is where a person allows his name to be used by the partnership (e.g., on notepaper) after he has ceased to be a partner (as to which, see **5.3.3**).

A person cannot be held liable under s. 14 unless he has in some way contributed to the mistake made by the person giving credit to the firm, for example by allowing his name to be given as a partner. It is not, however, necessary that he himself should have done anything to inform the person giving credit.

Section 14 only applies where credit is given to the firm. This is construed widely so that, for example, the apparent partner is liable where goods are delivered, as well as where cash is lent, to the firm.

3.5 Liability of new partners

Section 17(1) PA 1890 provides that 'a person who is admitted as a partner into an existing firm does not thereby become liable to the creditors of the firm for anything done before he became a partner'. This provision ensures that an incoming partner is not liable to the existing creditors of the firm merely because he has become a partner.

As between himself and the existing partners the incoming partner may agree to pay a share of debts owed to existing creditors. This does not make him liable to the existing creditors as they are not privy to the contract. The new partner may become liable to existing creditors by a novation (that is, a tripartite contract between the old partners, the new partner and an outsider whereby the existing contract between the old partners and the outsider is discharged and replaced by a contract between the new firm, including the new partner, and the outsider). However, this will not be a regular occurrence.

3.6 Partners' liability in tort

A partner who himself commits a tort is liable according to general principles of the law of tort. The liability of the firm as a whole is governed by s. 10 PA 1890:

> Where, by any wrongful act or omission of any partner acting in the ordinary course of the business of the firm, or with the authority of his co-partners, loss or injury is caused to any person . . . the firm is liable . . . to the same extent as the partner so acting or omitting to act.

It should be noted that the firm (as opposed to the actual tortfeasor) is only liable if either the commission of the tort was authorised by the partners or was committed 'in the ordinary course of business'. A partnership is also liable to the same extent as other employers (under common-law principles of vicarious liability) for torts committed by its employees.

3.7 Suing or being sued

A partnership is not a separate legal entity. Nevertheless, the partners may sue or be sued in the firm's name under Ord. 81 of the Rules of the Supreme Court (now contained in Sch. 1 to the Civil Procedure Rules). All the partners at the date when the cause of action accrued are then parties to the action. Where an action is brought against a partnership in the firm's name the writ may be served on any partner, on any person having control or management of the business at the principal place of business or by post to the principal place of business.

A person who has a judgment against a partner for the partner's personal liability may enforce that judgment against the partner's share of partnership property by means of a charging order (s. 23(2) PA 1890). He may not enforce such a judgment against the partnership property by means of execution or garnishee proceedings (s. 23(1)). Where a charging order is made the other partners may discharge it by paying off the judgment debt; if a sale of the property is ordered, they may purchase it. A charging order gives the other partners a right to dissolve the partnership if they wish (s. 33(2)).

online resource centre

For further resources and online chapters please visit the Online Resource Centre at www.oxfordtextbooks.co.uk/orc/business13_14/.

4 Partnership disputes

This chapter covers the following topics:

4.1 Introduction

We saw in **Chapter 2** that a decision of the majority of the partners on an 'ordinary matter' is binding on the minority. The wishes of the majority prevail over those of the minority who object. However, partnership law provides some machinery for protecting the partner who is aggrieved by what the other partners have done.

In this chapter we will look at the remedies available to a partner, which include dissolution of the partnership, appointment of a receiver, and remedies available under the terms of the partnership agreement itself.

4.2 Dissolution by the court

Dissolution of a partnership may occur automatically (e.g., on the death of a partner) by notice (e.g., any partner can give notice dissolving a partnership at will) or by court order (e.g., in the case of permanent incapacity of a partner). The various circumstances in which dissolution takes place will be considered in **Chapter 5**. In this chapter we intend to consider only those types of dissolution which provide a remedy to a partner against his co-partners under s. 35(c), (d), or (f) PA 1890.

4.2.1 Section 35(c): conduct prejudicial to the business

Section 35(c) provides that a partner may apply to the court for dissolution:

> when a partner, other than the partner suing, has been guilty of such conduct as, in the opinion of the court, regard being had to the nature of the business, is calculated to prejudicially affect the carrying on of the business.

This paragraph may be relied upon even though the prejudicial conduct has nothing directly to do with the partnership. A conviction for dishonesty, for example, would be likely to be regarded as prejudicial conduct in the case of many professional partnerships even though the dishonesty did not relate to the practice as such. The test is an objective one so that it need not be shown that the guilty partner *intended* to affect the business (this is so despite the use of the word 'calculated' in s. 35(c)).

4.2.2 Section 35(d): breach of partnership agreement

Section 35(d) provides that a partner may apply to the court for dissolution:

> when a partner, other than the partner suing, wilfully or persistently commits a breach of the partnership agreement, or otherwise so conducts himself in matters relating to the partnership business that it is not reasonably practicable for the other partner or partners to carry on business in partnership with him.

This paragraph contemplates that the trust between partners has broken down. If this breakdown results from persistent breaches of the partnership agreement or conduct in relation to the business (although not conduct in relation to other matters), then the court can order dissolution. Many of the cases under this paragraph have revolved around financial irregularities (such as failure to account for money received on behalf of the partnership or payment of private debts from partnership money).

4.2.3 Section 35(f): just and equitable dissolution

Section 35(f) provides that a partner may apply to the court for dissolution 'whenever in any case circumstances have arisen which in the opinion of the court render it just and equitable that the partnership be dissolved'. This provision is the equivalent of s. 122(1)(g) Insolvency Act 1986, which is in essentially similar terms but applies only to companies. The cases decided under s. 122(1)(g) (and its predecessors) are relevant also to s. 35(f), especially where the company which was the subject of the petition was intended to be run as if it were a partnership. Deadlock or other irreconcilable differences between partners are the most likely grounds on which a successful petition could be based. Exclusion of a partner from management (contrary to s. 24(5)) would also be grounds for petition, although this case would also probably be covered by s. 35(d).

4.3 Appointment of a receiver

The court has power to appoint a receiver to run the business of a partnership for the protection of the partners. The receiver's duty is to carry on the business of the partnership for the benefit of the partners generally, not to realise a security, so that his position is quite different from that of a company receiver appointed by a debenture-holder. There is comparatively little authority as to when a receiver will be appointed, but it does seem to be an exceptional step and the court is particularly reluctant to make an appointment in the case of a professional partnership (*Floydd v Cheney* [1970] 2 WLR 314).

4.4 Arbitration

Disputes may be solved by arbitration if the partners agree to this. It is common to make provision for arbitration in the partnership agreement. As in other types of contract an arbitration clause cannot effectively oust the jurisdiction of the court altogether. A clause drawn widely in an attempt to oust the jurisdiction of the court entirely will be held to be void. If an action is commenced despite the presence of an arbitration clause the court has a discretion to stay the proceedings to enable the arbitration to take place.

The court action can continue without there being any question of a stay when, as a matter of construction, the court decides that the dispute which has arisen is not covered by the arbitration clause in the partnership agreement. The clause should expressly state that disputes arising during dissolution may be referred to arbitration and that the clause is binding on assignees of partners.

4.5 Expulsion of a partner

4.5.1 Introduction

We have seen in this chapter that it is possible for a partnership to be dissolved by the court as a way of giving the plaintiff partner a remedy against his co-partners. However, the circumstances of the dispute within the partnership may be such that some partners would prefer to get rid of one or more of their co-partners without fully dissolving the partnership.

4.5.2 Requirement for provision in partnership agreement

This is only possible if an appropriate provision is included in the partnership agreement, as s. 25 PA 1890 provides that: 'No majority of the partners can expel any partner unless a power to do so has been confirmed by express agreement between the partners.' The question as to whether expulsion should be provided for, and if so by what majority, is one of the issues which must be considered when a partnership agreement is being drafted (see **Chapter 6**).

4.5.3 Content of expulsion clause

Where an expulsion clause is included in the agreement it will normally state that specific activities (such as fraud) or breaches of certain terms of the partnership agreement (such as that requiring a partner not to compete with the partnership or to devote the whole of his time to the business) will justify expulsion. Bankruptcy of a partner is a ground for the automatic dissolution of the whole partnership (s. 33(2) PA 1890), but in order to avoid the consequences of dissolution it is common for the partnership agreement to provide that a bankruptcy will not cause dissolution, rather that it will justify expulsion.

An expulsion clause will generally deal with the manner in which the expulsion is to be effected. It is normal to provide that written notice must be given to the offending partner and that it is to have immediate effect. The partnership agreement will normally distinguish expulsion and retirement in respect of financial arrangements. Thus, if annuities are to be paid the agreement would normally provide that an expelled partner should forfeit his rights.

4.5.4 Exercise of expulsion clause

If an expulsion clause is included in the partnership agreement, then the power must be exercised strictly in accordance with the agreement and in a bona fide manner and for the benefit of the partnership as a whole (*Blisset v Daniel* (1853) 10 Hare 493).

online resource centre

For further resources and online chapters please visit the Online Resource Centre at www.oxfordtextbooks.co.uk/orc/business13_14/.

5

Termination of and retirement from a partnership

This chapter covers the following topics:

5.1 Introduction

An individual may cease to be a partner on the happening of one of the following events:

(a) the dissolution of the partnership;
(b) his retirement; or
(c) expulsion from the partnership.

If the partnership is dissolved, the partnership will come to an end and its assets and business dealt with accordingly. The situation is different on the retirement or expulsion of a partner. Here, the former partners can carry on the business, albeit through the medium of a newly constituted partnership.

In this chapter, we will consider the legal consequences of the occurrence of these events.

The taxation consequences of the events covered in this chapter will be considered in **Chapters 22** and **23**.

5.2 Dissolution of partnership

If an event occurs which causes a partnership to be dissolved, the partnership relationship ceases and any partner may demand that the assets of the business are realised. Under the Partnership Act 1890 certain events result in automatic dissolution unless the partnership agreement provides otherwise. Dissolution is such an extreme step that it is common for partners to provide expressly in their partnership agreement that dissolution is *not* to occur automatically on the occurrence of the events specified in the Partnership Act.

5.2.1 The methods of dissolving a partnership

5.2.1.1 Dissolution by notice

Under ss. 26 and 32(c) PA 1890, one or more partners can, at any time, give notice to their fellow partners to dissolve the partnership. This notice takes effect from the date specified in the notice but if the notice is silent on the point, it takes effect from the date when all partners received the notice. Dissolution under ss. 26 and 32(c) can result in an immediate dissolution of the partnership. This could have disastrous consequences for the business.

However, ss. 26 and 32(c) can be overridden if the partnership agreement contains provisions to the contrary. As a result, many partnership agreements require a minimum period of notice to be given before the partnership is dissolved.

5.2.1.2 Dissolution by agreement

The partnership agreement can specify circumstances which cause the partnership to be dissolved, such as the occurrence of a particular event. The agreement can also specify the manner in which the partnership will be dissolved.

5.2.1.3 Automatic dissolution

A number of events cause partnerships to dissolve automatically:

(a) *Bankruptcy, death or charge*

The death or bankruptcy of a partner causes the partnership to be automatically dissolved, unless the partnership agreement contains provisions to the contrary (s. 33(1) PA 1890). Since dissolution is a serious matter for the other partners, many partnership agreements provide that, instead of causing automatic dissolution, the death of a partner shall give rise to the same consequences as a retirement (see **5.3**). A bankruptcy is often treated in the same way as an expulsion (see **4.5**). If a partner allows his share of the partnership property to be charged for his personal debts, the other partners have an *option* to dissolve the partnership (s. 33(2) PA 1890).

(b) *Illegality*

Partnerships formed to carry out an illegal activity or which are contrary to public policy are automatically dissolved. A change of circumstances (including a change in the law) can subsequently make illegal a partnership initially formed for a legal purpose. In these circumstances, s. 34 PA 1890 provides that the partnership is dissolved on the happening of the event which makes the business unlawful (for example, the date the change in the law takes effect). A provision to the contrary in the partnership agreement will not override s. 34.

(c) *By expiration*

Under s. 32(a) and (b) PA 1890, a partnership is dissolved:

(i) if it was entered into for a fixed term, upon the expiration of that term;

(ii) if it was entered into for a single adventure or undertaking, upon the completion of that adventure or undertaking.

A provision to the contrary in the partnership agreement overrides s. 32(a) and (b).

If the agreement is silent and the partnership continues despite the occurrence of the events set out above, s. 27 provides that a partnership at will, dissolvable by notice, is brought into existence. Such a partnership is subject to the terms of the original agreement to the extent that these do not conflict with the incidents of a partnership at will.

5.2.1.4 Dissolution by the court

Finally, a partner may apply to the court for dissolution of the partnership provided one of the statutory grounds for dissolution by the court exists. This is only really an option when an easier method of dissolution is not available, either under the Partnership Act or under any partnership agreement.

Under s. 96 of the Mental Health Act (MHA) 1983, the court has power, if satisfied after considering medical evidence that a partner is a mental 'patient', to dissolve or give directions for the dissolution of any partnership of which a 'patient' is a member. A 'patient' is a person incapable, by reason of mental disorder, of managing his own property and affairs.

In addition to s. 96 MHA 1983, s. 35 PA 1890 sets out grounds for dissolution by the court. Those grounds which give the partners a remedy in the event of a dispute (that is to say, s. 35(c), (d), and (f)) have been considered in **4.2**. The full list of s. 35 grounds is as follows:

Section 35(a)
Repealed by the predecessor to the Mental Health Act 1983.

Section 35(b)
When a partner, other than the partner suing, becomes permanently incapable of performing his part of the partnership contract.

Whether or not a partner has become *permanently* incapable is a question of fact. Since there may be difficulties in proving either that the partner is incapable or that his incapacity is permanent, and since there will be difficulties in running a partnership where a partner has a long illness, it is common to include a term in the partnership agreement allowing expulsion or insisting on retirement once a partner has been absent through illness for more than a specified time.

Section 35(c)
When a partner, other than the partner suing, has been guilty of such conduct as, in the opinion of the court, regard being had to the nature of the business, is calculated to affect prejudicially the carrying on of the business (see **4.2**).

Section 35(d)
When a partner, other than the partner suing, wilfully or persistently commits a breach of the partnership agreement, or otherwise so conducts himself in matters relating to the partnership business that it is not reasonably practicable for the other partner or partners to carry on the business in partnership with him (see **4.2**).

Section 35(e)
When the business of the partnership can only be carried on at a loss.

This is arguably one of the most important grounds for dissolution. In order for s. 35(e) to be invoked, the circumstances must be such as to make it a practical impossibility for the partnership to make a profit. If the partners who find themselves in this position cannot agree to bring the partnership to an end, this may be a valuable right if a delay in terminating the partnership will increase the amount of the loss, for which all the partners will be personally liable. It is important to note that a partnership is not necessarily insolvent simply because it is making a loss. It may well have valuable assets which, when sold, will discharge all liabilities and provide a surplus for the partners.

Section 35(f)
Whenever, in the opinion of the court, it is just and equitable that the partnership be dissolved (see **4.2**).

5.2.2 The legal consequences of dissolution

5.2.2.1 Continuing authority of partners for purposes of winding up (s. 38 PA 1890)

The occurrence of one of the events set out in **5.2.1** will cause the partnership to be dissolved but there may be various steps which need to be taken to wind up the affairs of the firm. Section 38 provides that, after the dissolution, the authority of each partner to bind the firm (as well as the other rights and obligations of the partners) continues despite the dissolution but only to the extent necessary to wind up the affairs of the partnership, and to complete transactions begun but unfinished at the time of the dissolution. However, where the dissolution is by order of the court, this authority can be terminated by the appointment of a receiver (who will simply wind up the business) or of a receiver and manager (who will continue running the business but only with a view to the beneficial realisation of the assets by means of, for example, a sale of the business as a going concern). Such appointments are likely to be made where there is a likelihood of dispute if the former partners try to wind up the affairs of the partnership.

5.2.2.2 Realisation of partnership property on dissolution

Once the firm has been dissolved, the value of the assets owned by the partnership will be ascertained, as will the extent of the debts and liabilities owed to creditors. In so far as it is necessary, the assets will be sold to raise the funds to discharge the debts. The partners may merely sell the assets used in the business or they may decide to sell the business as a going concern. If the partners decide to adopt the latter course of action, they may be able to sell the business for more than the aggregate market value of the assets used in the business because the sale price may take into account the 'goodwill' attaching to the business. (It should be borne in mind that the purchasers in this instance may well be some of the partners from the dissolved firm who wish to continue the business under a new guise.)

Goodwill has been defined as 'the whole advantage, whatever it may be, of the reputation and connection of the firm' (*Trego v Hunt* [1896] AC 7). This 'advantage' can arise as a result of various factors. If the partners have considerable expertise in their chosen field, their customers may return repeatedly. This 'goodwill' may, however, be largely personal to the partners with the result that it would disappear if they ceased their involvement in the business. Conversely, if the firm is situated in a prime location (such as the main shopping street in the town), the business may be very successful because of the convenience of access for its customers. In this latter case, the goodwill may attach to the premises rather than the partners, and so may be a very valuable asset of the partnership since it can be passed on to successors.

If the firm has saleable goodwill, a value will be attached to it. The valuation of goodwill is somewhat speculative and any formula for determining its value is inevitably rather artificial. A common formula is to ascertain the net profits of the business for a particular year and then for the parties to agree to multiply the period's profits by an agreed number, often two or three.

Where goodwill is sold, the purchasers will want to protect their investment against the loss of custom arising from the former owners setting up in competition in the same vicinity. Accordingly, the purchaser may wish to include a restrictive covenant in the sale agreement to guard against this possibility. If the purchasers are some of the partners of the dissolved partnership, they too should consider including restrictive covenants to protect their interests.

5.2.2.3 Application of the partnership property on dissolution (ss. 39 and 44 PA 1890)

Once the assets and liabilities have been ascertained, s. 39 entitles each partner to have the property of the partnership applied so that the debts and liabilities of the firm are discharged first. Once these liabilities have been met, any surplus is distributed to the partners (after deducting any sums for which each partner is liable to contribute to the firm, such as contributions to make up losses or deficiencies of capital). In order to ensure that the assets of the partnership are not distributed to the partners personally before the outside creditors are paid off, s. 39 goes on to give each partner the right to apply to the court to wind up the business and affairs of the firm in such a way as to ensure that the s. 39 order for application of assets is observed.

Section 44 provides that once the creditors of the firm have been paid, subject to any contrary agreement, the assets of the firm shall be applied in the following order:

(a) in repaying advances received from partners;
(b) in repaying the amounts shown as standing to the credit of each partner on his capital account; and
(c) any balance being divided between the partners in accordance with the profit-sharing ratio.

If the partnership has made losses (including losses or deficiencies of capital), these shall be met in the following order:

(a) from profits;
(b) from capital;
(c) from contributions made by the partners in the proportion in which profits are divisible.

Both parts of s. 44 are subject to contrary agreement. In particular the partners may agree to share surplus assets and to contribute to capital losses in a ratio different from the normal profit-sharing.

5.2.2.4 Notification of the dissolution

Section 38 gives partners continued authority to bind the firm after dissolution for the purpose of winding up the business (see **5.2.2.1**). If a partner exceeds this authority, under s. 36(1) PA 1890 outsiders dealing with the firm after a change in the constitution are entitled to treat all apparent members of the firm as still being members until the outsider has notice of the change (see **5.3.3.3**).

In order to protect themselves from liability for unauthorised debts incurred after the dissolution, the partners in the dissolved firm are entitled publicly to notify the fact of the dissolution (s. 37 PA 1890). To obtain protection from liability on unauthorised debts incurred with *existing* customers, the former partners should give notice personally to the customer.

Notice in the *London Gazette* is sufficient to gain protection from liability on debts with *new* customers (this point is considered in more detail in relation to retirement in **5.3.3.3**).

5.2.3 Problems on dissolution

5.2.3.1 Introduction

When the value of the partnership business is insufficient to pay back all monies owing, problems can arise on a dissolution. Such a shortfall can result in two main outcomes: either the outside creditors can be paid off but there is insufficient cash to pay back partners' capital contributions; or there is not even enough to pay back outside liabilities. Each of these will be looked at in turn.

5.2.3.2 Insufficient funds to pay back partners' capital

This is best explained by reference to a number of examples.

EXAMPLE 1

A, B and C are in partnership sharing profits equally, each having contributed £50,000 to the partnership. If only £90,000 remains (after paying off creditors), then there is a shortfall (loss) of £60,000, which according to s. 44(a) should be borne equally.

Technically, each partner should pay into the business £20,000 so that each can draw out his £50,000 in full. It is plainly impractical to do this, however, and each partner would simply draw out £30,000.

EXAMPLE 2

Instead suppose that A, B and C are in partnership sharing profits equally, each having contributed £50,000, £40,000, and £10,000 respectively to the partnership. If only £40,000 remains to satisfy partners' contributions, then there is a shortfall (loss) of £60,000, which again should be borne equally. Here it is more crucial that each partner contribute to the loss because of their initial unequal contributions. Note, in particular, that C will have to pay in £20,000 to receive £10,000 back. In reality, however, A and B will pay nothing and C will contribute £10,000. (This figure is reached by setting off C's capital entitlement against the £20,000 contribution.) The resulting £50,000 will then be divided between A and B to give them £30,000 and £20,000 respectively, which amounts to their initial capital contributions less £20,000.

EXAMPLE 3

Suppose in example 2 that C could not, in fact, contribute any further money. According to *Garner v Murray* [1904] 1 Ch 57, A and B would not have to make good this deficiency but simply pay in £20,000 each in the usual way. The resulting £80,000 would then be distributed between A and B according to their ratio of contribution, i.e., 5:4. A would receive £44,444.45 ($5/9$ × £80,000) and B £35,555.55 ($4/9$ × £80,000).

It will be noted that there is a curious disparity between examples 2 and 3 in that in example 2, because he can contribute, C is worse off than in example 3. Because of this, it is crucial when advising potential partners in a business to consider whether or not they wish to avoid the effect of s. 44 and agree that the partner who contributes the most should bear the most loss.

5.2.3.3 Insufficient funds to meet liability to creditors

In **5.2.3.2** it has been assumed that creditors' and partners' loans have been fully satisfied. If the assets of a partnership prove insufficient to meet these liabilities first, the situation is much the same; any deficiency must be made up by partners according to their profit-sharing ratios (subject to any contrary agreement). Again the problem comes when a partner is unable to contribute. Here the situation is more pressing because the overriding effect of s. 9 means that outside creditors are not concerned with the niceties of s. 44 and the partners who can pay must pay to satisfy these liabilities. If this is not done, then the outside creditors will look to enforce their entitlements by legal means.

The inability of partners to pay off their creditors is a topic in itself—such partners will face potential bankruptcy (see **Chapter 25**). However, since the Insolvent Partnerships Order 1994 (amending the previous Order of 1986), it is possible for creditors to apply to have a partnership wound up as if it were an unregistered company. This procedure is essentially the same as for a registered company. However, for the most part, such an application is unlikely to be of use to a creditor unless it is in conjunction with bankruptcy petitions against the partners in question (see **26.10**).

5.3 Retirement of a partner

5.3.1 Circumstances when 'retirement' occurs

The term 'retirement' is most frequently applied to mean a person retiring from full-time work having reached the statutory age of retirement. However, in the partnership context 'retirement' simply means leaving the partnership voluntarily irrespective of the age of the partner in question.

5.3.2 Retirement under the Partnership Act 1890

Partnership agreements can, and should, contain provisions dealing with retirement by partners. This is because the Partnership Act 1890 does not specifically deal with retirement. Under the 1890 Act, the only option available to a partner is to give notice under s. 26. If a s. 26 notice is given the partnership will be *dissolved* (see **5.2.1.1**); the section does not permit a partner to retire leaving the partnership otherwise unaffected. To avoid this, suitable provisions must be included in the agreement. One common form of wording provides that the partner wishing to retire should give written notice of a specified length (say, six months or one year). On expiry of the notice period, the retiring partner will leave and may be entitled to some financial settlement from his former partners but otherwise the partnership continues unaffected.

Partnership agreements frequently provide that a deceased person is to be treated as having retired. Additional problems relating specifically to death are considered in **5.4**.

5.3.3 The legal consequences of retirement

5.3.3.1 Debts incurred before retirement

The mere fact that a partner retires does not release him from his obligations in respect of debts incurred while he was a partner. Section 17(2) PA 1890 provides that: 'A partner who retires from a firm does not thereby cease to be liable for partnership debts or obligations incurred before his retirement.'

To avoid the problems of having to meet such debts after retirement, the retiring partner should, if possible, ensure that the debts are paid before he leaves. Since this may be difficult in many cases, the partner will be concerned to gain protection in other ways. In some cases it may be agreed that he will be indemnified by his former partners or that he will be released from his obligations by the creditor.

5.3.3.2 Debts incurred after retirement

The general rule is that only partners are liable for debts incurred by the partnership and so ceasing to be a partner prevents the *former* partner becoming liable on future debts as the retirement terminates the agency relationship. However, this general rule is subject to ss. 36 and 14 PA 1890. Under these sections a former partner becomes liable for debts incurred *after* he has left the partnership in certain circumstances.

5.3.3.3 Section 36

Section 36(3) provides that the estate of a partner '. . . who, *not having been known to the person dealing with the firm to be a partner*, retires is not liable for partnership debts contracted after the date of the . . . retirement'.

The date at which knowledge is tested for the purposes of this subsection is the date of retirement. If a creditor does not know at that date of the retiring partner's connection with the firm, the former partner will not be liable; the fact that the creditor may subsequently discover the former membership cannot make the former partner liable.

The subsection was considered in *Tower Cabinet Co Ltd v Ingram* [1949] 2 KB 397. A and B were in partnership. A retired and B continued the business under the old name. After A's retirement, the business ordered goods from a new supplier and failed to pay. The supplier sought to enforce judgment against A. The only knowledge the supplier had of A's connection with the firm was that A's name appeared on headed notepaper which, contrary to A's express instructions, had not been destroyed. The court found that, as the customer had no knowledge prior to A's retirement that A was a partner in the firm, A was completely protected by s. 36(3). (A further question arose of A's possible liability under s. 14(1)—see below.)

In cases where creditors know of the partner's connection with the firm before the former partner retires, s. 36(3) is of no assistance. Section 36(1) provides that: 'Where a person deals with a firm after a change in its constitution, he is entitled to treat all apparent members of the old firm as still being members of the firm until he has notice of the change.' It is necessary to consider what constitutes 'notice' for this purpose; and what makes a former partner an 'apparent' member of the continuing firm.

(a) *Notice*

Section 36(2) provides that in respect of persons who had no dealings with the firm before the date of the dissolution or change a notice in the *London Gazette* (where the firm has its principal place of business in England and Wales) will be sufficient notice.

Thus, to protect himself from liability to new customers who knew of his connection with the firm a retiring partner should ensure that a notice is published in the *London Gazette*.

Notice in the *London Gazette* will not be sufficient to relieve the former partner from liability in respect of customers who had dealings with the firm prior to the dissolution or change. If the retiring partner wishes to be absolutely protected from liability for future debts he should give the customers formal notification.

(b) *Apparent membership*

Where persons dealing with the firm know that a person was a partner, that partner will be liable for new debts so long as he is an apparent member of the firm (and until he gives notice). Persons may be 'apparent members' either because a customer has had dealings with them before or because their names appear on the notepaper or on a sign on the door or because the customer has some indirect information about their being partners.

A retiring partner should ensure that his apparent membership of the firm is terminated. He should give actual notice to existing customers and should publish a notice in the *Gazette* to cover the situation where people have not had dealings with the firm but are aware of the partner's connection with the firm.

5.3.3.4 Section 14

Liability for subsequent debts may also arise under s. 14 PA 1890. It will be recalled from **3.4** that s. 14(1) provides that:

> Every one who by words spoken or written or by conduct represents himself, or who knowingly suffers himself to be represented, as a partner in a particular firm, is liable as a partner to any one who has on the faith of any such representation given credit to the firm, whether the representation has or has not been made or communicated to the person so giving credit by or with the knowledge of the apparent partner making the representation or suffering it to be made.

Therefore, even if no liability arises under s. 36, the former partner may be liable to any person (whether they had previous dealings with the firm or not) who has given 'credit' to the firm on the faith of a representation that he is still a partner which is made by the former partner or which he has 'knowingly' allowed to be made.

The word 'apparent' in s. 14(1) has the same meaning as in s. 36(1) so that the decision in the *Tower Cabinet* case (see above) is equally relevant in these circumstances. In the case, it was alleged that the former partner had allowed himself to be held out as a partner. However, since the former partner had not authorised the use of the old notepaper, he had not 'knowingly' allowed himself to be held out as an 'apparent' partner and so no liability under s. 14 arose.

A retiring partner should ensure that his name is removed from any signs and that any notepaper is destroyed in order to prevent an accusation that he knowingly allowed himself to be represented as a partner.

5.3.3.5 Compliance with Pt 14 CA 2006

After the change in the partnership, the notepaper will normally be changed and care should be taken to ensure that it complies with the relevant requirements of the Companies Act 2006 (which were considered in **1.8**).

5.3.3.6 Dealing with the finances

Once the partner has retired from the firm, the arrangements for severing, or changing the basis of, the financial connection with the firm will be of considerable importance. These matters are generally covered by the partnership agreement and usually relate to the provision for the partner (and for his dependants) of some form of pension (whether paid by the former partners, under an approved annuity contract, or under a consultancy arrangement). In addition, the arrangements will deal with the former partner's entitlement (if any) to payment for his share in the partnership assets (which may include goodwill).

If there is no agreement, the former partner has a right to receive the net value of his share in the partnership property from his former partners.

5.4 Death

5.4.1 Introduction

As we saw in **5.2.1.3** above, death causes the automatic dissolution of a partnership. In order to avoid inconvenience to the surviving partners it is common to provide in the partnership agreement that instead of causing an automatic dissolution of the partnership, a deceased partner shall be treated as if he had retired.

5.4.2 Right of estate to share in profits and obtain amounts due

Subject to contrary agreement, s. 42(1) PA 1890 provides for the situation where any member of a firm has died (or otherwise ceased to be a partner) and the surviving (or continuing) partners carry on the business of the firm without any final settlement of accounts as between the firm and the outgoing partner or his estate. The outgoing partner or his estate is entitled at the option of himself or his personal representatives to claim:

(a) such share of the profits made since the dissolution as the court may find to be attributable to the use of his share of the partnership assets; or

(b) interest at the rate of 5% p.a. on the amount of his share of the partnership assets.

Any amount due from the surviving partners to the deceased partner's personal representatives in respect of his share is a debt accruing at the date of the death (s. 43).

5.4.3 Treatment in the partnership agreement

Raising a large capital sum to pay to the estate of a deceased partner may strain the resources of a partnership which is continuing after the death of a partner. This issue is normally dealt with by the partners in the partnership agreement as follows:

(a) by taking out insurance cover;

(b) by providing that on death (and/or retirement) capital sums due should be paid by yearly instalments over a specified period—interest being payable on the amount outstanding;

(c) by providing for a method of calculating the amount due;

(d) by providing that the deceased (or retiring) partner is to be entitled to a fixed amount in lieu of a share of profits. This avoids the need to apportion profits to the date of death (or retirement).

5.4.4 Liability for debts

Every partner is jointly liable for debts and obligations of the firm incurred while he is a partner. In addition, s. 9 PA 1890 provides that the estate of a deceased person is severally liable for such debts and obligations so far as they remain unsatisfied *but* subject to the prior payment of the deceased partner's personal debts. A partnership creditor can, therefore, proceed against the estate of a deceased partner in respect of partnership debts (even after obtaining a judgment against the other partners) provided some part of the debt is unsatisfied. However, partnership creditors are postponed to the deceased partner's own creditors.

So far as subsequent debts are concerned, s. 36(3) PA 1890 provides that the deceased partner's estate is not liable for partnership debts contracted after the death. However, if the deceased partner's personal representatives take part in the management of the business they make themselves liable for debts incurred from the time their participation commences.

online resource centre

For further resources and online chapters please visit the Online Resource Centre at www.oxfordtextbooks.co.uk/orc/business13_14/.

6 The partnership agreement

This chapter covers the following topics:

6.1 Introduction

In this chapter we will look at the provisions which should be considered for inclusion in a partnership agreement. Much of the contents of a partnership agreement will address issues raised by the provisions of the Partnership Act 1890 which we considered in **Chapters 1** to **5**, or which may be relevant to the tax provisions applicable to partnership which will be considered in **Chapters 17, 22**, and **23**. Those detailed provisions should be borne in mind when reading this chapter.

Before we look at the possible contents of a partnership agreement, we will consider whether a formal, written agreement is necessary at all, and at the end of the chapter we have included a section dealing with the points which a prospective new partner might wish to consider before putting his signature to a partnership agreement.

6.2 Is a written partnership agreement necessary?

A written agreement is not required for the formation of a partnership. This contrasts with the position of a company where the memorandum and articles, which have contractual effect under s. 14 CA 1985, must not only be in writing but must also be registered with the Registrar of Companies.

In practice, many partnerships decide that the agreement between the partners, as to how the business is to be regulated, should be in the form of a written agreement. Such an agreement is often called a partnership agreement, a partnership deed or articles of partnership.

The draftsman of a partnership agreement should bear in mind that many provisions of the Partnership Act 1890 apply to regulate the relationship of the partners except to the extent that there is contrary agreement. However well intentioned and however well drafted such legislation is, it is unlikely that it will entirely coincide with the wishes of a particular group of businessmen setting up a partnership.

The draftsman's task in drafting a partnership agreement is more onerous than his task in drafting articles of association for a company. In the case of a company a 'model' set of articles (Model Articles) is provided, which will suit the needs of most companies with comparatively minor alterations. The provisions of the Partnership Act are both more out of date and less comprehensive than those of the Model Articles. The nature of a partnership agreement must, of course, depend upon the circumstances but we have set out in the next paragraph the most important matters which need to be considered.

6.3 The clauses of the partnership agreement

6.3.1 The parties

The parties to the agreement will be the partners, old and new.

6.3.2 The commencement date and term of the partnership

While most partnerships will be partnerships 'at will' (and so can last indefinitely subject to notice to dissolve the partnership being given), it is possible to specify the length of the partnership's 'life'. Although the date the partnership agreement was entered into can determine the commencement of the partnership (which could be a newly constituted partnership following the retirement or admission of partners), partnership agreements often include a term stating the date on which the partnership commenced.

6.3.3 The nature of the partnership's business

The *ultra vires* rule does not apply to a partnership. The business should, however, be specified so that a partner who objects to what is being done by way of new types of business can insist on the agreement being followed. Unless the partnership agreement provides to the contrary, the clause specifying what business is to be carried on can only be altered with the unanimous agreement of the partners (s. 24(8) PA 1890). This clause may also specify where the partnership is to carry on business.

6.3.4 The partnership name

The business name of the partnership should be specified. The requirements as to approval for and publicity of business names were dealt with in **1.8**.

6.3.5 The income of the partnership

If the partnership agreement is silent on the point, the partners will share the income (and liabilities) of the partnership equally. Even if this is in accord with the partners' wishes, it is best to state specifically the way in which the partnership's profits will be shared. However, in many partnerships, this simple position is not what the partners require. The share of profits between the partners may be unequal to reflect differing levels of contributions of capital, or differing levels of involvement in the partnership's business. Some partnerships may choose to build a mechanism into their partnership agreements for regular reviews of the profit-sharing ratios to take into account the relative achievements of the partners. Other partnerships adopt a 'lock step' arrangement by which a partner's share of the profits may increase by a fixed amount annually over a period of years. If the partners have agreed among themselves that some or all of them should receive 'interest' on capital or 'salary', these arrangements should be set out in the partnership agreement. However, care should be taken to ensure if a 'salary' is paid to the partner that the Revenue cannot argue that the recipient was, in reality, an employee rather than a full equity partner (if the latter is what the partners were trying to achieve).

6.3.6 The capital of the partnership

A clause (or group of clauses) should be included dealing with the financial relationships between the partners. This should state what investment each partner is to make in the business, how each partner will satisfy his obligation to contribute capital (for example, whether in cash or assets) and over what period (if the capital contribution is not to be made in full on admission to the partnership). Although it may be difficult to specify the circumstances, it is worth giving thought to the circumstances in which further capital might have to be introduced. The reverse of these provisions is what should happen to the capital when the partnership is dissolved or a partner retires. What are the arrangements for a partner to withdraw capital and how is the goodwill of the business to be dealt with when a partner leaves?

6.3.7 The property of the partnership

The partnership agreement should include provisions specifying which property is to be regarded as partnership property and which is to remain the property of individual partners.

6.3.8 The management of the partnership

Small partnerships of two or three people will usually be run by the partners (perhaps in conjunction with a small number of employees) and each partner will have an equal say in management. In a large partnership (especially a professional partnership where there may be dozens of partners), a more complex management structure may be considered desirable and the structure should be specified. In the absence of contrary agreement all partners have an equal say in management. Among the more mundane, but very vital, matters which should be considered under this heading are questions such as where will the partnership maintain its bank account, who should be entitled to sign cheques for the partnership, who will allocate work to the employees, what authority is each partner to have in relation to buying stock, paying bills and so on? In most cases, the clause dealing with management of the partnership should be stated in general terms. It is better, for example, to say that junior partners are to have such functions as are assigned to them by the managing or senior partners than to list in minute detail what they are to be authorised to do.

6.3.9 The effect of prolonged absence

It is now common to find included in partnership agreements clauses dealing with the consequences for a partner who is absent from the business for a prolonged period. This may be through illness, maternity leave or compassionate leave. The nature of the provisions will be determined by the necessity for the partners to balance the needs of the business with supporting their fellow partner. However, these provisions often mirror corresponding provisions found in employment contracts (so that a partner may be permitted to be away from the partnership's business for six months due to illness before he can be expelled, or the partnership agreement may provide maternity leave provisions similar to the statutory provisions which employees enjoy).

6.3.10 Restrictions

Terms may be included dealing with the partners' obligations to the firm. It is quite common, for example, to provide that the partners are to give their whole time to the business of the firm or to provide that they are only to take up other businesses with the approval of their partners. Consideration should also be given to the inclusion of a clause preventing competition with the firm during the lifetime of the partnership (even if the partners are not full time), although such competition would in any case normally be a breach of the partners' duty of good faith. Similarly, it is often desirable to include a restrictive covenant to prevent competition with the firm by a partner after he has left the firm. Such a term must be reasonable otherwise it may be declared void as being a term in unreasonable restraint of trade. The partners may also decide to place specific restrictions on the activities of particular partners in relation to the running of the business. For example, a partnership agreement could prevent an individual partner from charging or selling any of the partnership's assets.

6.3.11 Partnership disputes

It is sensible to anticipate that problems may arise within the partnership and so provide for how disputes should be resolved. Commonly, clauses dealing with disputes require the partners to refer the dispute (whatever the subject matter of the dispute may be) to an independent arbitrator. This approach may lead to the resolution of the dispute and thus avoid the dissolution of the partnership.

6.3.12 Dissolution, death, retirement, and admission of partners

It is sensible to set out the circumstances in which the partnership will be dissolved or in which a partner can be expelled from the partnership. If the partnership comes to an end, tax liabilities can arise (see **Chapter 23**) and the partnership agreement should include a provision as to whether the firm should set aside a proportion of each partner's profit share to provide a fund to discharge any tax liability which might arise. Any outgoing partner, if he is retiring, will be concerned to secure an income during his retirement. While the partner can create a fund from which a pension can be paid during his years as a partner, many partnerships provide annuity or consultancy arrangements for former partners. The terms of such arrangements should be set out in the partnership agreement. Secondly, since the election for assessment on the continuing basis can mean that an incoming partner can be taxed on a share of profits in excess of the amount he actually receives, it is also common for the incoming partner to be indemnified by the existing partners for any extra tax he suffers as a result. The agreement should specify how new partners are to be admitted to the partnership. In the absence of agreement to the contrary, new partners may only be admitted with the unanimous consent of the existing partners (s. 24(7) PA 1890).

6.4 Issues for an incoming partner

We have seen the legal consequences of admission to a partnership in **Chapter 3** and the tax consequences of admission will be considered in **Chapter 23**. However, before accepting the offer of a partnership, a prospective partner needs to consider whether the partnership's business, management, and finances are such as to justify the risk of taking on unlimited liability with his future fellow partners.

The partnership agreement will be a useful source of information about the way the partnership's affairs are handled but the agreement will be by no means the only document the prospective partner will want to examine. Other documents will include previous years' signed accounts, as well as previous years' budgets and management accounts (which will show whether the business has suffered an unexpected shortfall in income or cost overruns which will need to be explained). The prospective partner should try to anticipate any future financial problems the partnership may face by investigating whether there are any contingent liabilities, whether the firm's insurance cover is adequate, and what steps the firm is taking to make provision for bad debts. Perhaps the most significant protection against problems in the future would be if the firm has a carefully thought out, effective business strategy and the prospective partner will need to satisfy himself that he considers the strategy to be appropriate given the firm's position in its particular market place.

online resource centre

For further resources and online chapters please visit the Online Resource Centre at www.oxfordtextbooks.co.uk/orc/business13_14/.

Companies

7

Limited companies

This chapter covers the following topics:

7.1 Introduction

In this chapter we shall begin to look at the legal position of limited companies. Many businesses are run by limited companies. These range from international conglomerates to companies owned by one person running a small business. Before turning to the detailed legal rules about companies, we need to see how they fit into the complex pattern of institutions which the law has created. We shall also introduce the distinction between private and public companies. Further information about public companies can be found in **Chapter 16**.

7.2 Corporations

A 'company' is in law a corporation, that is, an artificial legal 'person' with rights and obligations distinct from those of its members. Business associations were occasionally made corporations by Royal Charter from about the sixteenth century (for example, the East India Company in 1600), but until the Industrial Revolution few businesses were incorporated. With the growth of the canal and railway systems, incorporations were permitted in increasing numbers under Acts of Parliament. Eventually the concept of the company as a medium for any business came into being with the introduction of the Companies Act 1862. Thereafter, numerous Companies Acts were introduced during the nineteenth and twentieth centuries, culminating in the current regime provided by the Companies Act 2006 (the 2006 Act or CA 2006).

7.3 Sources of company law

7.3.1 Legislation

For just over twenty years, the Companies Act 1985 was the most important source of company law. It consolidated legislation contained in earlier Companies Acts and other pieces of legislation dealing with company law.

After proposals came to the fore to reform company law, the Companies Bill was published in November 2005. This Bill became law when the Companies Act 2006 received Royal Assent on 8 November 2006.

The key theme behind the 2006 Act is to reflect the reality of companies in operation today. Much of the previous system was predicated on the basis of large companies being the norm, whereas, in fact, the vast majority of companies are owner-managed with five or fewer persons involved. Therefore, one of the stated aims of the reform was to simplify the creation and operation of private companies, based around a 'think small first' approach.

The 2006 Act came fully into force on 1 October 2009, although elements of the Act had been introduced on a staggered basis prior to this date.

Whilst the 2006 Act introduced many reforms, many of the basic concepts of company law remained unchanged and a sizeable percentage of the Companies Act 1985 was restated within the 2006 Act. This Act, therefore, both reforms and consolidates elements of company law.

The 2006 Act applies throughout the United Kingdom (s. 1299), although a number of provisions apply only to Scotland or only to England and Wales and Northern Ireland. (Previously, the Companies Act 1985 did not apply to Northern Ireland, which had its own separate companies legislation.)

Throughout this text, reference will be made to the 2006 Act only, unless specific reference to the 1985 Act is still thought appropriate.

7.3.2 Judicial decisions

Company law has been an amalgam of increasing statutory regulation and common law, the latter being particularly relevant to the obligations and duties of directors and the rights of minority shareholders. Judicial input has always been significant in assessing the impact of both these branches of company law.

The introduction of any new legislation brings with it possible unanswered questions, so it is anticipated that the role of the courts over the new few years will be crucial in clarifying any doubts which exist in respect of the effect of the 2006 Act.

7.3.3 Tax legislation

The taxation of companies is largely dealt with in the Corporation Tax Acts 2009 and 2010. Companies' capital gains are largely dealt with in accordance with the Taxation of Chargeable Gains Act 1992, as amended. Again, many decisions of the courts have interpreted the meaning of this legislation. The taxation of companies is examined in detail in **Chapter 18**.

7.3.4 The general law

It is worth pointing out that the general law applies to companies as it applies to individuals, except to the extent that it has been modified by specific rules of company law. The general law of contract, for example, applies to companies with very few modifications, as does the law of tort, competition, and so on. This is really just a consequence of the fact that a company is a corporation and, therefore, in law a 'person' with legal rights and obligations.

7.3.5 The company's own regulations: articles of association

Despite the vast amount of law which applies to companies, a great deal of freedom of choice is given to each individual company as to how it will organise itself. This is both desirable and inevitable because of the widely differing circumstances in which each company operates. To provide for its own internal administration each company must have a set of regulations known as *articles of association*. These may be specially prepared for the company by the lawyer who assists with its formation. It is also possible, however, to adopt standard articles stipulated by regulation.

Until the introduction of the Companies Act 2006, this form of standard articles was known as Table A. Since 1 October 2009, a new set of standard articles known as the Model Articles has superseded Table A. In practice, lawyers are most likely to come across companies which have adopted either of these sets of articles wholesale or which have based their articles substantially upon them. (For a more detailed discussion of this area, see **Chapter 14**.)

7.4 Registration

Companies are formed (or incorporated) by a process called *registration*. The conditions for registration are determined by the Companies Act 2006.

Registration involves sending a number of documents and a fee to the Registrar of Companies, the official responsible for registering companies. A company comes into existence on the issue of a *certificate of incorporation* by the Registrar.

The Registrar is also responsible for maintaining records relating to registered companies. These records contain information which companies are required by law to disclose in relation to a wide range of matters. Records are kept at Companies House, which for companies incorporated in England and Wales is in Cardiff. For companies registered in Scotland, a separate Companies House is based in Edinburgh. For those registered in Northern Ireland, the relevant office is based in Belfast. The reader will find the Companies House website a useful reference source—see www.companieshouse.gov.uk.

The process of registration is examined in more detail in **Chapter 8**.

7.5 Types of registered company

7.5.1 Companies limited by shares

Most registered companies are 'limited by shares'. This expression refers to the *liability* of the members (or shareholders—the terms are almost interchangeable) of the company for that company's debts on a liquidation. The effect of a company being limited by shares is that, on a liquidation, the liability of a member is limited to the amount, if any, which remains unpaid on his shares. This is described further below.

When a company issues shares, the person taking the shares must agree to pay the company for them. Usually payment will be made immediately but sometimes shares will be issued 'unpaid' (sometimes expressed as 'nil-paid') or 'partly-paid', in which case payment must be made later. If the company goes into liquidation and is insolvent, any member who has not fully paid for his shares is liable to pay the amount outstanding to the liquidator, who will apply such amount in paying the company's debts. That is the extent of that member's liability for the company's debts. In the case of a member who has paid in full for his shares, he will have no liability (in normal circumstances) for the company's debts.

EXAMPLE

Charles subscribes for 500 £1 shares in Regency Furnishings Limited ('Regency').

If Charles pays £500 for the shares, his shares are said to be fully-paid, so no further liability for Regency's debts can fall on Charles.

Instead, if Charles pays 50p per share, his shares are said to be partly-paid. In effect, £250 remains as an outstanding obligation to Regency. Regency's constitution may contain rules about how and when it can demand the outstanding balance, but, in any event, on any liquidation of Regency, Charles will be obliged to contribute the remaining £250.

The position of a shareholder in a limited company is quite different from the position of a member of a partnership (see **3.2**). If a partnership business fails, each of the partners stands to lose not only what he has invested but also any private wealth which he may have. Limited liability can be an enormous advantage to a businessman, although creditors (particularly those who have lent money to the company) may require personal guarantees of the company's debts from shareholders, thus reducing the advantage.

7.5.2 Companies limited by guarantee

A small number of companies are limited by guarantee rather than by shares. This means that each member undertakes to pay a specified amount if the company is wound up (i.e., the guarantee) while he is a member or within a year after he ceases to be a member. Most companies limited by guarantee are charities or other non-trading companies.

7.5.3 Unlimited companies

An unlimited company is one which is registered under the Companies Act but without any limit on the liability of the members. If an unlimited company goes into liquidation the members are liable to contribute the whole of their private wealth (if so much is needed) to the payment of the company's debts. The creditors cannot sue the members direct but must claim in the liquidation. The liquidator then calls for contributions from the members. For this reason, an unlimited company is not a suitable choice for a trading entity or one which will incur substantial obligations.

7.5.4 Public and private companies

Nearly all company law rules apply equally to all companies. There are, however, a number of rules which distinguish between 'public' companies and 'private' companies. The important issue to note is that public and private companies are creatures of statute and the differences between them are determined by the Companies Act. Any company will be private unless it is specifically incorporated as a public one. Bringing a public company into being is effectively an administrative task. The only substantive matter is that the company's share capital must satisfy certain minimum requirements—the aggregate nominal value of all shares in issue must be at least £50,000 and each share must be at least one quarter paid up. (In other words, the company must have received at least £12,500 from its shareholders for those shares.)

The vast majority of companies in existence are private. Public companies, being more regulated, are less attractive. This difference has been made more acute by the Companies Act 2006, which has sought to provide greater freedom to those who operate private companies. Probably the principal reason for wanting a public company is that only public companies can issue shares or debentures to the public (hence the description 'public company'): a private company is prohibited from so doing. Private companies which want to circumvent the prohibition will have to convert to public status first. (These issues are discussed in more detail in **Chapter 16**.)

7.5.5 Other definitions

All companies are public or private but there are a number of other categories of company to which special rules apply:

(a) *Listed company*

A company is in this category if its shares are listed with the UK Listing Authority and traded on a stock exchange. Because of UK Listing Authority and London Stock Exchange rules only public companies can obtain a listing. Listed companies are subject to a more stringent regulatory regime (see **16.3**). Listed companies may also be referred to as 'quoted' companies and in general parlance the two terms are synonymous. However, the Companies Act 2006 includes within it the use of the defined term 'quoted company', so care should be taken in the use of this term.

(b) *Close company*

This category is relevant only for tax purposes; special tax rules apply to close companies (see **18.5**). Virtually all private companies are close and so are some public companies. A company which is not close is sometimes called an 'open company' but 'non-close company' is more correct.

(c) *Small and medium-sized companies*

These are companies which, because of their relatively small size (in financial terms), are exempt from providing certain information in their accounts. In addition, certain categories of small companies are now exempt from the requirement to have an audit of their accounts. Further discussion of this topic can be found in **Chapter 15**.

7.6 Separate legal personality

As we have already seen, a company is a 'body corporate'; that is, it is a legal person distinct from its members and officers (i.e., its directors and secretary). Even if a company is 100% owned and controlled by a shareholder, that company has a completely separate legal personality from that of the shareholder. This is clearly illustrated in the leading case of *Salomon v A. Salomon and Co Ltd* [1897] AC 22.

A number of consequences flow from this separate legal personality, so that a company:

(a) is able to own property;

(b) is liable for its own debts;

(c) can sue its debtors;

(d) is liable to be sued by its creditors; and

(e) has 'perpetual succession'—this means that the company does not cease to exist just because a member (however many shares he may own) dies or otherwise ceases to be a member.

7.7 'Lifting the veil of incorporation'

There are a number of circumstances in which the court may be willing to ignore the fact that a company is a separate legal person. Legislation also sometimes ignores the distinction between a company and its members. These circumstances are rather fancifully described as 'lifting the veil of incorporation' because the law looks behind the legal 'veil' which separates the company from its members and officers.

The occasions when the veil of incorporation is lifted are hard to classify and limited. It is probably open to the courts to extend the circumstances in the future. However, the case of *Adams v Cape Industries* [1990] Ch 433 suggests considerable judicial reluctance to do so. It is, of course, open to Parliament to do so by legislation.

7.7.1 Company legislation

The Companies Act 2006 and the Insolvency Act 1986 (IA 1986) contain a number of rules which depart from the general principle of separate legal personality; for example:

(a) *Fraudulent trading*

Section 213 IA 1986 provides that any person who is or was knowingly a party to fraudulent trading by a company whose business is being carried on with intent to defraud creditors or other persons, may be liable to pay the debts of the company. This liability arises only if the company is being wound up (although criminal penalties may be imposed for fraudulent trading under s. 993 of the 2006 Act even if the company is not being wound up).

(b) *Wrongful trading*

Section 214 IA 1986 provides that directors of the company may be personally liable in cases of wrongful trading. This arises where a company becomes insolvent and the directors then fail to take steps to protect creditors. This type of liability only arises if the company is being wound up.

Section 214 is discussed further in **Chapter 27**.

(c) *Group accounts*

Where companies are members of a group, group accounts must be produced to reflect that the financial transactions of the subsidiaries are in reality activities of the holding company (s. 399 CA 2006).

7.7.2 Decisions of the courts

7.7.2.1 Attempts to avoid legal obligations

The courts have occasionally lifted the veil of incorporation by making orders against companies where the proprietors have used a company as a means of avoiding a personal legal obligation; that is, where the company in question is being used as a deliberate facade to obscure the reality of the situation. For example, in *Jones v Lipman* [1962] 1 WLR 832 the defendant had contracted to sell land to the plaintiff and later conveyed it to a company in an attempt to avoid the possibility of an order of specific performance (an order of specific performance cannot normally be made once a third party has acquired rights in the subject matter of the contract). The company was owned and controlled by the defendant and so an order of specific performance was made against the company as well as the vendor.

7.7.2.2 Agency and trusts

In a few cases the court has held that a company is either an agent for its shareholders or their trustee. The exact scope of these decisions, however, is rather unclear and these cases ought to be regarded as providing exceptions rather than general rules. A company will *not* generally be regarded as either an agent for, or trustee of, its members.

7.7.3 Tax legislation

Tax legislation often imposes tax liability on shareholders to reflect the fact that transactions of their company are in reality transactions conducted on their behalf. It is not proposed to deal with all the rules involved but the following examples should be sufficient to indicate their scope:

(a) The companies in a 'group' of companies (i.e., broadly speaking, a holding company and its subsidiaries) are in many ways treated as one company for corporation tax purposes. Thus the rate of tax depends on the size of the group's profits rather than on the size of each company's profits, losses made by one member of a group can generally be offset against profits made by others, and dividend payments within the group may be ignored for tax purposes.

(b) Gifts made by a close company are treated as made by its members for the purpose of inheritance tax. This prevents people using corporate structures to try to avoid inheritance tax.

(c) The sale of a business to a company in return for shares can usually be ignored for capital gains tax purposes.

online resource centre

For further resources and online chapters please visit the Online Resource Centre at www.oxfordtextbooks.co.uk/orc/business13_14/.

8

Formation of a limited company

This chapter covers the following topics:

8.1 Introduction

In this chapter, we shall look at the process by which a limited company is formed and the steps required both for and following its formation. We shall also look at shelf companies, as an alternative means of providing a company to a client, and the related changes which can be made to a company's main features.

Whatever the reason for a new company, the process of registering a company is governed by the Companies Act 2006 (the 2006 Act or CA 2006). However, as many of the companies currently in existence will have been registered under the 1985 Act, this chapter considers both regimes, as appropriate. (The processes are fundamentally the same, but 1985 Act companies and 2006 Act companies show a number of differences in their make-up, which can have specific consequences for each type of company.) Note that we will consider the formation of private limited companies only. For the formation of public companies, please refer to **Chapter 16**.

8.2 Promoters

Those who wish to form a company are usually known as the 'promoters' of the company. There is no legal definition of a promoter; whether someone is a promoter is a question of fact. However, it is generally accepted that a promoter owes certain duties to the company which he seeks to create. These include duties of good faith and disclosure. It is important to advise promoters of their potential liability for any contracts which they might enter into on behalf of the proposed company prior to its incorporation (see **8.3**).

For the purposes of this chapter, we have used the term 'promoters' to mean any person or persons wishing to set up a company which will be used as a vehicle for their business.

A solicitor advising a client on the formation of a new business or on changing an existing business into a company would first discuss the advisability of incorporation compared to the alternatives of remaining a sole trader or forming a partnership. This requires a detailed knowledge of partnership law, company law, and relevant tax considerations. We therefore leave the topic of choice of business medium until **Chapter 28**.

Solicitors may also set up companies for their clients as part of a transaction. For example, a company may be set up to carry out a specific activity within a transaction, or trading assets may be hived into a newly formed company and that company sold on rather than the assets themselves being sold.

8.3 Pre-incorporation contracts

Difficulties may arise in relation to contracts made by the promoters on behalf of a proposed company. They may wish to make contracts to acquire premises, machinery, stationery and so on, prior to the company becoming incorporated. This may be due to a desire to have things 'up and running', so that trading can commence immediately the company is incorporated. This creates a problem as the company cannot enter into contracts until it has been incorporated as, until such time, it is not a legal person. The promoters cannot act as its agents since the principal does not exist.

Should the promoters purport to enter into a contract *on behalf of* the unformed company, s. 51 CA 2006 will apply. This provides that:

> A contract that purports to be made by or on behalf of a company at a time when the company has not been formed has effect, subject to any agreement to the contrary, as one made with the person purporting to act for the company or as agent for it, and he is personally liable on the contract accordingly.

The threat of personal liability means that the safest course is to enter into contracts only after incorporation when they can be entered into by the company. If this is not possible, then the following may be considered:

(a) preparing a draft contract which will be entered into by the company following incorporation;

(b) entering into a binding contract under which the promoters are personally liable until incorporation, at which time the contract is novated, i.e., a new contract on the same terms is entered into between the company and the third party (note that the third party's consent to novation will be required); or

(c) entering into a binding contract under which the promoters are personally liable until incorporation, at which time the promoters transfer the benefit of the contract to the company in return for the company's agreement to indemnify them in respect of their liability to the third party.

8.4 Methods of providing the client with a company

There are two main methods by which a client can be provided with a company. The solicitor may form a new company *from scratch*. In doing so, he can ensure that the company meets the client's particular requirements in every way, i.e., the company is effectively 'tailor-made' and brought into existence for the client.

Alternatively, the solicitor can arrange for the client to acquire a 'shelf' company. This type of company *has already been incorporated* either by law stationers or, sometimes, by the firm of solicitors itself. Since the company already exists, it must be transferred over to the client.

These methods are compared later in **8.11**. For the moment, we shall look at the steps required for the incorporation of a company from scratch.

8.5 Steps leading to incorporation

All new companies are set up under the provisions of the Companies Act 2006. The main relevant provisions are to be found in Pts 2 and 3 of the 2006 Act. Any promoter of a new company must subscribe their name to a memorandum of association and comply with the requirements for registration (s. 7 CA 2006). (See below at **8.6.2** for further discussion of the memorandum of association.) For this reason, the promoters are more properly referred to as subscribers.

Perhaps the most significant document in the process is the application for registration (s. 9 CA 2006) known as form IN01. The application for registration must state:

(a) The proposed name of the company.

(b) The proposed situation of the company's registered office, e.g., England, Wales, Scotland, or Northern Ireland.

(c) Whether or not the liability of the members is to be limited (either by shares or guarantee), which will normally be the case.

(d) Whether or not the company is to be public or private.

Additionally, the application must also contain:

(a) A statement of share capital and initial shareholdings.

(b) A statement of the company's proposed officers.

(c) A statement of the intended address of the company's registered office.

Section 13 CA 2006 requires a statement of compliance to be submitted with the application, which is confirmation by all the relevant subscribers that all requirements as to registration have been complied with. This statement is included within form IN01.

If particular articles of association are required (see **7.3.5** and **Chapter 14**), they should be submitted with the application for registration (s. 9(5)(b)). If this is not done, the relevant Model Articles will be deemed to be the articles of the company by default (s. 20 CA 2006). (See further discussion below at **8.6.8.**)

All these documents must be sent to the Registrar of Companies together with the relevant fee. The size of the fee will be determined by the nature of the application. A 'standard' application is in paper form and will take approximately five days to process. If the new company is required urgently it is possible to pay a higher fee which guarantees same-day incorporation.

However, electronic incorporation is now arguably the preferred method. The fee is less for the same type of service.

Details of relevant fees can be found in the Appendix to this chapter.

8.6 Issues to be considered on registration

8.6.1 Introduction

We shall now consider the specific issues which the process of registration raises. There are a number of features of a company which need to be confirmed by a lawyer to ensure that the proposed company meets the client's requirements.

8.6.2 Memorandum of association

Every company must have a memorandum. Historically its principal function was to set out the *raison d'être* of the company and to regulate its dealings with outsiders. Together with the articles, the memorandum formed the constitution of a company.

The position under the 2006 Act is very different; the significance of the memorandum has been substantially reduced for newly registered companies and it is now only relevant to the application for registration (s. 9(1)). Once a company has been registered, the memorandum is of historical interest only and is not part of the company's constitution. The memorandum needs to contain only two clauses (s. 8 CA 2006):

(a) a statement of intent of the subscribers (promoters) to form a company;

(b) a statement by the subscribers (promoters) that they agree to become members of the company and to take at least one share each. (In the case of a single member company, there will obviously only be one subscriber.)

Specimen Companies Act 2006 Memorandum

Companies Act 2006

COMPANY HAVING A SHARE CAPITAL

Memorandum of Association of OXP (222) Limited

Each subscriber to this memorandum of association wishes to form a company under the Companies Act 2006 and agrees to become a member of the company and to take at least one share.

Name of each subscriber	Authentication by each subscriber
[ ]	[ ]

[DETAILS OF SUBSCRIBERS NOT SUPPLIED]

Dated:

Prior to the advent of the Companies Act 2006, five compulsory clauses had to be included in the memorandum. These related to:

(a) the name of the company;

(b) the *situs* of the registered office;

(c) the objects of the company, that is, what its purpose was;

(d) the liability of the members, that is, whether or not it was limited;

(e) the authorised share capital of the company, that is, the initial pool of shares out of which shares could be allotted by the company to prospective shareholders.

Specimen Companies Act 1985 Memorandum

THE COMPANIES ACTS 1985 & 1989

PRIVATE COMPANY LIMITED BY SHARES

MEMORANDUM OF ASSOCIATION

OF

OXP (777) LIMITED

1. The Company's name is "OXP (777) Limited".

2. The Company's registered office is to be situated in England and Wales.

3. The object of the Company is to carry on business as a general commercial company.

4. The liability of the members is limited.

5. The Company's share capital is £10,000 divided into 10,000 shares of £1 each.

WE, the subscribers to this Memorandum of Association, wish to be formed into a Company pursuant to this Memorandum; and we agree to take the number of shares shown opposite our respective names.

Names and Addresses of Subscribers		Number of shares taken by each Subscriber
[ ]		[ ]
[ ]		[ ]
	Total shares taken	[ ]

[DETAILS OF SUBSCRIBERS NOT SUPPLIED]

Dated: [ ]

Witness to the above signatures: [ ]

The Companies Act 2006 has not, however, downgraded the significance of the memoranda of companies set up under the 1985 Act. Instead, those elements which are no longer required for inclusion in a valid memorandum will be deemed to be included within the articles (s. 28 CA 2006), most notably the objects clause and the share capital clause. In this way, they still have constitutional effect. For this reason, it is not possible to ignore the contents of the memorandum of a 1985 Act company.

8.6.3 The name of a company

8.6.3.1 Choice of name

Generally, the promoters have freedom of choice as far as the company's name is concerned. The purpose of a company's name is to differentiate the company from all other registered companies. The Companies Act 2006, therefore, prohibits the Registrar from registering a company with a name which:

(a) does not end with the word 'limited' (or its Welsh equivalent 'cyfyngedig' if appropriate) if the company is a private limited company (s. 59 CA 2006);

(b) is the same as that of an existing registered company (s. 66(1) CA 2006); or

(c) in the opinion of the Secretary of State constitutes a criminal offence, or is offensive (s. 53 CA 2006).

In addition, the approval of the Secretary of State is necessary for the registration of a company under a name which suggests a connection with the Government or a local or public authority (s. 54 CA 2006). Furthermore, the inclusion in a company's name of particular words specified in regulations made under s. 55 CA 2006 (so-called 'sensitive' words) will also require the approval of the Secretary of State. In either instance, consultation with the relevant government department or institution specified in the regulations is sometimes required before the Registrar gives its approval.

If a name is rejected by the Registrar, a certain amount of expense and delay is bound to occur as the promoters or solicitor will have to submit a further set of documents applying for formation with a new name. Therefore, to minimise the risk of a name being rejected the promoters or solicitor should consult the index of company names kept by the Registrar of Companies shortly before the application for registration. If the name is already in use a new name should be chosen. If the name is not in use then the application should progress quickly as there is no procedure for reserving a name.

8.6.3.2 Power of Secretary of State to order change of name

The Secretary of State has power to direct a company to change its name in the following circumstances:

(a) within 12 months of registration, if the name is the same as or, in the opinion of the Secretary of State, too like a name appearing in the index of names at the time of registration, or is the same as a name which should have been in the index at that time (ss. 67 and 68 CA 2006);

(b) within five years of registration, if misleading information was given at the time of registration for the purposes of a company's registration by a particular name (s. 75 CA 2006); and

(c) at any time, if the name gives 'so misleading an indication of the nature of the company's activities as to be likely to cause harm to the public' (s. 76 CA 2006).

8.6.3.3 Passing-off

Registration of a company with a particular name does not give the company any protection against a passing-off action if an existing business trades under a similar name and its business is likely to be affected by the similarity.

Additionally, third parties are able to object to a company's registered name on the basis that they already have goodwill in the same or a similar name (s. 69 CA 2006). Such an objection will have to be made to a company names adjudicator, which is a new office created by the 2006 Act (s. 70 CA 2006).

8.6.3.4 Trade marks

If a company registered a name which included a registered trade mark of another business, it would be open to an action for infringement of such trade mark. It may therefore be prudent for the promoters or their solicitor to inspect the trade marks register before applying for registration, should there be any concern in this regard.

8.6.4 Registered office

A company's registered office determines the jurisdiction under which it is formed. For a company to be registered under the CA 2006, its registered office must be situated and remain in the UK. This requirement is satisfied by the need to state both the intended situation of the company's registered office and its actual address in the application for registration (ss. 9(2)(b) and 9(5)(a) CA 2006).

Under the 1985 Act, the memorandum had to state that the company's registered office would be situated in England (which includes Wales for this purpose) or Wales (to the exclusion of England) or Scotland (for a Scottish registered company), as appropriate. The function of this clause was therefore to determine the company's domicile. The specific address of a company's registered office was then included in the details provided in Form 10, as part of the registration process.

8.6.5 A company's objects and the *ultra vires* doctrine

Because a company is an artificial person, there exists the concept of a company's objects, or purposes, and the powers it is to have. The wording and location of a company's objects can differ from company to company, due to the historical development of this concept. It is, therefore, important to analyse it chronologically.

For well over a century, until the introduction of the CA 2006, the objects had to be stated in the memorandum. Originally any contracts made, or acts done, by a company not within its stated objects, or reasonably incidental thereto, used to be void on the basis that they were *ultra vires*. Because of this rule, objects clauses were traditionally drafted very widely. In particular, it is usual to find in older memoranda many sub-clauses which seek to list all the businesses and activities which the company could conceivably wish to undertake at any time. These would also be followed by a statement that the sub-clauses should be construed as independent of each other.

Certain decisions of the courts sought to temper the impact of the *ultra vires* rule for companies. However, it remained problematic and lawyers continued to draft wide, and very long, objects clauses.

The introduction of s. 35 CA 1985 all but abolished the rule in relation to transactions between *a company and an outsider*. (This provision is carried over into s. 39 CA 2006.) Despite this, many companies still submitted a long form of objects clause when they registered.

An alternative, short form objects clause was possible under s. 3A CA 1985 which provided:

Where the company's memorandum states that the object of the company is to carry on business as a general commercial company—

(a) the object of the company is to carry on any trade or business whatsoever, and

(b) the company has power to do all such things as are incidental or conducive to the carrying on of any trade or business by it.

Where a company adopted this simple form of objects clause, the powers of the company would include the power to carry on any trade or business. The intention behind this statutory 'shorthand' was to allow companies to replace their extensive objects clauses with a single sentence.

However, due to uncertainty about the ambit of the phrase 'trade or business' many companies adopted a 'belt and braces' approach and had both the new form of clause and a traditional long form objects clause following it.

The position has now been reversed under the CA 2006; the objects of any company now registered will be completely unrestricted, unless a specific provision to the contrary is included in a company's articles (s. 31 CA 2006). For this reason, the revised form of memorandum no longer has to contain an objects clause.

It is likely that most companies will take advantage of this situation and rely upon the statutory implication. However, it may be that in certain situations (for example, where a company is being created with a definite objective in mind) those setting up a company will require or deem it necessary to delineate a company's objects in the articles.

For companies set up otherwise than under the 2006 Act, the importation of the objects clause from the memorandum into the articles (s. 28 CA 2006) will have the effect of continuing to impose limits on the company's objects. Therefore, such companies may wish to alter their articles to remove any such restriction and take advantage of the approach offered by the new Act.

To impose, change, or remove any restriction on its objects, a company will have to change its articles by special resolution (s. 21(1) CA 2006). In turn, the company will be obliged to send to the Registrar of Companies an amended copy of the articles (s. 26(1) CA 2006), together with a copy of the special resolution (s. 30(1) CA 2006). Section 31(2) CA 2006 also imposes a separate obligation to notify the Registrar of any such change; the change will not be effective until it is registered.

Overall, the significance of a company's objects is now somewhat minimal, especially for those registered under the 2006 Act with unrestricted objects. However, directors are under a duty to observe a company's constitution (s. 171 CA 2006), so, in relevant circumstances, lawyers must continue to determine whether or not a company's constitution restricts its activities in any way.

8.6.6 Limited liability

There exists the possibility of both limited and unlimited companies (see 7.5). As such, it is necessary to determine the status of a company's shareholders at the time of registration. (For most purposes, shareholders will want the benefit of limited liability.) It is necessary, therefore, to make a statement to this effect in the application for registration (s. 9(2)(c) CA 2006).

Previously, under the 1985 Act (and before), the same outcome was achieved by a limited liability clause being included in the memorandum of association which was submitted for registration purposes. This clause is no longer necessary in memoranda under the 2006 Act.

8.6.7 Initial shareholders and share capital

Most companies will be created with a share capital. In turn, this means that those companies must be created with shareholders, although it is possible to set up a company with only one shareholder (s. 7(1) CA 2006). A company's initial shareholders will be the subscribers to the memorandum, who must agree to take a minimum of one share each (s. 8(1)(b) CA 2006).

Specific details of the subscribers' shareholdings must be set out in the statement of capital and initial shareholdings, which forms part of form IN01. This statement will provide details of:

(i) the total number of shares taken on formation by the subscribers;

(ii) the aggregate nominal value of those shares;

(iii) the rights attaching to those shares;

(iv) the number, nominal value and class of shares taken by each subscriber and the amount paid up on each share.

Specific discussion of a company's share capital is contained in **Chapter 11**. For these purposes, it is sufficient to recognise that all shares must have a nominal, financial value attributed to them, normally denominated in Pounds Sterling. In turn, the relevant shareholder will normally agree to pay the company an amount at least equivalent to the nominal value of the shares subscribed for.

EXAMPLE

Charles and William set up a company by subscribing to the memorandum. They each agree to take 50 shares fully-paid with a nominal value each of £1. As a consequence:

(i) The total nominal value of shares taken by Charles and William is £100.

(ii) Each of Charles and William will have a shareholding with a nominal value of £50 and will, accordingly, each have to pay to the company £50.

8.6.8 The articles of association

This important topic has already been considered briefly at **7.3.5** and a fuller discussion can be found in **Chapter 14**, to which the reader should refer. This section, therefore, simply introduces some of the main relevant issues on incorporation.

The articles are the main constitutional document of a company (s. 17 CA 2006). These regulate the company's internal affairs and contain provisions dealing with such matters as directors' powers, proceedings at members' meetings, conduct at board meetings and so on. By statutory implication, a company and all its members are bound into the provisions of the articles (s. 33(1) CA 2006). When preparing to incorporate a company, one of the most important matters to discuss with the promoters is the contents of the articles and their effect.

A company is able to choose the type of articles it thinks appropriate, but standard form articles have been provided by statutory instrument for companies for many years to assist with the process. The latest versions of these are referred to as the Model Articles and are set out in the Companies (Model Articles) Regulations 2008.

Effectively, a company has four choices:

(a) It can have prepared specially drafted articles from scratch. (This is likely to be a rare occurrence and will be expensive.)

(b) It can adopt standard articles supplied by its legal advisers with or without amendment. (Many law firms will have these as a standard precedent which they can recommend to clients.)

(c) It can adopt the Model Articles wholesale with no amendments.

(d) It can adopt the Model Articles but with bespoke amendments.

With the exception of choice (c), a company must register its chosen articles as part of its application for registration. A failure to do so will mean that the Model Articles will apply to the company by default (s. 20 CA 2006).

8.7 The certificate of incorporation

Upon receipt of an application for registration of a company, Companies House will examine the registration documents and, provided they are in order and the chosen name is still available, will sign a certificate of incorporation stating that the company is incorporated on a particular date and that it is limited (if appropriate). The Registrar of Companies specifies the company's unique registered number on the certificate and this must be quoted on all official documents and business letters.

From the date of incorporation the company becomes a legal entity (s. 16(3) CA 2006). At the same time as the Registrar issues the certificate, he must (under s. 1064 CA 2006) 'officially notify' the fact of issue. This means he must place a notice to this effect in the Government's official newspaper (in England and Wales, the *London Gazette*).

8.8 Steps necessary after incorporation

Once the certificate of incorporation has been issued the company's existence begins. One of the first things which is likely to happen is for the board of directors to conduct its first meeting. The agenda for this will include such matters as:

(a) The approval and execution of any service contracts for board members.

(b) The allotment of any shares over and above those allocated to the subscribers to the memorandum.

(c) The appointment of auditors to the company (if thought necessary).

(d) The appointment of bankers to the company.

(e) Instructions to make the necessary entries in the relevant registers of the company, e.g., the registers of members and the registers of directors.

(f) Alteration of the company's automatically designated accounting reference date (if thought necessary).

In turn, items (a) and (b) may require reference to the shareholders, so a general meeting would also have to be called to coincide with the board meeting.

8.9 Publication of a company's name

There are a number of statutory provisions concerning publication of a company's name. Note, however, that whilst the 2006 Act imposes the obligation to make disclosures, the detailed provisions are contained within the Companies (Trading Disclosures) Regulations 2008.

8.9.1 Disclosure of registered name

A company is required to:

(a) display its registered name at its registered office and any other place of business in which its business is carried on, in a position which can be seen by any visitor to such places and in letters which can be read by the naked eye;

(b) ensure that its name appears on business letters, correspondence and documentation, notices, official publications, cheques, orders for money or goods, invoices, and websites.

8.9.2 Additional disclosures

A company's business letters, order forms, and website should also contain the following information:

(a) the place (i.e., country) of registration of the company;

(b) its registered number;

(c) the address of its registered office.

There is no need to include the names of directors on a company's stationery, but if the name of *any* director appears on a business letter (other than in the text or as a signatory) on which the company's name appears, then the names of *all* the directors who are individuals and the corporate names of all the corporate directors must appear in legible characters.

8.9.3 Penalties for default

Failure to comply with any of the above disclosure requirements without reasonable excuse makes the company and every officer authorising the issue of a letter, etc., liable to a fine.

8.10 Statutory registers

8.10.1 The registers

Companies are required by the Companies Act 2006 to keep certain registers—often referred to as the company's 'books'.

There is no required format for registers and they may be kept in hard copy or electronic format (s. 1135 CA 2006), so the term 'books' is somewhat of a misnomer.

As far as a private limited company is concerned, the two most important registers it must keep at its registered office are:

(a) A *register of members* (s. 113 CA 2006) containing each member's name, address, dates of entry on the register, and cessation of membership together with details of the shares held. (Note that s. 115 CA 2006 requires an index of members to be kept if a company has more than 50 members and the register is not already kept in the form of an index.)

(b) A *register of directors* (s. 162 CA 2006) setting out in respect of each director their name, service address, country of residence, nationality, and date of birth. A separate register of directors' residential addresses must also be maintained (s. 165 CA 2006). Failure to maintain either of these registers is an offence by both the company and any officer in default and is punishable by a fine.

8.10.2 Inspection of company books

Both the register of members and register of directors must be kept available for inspection by members and the general public at the registered office. (They may also be kept at a place other than the registered office provided the Registrar is notified.) Inspection of registers by members is free; all other persons must pay a prescribed fee. It is also possible for either members or outsiders to request a copy of the register of members on payment of a fee. (The rights for outsiders to see the register of members is of particular use in takeover situations when the company is a possible target for a bid and the bidder wishes to find out more about that company's shareholders.)

In recent years there has been some sensitivity about the availability of directors' home addresses to the public through the right to inspect a company's registers. For this reason, the 2006 Act only requires that the register of directors includes a service address, which can obviously be different from a home one. The separate register of residential addresses is not available for public inspection.

8.10.3 Other documents to be kept by a company

Other documents which should be kept at the registered office include:

(a) directors' service contracts (s. 228 CA 2006), which can be inspected by members free of charge. Members can also, on payment of a fee, ask to be supplied with a copy of any service contract;

(b) records of shareholder resolutions of the company (passed at general meetings or otherwise) for a period of 10 years (s. 358 CA 2006), which can be inspected by members free of charge.

Companies are also obliged to record and maintain minutes of all directors' meetings for 10 years (s. 248 CA 2006). However, the Act does not require these to be maintained at the registered office for inspection.

8.11 Comparison of 'tailor-made' with 'shelf' company

8.11.1 The tailor-made company

This is a company formed following the procedure outlined above. The documentation will be tailored to the promoters' requirements, with the memorandum and articles including provisions appropriate to the particular circumstances of the case. The promoters will most likely be the subscribers to the memorandum (the company's first members) and may also be the company's first directors and secretary.

This method can be relatively expensive, as every application for registration will be unique to the client. In addition, there will be the time involved in waiting for Companies House to process the application, which can take around five days although an expedited, same-day, incorporation service is available for a higher fee. (See the Appendix to this Chapter for further details of relevant fees.)

8.11.2 The shelf company

This is a company which has already been incorporated—normally by a company formation specialist, law stationers, or a firm of solicitors—from whom it is then purchased by the promoters. In other words, the promoters do not seek to register their own company from scratch, they simply take over a company which has already been formed, but which will have carried on no commercial functions.

Shelf companies are invariably set up according to a standard formula, such that they are relatively inexpensive to create and 'bulk' applications can be made. (A law stationers, for example, may set up thousands of companies in this way each year.)

These companies are, however, no different to any other company, in that they must fulfil all the requirements for registration. A shelf company will, therefore, have directors, shareholders, a registered office, a name, and a memorandum and articles. Most or all of these aspects of the shelf company will have to be altered to suit the needs of the relevant promoters and ownership of the company must be transferred to the promoters.

In the remainder of this section, we will consider the issues surrounding the necessary conversion of each of the elements of a shelf company. This process of conversion normally involves decisions of both the directors and shareholders of the shelf company, but, as these decisions are very often a standard requirement, supporting pro forma documentation will ensure that the process is effectively an administrative one.

8.11.2.1 Memorandum of association

As a company's memorandum ceases to have any relevance beyond its initial registration, that of the shelf company will be of no consequence to those taking it over.

8.11.2.2 Company name

Shelf companies are generally created with wholly imaginary and often unusual names. (This is to avoid any application being rejected on the basis that a company is already registered with the same name.) As a result, the name of the chosen shelf company will have no connection with the promoters or their business. If the name of their company is unimportant to the promoters, this will cause no problems. However, if they wish their company to trade under their own names or a chosen name, it will have to be changed. (See **8.12** for further discussion of the process of changing a company's name.)

8.11.2.3 Articles of association

As regards the articles, the shelf company is likely to have been incorporated with either Model Articles or with standard amended articles. Great care must be taken to ensure that the articles are suitable for the promoters' wishes. If they are not, they will have to be amended in accordance with the Companies Act, which requires the members to pass a special resolution approving the change (see **Chapter 14** for further discussion of this area).

8.11.2.4 Directors and shareholders

Representatives of the entity which formed the shelf company will have signed the memorandum as subscribers, and will have been named in the registration documentation as officers of the company. This means that they become the first members, directors, and secretary (if any) of the company, and their names should appear in the company's books as such. (It is likely that there will be only one or two subscribers and/or directors of the shelf company.)

In order for ownership and control of the shelf company to be passed to the promoters, it is necessary that:

(a) the first members *transfer* their shares to the promoters;

(b) the first directors and secretary (if any) *resign* their positions; and

(c) the promoters are appointed as new directors and secretary (if one is required).

An alternative means by which ownership and control can be vested in the promoters is for a 'letter of renunciation' to be supplied with the shelf company. This letter contains a renunciation of rights as shareholders and company officers in favour of the promoters, which avoids the need for formal transfer of the shares and resignation of the existing directors.

8.11.2.5 Accounting reference date

The date of registration of the shelf company will determine its accounting reference date, that is, the date on which its accounting year ends. If this is not suitable, it will have to be changed to meet the promoters' needs. (See **8.13** for further discussion of this issue.)

8.11.2.6 Registered office

As part of the process of registration of the shelf company, details of the company's first registered office will have been supplied (normally the address of the law stationers or the solicitors' firm which has set up the company). If this is not suitable, it will have to be changed to meet the promoters' needs. (See **8.14** for further discussion of this issue.)

8.11.3 Advantages and disadvantages

The greatest advantage of utilising a shelf company is generally considered to be speed and certainty. The promoters may obtain a company immediately, often for a comparatively low price.

A tailor-made company will inevitably take longer to form (even using the same-day service) due to the need to take instructions and complete documentation. The cost of the latter will almost certainly be greater than the initial cost of a shelf company. However, it is possible to set up a company from scratch using relatively standard documentation, after which discussions can take place with the client about the particular suitability of, say, the articles, which can be amended subsequently. Also, the promoters may prefer a company set up from scratch, as it has no prior history.

There are no hard and fast rules as to when a tailor-made or shelf company should be used. The advantages and disadvantages above should be considered in conjunction with the circumstances of the particular case, including any time or budget limitations of the promoters.

8.12 Change of name

8.12.1 Introduction

As seen above, it may be that the name of a shelf company has to be changed to suit a client's purposes. By contrast, if a company is tailor-made for a client, it is unlikely that it will want to change its name for the foreseeable future. However, at some future date, it may be thought desirable to make such a change.

8.12.2 Choice of name

As on incorporation, a company has general freedom to choose whatever name it likes, but this is subject to the same restrictions which apply on incorporation and the powers of the Secretary of State to direct a change of name (detailed in **8.6.3**).

8.12.3 Procedure

Section 77 CA 2006 allows two methods by which a company may change its name: either by special resolution or by any alternative method stipulated in a company's articles. Such a method could be simpler or more difficult than by special resolution, so could include, for example, either a majority or unanimous decision of the directors or the shareholders.

Note that the Model Articles do not contain any specific provision dealing with change of name. In addition, companies which were set up prior to s. 77 coming into effect (that is, companies incorporated prior to 1 October 2009) are unlikely to include any such provision, as it was not possible to do so under the 1985 Act. In default of any positive action, therefore, it may be the case that many companies will have to change their names by special resolution.

Any change of name must be notified to the Registrar of Companies. The method of notification will depend upon the method by which the company's name was changed. If a special resolution is used, both notice of the change to the name on form NM01 and a copy of the resolution must be sent to the Registrar (s. 78 CA 2006). Where the change is effected by a method in the articles, the company must give notice that this is the case and notice of the change itself on form NM04 (s. 79 CA 2006). A fee is also payable, in either circumstance. (See the Appendix to this Chapter for further details of relevant fees.)

If the change is satisfactory in the opinion of the Registrar, a certificate of incorporation on change of name will be issued (s. 80 CA 2006), at which point the change of name is effective (s. 81(a) CA 2006). It is important, therefore, to recognise that the change does not take effect at the time the decision is made.

Once the name has been changed, it must be used on the company's notepaper and other documents in accordance with the disclosure requirements discussed at **8.9**.

8.12.4 Use of business name

For some companies, the registered name is somewhat of a statutory formality, as they may choose to trade under a business name for the purposes of their public image. (Effectively, this will be a trade mark of the business. There are many examples on the high street, for example, of business names.) To avoid companies defeating the restrictions on corporate names through the use of business names, they are regulated by Pt 41 CA 2006 (and related regulations), which impose the same restrictions on the use of business names as for corporate names.

The advantage of a business name is that any change to it is not regulated by the Companies Act, so it can be changed at any time by board resolution. Additionally, the change does not have to be registered at Companies House (although, if the business name is also a registered trade mark, a new registration would have to be made to the Trade Marks Registry).

8.13 Change of accounting reference date

8.13.1 Introduction

A company's accounting reference period is the period for which a company must produce annual accounts, as required by the Companies Act 2006. The accounting reference period of a company is determined according to its accounting reference date (ARD).

8.13.2 Accounting reference date of a company

A company's ARD is determined by its date of incorporation (s. 391 CA 2006). The situation is somewhat complicated because the date of incorporation can result in different rules being applied. However, for our purposes, the most important of these rules is that for any company incorporated after 1 April 1996 (either under the provisions of the 1985 Act or those of the 2006 Act) its ARD will be the last day of the month in which the anniversary of its incorporation falls. Therefore, a relevant company incorporated on 14 July would have 31 July as its ARD and its first set of accounts would have to reflect the period from incorporation until the following 31 July. Thereafter, each set of accounts would represent the period from 1 August to the following 31 July.

8.13.3 Altering the accounting reference date

8.13.3.1 Reasons

A company may wish to alter its ARD for various reasons. Many companies wish to have their accounting period end at the end of the calendar or financial year. Others may be or become part of a group of companies where it makes administrative sense for each company in the group to have the same ARD and hence the same accounting period.

8.13.3.2 Method

A company may alter its ARD by giving notice to the Registrar of Companies on form AA01 pursuant to s. 392 CA 2006. The decision to alter a company's ARD will usually be taken by its board of directors.

Any alteration to the ARD will result either in a shortening or lengthening of the current accounting period. There are two important rules to bear in mind:

(a) If any alteration is to affect a company's initial accounting reference period, this should neither be shortened to less than six months nor lengthened to more than 18 months from the date of its incorporation.

(b) Any alteration to a subsequent accounting reference period must not lengthen it by more than 18 months.

EXAMPLE

Quartz Limited is incorporated on 13 October 2008. Its ARD is, therefore, determined as 31 October. Its first accounts will have to be made up to 31 October 2009. If this is unsuitable, Quartz must notify Companies House of the desired change.

If the preferred date for its ARD is 30 April, Quartz must notify of this change and apply to have its first accounting reference period end on 30 April 2009, i.e., shorten the relevant period. (The alternative would result in an accounting reference period in excess of 18 months.)

Instead, if the preferred date for its ARD is 31 December, Quartz must notify of this change and apply to have its first accounting reference period end on 31 December 2009, i.e., lengthen the relevant period. (The alternative would result in an accounting reference period shorter than six months.)

8.14 Change of registered office

A company's registered office may be changed by giving relevant notice on form AD01 to the Registrar, pursuant to s. 87 CA 2006. (Effectively this is a decision for the board of directors.)

The change is effective in relation to service of documents when registered by the Registrar, although service of documents at the old registered office remains valid for a further 14 days after registration.

online resource centre

Interactive online exercises (Student Learning Activities) which complement the topics covered in this chapter are available at www.oxfordtextbooks.co.uk/orc/business12_13/.

APPENDIX
COMPANIES HOUSE FORMS AND FEES

The following two tables set out some of the more common forms and fees which a company may have to submit to Companies House in its lifetime. Some have already been referred to in this chapter. Others, such as the annual return and the registration of a mortgage, are relevant to other elements of the book.

Main Companies House forms

Form	CA Section	Purpose	Fee (see below)
IN01	9	Application to Register	Yes
AR01	854	Annual Return	Yes
AA01	392	Change of Accounting Reference Date	No
NM01	78	Change of Name by Special Resolution	Yes
NM04	79	Change of Name by Method in Articles	Yes
AD01	87	Change of Registered Office	No
AP01	167	Appointment of Director	No
AP03	276	Appointment of Secretary	No
TM01	167	Termination of Director's Appointment	No
TM02	276	Termination of Secretary's Appointment	No
MR01	859A	Registration of Particulars of a Charge	Yes
SH01	555	Return of Allotment of Shares	No
SH03	707	Return of Buy-back	No – but attracts stamp duty
SH06	708	Notice of Cancellation of Shares (post buy-back)	No

Notes:

(a) All forms are titled according to their purpose: for example, the prefix 'SH' stands for 'shares'; the prefix 'AP' stands for appointment.

(b) Every form has a statutory premise, which will be referred to on the face of the form.

(c) Where a fee is payable, the form will provide details.

(d) All forms contain a checklist on the final page, which should not be overlooked when completing a form.

(e) It is usually a director or the secretary (if one appointed) who signs a form on the company's behalf. If, however, the company is insolvent, the signatory will normally be the liquidator or administrator.

Main Companies House fees

	Paper Filing	Electronic Filing
Incorporation	£40.00	£14.00
Same-day Incorporation	£100.00	£30.00
Change of name	£10.00	£8.00
Same-day change of name	£50.00	£30.00
Annual Return	£40.00	£14.00
Registration of mortgage or charge	£13.00	£10.00

online resource centre

For further resources and online chapters please visit the Online Resource Centre at www.oxfordtextbooks.co.uk/orc/business13_14/.

9

Directors and secretary

This chapter covers the following topics:

9.1 Introduction

In this chapter, we shall look at the law relating to a company's officers. This is a combination of statute, common law, and regulations under a company's articles of association. In respect of this last limb, we will consider both Table A and the Model Articles for Private Companies, as both are likely to be encountered in practice. (Further relevant discussion of the articles can be found in **14.4**.)

9.2 Division of powers within a company

The power to take decisions on behalf of a company is divided between the directors and members. There are a number of powers which are exercisable only by the members under various provisions of the Companies Act 2006 (the 2006 Act or CA 2006), for example, the power to change the articles. Furthermore, the directors may have to seek authorisation from shareholders prior to committing the company to a transaction, for example, a buy-back of shares. However, in most instances, the directors will be able to conduct the business of and manage the company without reference to the shareholders. This is because there will be a general delegation of such authority from the company to the directors through the articles of association (see **9.9.1** for further discussion).

9.3 Appointment of directors

9.3.1 Introduction

The first directors of a company are the people who are named as such and whose details are provided to the Registrar as part of the process of registration; they automatically become directors on the company's incorporation (s. 16(6) CA 2006). Section 154 CA 2006 provides that a private company must have at least one director and that a public company must have at least two directors. For both private and public companies at least one director is required to be a 'natural person', that is, not a company or corporation (s. 155 CA 2006). (Previously, it was possible for a private company to exist with simply one corporate director and for a public company to exist with two such directors. Any companies set up in this way will have had to effect the appointment of a 'human' director either to replace or in addition to a corporate one.)

From time to time, it will be necessary to appoint further directors, either because one of the directors has ceased to hold office or because it is decided to increase the size of the board. Apart from a few statutory restrictions (dealt with below), the company is free to make whatever provision it wishes in its articles as to the appointment of directors. In particular, there is no general requirement that the directors should be shareholders, nor that they should be chosen by the shareholders.

The appointment of any director, other than on incorporation, will trigger an obligation on the company under s. 167 CA 2006 to notify the Registrar of Companies on form AP01 within 14 days of the appointment (see **9.11.1.2**).

9.3.2 Provision for appointment in a company's articles

Statute makes no special provision for the method of appointing directors. It is, therefore, a matter for the articles. Companies may adopt various methods to deal with this issue. What follows, therefore, is a general summary of the more common approaches.

Normally the main power to appoint directors is given to the members. This provides for appointment by ordinary resolution (that is, by a simple majority of the members).

Appointments to fill vacancies on the board and appointments of additional directors may also normally be made by the board itself. The articles may specify that persons co-opted in this way hold office until the following annual general meeting (assuming the company holds such meetings), at which point their appointment should be confirmed by ordinary resolution. However, this can be a cumbersome device and the articles may allow any appointment by the board to be as permanent as that by the shareholders. For example Article 17 of the Model Articles for Private Companies allows a permanent appointment to be made either by ordinary resolution of the members or by a decision of the directors.

It should be noted that neither the previous Table A nor the Model Articles require a director to be a shareholder. If the company wants to restrict membership of the board to shareholders, an article to that effect must be adopted on formation or by later amendment.

9.3.3 Service contracts

It is common for managing directors (see **9.4**) and other executive directors to enter into service contracts with a company on their appointment to the board. Notwithstanding that both events will usually occur within very close proximity to each other, it is important to understand the distinction between a person

(a) being *appointed* to the *office* of director; and

(b) *entering* into a *service contract*.

On being appointed to the office of director, the director's conduct is defined primarily by the company's articles, common law, and legislation. He may receive a *fee* for holding office. On entering into a service contract to carry out an executive role, the director has various rights and obligations defined primarily by the terms of the contract as negotiated with the company. (The director will normally also be entitled to those rights which the law affords all employees.)

The distinction is of particular importance should a director be removed from office (see **9.8.1.3**).

One of the main rights under the service contract will be that of receiving a *salary* and related remuneration in return for carrying out the defined obligations. However, because directors are in a fiduciary relationship with their companies, they are technically not permitted to be rewarded for their services. However, an express provision in the articles will displace this presumption. For example, regulation 82 of Table A allows directors' remuneration to be determined by ordinary resolution. However, the pay of any director who is appointed to perform an executive function may be determined by the directors under regulation 84. By contrast, article 19 of the Model Articles for Private Companies adopts a simpler approach and allows all forms of directors' remuneration to be determined by the board.

9.4 Managing directors

9.4.1 Appointment and powers

It is very common for one of the directors of a company to be appointed managing director. The functions actually performed by the managing director vary from company to company, but in practice he will usually be either the most senior executive director in the company's hierarchy or second in command to the chairman. A managing director cannot be appointed unless the articles so provide. For example, Table A, article 84 does so provide and additionally article 72 provides that: '[the directors] may . . . delegate to any managing director . . . such of their powers as they consider desirable to be exercised by him'. The Model Articles contain wider powers of delegation, allowing directors to delegate 'to such persons . . . to such an extent . . . as they think fit' (article 5). (See **9.9** for discussion of directors' powers generally.)

9.4.2 Service contract

The managing director will usually have a service contract. The terms of the contract will be negotiated by the managing director and the board; the members' approval will be required if he is given security of tenure for longer than two years (s. 188 CA 2006—see **9.11.2.1**). The managing director is both a director and an employee of the company. Like other employees he has certain statutory rights against the company if he is unfairly dismissed or made redundant. Since he automatically ceases to be managing director if he ceases to be a director, the members can remove him from both offices by passing an ordinary resolution (s. 168 CA 2006), but this may result in heavy damages being payable by the company for breach of the service contract (see **9.8.1.3**).

9.5 Alternate directors

The articles can give a director power to appoint (subject to the approval of the board) an alternate director. Once appointed, the alternate director has all the powers of the appointing director until he is removed by the appointing director or the appointing director ceases to be a director. However, the alternate director is not entitled to receive remuneration from the company for his services.

The Model Articles for Private Companies do not contain provision for alternate directors, as it is thought unlikely that directors of private companies would wish to appoint alternates. The equivalent articles for public companies do contain such a provision and this could be adopted by private companies if the need arose.

9.6 Shadow directors

A 'shadow director' is defined by s. 251(1) CA 2006 as 'any person in accordance with whose directions or instructions the directors of a company are accustomed to act'. However, a person who gives advice in a professional capacity to the directors is not to be taken to be a shadow director. Similar provisions are contained in s. 251 Insolvency Act 1986.

Under a number of provisions of the 2006 Act, shadow directors are treated as directors of the company. Examples of the provisions which apply to shadow directors are:

(a) the general duties of directors (see **9.10**);

(b) the statutory restrictions on substantial property transactions and loans (see **9.11.2.2** and **9.11.2.3**);

(c) the requirement to disclose interests in contracts with the company to the board (see **9.10.1.8**); and

(d) the provisions relating to service contracts (see **9.11.2.1**).

In addition, and perhaps more significantly, shadow directors are deemed to be directors for the purpose of wrongful trading under s. 214 Insolvency Act 1986 (see **27.1**), by which they may become personally liable for the debts of an insolvent company. Under the Company Directors Disqualification Act 1986, shadow directors may also be disqualified from holding office or being concerned in the management of a company, as if they were directors.

9.7 Retirement of directors

9.7.1 Retirement by notice

The most straightforward way in which a director may vacate office is to retire by giving notice to the company. Usually this takes the form of a letter to the board.

9.7.2 Retirement by rotation

As a way of providing shareholders control over the board on an ongoing basis, the articles may contain a provision which obliges a designated percentage of directors to retire from office on an annual basis.

In the case of a private company, provisions for retirement by rotation are unnecessarily cumbersome and are often not included so that, once appointed, directors hold office permanently until death, voluntary retirement, disqualification, or removal from office under s. 168 CA 2006 (see **9.8.1**). The Model Articles for Private Companies recognise this and do not contain any provision for retirement by rotation. By contrast, Table A does contain such provisions—see regulations 73–74.

It should be noted, however, that Table A also states that managing directors and directors holding any other executive office are not subject to retirement by rotation—see regulation 84 of Table A.

9.8 Removal of directors from office

9.8.1 Removal of directors under s. 168 CA 2006

9.8.1.1 Power to remove by ordinary resolution

Section 168 CA 2006 provides for removal of directors by ordinary resolution (i.e., by a majority vote of the shareholders). The power given by the section overrides anything in the company's articles (even, for example, an article naming a life director) or in an agreement with the director. Section 168 provides the most effective means by which majority shareholders who object to the way in which their company is being run can keep control of the company. Where the directors themselves are the majority shareholders, as they very frequently will be in the case of a private company, the other (minority) shareholders have limited rights to object to the way the board is running the company.

9.8.1.2 Procedure

No resolution purporting to remove a director from office is valid unless special notice has first been given to the company of an intention to remove a particular director. This usually emanates from the shareholder or shareholders who wish to remove the director. In effect, this gives the company a minimum period of 28 days' 'grace' before any steps are taken by the shareholders in question to remove the director (s. 312(1) CA 2006, superseding the similar provision in s. 379 CA 1985). On receipt of the notice, a company is obliged to send a copy to the director whose removal is proposed.

However, special notice is not sufficient to cause a meeting to be held at which the necessary resolution can be proposed or to have such a resolution included on the agenda of any forthcoming meeting (see *Pedley v Inland Waterways Association* [1977] 1 All ER 209). Unless the board is sympathetic to the proposal and calls a general meeting itself, the shareholders concerned must invoke their right under s. 303 CA 2006, or any special right they may have under the company's articles of association, to cause the directors to call a general meeting for the purpose of considering the director's removal.

9.8.1.3 Director's right to compensation and damages on removal

The shareholders have an absolute right to remove a director. However, this does not deprive the director of any rights to compensation or damages he may have (s. 168(5) CA 2006). When considering these rights, it is important to maintain a distinction between the right to a payment for loss of office and the right to claim damages where there is a service contract between the director and the company.

Should the director be removed *from office*, then the only compensation for such loss of office he may receive is a payment approved by the company under s. 217 CA 2006. However, removal from office will almost certainly terminate any service contract as it will be impossible for the director to fulfil his obligations. Depending on the terms of the director's remuneration under the contract, damages could be extensive. (Payment of damages does not require shareholder approval, as the company is legally bound to pay them.) It is therefore important for the shareholders to consider the financial cost of removing a director.

9.8.1.4 Special voting rights on resolution to remove director

The articles may validly give special voting rights to some of the shareholders either generally or in particular circumstances. In the case of *Bushell v Faith* [1970] AC 1099, the articles provided that:

> in the event of a resolution being proposed at any general meeting of the company for the removal from office of any director, any shares held by that director shall on a poll in respect of such resolution carry the right to three votes per share . . .

The director whose removal was proposed owned one third of the shares and so could not be removed. Nevertheless, the article was held to be valid, since all that the Act lays down is that an ordinary resolution may be used to remove a director and an ordinary resolution is one requiring a simple majority of votes. A clause of this type does not, therefore, prevent a resolution from being an ordinary resolution but effectively makes it impossible to remove the director without his consent.

The decision in *Bushell v Faith* has been criticised, but there are some circumstances where it may be appropriate to include in the articles a regulation which makes it impossible for the majority shareholders to get rid of a director who owns a minority of the shares. Such a regulation should be considered, for example, where a small number of people wish to run a company as a 'quasi-partnership'—that is, where they all intend to have a continuing right to take part in management. In other circumstances it may be appropriate to give the shareholders wider powers to remove directors than are given by s. 168 so that, for example, removal by ordinary resolution *without* special notice may be considered appropriate.

9.8.2 Disqualification

9.8.2.1 Company Directors Disqualification Act 1986

Companies legislation contains a number of provisions under which directors are disqualified either automatically or by court order. The most important of these are contained in the Company Directors Disqualification Act 1986 (CDDA 1986). This Act provides for disqualification from acting as a director, liquidator, receiver, or manager of a company and from being concerned with the management of a company for up to 15 years (five years if the order is made by a magistrates' court). Disqualification can be imposed following:

(a) conviction for an indictable offence in connection with the management of a company;

(b) a finding that an offence involving fraud has been committed in the course of winding up a company;

(c) persistent default in filing returns with the Registrar (persistent default is conclusively presumed following three convictions for failure to file returns within five years); the maximum period of disqualification in this case is five years even if the penalty is imposed by a court other than a magistrates' court;

(d) a finding that a person is 'unfit' to be concerned in the management of a company. The order may only be made against a person who is or has been a director of a company which has become insolvent while or after he was a director. For these purposes a company is insolvent if it goes into insolvent liquidation, an administration order is made against it or an administrative receiver is appointed. Where an order is made on the ground of unfitness, the disqualification period must be for a minimum of two years and a maximum of 15.

The CDDA 1986 also contains a provision allowing directors to give an undertaking to the Secretary of State for Business, Innovation and Skills not to be involved in the management of a company for a specified period of time. This process of 'fast track' disqualification avoids the need for court proceedings and is intended to increase efficiency in dealing with errant directors.

9.8.2.2 Disqualification under the articles

The articles of a company may make provision for disqualification or automatic retirement in circumstances other than those specified in the Act, for example, if a director:

(a) becomes bankrupt;

(b) is or may be suffering from mental disorder and is admitted to hospital under the Mental Health Act or a court order is made against him on matters concerning mental disorder;

(c) is absent from directors' meetings (without the board's permission) for at least six months and the directors resolve that the office be vacated.

The articles also normally provide for the resignation of directors by their giving written notice to the company. No particular period of notice is required. If the director has a service contract, as, for example, in the case of most full-time directors, there is an implied obligation to give reasonable notice but for the sake of certainty it is better to include a specific period in the contract. Similar provisions to those described above are contained in the Model Articles.

Neither Table A nor the Model Articles contain any express power for the directors to remove one of their kind. However, it is possible for articles of association to reserve such a power either by a majority decision of the board or by a written request from all other directors, for example, a provision stating that a person will cease to be a director if that person receives notice signed by all the other directors stating that that person should cease to be a director. There is judicial authority for the fact that such a power is fiduciary and must be exercised in the best interests of the company (see *Samuel Tak Lee v Chou Wen Hsien* [1984] 1 WLR 1202). On this basis, it is expected that the statutory duties of directors under the 2006 Act (see **9.10**) would also apply to the exercise of this power.

9.9 Powers of directors

9.9.1 Defining directors' powers

The powers of the directors are delegated to them through the articles, including, in particular, power to manage the business of the company. For example, article 3 of the Model Articles for Private Companies provides that:

> Subject to the articles, the directors are responsible for the management of the company's business, for which purpose they may exercise all the powers of the company.

However, article 4 contains a qualification to this delegation in that:

> The shareholders may, by special resolution, direct the directors to take, or refrain from taking, specified action.

Article 70 of Table A produces a very similar result, albeit with less concise wording:

> Subject to the provisions of the Act, the memorandum and the articles and to any directions given by special resolution, the business of the company shall be managed by the directors who may exercise all the powers of the company. No alteration of the memorandum or articles and no such direction shall invalidate any prior act of the directors which would have been valid if that alteration had not been made or that direction had not been given. The powers given by this regulation shall not be limited by any special power given to the directors by the articles and a meeting of directors at which a quorum is present may exercise all powers exercisable by the directors.

9.9.2 Exercise of powers

9.9.2.1 Introduction

Decisions of the directors must normally be taken either at a board meeting at which a quorum is present or by unanimous written agreement. This is, however, subject to the directors' power to delegate (e.g., to a managing director, committee of directors, or appointed agent—see **9.4.1** and **9.12.3**).

9.9.2.2 Calling a board meeting

Article 9 of the Model Articles provides that any director may call a board meeting or require the company secretary (if one exists) to do so at any time. No particular period of notice is required, so that a meeting will be validly held if reasonable notice is given. Notice need not be in writing, but it must contain details of when and where the meeting is to be held. Also, in recognition of the use of AV technology to enable meetings to take place, if it is anticipated that directors will not all be in the same place for the meeting, details of how communication will take place should be provided.

The equivalent provision of Table A is article 88, although this deals with more than just notice of a board meeting and it also provides that notice need not be given to a director who is absent from the UK.

9.9.2.3 What constitutes a meeting?

At face value, a meeting will require the presence of directors in the same venue. However, this can be restrictive and can result in practical difficulties for the board. It also does not allow the use of modern communication methods. A company's articles may, therefore, recognise a wider concept of what a board meeting may be. For example, article 10 of the Model Articles for Private Companies treats any director as participating in a board meeting if he can communicate to other directors any information or opinions he has on the business being discussed. Furthermore, any method of communication is acceptable and the location of any director is irrelevant as to whether or not he is participating in the meeting.

9.9.2.4 Decisions at board meetings

Decisions at board meetings are taken by majority vote; if there is an equality of votes, the chairman may be given a casting vote. The chairman is chosen by the directors from among themselves. The chairman's casting vote prevents deadlock (without it a resolution fails if there is an equality of votes), but it also means that the director who is the chairman has considerably more power than the others.

Both the Model Articles and Table A allow the chairman to have a casting vote.

9.9.2.5 Prohibition on director voting on resolution in which he is interested

Previously under the common law and now under s. 175 CA 2006 directors should avoid a conflict of interest with their respective company. As a way of reinforcing this duty, the articles may impose a prohibition on directors' voting and counting in the quorum in a conflict situation which is to be voted on at a board meeting. Such a provision can be found in both the Model Articles (art. 14) and Table A (arts 94–96).

The relevant articles are some of the most complicated to be found in either the Model Articles or Table A. However, they break down into three main elements:

(1) the situation in which the prohibition applies;

(2) any carve-outs or exceptions to the prohibition;

(3) a mechanism to allow the prohibition to be disapplied.

The following table demonstrates this.

Provision	**Model Articles**	**Table A**
Prohibition	Art. 14(1): director cannot count in quorum or vote on a decision of the directors which concerns an actual or proposed transaction with the company in which the director is interested. Art. 14(3)(b): prohibition does not apply where the director's interest cannot reasonably be regarded as likely to give rise to a conflict of interest.	Art. 94: prohibits a director from voting on any resolution concerning a matter in which that director has an interest or duty which is material and conflicts or may conflict with the interests of the company. Art. 95: prohibits a director from counting in the quorum on which he is forbidden from voting.
Exceptions	Art. 14(3)(c): prohibition does not apply, even if conflict, when that director's conflict of interest arises from a 'permitted cause'. Art. 14(4): permitted causes are: (a) guarantee given by or to a director in respect of an obligation incurred by or on behalf of the company; (b) subscription for shares/securities of the company or the underwriting or guaranteeing of a subscription for shares/securities; (c) arrangements for providing benefits to employees or directors which do not provide special benefits to directors.	Art. 94: restriction on voting does not apply to any interest or duty of a director arising in respect of either: (a) a resolution concerning any guarantee, security or indemnity to be given to the director in respect of money lent to the company, or an obligation incurred by the director for the benefit of the company; (b) an arrangement whereby the company gives a guarantee, security, or indemnity to a third party in respect of an obligation of the company guaranteed or indemnified by the director; (c) an interest arising from his buying any shares or other securities from the company; or (d) a resolution relating to a retirement benefits scheme.
Disapplication	Art. 14(3)(a): effect of art. 14(1) can be disapplied by ordinary resolution.	Art. 96: effect of art. 94 can be disapplied by ordinary resolution.

The application of these articles requires detailed analysis and interpretation, which may not produce a definitive answer. If there is any doubt about a director's capacity to vote, it is probably preferable to err on the side of caution, especially if there are other directors who can constitute a quorum and pass the necessary resolution. (Note that the relevant director will only be excluded from the relevant resolution out of which the conflict arises; in all other aspects of the board meeting, the director can take full part.)

This type of article can, however, cause problems where a company has, for example, only two directors, one or both of whom are interested in specific resolutions. Prima facie, the relevant board meeting will be inquorate and the resolution will not be able to be passed validly. The short-term solution would be to seek the disapplication of the prohibition by the shareholders. Alternatively, if it is thought that the problem will recur, this type of article could be removed by special resolution or not adopted at the outset of a company's registration.

Irrespective of which of the above prohibitions applies, it should always be remembered that, independently of the articles, a director is obliged by s. 177 CA 2006 to make a declaration of any interest he may have in a transaction with the company.

9.9.2.6 Decision by way of written resolution

The articles may allow the directors to pass valid resolutions without holding a board meeting. For example, article 93 of Table A provides that if *all* the directors entitled to receive notice of meetings sign a written resolution, this decision is valid and effective as if it had been passed at a board meeting. Article 8 of the Model Articles also permits the similar use of a written resolution by the directors, but also treats as valid a decision where 'all eligible directors indicate to each other *by any means* that they share a common view on a matter', which would presumably include such things as the use of text messaging or e-mail exchange. Such informality does have practical benefits, but for evidential purposes a written record of any such decision would still be appropriate.

9.10 Directors' duties

9.10.1 Statutory duties under CA 2006

9.10.1.1 Introduction

One of the most potentially significant changes introduced by the Companies Act 2006 is the statutory statement of the duties owed by directors to a company. Previously, the majority of directors' duties were founded on common law rules and equitable principles. The statutory duties have been based on these principles and are stated in s. 170(3) CA 2006 to 'have effect in place of those rules and principles as regards the duties owed to a company by a director'. The common law rules and equitable principles will continue to have relevance. Section 170(4) CA 2006 states that the statutory duties:

> shall be interpreted and applied in the same way as the common law rules or equitable principles, and regard shall be had to the corresponding common law rules and equitable principles in interpreting and applying the . . . duties.

In addition, whilst the statutory duties are said to take effect in place of the common law rules and equitable principles, the Act falls short of stating that no common law rules will continue to apply. For these reasons, an outline is provided below (see **9.10.2**) of some of the major fiduciary duties owed by directors to a company. First, however, we shall consider the statutory duties under CA 2006. Each will be considered separately but to summarise them, they are:

(a) to act within the company's constitution and to exercise their powers for proper purposes;

(b) to promote the success of the company;

(c) to exercise independent judgement;

(d) to exercise reasonable care, skill, and diligence;

(e) to avoid conflicts of interest;

(f) not to accept benefits from third parties;

(g) to declare interests in existing and proposed transactions or arrangements.

9.10.1.2 Duty to act within powers

Section 171 CA 2006 requires that a director must:

(a) act in accordance with the company's constitution; and

(b) only exercise powers for the purposes for which they were conferred.

This provision is based on a common law principle illustrated in the case of *Hogg v Cramphorn Ltd* [1967] Ch 254 (see **9.10.2.2**).

9.10.1.3 Duty to promote the success of the company

Under s. 172 CA 2006, a director must act in the way in which he considers, in good faith, would be most likely to promote the success of the company for the benefit of the members as a whole. In doing so, he should have regard (amongst other matters) to:

(a) the likely long-term consequences of any decision;

(b) the interests of the employees;

(c) the need to foster relationships with suppliers, customers, and others;

(d) the impact of operations on the community and the environment;

(e) the need to maintain a reputation for high standards of business conduct;

(f) the need to act fairly as between members of the company.

These requirements appear to be wider than the duties under the previous regime. These were, predominantly, to act in the best interests of the company (being the members, present and future) and, under s. 309 CA 1985, to have regard to the interests of the company's employees. One of the main intentions behind the new regime is the development of a principle of 'enlightened shareholder value'. This is designed to result in companies taking account of a wide range of stakeholders who are potentially affected by their business activities. What remains to be seen is the extent to which directors are going to feel the need to be seen to be complying with the new regime. That is, will board minutes of decisions expressly refer to the fact that each of the above matters was considered? The business community is not in favour of this as it will increase bureaucracy and costs. Two points are likely to support a lower key approach. First, the fact that the overriding duty under s. 172 remains that of acting for the benefit of the members as a whole, as under the previous regime. Secondly, guidance provided by the DTI has stated that, subject to good faith, the decision as to what will promote success is to remain one for a company's directors, not the courts.

9.10.1.4 Duty to exercise independent judgement

This duty is set out in s. 173 CA 2006. The duty will not be infringed by a director where he acts in accordance with an agreement duly entered into by the company or in accordance with the company's constitution.

9.10.1.5 Duty to exercise reasonable care, skill, and diligence

This duty, required by s. 174 CA 2006, is to be judged by reference to the care, skill, and diligence that would be exercised by a reasonably diligent person with:

(a) the general knowledge, skill, and experience that may reasonably be expected of a person carrying out the functions carried out by the director in relation to the company; and

(b) the general knowledge, skill, and experience that the director has.

This test, which combines objective and subjective views, is similar to that applied in judging conduct in relation to wrongful trading under s. 214 Insolvency Act 1986.

9.10.1.6 Duty to avoid conflicts of interest

A director is required, by s. 175 CA 2006, to avoid a situation where he has, or can have, a direct or indirect interest that conflicts, or possibly may conflict, with the interests of the company. The section makes specific reference to situations involving the exploitation of any property, information, or opportunity, whether or not the company could itself take advantage of such situation. It is important to note, however, that the section is of no relevance to situations involving contracts with the company itself (s. 175(3) CA 2006). Moreover, if the situation in question is one which cannot reasonably be regarded as likely to give rise to a conflict of interest, the duty is not infringed.

Any potential conflict of interest can, however, be authorised by a quorum of non-conflicted directors (the director with the conflict is not to be counted in the quorum). Under the 2006 Act the right is given to private companies by statute, provided that their articles do not contain more restrictive provisions. The Model Articles for private companies do not displace this right. The right is also available to public companies, but only if their constitutions expressly provide for such right.

9.10.1.7 Duty not to accept benefits from third parties

A director of a company is prohibited, by s. 176 CA 2006, from accepting a benefit from a third party conferred by reason of his being a director or his doing (or not doing) anything as a director. There is an exception to this prohibition if the acceptance of the benefit cannot reasonably be regarded as likely to give rise to a conflict of interest. This duty is a statutory version of the previous common law duty not to make a secret profit (see **9.10.2.1**).

9.10.1.8 Duty to declare interest in proposed or existing transactions or arrangements

A director is obliged to declare the nature and extent of his interest in any proposed transaction or arrangement with the company before the company enters into this arrangement (s. 177 CA 2006). (This deals with the apparent gap in s. 175, excluding such contracts from the ambit of that section.) The declaration may be made at a board meeting or by notice in writing to all directors (s. 177(2) CA 2006). A general notice may also be given by a director, under s. 185 CA 2006, to the effect that he is connected with a particular company or specified person, and should therefore be regarded as interested in any transaction or arrangement that may, after the date of the general notice, be made with that company or person.

The obligation is, however, waived if:

(a) The director's interest cannot reasonably be regarded as likely to give rise to a conflict of interest.

(b) The other directors are already aware of the interest or, at least, ought reasonably to be aware of it.

(c) The interest arises out of the terms of the director's service contract with the company, which have been or are to be considered by the board.

It is believed that where the making of a declaration is effectively of neutral consequence, a director is likely to make it, rather than rely upon the above exceptions. However, where a director (possibly for reasons of an obligation of confidentiality) would prefer not to make a declaration, these exceptions and their ambit are much more significant. Finally, in those instances where directors are simply unaware of their obligation or neglect to fulfil it, these exceptions may be relied upon as a defence in any action for breach of duty.

The s. 177 declaration should be contrasted with the alternative declaration to be made pursuant to s. 182 CA 2006 in relation to pre-existing arrangements entered into by the company, in which a director is interested. (This obligation is particularly relevant at the moment a director is appointed.) Whilst the method for making this declaration and the exceptions to doing so are very similar to those under s. 177, this is not technically a duty, and so the consequences of failing to comply with s. 182 are different. Instead of this being a breach of duty, it is a criminal offence punishable by a fine (s. 183 CA 2006).

9.10.1.9 Breach of directors' duties

The consequences of a breach (or threatened breach) of the above statutory duties are the same as if the corresponding common law rule or equitable principle applied. Hence, the duties are enforceable in the same way as any other fiduciary duty owed to a company by its directors. Members will therefore be able, with court approval, to commence derivative actions (see **10.6.2**). Where a director has breached a duty or trust, or has conducted himself in a negligent manner, this conduct may be ratified by an ordinary resolution of the members of the company (s. 239 CA 2006).

9.10.2 Fiduciary duties under the common law

The new statutory duties of directors are, under s. 170 CA 2006, to have effect in place of common rules and equitable principles. However, s. 170(4) states that regard should be had to such rules and principles in interpreting and applying the general statutory duties. It therefore appears that it will remain important to understand the fiduciary duties owed by directors to a company. In this section we will, therefore, briefly consider the previous common law position.

Directors do not hold the property of their company on trust since the company is a separate legal entity and therefore is able to own property directly. However, directors do owe fiduciary duties to their company. That is, they are in the same position in respect of their powers as trustees or agents with respect to the company. Under the common law, the two main duties for directors to observe were the duty not to make any secret profit from their position and the duty to exercise the powers given to them bona fide for the benefit of the company.

The liability of directors for breach of duty is personal. However, the advice they receive may be relevant to whether they are in breach of duty. In *Norman v Theodore Goddard* [1992] BCC 14 it was held that a director was not liable for breach of fiduciary duty when he reasonably relied on advice given to him by a partner in a firm of solicitors.

9.10.2.1 Secret profit

Profit from position as director

The concept of secret profit is a rather intangible one; it does not, of course, prevent directors from receiving remuneration for their services. A profit is a secret profit if it comes to the director because of his position as a director:

In *Cook v Deeks* [1916] 1 AC 554, two directors of a company negotiated a construction contract with the Canadian Pacific Railroad on behalf of their company. At a late stage in the negotiations they decided to take the contract in their own names. The Privy Council held that they were accountable to their company for the profit; it was only through their position as directors of the company (which had previously contracted with the Canadian Pacific) that they were able to make the profit.

'Secret' means failure to obtain permission

Although the fiduciary duty is to hand over what are described as secret profits, it seems that secrecy in this context means failure to obtain permission rather than actual secrecy:

In *Regal (Hastings) Ltd v Gulliver* [1967] 2 AC 134, the plaintiff company owned a cinema and wished to buy two others in the same town with a view to selling all three together. The company could not raise sufficient money to buy the other cinemas and so another company was set up partly owned by Regal (Hastings) Ltd and partly by some of the directors of Regal (Hastings) Ltd who had money of their own to invest. The new company then purchased the other two cinemas. The purchasers who wished to acquire all three cinemas then purchased all the shares in Regal

(Hastings) Ltd and in the new company, thus acquiring control of the companies. The new board of directors then instituted proceedings on behalf of Regal (Hastings) Ltd against its former directors. It was held by the House of Lords that a secret profit had been made since the opportunity to invest in the new company only came to the defendants because they were directors of Regal (Hastings) Ltd. This profit was ordered to be paid to Regal (Hastings) Ltd even though that company had been unable to raise all the money needed for the purchase itself and even though, realistically, the consequence of the order was that the purchaser who had negotiated the purchase of the shares at a fair price got some of the purchase price repaid to their own company.

Secret profit to be paid to company

A secret profit must be paid over to the company even if the company itself could not have made the profit:

In *Boston Deep Sea Fishing Co v Ansell* (1888) 39 ChD 339, the defendant was a director of the plaintiff company and negotiated a contract on its behalf for the supply of ice to a fleet of fishing smacks owned by the company. The defendant was a shareholder in the ice-making company which had a policy of paying 'bonuses' to any of its shareholders who introduced work to it. The court held that the defendant was liable to the company for the bonuses even though the company itself could not have obtained them since it was not a shareholder in the ice-making company.

9.10.2.2 Exercise of powers bona fide in the interests of the company as a whole

The second requirement of directors' fiduciary duties is that the directors must exercise their powers bona fide in the interests of the company as a whole. This involves two separate restrictions on directors' powers:

(a) Directors must not exercise their powers other than for the purpose for which they were given; if they exercise their powers for some other reason, their decisions may be challenged.

In *Hogg v Cramphorn Ltd* [1967] Ch 254, directors issued shares to trustees for the benefit of employees. The purpose of the directors in issuing the shares was found to be the prevention of a takeover of the company. It was held that the issue could be challenged (even though the directors believed it to be in the interests of the company as a whole), since the purpose of giving directors the power to issue shares is to enable them to raise capital.

(b) Directors must not exercise their powers for motives of personal gain (this often overlaps with the rule against directors making secret profits).

In *Piercy v S. Mills & Co Ltd* [1920] 1 Ch 77, shares were issued, at a time when capital was not needed, purely for the purpose of strengthening and maintaining the directors' control of the company. The issue was held to be invalid.

(Many of the cases on this type of breach of duty have been concerned with the issue of shares by directors, which power is now much restricted by legislation—see **Chapter 11**.)

9.10.3 Duty to make returns

The duty to make returns to the Registrar of Companies will normally be performed on behalf of a company by its secretary, but directors are in some circumstances also liable to a fine if returns are not made and persistent default can lead to disqualification. The directors are also under a duty to keep minutes of their own meetings and to deliver accounts.

9.10.4 Directors' duties to third parties

A director does not generally owe any direct duty to a person dealing with his company, notwithstanding the requirement under s. 172 CA 2006 to have regard to various third parties' interests. (The duty to have regard to these interests is in fact owed to the company's members.) However, a director can make himself liable to a third party in a particular case if he claims an authority to bind his company which he does not have. The action resulting from such a liability is called an action for breach of warranty of authority (see **9.12**).

9.11 Statutory controls on directors

Because of the very high degree of control which directors are able to exercise over their companies, over time an increasing number of statutory provisions were included in the Companies Acts for the protection of shareholders and the public generally. These provisions are all now to be found in the 2006 Act.

9.11.1 Disclosure of information

9.11.1.1 Register of directors

Section 162 CA 2006 requires every company to keep at its registered office a register of directors. In respect of each director (including any shadow director) the following information must be given:

(a) present forename(s) and surname, and any former name;

(b) a service address;

(c) the country or state (or part of the UK) in which he is usually resident;

(d) nationality;

(e) business occupation (if any);

(f) date of birth.

Further, s. 165 imposes an obligation on companies to maintain a register of directors' residential addresses. (This is to cover the fact that such addresses do not feature in the register of directors, which is available for inspection by both shareholders and outsiders (s. 162(5)).)

Obviously any appointment, retirement, or removal of a director will necessitate a change to these two registers.

9.11.1.2 Notification to the registrar of companies

Details of directors must feature on the public record. Section 12 CA 2006 requires notification of particulars of the first directors. Where there is any change in directors or directors' particulars (whether because a director is appointed or ceases to hold office, or because of changes in the particulars of the continuing directors), notice must be given to the Registrar within 14 days of any such change on either form AP01 (appointment) or form TM01 (termination of office). This duty arises under s. 167 CA 2006.

9.11.1.3 Service contracts

Copies of directors' service contracts must be available for inspection by the members (s. 228 CA 2006). If a director does not have a written service contract, then a written memorandum of his terms of service must be kept instead.

9.11.2 Restrictions on freedom of contract

9.11.2.1 Directors' service contracts

The terms of directors' service contracts will usually be determined by the board although members are entitled to information about the terms of such contracts. Section 188 CA 2006 requires the approval of the members by ordinary resolution of any provision in a director's service contract which provides for a guaranteed term exceeding two years. Approval is also required where an existing contract is extended if the aggregate term exceeds two years.

EXAMPLE

(a) D's service contract is for a fixed period of four years and contains no provision for early termination by the company. This contract would require shareholder approval.

(b) D's service contract is for an indefinite period, terminable at any time by the company on six months' notice. This contract would not require shareholder approval.

(c) Alternatively, D's service contract is for an indefinite period, terminable at any time by the company on three years' notice. This contract would require shareholder approval.

If a company agrees to a provision in contravention of s. 188, the provision is void to the extent of the contravention and the company is deemed to be able to terminate the contract by reasonable notice.

9.11.2.2 Substantial property transactions

Section 190 CA 2006 controls arrangements whereby:

(a) a director of a company (or its holding company), or a person connected with that director, is to acquire from the company a substantial non-cash asset; or

(b) the company is to acquire a substantial non-cash asset from one of its directors (or a director of its holding company) or a person connected with that director.

EXAMPLE

The main situations s. 190 is concerned with are:

(a) Co A buys from or sells to X, a director of Co A.

(b) Co A buys from or sells to T, a person connected with a director of Co A.

(c) Co A buys from or sells to Y, a director of the holding company of Co A.

(d) Co A buys from or sells to F, a person connected with a director of the holding company of Co A.

For the purposes of s. 190 a connected person includes (among others) a director's spouse, child, or step-child (ss. 252 and 253 CA 2006). Additionally, there are complicated rules for determining the extent to which a company is connected with a director. Put simply, if a director owns at least 20% of the share capital of a company, that company is connected with him (s. 254(2) CA 2006).

A substantial non-cash asset is defined by s. 191 CA 2006 as an asset which has a value which, at the time of the relevant arrangement:

(a) exceeds 10% of the company's net asset value and is more than £5,000; or

(b) exceeds £100,000.

A company's asset value will normally be determined by reference to the company's most recent statutory accounts.

EXAMPLE

EG 123 Limited has a net asset value of £330,000. It proposes to buy an asset from a director.

(a) If the asset is worth £4,000, it will not be substantial, as it is worth less than £5,000.

(b) If the asset is worth £114,000, it will be substantial, as it is worth more than £100,000.

(c) If the asset is worth £20,000, it will not be substantial, as its value does not exceed 10% of the company's asset value, despite being worth more than £5,000.

(d) If the asset is worth £52,000, it will be substantial, as its value exceeds 10% of the company's asset value, and is worth more than £5,000.

The value to be attributed to the asset in question raises two interesting issues. The first is that this value must be the market value of the asset, otherwise directors could manipulate the price paid to fall outside the ambit of the section. Secondly, should the market value be adjudged by reference to any special value which the asset may have to the relevant director? In *Micro Leisure Ltd v County Properties and Developments* [2000] TLR 12, this question was answered in the affirmative. Lord Hamilton put forward the example of a ransom strip of land which, when purchased by a director, would substantially increase the development potential of the director's existing land. It is submitted, however, that situations where the objective market value and the 'director-specific' value are different will be rare.

Any arrangement to which s. 190 does apply must be approved by the company's members by ordinary resolution in advance or must be made on the basis that such approval will subsequently be given. (This requirement does not apply, however, where the company in question is a wholly-owned subsidiary (s. 190(4)(b) CA 2006).)

Additionally, if the relevant director or person connected with that director is:

(a) a director of the company's holding company; or

(b) a person connected with a director of the company's holding company

an ordinary resolution of the members of that holding company must also be obtained or the transaction must be made on the basis that such approval will subsequently be given.

EXAMPLE

(a) B Limited is a wholly-owned subsidiary of A Limited. Zahid is a director of both companies.

If B Limited were to sell a substantial asset to Zahid, an ordinary resolution of A Limited would be necessary, but not one of the shareholders of B Limited itself (as it is 100% owned). (Although the board of B Limited would have to resolve to sell the asset, in any event.)

(b) S Limited is an 80% subsidiary of T Limited. Cecil is a director of T Limited only.

If S Limited were to sell a substantial asset to Cecil, an ordinary resolution of both T Limited and S Limited would be necessary—the sale is to a director of S Limited's holding company and S Limited is not wholly-owned. (As in the above example, the board of S Limited would have to resolve to sell the asset, in any event.)

Any contract made in contravention of the above requirements is voidable by the company unless:

(a) the contract is subsequently affirmed within a reasonable time by ordinary resolution of the members of the company and any holding company, as necessary;

(b) restitution of the money paid or the relevant asset is no longer possible;

(c) the company has been indemnified by any other persons for the loss or damage suffered by it; or

(d) third party rights (acquired for value without notice) would be affected by avoidance.

In respect of any transaction which contravenes s. 190, the following are potentially liable to account to the company which entered into the transaction for any gain that they made and to indemnify that company for any loss which it suffered as a result of the transaction:

(a) any director of the company or its holding company who was a party to the transaction

(b) any person with whom the company entered into the arrangement who is connected with a director of the company or its holding company;

(c) the director of the company or holding company with whom any such person is connected; and

(d) any other director of the company who authorised the transaction.

Liability may be avoided by a director where the transaction was with a person connected with a director of a company or its holding company and the director shows he took all reasonable steps to secure the company's compliance with s. 190. In addition, the parties detailed at (b) and (d) above will not be liable if, at the time of the transaction, they were unaware of the circumstances constituting the contravention of s. 190.

The main purpose of s. 190 is to prevent directors from making substantial profits in transactions with their companies and so reinforces the rules about conflicts of interest. One fairly common type of contract which is subject to its provisions is a contract under which a director receives shares in return for assets. For example, if a director who owns business premises (of the requisite value) wishes to transfer them to the company in return for shares, the approval of the members in general meeting must first be obtained.

9.11.2.3 Loans to directors

The Companies Act 2006 has removed some of the previous statutory restrictions on companies making loans to directors, whilst preserving controls on such transactions. The provisions relating to loans and similar indirect transactions (quasi-loans and credit transactions) are contained in ss. 197–214 CA 2006.

Any company may not make a loan to a director of the company or its holding company nor may it guarantee or provide security in connection with a loan made by any person to such a director, unless the transaction has been approved by ordinary resolution (s. 197(1) CA 2006). (This requirement does not apply, however, where the company in question is a wholly-owned subsidiary (s. 197(5)(b) CA 2006).)

In addition, in those instances where the relevant director is a director of the company's holding company, an ordinary resolution of that company's shareholders is required.

EXAMPLE

Carrington Limited lends money to a director—an ordinary resolution of the shareholders of Carrington is required.

Carrington Limited guarantees a loan made by Credit Bank to a director—an ordinary resolution of the shareholders of Carrington is required.

Carrington Limited lends money to a director of its holding company—an ordinary resolution of the shareholders of the holding company is required. Whether or not the shareholders of Carrington must also approve the loan will depend upon whether or not it is a wholly-owned subsidiary.

Public companies are subject to greater regulation in a number of ways. First they must seek shareholder approval for:

(a) any loan made to a person connected with a director or with a director of any holding company; or

(b) any guarantee or security provided in connection with a loan made by any person to such a connected person.

Secondly, they must also seek shareholder approval before entering into any arrangement with a director or with a director of its holding company or with any person connected with either of those persons which amounts to a quasi-loan. The same is true for any guarantee or security provided by the company in respect of a quasi-loan made by any person to any of those such persons.

Quasi-loans (as defined by s. 199 CA 2006) are effectively situations where a director incurs a payment obligation and the company agrees to meet that obligation on the director's behalf or agrees to reimburse the relevant amount to the director, on the understanding that the director will repay the sum in question to the company.

Thirdly, public companies must also seek shareholder approval before entering into any arrangement with a director or with a director of its holding company or with any person connected with either of those persons which amounts to a credit transaction. The same is true for any guarantee or security provided by the company in respect of a credit transaction entered into by any person for the benefit of any of those such persons.

Credit transactions (as defined by s. 202 CA 2006) are effectively situations where the company (or a third party) sells or leases an asset to the director in return for payment by the director in instalments or on the basis that payment is to be deferred.

EXAMPLE

Partington plc agrees to guarantee a loan made by Credit Bank to the husband of one of its directors. In contrast to a private company, where shareholder approval would not be necessary for the guarantee of a loan made to a connected person, an ordinary resolution would be necessary here.

If Partington plc were to enter into a credit transaction with any of the following:

(a) a director;

(b) a director of its holding company;

(c) a person connected with a director of its holding company;

shareholder approval would be necessary as follows:

(i) in respect of example (a), an ordinary resolution of Partington's shareholders, unless Partington was a wholly-owned subsidiary;

(ii) in respect of example (b), an ordinary resolution of the shareholders of the holding company and of Partington's shareholders, unless Partington was a wholly-owned subsidiary;

(iii) in respect of example (c), an ordinary resolution of the shareholders of the holding company and of Partington's shareholders, unless Partington was a wholly-owned subsidiary.

In all instances where shareholder approval is required, a memorandum setting out prescribed details of the relevant transaction must be made available to the members in advance of the resolution being passed.

There are a number of exceptions to the above, most notably:

(a) Any company may, without member approval, provide a director (or a director of its holding company) with funds to meet expenditure incurred or to be incurred by him for the purposes of the company or for the purpose of enabling him properly to perform his duties, provided that the aggregate value of any such transactions with a director does not exceed £50,000 (s. 204).

(b) Companies need not seek shareholder approval for any loan, guarantee, security, or quasi-loan if the value of that transaction, together with any other similar transactions, does not exceed £10,000 (s. 207(1)).

(c) Companies need not seek shareholder approval for any credit transaction or guarantee or security related to a credit transaction, if the value of that transaction, together with any other similar transactions, does not exceed £15,000 (s. 207(2)).

(d) Any company may, without member approval, provide a director (or a director of its holding company) with funds to meet expenditure incurred or to be incurred by him for the purposes of defending (or avoiding) criminal or civil proceedings which arise out of any alleged negligence or breach of duty or trust of that director in relation to the company (s. 205). (Note that there are a number of detailed conditions which must be fulfilled for the loan to fall within this exception.)

The consequences of failing to obtain the necessary shareholders' approval for a loan, quasi-loan, or credit transaction are similar to those in respect of substantial property transactions, namely:

(a) The transaction or arrangement is voidable at the company's instance (subject to issues of impossibility or third-party rights acquired in good faith) (s. 213(2)).

(b) The relevant director of the company or its holding company and any other director of the company who authorised the transaction is liable to account to the company which entered into the transaction for any gain that they made and to indemnify that company for any loss which it suffered as a result of the transaction (s. 213(3) and (4)). (This provision extends to relevant connected persons in respect of loans, quasi-loans, and credit transactions or related guarantees or security made or granted by public companies.)

As with substantial property transactions, subsequent affirmation by ordinary resolution is also possible (s. 214).

9.11.3 Summary

Matters which directly involve directors should always be considered carefully. First, the particular transaction with the director needs to be categorised to assess if it is:

(a) a substantial property transaction requiring shareholders' approval;

(b) a loan or other credit arrangement requiring shareholders' approval;

(c) a term of duration of a service contract requiring shareholders' approval; or

(d) a payment for loss of office requiring shareholders' approval.

Secondly, in terms of any board approval of the transaction, it must be established whether:

(a) the company's articles impose any restriction on the relevant director voting and the consequences of this in the decision-making process;

(b) the director is obliged to make a declaration of his interest in the matter to the company.

Finally, both in terms of the director in question and the board as a whole, the nature of any obligation to comply with their duties generally must also be confirmed.

9.12 The directors and protection of outsiders

9.12.1 Introduction

A company is not a natural person and so can only exercise its powers through agents. Usually contracts will be made on behalf of the company either by the directors or by managers acting on the directors' authority. If a contract is made in accordance with the articles of the company it will be binding on the company, so that the third party with whom the company is dealing can sue the company if it fails to perform the contract. Where, however, a contract is made by the wrong people (e.g., the directors exercise a power which is vested in the shareholders, or an employee acts without the authority of the directors), or in the wrong way (e.g., a meeting is held but it has not been properly convened), the whole transaction is, prima facie, void. Contracts and other transactions decided upon without proper authority (or without a proper exercise of authority) are described as 'irregular'.

In dealing with irregular contracts the law is faced with a dilemma. If the contract is declared irregular and void, the outsider will not be able to enforce it against the company, even though he may be unaware of the irregularity. On the other hand, if the company is held to be bound by irregular contracts, the directors will, in effect, be able to ignore the requirements of the company's constitution to the possible detriment of the shareholders. The law deals with this dilemma by providing that irregular contracts, though prima facie void, are often binding on the company in certain circumstances. These circumstances result partly from statute and partly from the general law of agency.

9.12.2 Statutory protection

Section 40(1) CA 2006 provides:

In favour of a person dealing with a company in good faith, the power of the directors to bind the company, or authorise others to do so, is deemed free of any limitation under the company's constitution.

The sphere of directors' actions can be limited by a company's constitution in two main ways

(a) any restrictions on a company's objects contained within the articles, which directors have a duty to observe; and
(b) any regulations governing directors' activities contained within its articles, such as a requirement for the board to seek shareholder approval for certain transactions or for it to act in accordance with instructions provided by special resolution.

In respect of the first issue, the following should be borne in mind:

(a) Companies which are set up under the 2006 regime will no longer have any objects clause in their memoranda; their objects will be unrestricted, unless any contrary statement appears in the articles. On the basis that few companies will want to restrict their objects, the possibility of directors committing those companies to an action outside its objects will not be an issue.
(b) The objects clauses of companies set up under the 1985 Act will be deemed to be absorbed into the articles. Directors of those companies will still, therefore, have to consider the ambit of the objects clause, unless their company chooses to remove the objects clause altogether from the articles.

The effect of s. 40 CA 2006 is that:

(a) where an unconnected third party;
(b) acting in good faith;
(c) enters into a contract with a company;
(d) which contract has been decided on or authorised by the board of that company then notwithstanding any restrictions on the board's powers under the company's constitution (and whether or not the third party is aware of any such restriction), the contract will be valid. However, the directors may be liable to the company for any loss caused on the basis that they have breached their duty to the company.

It should be noted that under s. 40(2)(a), a person dealing with the company is not under an obligation to enquire as to any limitation that the directors may be subject to.

Requirements of good faith
The protection of s. 40 is given only to persons who act in good faith. However, good faith is presumed unless the contrary is proved (s. 40(2)(b)(ii)) and knowledge that the directors are acting beyond their powers is not of itself sufficient proof of bad faith (s. 40(2)(b)(iii)).

Transaction with connected party
Section 41 CA 2006 makes a limited exception to s. 40. This applies where the board of a company exceeds its powers in a transaction with a director or a person connected with a director In such cases the transaction is voidable by the company, that is, the company has the option to avoid the contract, but the contract is not void per se.

Whether or not it is avoided, the director or connected person and any director who authorised the transaction is liable to account to the company for any gain he makes and to indemnify the company against any loss. Where a transaction is irregular and is made between the company, a director, and one or more third parties, the court has a wide discretion which enables it to protect any innocent third party.

Note that the company's right to avoid a contract under s. 41 is lost if:

(a) restitution becomes impossible;

(b) a third party who has acquired rights bona fide for value would be affected;

(c) the transaction is affirmed by the shareholders; or

(d) the company has been fully compensated by an indemnity against any loss or damage.

9.12.3 Agency

9.12.3.1 General position

A company can only act through agents; the authority of agents to act for a company depends on the general law of agency. The actions of an agent are binding on a principal if the agent has actual authority or authority arising from estoppel. The agent may also be personally liable to the third party (i.e., to the outsider) if the principal (i.e., the company) is not liable.

9.12.3.2 Actual authority

The scope of the actual authority of a company's agents depends upon the constitution of the company. The board of directors, acting collectively, usually has very wide powers to act on behalf of the company. The articles will usually permit delegation to committees of directors and to a managing director (or to other directors exercising similar executive functions).

Of fundamental concern, therefore, is the status of the agent director. Section 161 CA 2006 provides that the acts of a director are valid notwithstanding that it is afterwards discovered:

(a) that there was a defect in his appointment;

(b) that he was disqualified from holding office;

(c) that he had ceased to hold office;

(d) that he was not entitled to vote on the matter in question.

This section protects an outsider dealing with a company and means that it does not have to be concerned with any procedural or legal irregularities which may have occurred and which that outsider may not have been aware of or able to discover when dealing with the director.

9.12.3.3 Agency by estoppel

A company may be bound by the acts of a person acting on its behalf when it is estopped from denying that person's authority. The estoppel may prevent the company from denying that the alleged agent is its agent or that he has power to bind the company in a particular way.

Agency by estoppel may result either from 'holding out' (that is, a representation that the agent has authority, even if no actual authority existed) or from a representation that the agent is a member of a particular class of agent which is recognised to have certain powers to bind its principals.

'Apparent authority'

Directors do not generally have authority to act alone, so a company is prima facie not bound by the actions of a single director, unless the board has conferred upon him actual authority by formal delegation of that authority in accordance with the articles. However, directors may conduct company business in all manner of contexts, either as a board or individually. Contracting third parties need the comfort of knowing that whenever they deal with a director, the director's actions can be relied upon. Effectively, apparent authority serves this purpose and ensures that the company is still bound, irrespective of the existence or otherwise of actual authority.

The main requirement is that the board has represented to the third party that the director has authority in the particular transaction. The representation does not need to be formal or active; often it will simply be the fact that the director is allowed to conduct himself in a particular way.

Possibly the leading case on this is *Freeman and Lockyer v Buckhurst Park Properties* [1964] 1 All ER 630, where a director was often left in overall charge of the company due to the absence overseas of the other main board member. The director in question had engaged the services of a firm of surveyors, without reference to his fellow board members, due to the circumstances described. The company in due course refused to pay the surveyors' fees on the basis that the director had engaged the surveyors without actual authority to do so. The Court of Appeal held that the company was so bound, due to the apparent authority of the director.

Usual authority

It is a well-established rule of the law of agency that a principal is estopped from denying that an agent of certain recognised classes has the authority normally associated with that class (unless, of course, he tells the third party that there is a restriction on the power of the agent). In relation to companies, this rule has been applied to managing directors. If a company describes one of the directors as a managing director, it is estopped from denying that he is a managing director (even if he has not been appointed) and that he has the authority of a managing director (even if his appointment includes terms restricting his authority). This type of authority is best described as 'usual authority'.

A director may also have an authority because of some other office which he holds. For example, in *First Energy (UK) v Hungarian International Bank* [1993] 2 Lloyd's Rep 194, a bank manager was held to have authority (by reason of his office) to make a statement as to a loan agreement which was binding on the bank. The bank manager in question was not a director but his authority would have been the same if he had been.

The company secretary has been held to have usual authority to bind the company to contracts concerning administration.

9.12.3.4 Liability of agent to third party

A person purporting to act as agent for a company will be personally liable to a third party for breach of warranty of authority if it turns out that he had no authority to bind the company.

9.12.3.5 Ratification

If a contract is made by an agent without authority so that the company is not bound by the contract, the company can ratify, and thus retrospectively validate, the contract. Ratification may be effected by the people with actual authority to bind the company (i.e., normally the board, but in some cases the members in general meeting—see s. 239 CA 2006). Ratification will usually be implied where the company has accepted performance of the contract.

9.13 The company secretary

9.13.1 Appointment

As from 6 April 2008, s. 270 CA 2006 removed the requirement for a private company to have a secretary. (It remains a requirement under s. 271, however, for *public* companies to have a secretary.) Private companies therefore have the option of incorporating with or without an appointed secretary. In the latter instance, a secretary may be appointed at a later date. Companies set up prior to this date would already have one appointed. They may either keep a secretary in post or bring this appointment to an end.

9.13.2 Responsibilities and powers

The secretary is responsible for keeping the various records of the company, such as minutes of board and general meetings and the various records which must be kept at the registered office. A secretary is also an officer of the company and so is liable to a fine if the company is in breach of the provisions of the Companies Act which require information to be filed with the Registrar of Companies.

Where a private company has no secretary, the duties of a secretary may be carried out by a director or any person authorised by the directors to carry out such duties.

Many company secretaries are given powers far in excess of those contemplated by the Companies Act. Often the secretary is responsible for the administration of the company and performs the functions of an office manager as well as of a record-keeper. The courts have, therefore, recognised that an outsider is entitled to rely on a decision taken by the secretary which relates to administration even if it turns out that the decision was not authorised by the board (i.e., the secretary has usual authority to make such contracts). Thus, in *Panorama (Developments) Guildford Ltd v Fidelis Furnishing Fabrics Ltd* [1971] 2 QB 711, the Court of Appeal held that a company was bound to pay for the use of cars hired by the secretary purportedly on behalf of the company but in fact for his own use.

9.13.3 Register

Companies are required to keep a register of secretaries (where appointed) and to notify the Registrar of Companies within 14 days of any change (ss. 275 and 276 CA 2006 respectively). Any appointment of a secretary must be notified to the registrar on form AP03; the termination of a secretary's appointment must be notified on form TM02. (The appointment and removal of secretaries is a matter for the board of directors.)

online resource centre

For further resources and online chapters please visit the Online Resource Centre at www.oxfordtextbooks.co.uk/orc/business13_14/.

10 Shareholders

This chapter covers the following topics:

10.1 Introduction

This chapter will deal with the position of shareholders in relation to a company. We will look at the following issues:

(a) registration of membership;
(b) the powers of shareholders in relation to their company;
(c) the legal protection given to shareholders by the rules of equity and by the Companies Act 2006 (the 2006 Act or CA 2006);
(d) the payment of dividends to shareholders.

You will find references to shareholders throughout this book so this chapter is intended to deal with their position in the company in general terms.

10.1.1 The right to membership

It has already been explained (see **Chapters 7** and **8**) that all private companies must have at least one 'member'. Section 112 CA 2006 provides that:

(1) The subscribers of a company's memorandum are deemed to have agreed to become members of the company, and on its registration become members and must be entered as such in its register of members.
(2) Every other person who agrees to become a member of a company, and whose name is entered in its register of members, is a member of the company.

This means that membership begins either:

(a) when a company is registered, in respect of the subscribers to the memorandum; or
(b) when the shareholder's name is entered in the register of members, in any other instance.

In respect of this second instance, the *right* to become a member may result from a contract between the company and the purchaser of new shares (this is called an allotment or issue of shares; see **Chapter 11**). The right may also arise because an existing shareholder transfers shares to someone else by sale or gift. It may also arise when a member dies or becomes bankrupt. At that time the shares are automatically transmitted to the personal representative or trustee in bankruptcy. From this we can see that it is the ownership of shares which entitles the shareholder to become a member of a company, but a company must formally register that person as a member for their membership to take effect. (This is particularly important in the area of buying and selling shares; see **Chapter 12** for further details.) Hence, the terms 'member' and 'shareholder' mean almost the same thing, but there is a technical difference.

When someone becomes a shareholder and is registered as a member that person normally acquires some influence over the company's activities through the votes which attach to his shares, as well as ownership of a percentage of the company.

10.2 Registration of membership

10.2.1 Contents of the register

Every company must keep a register of its members and their shareholdings (s. 113 CA 2006). The following information must be recorded:

(a) the names and addresses of the members;

(b) the number of shares held and, where the company has more than one class of issued shares, the number of each class held by each member;

(c) the amount paid or agreed to be considered as paid on the shares of each member;

(d) the date at which each member was entered in the register;

(e) the date at which each member ceased to be a member.

Additionally, pursuant to s. 123 CA 2006, if the company has only one member, the register must also contain:

(a) a statement to that effect and of the date when this occurred;

(b) if the company formerly had only one member, a statement that the number has increased to two or more and the date when this occurred.

The register must normally be kept at the registered office of the company and, if kept elsewhere, the Registrar of Companies must be notified (s. 114 CA 2006). The register of members itself is not sent to the Registrar but the annual return made by a company contains details of the membership.

No particular form of register is required, but under s. 115 CA 2006 an index is required if the register is not kept in the form of an index and there are more than 50 members. (This provision is of little relevance to private companies since very few of them have more than 50 members.)

10.2.2 Trusts

In certain instances, the legal and beneficial title to shares is split by the beneficial owner appointing a nominee to hold the legal title in the shares on their behalf, normally for reasons of anonymity or convenience. Section 126 CA 2006 provides that 'no notice of any trust . . . shall be entered on the register of members . . . '. The effect of this is that the company need only deal with the nominee, as the legal owner of shares, even if it knows that they are held on trust. The company must, therefore, pay dividends to the nominee and allow the nominee to exercise any voting powers attached to the shares. Accordingly, the beneficial owner is technically disenfranchised. (Although this situation does not, of course, affect the position as between the nominee and the true owner. The nominee must, therefore, hand over to the beneficial owner any dividend he receives and vote in accordance with the owner's wishes.)

The 2006 Act has introduced a new concept whereby a shareholder (i.e., the nominee) may appoint another person, that is, the beneficial owner, to enjoy or exercise their rights, if the articles so permit (Part 9 CA 2006). It is not expected that many closely-held, private companies will want to take advantage of this possibility, but it may have more relevance to listed companies, where a number of their investors may hold their shareholdings through nominees.

Additionally, shareholders in listed companies will automatically enjoy the ability to nominate another to enjoy 'information rights', that is, to receive copies of all communications from the company to its shareholders. In this way, a beneficial owner can be kept informed of relevant activity within the company.

10.3 Powers and duties of shareholders

10.3.1 Sources of shareholders' powers

In most companies, it is the directors who actually run the company (see **Chapter 9**). To ensure that shareholders have a measure of influence over the board, the law steps in to provide shareholders with specific influence over certain designated company activities, either through the Companies Act or through the articles. For instance, shareholders are normally granted the right to appoint directors in the articles. Additionally, the 2006 Act stipulates that a loan to be made by a company to one of its directors will usually require the prior approval of the shareholders to be lawful (see **9.11.2.3**).

10.3.2 Powers of control

The powers of shareholders are normally exercised by passing a specified resolution at a general meeting. Alternatively, a written resolution may be used, unless the company is public. (Company meetings and resolutions are dealt with in detail in **Chapter 13**.)

As such, the size of a shareholder's holding will determine how influential he can be over such a resolution. Most resolutions must be passed by a simple majority as ordinary resolutions, but a small number of decisions require a special resolution, which must be passed by at least a 75% majority. A shareholder who controls 75% of the votes is, therefore, able to exercise powers which a shareholder with a simple majority (that is, over 50%) could not exercise alone. Conversely, a shareholder with more than 25% but less than 50% of the votes can block a special resolution even though he does not have enough votes to be in control of the company. (This is sometimes called negative control.)

In practical terms, any shareholding in excess of 50% is regarded as a majority shareholding which would grant the holder *de facto* control over the company. By contrast, a minority shareholder often has no real power (unless he is a director and/or can persuade the majority to agree with him), but his position is protected by a number of rights, mostly statutory, some of the most important of which are discussed later in this chapter.

10.3.3 Duties of shareholders

Just as the powers and rights of members largely depend on the proportion of votes that they control, so the duties of members differ depending on whether or not they are in control of the company. The basic rule is that members (whether or not in control) can exercise their right to vote as they wish, so that they can take account of their own interests to the exclusion of conflicting interest of other shareholders. However, this does not mean that shareholders are *entirely* free to vote as they please; as we shall see in the sections which follow, acting purely out of naked self-interest may entitle those affected by such actions to bring an action in the courts.

10.4 Internal disputes—introduction

The courts are very reluctant to get involved in disputes within a company. In particular, they are not willing to do anything which might amount to interference with business decisions. As such, the grounds for complaining about the way a company is run are relatively limited.

In this section, we will look at the way in which shareholders may complain about perceived irregularities in their companies. At the outset of this discussion, it is important to recognise that there are two main methods of shareholder protection: either a shareholder will be relying upon his contractual rights which derive from the company's constitution or he will be seeking a statutory remedy.

10.5 The constitution as a contract

10.5.1 Contract between members and company

Section 33 CA 2006 states that:

The provisions of a company's constitution bind the company and its members to the same extent as if there were covenants on the part of the company and of each member to observe those provisions.

In turn, s. 17 defines the constitution as including the articles and any special resolutions of the shareholders. (Note that for companies incorporated under the 1985 Act regime, the influence of the memorandum will continue to be felt through the impact of s. 28 CA 2006, which will deem relevant provisions of the memorandum as part of the articles.)

The effect of this important section is that the constitution forms an agreement which contractually binds:

(a) a company to each of its members; and

(b) the members of the company to each other.

Thus, if specific provisions are not observed, an action may be taken to enforce the obligations imposed by the company's constitution. The extent to which obligations are enforceable is considered further below.

10.5.2 Membership rights

An obligation imposed by the constitution on a member or on the company for the benefit of a member is only enforceable if it relates to membership rights. The most obvious examples of membership rights which have been enforced as a result of actions based on the section include:

(a) the right to a dividend once lawfully declared (*Wood v Odessa Waterworks Co* (1889) 42 Ch D 636);

(b) the right to share in surplus capital on a winding up (*Griffith v Paget* (1877) 5 Ch D 894); and

(c) the right to vote at meetings (*Pender v Lushington* (1877) 6 Ch D 70).

The most obvious obligation of a member which may be enforced by a company is the obligation to pay for shares issued by it.

It should be noted that a company's articles are a contract complete in themselves. The court will not normally, therefore, imply any additional terms into the articles. A good example of this rule is found in *Bratton Seymour Service Co v Oxborough* [1992] BCC 471, where the rule worked in favour of the members, as the company, which was set up to manage a development of flats, claimed unsuccessfully that the members had an implied obligation to contribute to the upkeep of certain communal areas related to the flats.

10.5.3 Other rights

Obligations imposed by the constitution which do not relate to membership rights are not enforceable under s. 33. A member may, therefore, be left without any remedy, even though the company has failed to observe an article which would have benefited him. This is illustrated by the case of *Eley v Positive Government Security Life Assurance Co* (1876) 1 ExD 88. When the company was formed a provision was included in the articles naming the plaintiff as solicitor of the company. He was never, in fact, appointed to the office but did become a member of the company. It was held that he could not sue the company (under the provisions of earlier corresponding legislation) because the right to be appointed as solicitor was not a *membership right* of the plaintiff.

Similarly, in *Beattie v E. and F. Beattie Ltd* [1938] Ch 708, a dispute arose between a company and one of its directors concerning the repayment of sums improperly paid to the director. The director wished to refer the matter to arbitration in accordance with an article requiring arbitration of disputes with members, but was held not entitled to insist on arbitration since the dispute was between the company and the plaintiff in his capacity as *director,* not in his capacity as shareholder.

10.5.4 Implied contracts

The terms laid down in the constitution may be impliedly incorporated into a contract made with the company. For example, in *Re New British Iron Company, ex parte P. Beckwith* [1898] 1 Ch 324, there was no express agreement between the directors and the company regarding their remuneration. However, the articles stated that the board was to receive an annual sum of £1,000. This was held to be a binding obligation on the company, even though the directors were not claiming in their capacity as members.

10.5.5 Shareholders' agreements

Shareholders may wish to regulate their dealings with each other outside the articles (or as a supplement to them). For example, they may wish to stipulate that there must be unanimity between them regarding the appointment of a new director, irrespective of the mechanism for appointment of directors in the articles. Such provisions can be enshrined in a shareholders' agreement, rather than the articles. The important thing to note is that such an agreement will only bind those shareholders who are parties to it. The constitution binds all shareholders at any time in the life of the company. (Further discussion of this topic is found in **Chapter 32**.)

10.6 Actions by shareholders

10.6.1 Personal or representative action

When a member sues to enforce his rights under the constitution under s. 33 CA 2006, he is effectively bringing an action for breach of contract. Any judgment he obtains will be directly enforceable by him and binding on the company. This type of action can be contrasted with a situation where the company has suffered a wrong and the shareholder is seeking redress on the company's behalf. This type of action will be considered next.

10.6.2 Derivative action

10.6.2.1 History of the derivative action

A shareholder is not usually permitted to sue where a wrong is done to the company of which he is a member. This rule was known as the rule in *Foss v Harbottle* (1843) 2 Hare 461, and there were two justifications for it. First, since a company is a separate legal person distinct from its members, the company is the proper plaintiff in an action where a wrong has been done to the company. Secondly, the decision whether or not to sue can be taken either by the directors or by the members in general meeting, and the court is unwilling to interfere with this decision by imposing its own views on the company At the same time, however, the courts did recognise that in some exceptional circumstances it was appropriate to allow a shareholder to sue on behalf of the company, since otherwise justice could not be done, for example, where the majority shareholders were using their position of power within the company to obtain a direct personal advantage or where the actions of the board had produced a result which was injurious to the interests of the company or the members as a whole. Therefore, a number of exceptions to the rule in *Foss v Harbottle* developed on a case-by-case basis, under which a shareholder could bring an action if the company would not. This type of action was normally described as a 'derivative action' because the right of the member to sue was not personal to him but derived from the right to sue which the company had failed to exercise.

These exceptional cases should be contrasted with cases where the personal rights of a shareholder are affected. In such cases, the shareholder does not need to rely upon an exception to *Foss v Harbottle* at all, but can sue because of the contractual rights which he has under s. 33 (*Pender v Lushington* (1877) 6 Ch D 70). It was not always easy to decide whether or not a shareholder had a right of action under the exceptions to *Foss v Harbottle* or under s. 33. The distinction was crucial, however, as a shareholder always has *locus standi* to enforce his own personal rights, but only a very limited right to sue on behalf of the company. Secondly, wrongs done to a company could be ratifiable by the majority and a court would bow to the wishes of the majority in such situations. (Occasionally, however, ratification itself could amount to wrongdoing, justifying a derivative action (*Cook v Deeks* [1916] 1 AC 554).)

10.6.2.2 Impact of the Companies Act 2006

The Companies Act 2006 has now codified derivative actions (Chapter 1, Pt 11 CA 2006) and all derivative actions now have to be brought under the statutory provisions. (The relevant sections came into force on 1 October 2007.)

Section 260(3) states that a derivative action must be brought in respect of a cause of action arising from an actual or proposed act or omission involving negligence, default, breach of duty, or breach of trust by a director. The common view of this is that it expands the opportunities for derivative actions in three ways (although the possibility to complain specifically about the actions of the majority shareholders has been removed, on the basis that the more appropriate claim is for unfair prejudice; see 10.7). First, under the common law any misfeasance by a director which was ratifiable by the majority was not sufficient grounds to found an action (on the basis that the majority should be allowed to determine the issue). The distinction between ratifiable and non-ratifiable actions is no longer an issue; all default and breaches by directors are arguably grounds to bring an action. Secondly, it was previously very difficult to bring a derivative action for directors' negligence (*Pavlides v Jensen* [1956] 2 All ER 518). The Act now specifically includes this as an actionable ground.

Finally, the Act does not stipulate the need to prove, for example, wrongdoer control or fraud on the minority (that is, the exercise of power for dubious or personal ends). At first glance, therefore, it would appear that in all instances of breach or default by a director, any shareholder would automatically have the ability to launch a derivative action. However, s. 261 imposes a 'screening process', under which such a shareholder must apply to the court for permission to pursue a claim and must demonstrate a prima facie case for such permission to be granted. In making its decision, a court must take into account the matters set out in s. 263, which include:

(a) whether or not a person acting to promote the interests of the company would or would not continue the claim;

(b) the good faith of the shareholder bringing the claim;

(c) any prior authorisation or ratification of the act or the possibility of subsequent ratification;

(d) in particular, the views of shareholders with no interest, direct or indirect, in the matter.

Most of these concepts are new and it remains to be seen how far the existing jurisprudence regarding derivative actions will be considered relevant or influential in determining them. It is suggested that the applications for permission to prosecute a claim may in themselves end up as significant as the trial of the substantive issue itself.

Finally, any shareholder bringing a derivative action must consider three practical points:

(a) If the action is successful, the judgment will give a remedy to the company (which has been wronged) rather than to the claimant.

(b) Any internal dispute in a company can deflect the attention and energies of those involved away from the proper business of running the company.

(c) Professional costs will be incurred by all parties, including the shareholder.

Under the previous regime, it was generally accepted that any reasonable claim brought in good faith would entitle the shareholder to an indemnity for costs from the company. However, irrespective of this issue, if the company does end up meeting some or all of the costs of the action, this may simply erode the benefit of the action brought.

10.7 Unfair prejudice

10.7.1 Introduction

In addition to the derivative action, statute has afforded shareholders the possibility to complain about conduct of others within a company since the introduction of s. 210 CA 1948. This became (in revised form) s. 75 CA 1980 and this, in turn, became s. 459 CA 1985. The latest statement of this right is found in s. 994 CA 2006, which provides that:

> A member of a company may apply to the court by petition for an order . . . on the ground (a) that the company's affairs are being or have been conducted in a manner that is unfairly prejudicial to the interests of the members generally or of some part of its members (including at least himself) or (b) that an actual or proposed act or omission of the company (including an act or omission on its behalf) is or would be so prejudicial.

Section 994 is effectively the same as the previous s. 459, so cases decided under the previous section are likely to be valid in interpreting its effect.

10.7.1.1 Grounds

A shareholder may petition under s. 994 if he can show that he has suffered unfair prejudice. As will be seen from the wording of the section, the prejudice must have arisen from the way in which the affairs of the company were being conducted or from an actual or proposed act or omission by the company. The prejudice must have affected the interests of at least some of the members of the company (but it can affect them all equally). If these things can be shown then the court will have to consider what remedy would be appropriate.

10.7.1.2 Rights as shareholder must have been prejudiced

If the petitioner is to succeed he must show that his rights as a shareholder have been prejudiced. In *Re Postgate and Denby* [1987] BCLC 8, it was held that such rights include all rights given under the company's memorandum and articles, statutory rights, and also rights arising out of agreements and understandings between members. The Law Commission reviewed shareholder remedies in 1997 (Law Com No. 246, para. 1.9). In this report a number of guiding principles were iterated, one of which was:

> A member is taken to have agreed to the terms of the memorandum and articles of association when he became a member, whether or not he appreciated what they meant at the time. The law should continue to treat him as so bound unless he shows that the parties have come to some other agreement or understanding which is not reflected in the articles or memorandum. Failure to do so will create unacceptable commercial uncertainty. The corollary of this is that the best protection for a shareholder is appropriate protection in the articles themselves.

(It is likely that this viewpoint was influential on the House of Lords' decision in *O'Neill v Phillips*, discussed below.)

Thus, in *Re A Company (No. 004377 of 1986)* [1987] 1 WLR 102, the petition failed as the articles of the company laid down exactly what was to happen if the quasi-partnership ended for any reason. This included a right for a majority shareholder to buy the shares of the minority. The minority shareholder might indeed be prejudiced by such a provision but he could not claim that the prejudice was unfair as he had (by joining the company) agreed to this in advance.

10.7.1.3 Test for unfair prejudice

The test as to what amounts to unfair prejudice is primarily objective. In the leading case in this area, *O'Neill v Phillips* [1999] 2 All ER 961 (a case on s. 459), Lord Hoffmann explained that '. . . a balance has to be struck between the breadth of the discretion given to the court and the principle of legal certainty . . . It is highly desirable that lawyers should be able to advise their clients whether or not a petition is likely to succeed.' Moreover, he was opposed to the application of a 'wholly indefinite notion of fairness'. In order to provide objectivity in the concept, his Lordship relied upon the fact that 'the manner in which the affairs of the company may be conducted is closely regulated by rules to which the shareholders have agreed' (effectively the company's constitution, but also formal and informal agreements or understandings between members). On this basis, he came to two conclusions about unfair prejudice:

(a) A member will not ordinarily be entitled to complain of unfairness unless there has been some breach of the terms on which he agreed that the affairs of the company should be conducted.

(b) There will, however, be cases in which equitable considerations make it unfair for those conducting the affairs of the company to rely upon their strict legal powers.

For these reasons, Mr O'Neill's claim failed. He may have had a legitimate expectation that Mr Phillips, the majority shareholder, would confer various benefits upon him (such as an increased share in profits and more shares in the company), but he had no formal grounds upon which to base a claim. It is submitted, therefore, that Lord Hoffmann's approach has narrowed the scope of a claim under s. 994 for the simple reason that one must, in fact, establish the specific terms upon which it was agreed that the company's affairs be conducted (which may well be outside the company's articles of association). Furthermore, one must prove an actual breach of such terms or show that they were being used in a way which offends against equitable considerations.

10.7.2 Powers of court

10.7.2.1 Orders

If a petition under s. 994 is successful the court 'may make such order as it thinks fit for giving relief in respect of the matters complained of' (s. 996(1)). Section 996(2) lists particular types of order which may be made but is expressly stated to be without prejudice to the general power given by s. 996(1). The powers listed in s. 996(2) are to:

(a) regulate the conduct of the company's affairs in the future;

(b) require the company to refrain from doing or continuing an act complained of by the petitioner or to do an act which the petitioner has complained it has omitted to do;

(c) authorise civil proceedings to be brought in the name and on behalf of the company by such person or persons and on such terms as the court may direct;

(d) require the company not to alter its articles without leave of the court;

(e) provide for the purchase of the shares of any members of the company by other members or by the company itself and, in the case of a purchase by the company itself, the reduction of the company's capital accordingly.

10.7.2.2 Power to authorise civil proceedings

The power to authorise civil proceedings subject to terms may prove particularly useful. A shareholder may be deterred from bringing a derivative action by the prospect of heavy costs. It may, therefore, be attractive to petition under s. 994 in the hope of obtaining an order for the action to be pursued by the company. The court will ensure that such a petition can be dealt with (in suitable cases) without the substantive issue being tried in the s. 994 proceedings.

10.7.2.3 Purchase of petitioner's shares

In practice, the most common remedy awarded to a successful petitioner is that his shares should be purchased by the wrongdoers who have caused the unfair prejudice. The question of valuation causes considerable problems in such cases. The courts have held that the shares should be valued as at whatever date is fair to the petitioner. This usually means that the shares are valued at the date when the prejudice to the petitioner began. If a different date is chosen the court will usually order that the valuer should value the shares as if the prejudice had not taken place.

10.8 Just and equitable winding up

Companies may be wound up on a number of grounds. Winding up is the process by which a company's existence is brought to an end; it usually results from the insolvency of the company. However, one type of winding up is available as a remedy to shareholders of solvent companies—this is winding up under s. 122(1)(g) Insolvency Act 1986, which provides for winding up where 'the court is of the opinion that it is just and equitable that the company should be wound up'. Winding up is a rather drastic solution to problems arising within a company and is now much less important, due to the remedy for shareholders available for cases of unfair prejudice.

10.9 Shareholders and profits

Basically there are four ways in which a company can deal with its profits:

(a) retain them in the business;

(b) use them to pay interest on debentures and other borrowings;

(c) pay directors' fees (and bonuses);

(d) pay them as dividends to the shareholders.

If profits are retained in the business the shareholders ought to benefit in the long run, since the capital value of the company (and thus of the shares in it) will increase. A payment of interest on borrowings will often be a payment to an outsider, which reduces profits available to the shareholders. However, most such payments are tax-deductible, so can contribute towards the reduction of a company's taxation liabilities. Directors' fees are expenses of the business which an accountant would regard as reducing the profit available to shareholders, but in the case of many small, private companies the directors and shareholders are the same people; thus a payment of directors' fees can be, in a commercial sense, equivalent to a payment of profit to the shareholders. However, the tax consequences are quite different. In simple terms, dividends are paid out of after-tax profits in the company's hands and will be taxed again as an income receipt in the hands of the recipient shareholder. The payment of a bonus or increased salary will be treated as an income expense of the company, which can be set against its taxable profits, but will again be taxed as an income receipt in the hands of the recipient director. The tax-deductible nature of salaries/bonuses can make them more attractive than payment of a dividend.

A company is, in any event, not entirely free to choose between the four different uses of profits for the following reasons:

(a) It will often be contractually bound to make payments of interest and directors' fees.

(b) There are company law rules which prevent the company from paying dividends except to the extent of 'profits available for the purpose'. (The reason for this is that the original investment made in the company by shareholders may not be returned to them, except in limited circumstances, until the company is wound up.)

(c) It will often be commercially unwise for the company to pay out all its profits, since some will be required to provide for future contingencies or for the expansion of the business.

10.10 Declaration and payment of dividends

A dividend is a payment to the shareholders of the company which provides them with a return on their investment. It is not a payment of interest on the money invested, since the shareholder does not have an automatic right to the dividend—as we shall see, it becomes payable only if 'declared' by the company (or otherwise authorised under the articles) and only if the Companies Act permits payment in the circumstances (see **10.11**).

The method of declaration of a dividend is essentially an internal matter for a company determined by its articles. By way of example, therefore, we shall focus on the method set out in article 30 of the Model Articles for Private Companies, which contains a relatively common approach to dividends. However, in all circumstances the articles of the relevant company should be referred to.

10.10.1 Procedure

10.10.1.1 Final or year-end dividends

The payment of a dividend must be made out of profits available for this purpose (s. 830 CA 2006). In turn, any such payment must be made by reference to relevant accounts (s. 836 CA 2006). It is usual, therefore, for dividends to be paid by reference to the year-end accounts of a company. A dividend can only be paid once it has been *declared* by ordinary resolution (art. 30(1)). However, no declaration can take place unless a dividend has first been *recommended* by the board (art. 30(2)). The process, therefore, would be:

(a) After the accounts have been prepared the directors will consider what dividend, if any, ought to be declared, and will make a recommendation of that amount.

(b) A meeting of the shareholders will be held at which the question of declaring a dividend will be considered. (Alternatively, a written resolution could be used.) The members may reject the directors' recommendation or declare a dividend smaller than that recommended, but article 30(2) prevents them exceeding the amount recommended by the directors.

Once the dividend has been declared, the members will be paid the dividend by the company. The amount of dividend paid to each member depends on the nominal value of the shares held, no account being taken of any premium paid on the shares.

The reason why the members cannot declare a dividend in excess of the directors' recommendation is that the directors are the managers of the company's business, and so are in a better position than the members to assess the economic ability of the company to pay dividends; it is therefore probably a sensible provision to include in the articles. If members with a majority of the votes object to the dividend policy of the directors they can exercise their right to remove the directors from office under s. 168 CA 2006.

Traditionally, the declaration of a dividend was a standing item on the agenda of the AGM. The demise of the AGM for private companies (see **13.1**) has altered practice in this area and may result in a greater opportunity or need for the board to declare dividends independently of the members, normally as interim dividends (see below).

10.10.1.2 Interim dividends

During the course of an accounting period (i.e., a 12-month period in respect of which the company's accounts are prepared), the directors may decide to pay an interim dividend (art 30(1)). It is not necessary for such dividends to be formally declared by ordinary resolution of the shareholders. However, the same legal safeguards apply to interim dividends as final ones (See **10.11** for a full discussion.)

10.10.2 Classes of share

If there are different classes of share they may have different rights to dividends. Thus, if there are preference shares, the ordinary shareholders will usually not be entitled to any dividend until the preference shareholders have received their dividend (which will be expressed as a fixed amount per share or a fixed percentage).

EXAMPLE

A company has 2,000 £1 shares of which 1,000 are ordinary shares and 1,000 are 10% preference shares; the company declares a dividend of £150. The preference shareholders are entitled to their 10% (i.e., £100) and the ordinary shareholders get the balance (i.e., £50 or 5p per share).

The payment of an *interim* dividend can potentially eat into profits which should be first used for the payment of preferential dividends. As such, if any preferred dividends are in arrears, no interim dividend can be paid in respect of other shares (art. 30(5)).

10.10.3 Legal entitlement to dividend

Once declared by the members in general meeting, a dividend is a debt due to the members from the company. The member is, therefore, entitled to sue the company if the dividend is not paid. An interim dividend is not, however, a debt due from the company, so that the members have no right to it until it is actually paid.

10.11 Restrictions on sources of dividends

10.11.1 The basic rule

So as to ensure that money invested by shareholders is not returned to them before the company is wound up, there have always been rules based on judicial decisions preventing the payment of dividends other than out of profits. Statute now lays down clear rules as to what funds are available for the payment of dividends. These rules, which were first introduced in 1980, are designed to implement the European Communities' Second Directive on Company Law and differ somewhat from the rules previously established by the courts—the statutory rules (now contained in the Companies Act 2006) are generally more restrictive.

Section 830(1) CA 2006 provides that: 'A company shall not make a distribution except out of profits available for the purpose.' The term 'distribution' is defined by s. 829 and includes all distributions of assets to members except:

(a) the issue of bonus shares;

(b) the redemption or purchase of its own shares by the company (see **12.4**);

(c) reduction of capital (see **11.3.2**); or

(d) a distribution on winding up.

Most dividends are paid in cash and are included in the definition of 'distributions', since cash is just as much an asset as other types of property.

10.11.2 'Profits available'

10.11.2.1 Definition

'Profits available for the purpose' of paying dividends are defined by s. 830(2) as 'accumulated, realised profits, so far as not previously utilised by distribution . . . less . . . accumulated, realised losses . . . '. This means that each year it is necessary to calculate the company's trading profit and any capital profits that have been made on the disposal of fixed assets. These are the 'realised profits' from which must be deducted any realised losses, that is, any trading loss or loss made on the disposal of a fixed asset. However, a dividend is only payable if there are *accumulated* realised profits in excess of *accumulated* realised losses. This means that the balance of realised profits can be carried forward from year to year. It is not, therefore, necessary to make a profit every year in order to pay a dividend—all that is required is that there should be a balance of profits taking this year and previous years together.

EXAMPLE

	Realised profit/(loss)	*Dividend*	*Balance to carry forward*
Year 1	4,000	1,000	3,000
Year 2	2,000	1,000	4,000
Year 3	(3,000)	1,000	nil

The dividend in year 3 is lawful because in year 1 the realised profits were £4,000 and the dividend only £1,000, so that £3,000 worth of profits could be carried forward. In year 2, the realised profits were £2,000 and the dividend £1,000, so that a further £1,000 could be carried forward. In year 3, there was a realised loss of £3,000 which had to be deducted from the accumulated profits of £4,000, thus leaving £1,000 for a dividend.

Just as realised profits not used to pay dividends may be carried forward to later years and used to pay dividends in those later years, so realised losses which are not balanced by realised profits accumulated from previous years must be carried forward to later years and set off against realised profits before a dividend can be paid. Thus (continuing the example above):

	Realised profit/(loss)	*Dividend*	*Balance to carry forward*
Year 4	(2,000)	nil	(2,000)
Year 5	1,000	nil	(1,000)
Year 6	2,000	1,000	nil

In year 4, there was a loss, and since no accumulated profits were available from years 1 to 3, no dividend could be paid. In year 5, a profit of £1,000 was made but this could not be used to pay a dividend since the accumulated realised loss (£2,000 from year 4) was more than the realised profit. In year 6, the £1,000 dividend was the maximum which could be paid because £1,000 of the loss from year 4 had to be set off against the profit.

10.11.2.2 Unrealised losses

It should be noted that, although realised losses must be made good out of realised profits before a dividend can be paid, there is no requirement that *unrealised* losses must be made good. For example, if a company owns land which it knows to be declining in value, it can still go on paying dividends out of realised profits, since the loss on the land is only realised when the land is sold. Similarly an unrealised profit cannot be used to pay a dividend. A company which is making small realised losses cannot, therefore, pay a dividend even if it knows its land is increasing in value by more than the losses.

10.11.2.3 Calculation of profits and losses

Section 830 does not lay down particular rules as to how profits and losses are to be calculated; normal accountancy practice must be applied in deciding whether a profit or loss has been realised.

10.11.3 Justification of distribution by reference to the 'relevant accounts'

10.11.3.1 The 'relevant accounts'

Whether a company has any profits available for distribution can only be judged by reference to properly drawn-up accounts. Section 836 CA 2006 lays down rules as to which accounts are to be used at any particular time for deciding whether there are profits available. Usually the company must rely on the last set of accounts prepared in accordance with the duty imposed on the company under Chapter 4, Pt 15 CA 2006 and circulated to members pursuant to s. 423 CA 2006.

In *Bairstow v Queen's Moat Houses plc* [2001] 2 BCLC 531, the Court of Appeal emphasised the fact that failure to comply with this requirement would render any distribution unlawful, even if there existed available profits in reality.

10.11.3.2 Interim and initial accounts

If the company wants to pay a dividend which is not justified by its last accounts it can prepare 'interim' accounts specially for the purpose of showing that profits are available for distribution (s. 836(2)(a)). This might be done, for example, if the company had made a loss and so could not pay a dividend but has now started to make profits again and does not want to wait until the next full set of accounts are produced. Similarly, if a company wishes to pay a dividend before it has prepared *any* accounts (i.e., broadly speaking, during its first year after incorporation) it can prepare 'initial' accounts to justify the dividend payment (s. 836(2)(b)).

Interim and initial accounts must be prepared in much the same way as the normal final accounts of the company. Also, these accounts must enable a reasonable judgement to be made as to the amount of profits, losses, assets, and liabilities of the company at the time (ss. 838(1) and 839(1) CA 2006). Because of the expense involved in preparing such accounts, it will usually be better to wait until accounts are produced in the normal way before paying the dividend.

10.11.4 Consequences of unlawful distributions

Section 847(2) CA 2006 requires any member to repay a distribution which he 'knows or has reasonable grounds for believing' to be unlawful. Additionally, if a dividend is paid unlawfully, the directors will normally be personally liable to the company, since they will have recommended and paid (or permitted payment of) the dividend in breach of their duty as trustees of the company's assets. (See, for example, *Bairstow v Queen's Moat Houses plc* [2001] 2 BCLC 531.)

online resource centre

For further resources and online chapters please visit the Online Resource Centre at www.oxfordtextbooks.co.uk/orc/business13_14/.

11

Company finance

This chapter covers the following topics:

11.1 Introduction

Once a company is formed it will need to spend money to get its business going. It may need to buy stock, buy or rent premises, pay wages, advertise, and pay the general expenses involved in running a business. The money that the company needs to start its business is often called capital. Technically, however, 'capital' is the liability of the company to the people who have provided it with money on a long-term basis, effectively the shareholders.

A company can raise money either in the form of an investment by shareholders ('equity finance') or in the form of borrowing ('debt finance'). Once the business is established, profits may be retained in the business, thus producing a third source of finance. (Retained profits may be paid out to shareholders in the form of dividends. As such, they need to be represented as part of the capital of the company in the accounts.)

This chapter will look at how companies raise money through a combination of equity and debt finance. It is important to note that an important source of information as to how a company is capitalised is the balance sheet, which will provide details of both debt and share funding.

EXAMPLE

A Limited is funded in the following manner:

Share capital	£ 1,000
Retained profits	£25,000
Borrowings	£10,000

A total, therefore, of £36,000 has gone into the company, but there is also a corresponding liability to pay back the borrowings. In very simple terms, the assets would be represented as follows in A Limited's balance sheet:

ASSETS	
Cash	£36,000
Liabilities	£10,000
Net Assets	£26,000
CAPITAL	
Share capital	£ 1,000
Retained profit	£25,000
Total	£26,000

Note how the assets match the capital, hence the fact that the figures 'balance'. (It is recommended that **15.7**, which looks at the balance sheet in more detail, is read in conjunction with this chapter.) It should also be noted that the relationship between a company's asset base and the debt and equity finance which has produced it is called 'gearing'. In very simple terms, if a company is capitalised with a substantial amount of debt in comparison to the money raised from its shareholders, it is said to be highly geared.

EXAMPLE

Magnolia Limited has an asset base of £15,000. Its shareholders have contributed £5,000 and its borrowings amount to £10,000.

Effectively, Magnolia's equity finance would have to increase by 300% to match its asset base, so it can be considered as highly geared.

Alternatively, if Magnolia Limited had an asset base of £10,000, of which £8,000 was made up of equity funding and the balance through borrowing, its equity funding would only have to increase by 25%, so it would be considered as having relatively low gearing.

(In a case where equity finance matches asset value, a company would then be considered as zero geared, as no increase in its equity funding would be necessary.)

11.2 Issue of shares

11.2.1 Legal nature of shares

A share in a company is a chose in action. Its value to the shareholder depends on the particular contractual rights which he obtains from owning the share. These contractual rights are obtained when the shares are issued to him by the company, if he is the original owner, or when they are transferred or transmitted to him. This section is concerned with the issue of shares by a company; transfer and transmission are dealt with in **Chapter 12**.

11.2.2 Rights attaching to shares

The rights attached to shares vary from company to company and a company may issue different classes of shares with different rights attached to them. It is, therefore, difficult to generalise about the exact nature of a share, but the following points may be of assistance:

(a) Nearly all shares give the shareholder a *right to a dividend* (i.e., a share in profits), but a dividend is only payable if the company has made profits and it is decided to declare a dividend (see **Chapter 10**).

(b) Most, but not all, shares give the shareholder a *right to vote* at general meetings of the company.

(c) If the company is wound up the shareholder will have a *right to repayment* of his investment (in the comparatively unlikely event that the company is then solvent) and in most cases a *right to participate* in any undistributed profit.

(d) The Stock Transfer Act 1963 lays down a procedure for the transfer of shares but does not guarantee the shareholder a *right to transfer*.

(e) Shareholders are given certain *rights as a matter of law* by the Companies Act. Many of these rights are, however, only given to shareholders who have a right to vote at company meetings (e.g., the rights to remove directors and to appoint and remove auditors referred to in **Chapter** 9).

In the case of a private company the voting rights will often be as important as the financial rights. This is especially so in the case of a shareholding which gives voting control, since it effectively carries with it the right to control many major decisions of the company.

11.2.3 The value of shares

The value of shares clearly depends to some extent on the rights attached to them but it also depends on other factors—particularly the profitability of the company and its asset worth.

All shares must have a 'nominal value' (also called 'par value'). (For most English registered companies, the nominal value chosen is normally £1, for obvious reasons.) This figure says little about the true value of the shares, since shares can be issued for more (but not less) than nominal value and, once issued, their true value will fluctuate either upwards or downwards as the company is more or less successful.

EXAMPLE

Control Systems Limited has 1,000 ordinary shares of £1 each in issue. Accordingly, these shares have a nominal value of £1 each. However, if Control Systems, as a business entity, is worth £2,000,000, to buy all the shares in this company and, thus, assume total control over it, would cost this amount. Therefore, each share has an actual worth of £2,000.

11.2.4 Procedure for the issue of shares

When new shares are created by a company they are said to be 'issued' or 'allotted' by the company to the people who have contracted to buy them. Any proposed issue of shares is likely to raise a number of complex legal matters. These will be now considered in turn.

11.2.4.1 Limit on the size of the allotment

The relevant share capital of a company (its issued or allotted share capital—s. 546 CA 2006) will be increased automatically every time an allotment of shares is made by the size of the fresh allotment (s. 617(2)(a) CA 2006). The 'default position', therefore, is that companies are free to make allotments of any size at any time. However, it is always possible for a company to impose a restriction on its issued share capital in its articles; for example, a ceiling limit on the number of shares which can be allotted over a designated time span.

However, companies incorporated under the 1985 Act are still bound by the limit imposed by the authorised share capital clause contained in their memoranda, which is deemed to be incorporated into the articles. If this clause would prohibit any subsequent allotment, the solution will be for a company to alter its articles to remove this restriction or to amend upwards the limit imposed. Although this is technically a change to the articles, it can be achieved by ordinary, rather than special, resolution.

EXAMPLE

Cranwell Limited was formed under the Companies Act 1985. Accordingly, it has a memorandum which complies with that Act, including a share capital clause which states that: 'The share capital of the company is £1,000 divided into 1,000 shares of £1 each.'

Cranwell has 800 shares in issue and wishes to allot a further 400 shares. The above clause, therefore, prevents this; the balance of share capital from which to make the allotment stands at 200 shares. The two solutions, therefore, are either:

(a) amend the clause to increase the amount stated to at least 1,200 shares (or such higher amount as is desirable); or

(b) delete the clause entirely to remove the restriction totally.

11.2.4.2 Directors' authorisation

For private companies with only one class of share in issue, directors are free to allot further shares of the same class without prior reference to the shareholders, subject to any restriction imposed upon them in the articles (s. 550 CA 2006). However, where the company is public or where there are different classes of shares in issue or the proposed allotment will result in such a situation, the advance consent of shareholders by ordinary resolution or authority from the articles will be required (s. 551 CA 2006).

EXAMPLE

Proposed Allotment	*Applicability of s. 550 CA 2006*	*Applicability of s. 551 CA 2006*
A Limited was registered on 30 November 2009 under the Companies Act 2006. It has 150 ordinary shares of £1 each in issue. The board of directors wishes to allot a further 50 ordinary shares of £1 each. There are no restrictions in its articles on the size of future allotments.	The section applies. There will only be ordinary shares in issue both prior to and after the proposed allotment. The board may make the allotment without any prior authorisation from the shareholders.	N/A

Proposed Allotment	*Applicability of s. 550 CA 2006*	*Applicability of s. 551 CA 2006*
A Limited was registered on 30 November 2009 under the Companies Act 2006. It has 150 ordinary shares of £1 each in issue. The board of directors wishes to allot 50 preference shares of £5 each. There are no restrictions in its articles on the size of future allotments.	N/A	The section applies. There will be both ordinary shares and preference shares in issue after the proposed allotment. The board may only make the allotment with the prior authorisation of the shareholders, either in the form of an ordinary resolution or from authority contained in the articles.
B Limited was registered on 30 February 2010 under the Companies Act 2006. It has 100 ordinary shares of £1 each and 100 preference shares of £10 each in issue. The board of directors wishes to allot a further 50 ordinary shares of £1 each. There are no restrictions in its articles on the size of future allotments.	N/A	The section applies. There are both ordinary shares and preference shares in issue prior to the proposed allotment. The board may only make the allotment with the prior authorisation of the shareholders, either in the form of an ordinary resolution or from authority contained in the articles.

There is, however, one caveat to the general applicability of s. 550. It only applies automatically to companies formed on or after 1 October 2009. For all other private companies it will be necessary for the shareholders to pass an ordinary resolution allowing the directors to take advantage of the section; effectively as a one-off 'trigger' event.

Any necessary authorisation to allow an allotment may be given either for a particular exercise of the directors' power or generally, and may be unconditional or subject to conditions. Whether the authorisation is given by ordinary resolution of the members in general meeting or by the articles, it must state the maximum amount of shares which the directors may issue and the date when the authority will expire. The authority cannot be given for more than five years from formation of the company or the passing of the resolution (as the case may be) and can be revoked or varied by the company in general meeting at any time. Once given, the authority can be extended by up to five years by a further resolution of the company.

If the directors issue shares without authority they commit an offence (s. 549(4)) (and presumably would be liable to the company for breach of duty) but the issue of shares remains valid (s. 549(5)).

Some companies may have in their articles pre-existing authority to allot shares up to a specified amount, which will have been granted under the predecessor to s. 551, namely s. 80 CA 1985. If this authority has not expired, it will continue to be valid authority for the directors, but they will still have to comply with the limits specified therein. If this would be problematic, the company can either change its articles by special resolution or vary the authority (or grant fresh authority) by ordinary resolution.

11.2.4.3 Rights of pre-emption

Under s. 561 CA 2006, if it is proposed to issue shares to any person, they must first be offered to the existing shareholders, in proportion to their existing holdings, on terms at least as favourable as those proposed for the issue to that person. Section 562 stipulates the manner in which offers under s. 561 must be made; in particular, the members must be given at least 14 days to accept the offer or reject it (s. 562(4) and (5)).

This right of pre-emption does not apply if the shares are to be issued wholly or partly for non-cash consideration (s. 565).

Furthermore, s. 561 will only apply if the shares to be allotted are 'equity shares', as defined by s. 560. What constitutes an equity share depends upon the rights which the share does or does not enjoy, and, therefore, understanding the concept first requires a sound knowledge of such potential rights. However, put simply, shares which enjoy only fixed entitlements in respect of both dividends and a return of capital are not equity shares and are not subject to s. 561. (See **11.2.2** and **11.5** for more specific discussion of rights which shares may enjoy.)

Section 561 gives shareholders a useful degree of protection in cases where the effect of issuing shares would be to water down their influence within the company and their entitlement to dividends. A still higher degree of protection can be given if the articles provide for pre-emption rights on *any* issue of shares, so that the company will not be able to offer shares for a non-cash consideration unless the members are willing to give up their rights.

It should be noted that s. 561 is only concerned with the *issue* of shares. It should not be confused with any provision in a company's articles which provides for pre-emption rights where an existing shareholder wants to *transfer* his shares (see **Chapter 12**).

A failure to comply with either s. 561 or s. 562 will result in any director who knowingly authorised or permitted such failure being liable to compensate any shareholder to whom an offer should have been made for any loss, damage, costs, or expenses.

11.2.4.4 Excluding rights of pre-emption

Section 567 allows *private* companies the possibility of excluding the effect of ss. 561 and 562, either wholly or partially, through a provision in the articles. Additionally, companies can disapply the effect of s. 561 in respect of specific allotments, either through a special resolution or provision in the articles, although it is important to distinguish between allotments where the directors do and do not require shareholders' authority and the extent and nature of that authority (contrast ss. 569, 570 and 571).

Note that the articles of some companies may have taken advantage of the similar regime which existed under the Companies Act 1985 to disapply the pre-emption rights previously imposed by s. 89 CA 1985—see ss. 89–95 CA 1985. In those cases, such disapplication is treated as continuing in effect, as if it were made under the relevant section of the Companies Act 2006 (paras 50–53 Companies Act 2006 (Commencement No 8, Transitional Provisions and Savings) Order 2008).

11.2.4.5 Directors' fiduciary duties

The directors may not issue shares in breach of their fiduciary duty, so that the approval of the members is required if the motive behind the issue is anything other than the raising of further investment in the company.

Very often the courts have, in such circumstances, been prepared to declare such allotments unlawful (see **9.10.2.2**). It is a moot point as to whether or not, if a s. 551 authority is obtained, a separate approval of the shareholders is required to cover this point. It is submitted that it is not. However, there may be circumstances where such a rule does not hold true; for example, if the s. 551 authority is obtained by deception, or if it was granted some time before the actual allotment takes place and the company's circumstances have changed to such an extent that, if asked again, the shareholders may not grant such an authority.

11.2.5 Payment for shares

11.2.5.1 Consideration

A contract for the issue of shares may provide for payment in cash or for some other consideration. If the full nominal amount is paid at the time of the allotment, the shares are said to be 'fully paid up'. If not, they are 'partly-paid'. In this case, the outstanding amount can be asked for by the company making a 'call'. (The details of such a device will normally be specific to the company's articles.) Additionally, if the company goes into liquidation, the shareholder is obliged to contribute the outstanding sum to the company. (See **7.5.1** for further discussion of this area.) Payment in full on issue of the shares is usually required, so that partly-paid shares are rather uncommon.

Companies may not issue shares at a discount to their nominal value. This is prohibited by s. 580 CA 2006, which makes the allottee liable to the company for the shortfall. As such, it is impossible to pay less than the nominal value of a share and for that share to be treated as fully paid up by the company.

EXAMPLE

Sage Pharmacies Limited purports to allot to Constance 2,000 £1 ordinary shares as fully-paid Constance only pays 60 pence per share. As such, Constance still owes 40 pence per share.

11.2.5.2 Premium

Shares can be issued at a premium, that is, for more than their nominal value. (For the accounting consequences of this, see **11.3.4**.)

EXAMPLE

Sage Pharmacies Limited allots to Cedric 200 £1 ordinary shares at a premium of £4 per share Cedric, therefore, will pay a total of £1,000 for these shares, i.e., £5 for each share.

11.2.6 Registration of allotments

Section 555(2) CA 2006 requires a return of allotment to be made to the Registrar of Companies within one month of the issue of shares. This return effectively details the allotment which has taken place. The return must also be accompanied by a statement of capital, giving details of the company's share capital at that time (s. 555(4)). This registration obligation is achieved by the completion and submission of Form SH01.

Copies of several shareholder resolutions may need to be submitted to the Registrar within 15 days of the allotment, depending upon whether or not they were necessary to effect the allotment. Such resolutions may be:

(a) Any special resolution passed to disapply pre-emption rights.

(b) Any ordinary resolution passed pursuant to s. 551 to grant directors authority to make the allotment.

(c) Any ordinary resolution passed to amend or revoke the share capital clause carried over from the company's memorandum of association.

(d) Any ordinary resolution passed by a 1985 Act company to trigger the availability of s. 550.

Section 554 imposes on companies an obligation to register any allotment in the *internal* register of members within two months of its occurrence. Further, s. 769 requires a company within the same time period to have share certificates ready for delivery to the relevant shareholders.

11.2.7 Issue of shares to the public

Section 755 CA 2006 prohibits a private company from offering shares (or debentures) to the public or from issuing them with a view to an offer for sale to the public. Any action in contravention of this prohibition can result in a court ordering that the company in question re-register as a public company (ss. 757 and 758). (An application to the court in this instance can be made by either a member or creditor of the company or the Secretary of State.)

11.2.8 Allotment of shares: summary

11.2.8.1 Introduction

The following is a summary of the main issues already discussed in respect of a proposed allotment of shares by a *private* company. Please note the following:

(a) This is only a summary—there is no substitute for direct reference both to the Companies Act and the relevant company's articles.

(b) Different issues arise in respect of companies formed under the 1985 Act and companies formed under the 2006 Act. Accordingly, they are considered separately.

(c) In respect of 1985 Act companies, the Companies Act 2006 (Commencement No 8 Transitional Provisions and Savings) Order 2008 must also be consulted, particularly paras 42–55.

Usually there are three main questions to consider:

(i) Do the articles need to be amended to deal with a numerical restriction on issued shares?

(ii) Do the directors need shareholders' authorisation by ordinary resolution to effect the allotment?

(iii) Do pre-emption rights apply to the allotment, in which case, must they be disapplied?

11.2.8.2 Private company incorporated under the Companies Act 2006

1. Do the articles contain any restriction on the number of shares which the company may issue? If yes, would the proposed allotment go beyond this restriction? Special resolution is required to alter the articles to increase or remove this restriction. (It is highly unlikely that a 2006 Act company will include such a restriction in its articles. The Model Articles, for example, do not contain such a restriction.)
2. What types of share are currently in issue and what type of share is it proposed to issue? If only one type both before and after, s. 550 CA 2006 applies: permission to allot is

automatic. If more than one type either before or after, s. 551 CA 2006 applies: permission is required by ordinary resolution, unless the company's articles already contain a permission to the directors to make the allotment in question. (If the Model Articles are relevant, no such permission is included.)

3. Do the shares to be allotted fall within the definition of 'equity securities' in s. 560 CA 2006? If yes, s. 561 pre-emption rights apply and may have to be disapplied by special resolution, unless:
   (i) they are excluded already by the company's articles (the Model Articles contain no such exclusion);
   (ii) they are substituted by alternative pre-emption rights in the company's articles (the Model Articles do not include such rights); or
   (iii) consideration for the allotment is wholly or partly non-cash (s. 565 CA 2006).

11.2.8.3 Private Company incorporated under the Companies Act 1985

1. Do the company's articles contain any restriction on the number of shares which the company may issue? If yes, would the proposed allotment go beyond this restriction? It is possible that the authorised share capital clause of the company's memorandum, having been imported into the articles by s. 28(1) CA 2006, may have such an effect. An ordinary resolution (exception to the general rule) is required to alter the articles to increase or remove this restriction.
2. How many types of share are currently in issue and what type of share is it proposed to issue? If only one type both before and after, s. 550 CA 2006 applies: permission to allot is automatic. However, directors cannot benefit from the effect of s. 550 until an enabling ordinary resolution has been passed. If more than one type of share is in issue either before or after the allotment, s. 551 CA 2006 applies: permission is required by ordinary resolution, unless the articles already permit the directors to make the allotment in question. (If Table A is relevant, no such permission is included.)
3. Do the shares to be allotted fall within the definition of 'equity securities' in s. 560 CA 2006? If yes, s. 561 pre-emption rights apply and may have to be disapplied by special resolution, unless:
   (i) they are excluded already by the company's articles (Table A contains no such exclusion);
   (ii) they are substituted by alternative pre-emption rights in the company's articles (Table A does not include such substitute rights); or
   (iii) consideration for the allotment is wholly or partly non-cash (s. 565 CA 2006).

11.3 Share capital

11.3.1 Introduction

Once shares have been issued they are said to form part of the 'capital' of the company. Issued capital is measured by reference to the nominal value of the shares in question.

EXAMPLE

If 500 shares each with a nominal value of £1 have been issued, the issued capital is £500. If those shares have been issued at nominal or par value, the issued share capital will be matched by £500 cash received for the shares and this fact will be represented in the balance sheet. Whilst a massive over-simplification of what a balance sheet actually looks like, the accounting treatment would be as follows:

ASSETS
Current Assets £500

CAPITAL
Share capital £500

If, in fact, those shares were issued for more than their nominal value, for example, shareholders have paid £10 each for their shares (that is, at a premium of £9 per share), this will not affect the issued share capital figure. However, the company will have received a total of £5,000 for the issued shares.

To ensure that there is a matching correlation between the company's assets and the way the shareholders have contributed to those assets, the total amount of the premium (that is, £4,500) will have to be recorded in the balance sheet of the company to reflect this additional contribution by the shareholders. The issued share capital figure plus the share premium will then represent the £5,000 received. Again, by way of simple example, the accounting treatment would be as follows:

ASSETS	
Current Assets	£5,000
CAPITAL	
Share capital	£ 500
Share Premium	£4,500
	£5,000

(See **11.3.4** below for further discussion of the share premium account.)

(Issued) share capital is really a liability of a company to its shareholders, since the company will one day be liable to repay the shareholders' investment (usually, in fact, only when the company is wound up).

11.3.2 Alteration to share capital

Most instances of an alteration to a company's share capital under s. 617 will be brought about by an allotment of shares. However, it is also possible under that section to alter share capital in the following ways:

(a) by consolidation;

(b) by subdivision;

(c) by reduction.

Shares are consolidated if they are consolidated into a smaller number of shares of a larger nominal amount (e.g., 1,000 £1 shares become 100 £10 shares); subdivision is the opposite (1,000 £1 shares become 10,000 10p shares). Any consolidation or subdivision of share capital can be achieved by ordinary resolution of the shareholders, unless the company's articles prohibit or restrict such alteration.

Since the change brought about by any consolidation or subdivision is really only a nominal one, there will seldom be any advantage in making it, unless the value of each share is either extremely large or extremely small, in which case subdivision or consolidation may be of some cosmetic value.

Under ss. 641–653 CA 2006, companies may reduce their share capital. The reasons for wanting to do this vary and are often quite technical. For example, public companies are only permitted to pay dividends if their net assets exceed their share capital (s. 831 CA 2006). If this is not the case, one solution is to reduce the share capital. (For public companies listed on the Stock Exchange, a failure to pay out a dividend can be prejudicial to the share price of the company.)

It is beyond the scope of this book to deal with this issue in any detail. However, in order to have a basic understanding, the following important issues should be borne in mind:

(a) the shareholders must approve the reduction by special resolution;

(b) the reduction must be sanctioned by the court;

(c) in a number of circumstances, creditors have a right to object to the reduction;

(d) should the reduction affect separate classes of shareholders differently, there may be a class rights issue under s. 630 CA 2006.

This process is available to any company (s. 641(1)(b)). However, an alternative process is also available for private companies, which involves, instead, a special resolution to authorise the reduction, together with statements of solvency about the company from each relevant director (s. 641(1)(a)). This process was specifically introduced by the 2006 Act to make it simpler and cheaper for private companies, removing the need for an application to the court.

11.3.3 Maintenance of capital

For the protection of people dealing with the company, share capital has to be 'maintained' by the company. This does not mean that the money invested has to be deposited or set aside as a fund to guarantee the company's creditors. The money is available to be used by the company as 'working' capital, to pay for the expenses of its business. What maintaining capital means is that it must not, normally, be returned to the members in any way while the company is a going concern.

Two major consequences of this rule are:

(a) that dividends may only be paid out of profits (see **10.11**);

(b) that capital invested cannot be returned to the members except:

 (i) by a properly approved reduction in capital; or

 (ii) where the company redeems or purchases its own shares (see below and **Chapter 12**).

11.3.4 Share premium account

As has already been explained, it is common for shares to be issued for more than their nominal value. The excess is not strictly speaking share capital, but is required by s. 610(1) CA 2006 to be credited to a 'share premium account' (i.e., an account showing the company to be liable to the members for the amount of the premium). The share premium account has to be maintained in the same way as share capital; thus assets representing it cannot be returned to members. (The specimen balance sheet at **15.7** contains an example of the accounting treatment of a share premium.)

11.3.5 Company as member of itself and purchase of own shares

11.3.5.1 The company as its own shareholder

A company may not be registered as its own shareholder. However, shares can be transferred to a trustee or nominee for the company. In addition, a subsidiary is prohibited from owning shares in its holding company.

11.3.5.2 Original prohibition on purchase of own shares

The traditional position was that it was illegal for a company to buy its own shares (*Trevor v Whitworth* (1887) 12 App Cas 409). This is because use of its money by a company to purchase its own shares is in effect a return to the shareholder of his investment and so is a reduction of capital. Statute has since intervened to modify this restriction, by the recognition of both redeemable shares and buy-back of shares in defined circumstances.

11.3.5.3 Redeemable shares

Section 684 CA 2006 gives companies power to issue redeemable shares; that is, shares which can be bought back by the company at the option of the company or the shareholder. In the case of a private company, its articles may exclude or restrict this possibility; a public company, by contrast, must be authorised by its articles to issue redeemable shares. The terms of redemption must be set out in the articles or can be left to the directors to determine, so long as they do so prior to the allotment (s. 685). No share can be redeemed unless it is fully-paid (s. 686).

Any redemption has to be notified to the Registrar of Companies within 28 days of its happening (s. 689). A statement of capital must also be sent, which sets out details of the company's share capital after the redemption

11.3.5.4 Buy-back of shares

It is thought to be desirable for companies, particularly small family companies, to have the power to purchase their own shares as this provides an additional market for the shares. Section 690 CA 2006, therefore, gives companies power to purchase their own shares, unless this is displaced or restricted by a provision in its articles.

Examples of cases where the power is useful include buying out dissident shareholders and the provision of funds to the estate of a deceased shareholder to assist in the payment of inheritance tax. In fact, all companies have the possibility of buying back some of their shares and it is not uncommon to read in the financial press of major public companies doing so as a way of returning cash to shareholders. To reflect the diversity of companies which may effect buy-backs, the legislation distinguishes between 'off-market' and 'market' purchases (s. 693). The specifics of this distinction are beyond the scope of this book. Only a small number of companies whose shares are traded on an investment exchange, e.g., the London Stock Exchange, will have the option of undertaking a market purchase. What follows, therefore, is an explanation of the mechanics of an off-market purchase.

Certain controls on buy-backs were eased in April 2013 by amendments to Part 18 of the Companies Act 2006. Many of these changes were to meet the Government's aspirations for greater ease of employee investment and ownership in private companies. This has been achieved by a less onerous regime for buy-backs which facilitate employees' share schemes. Many of the changes are, therefore, outside the scope of this discussion. However, a number of the changes are of general application to buy-backs and are included in the explanation that follows.

As with redeemable shares, no share can be bought back unless it is fully-paid (s. 691(1)). The contract for purchase (between the company and the relevant shareholder) must be approved by ordinary resolution before the company enters into it (s. 694(1)). The members whose shares are to be purchased must not use the votes given to them by the shares which are to be purchased on that resolution (s. 695). The resolution will be invalid unless:

(a) where a general meeting has been called, a copy of the contract (or a memorandum of its terms) is made available for inspection by the members at the company's registered office for a period of at least 15 days ending with the date of the meeting and also at the meeting itself;

(b) where a written resolution is being used, a copy of the contract (or a memorandum of its terms) is sent to every eligible member at the same time as the written resolution (s. 696).

Once the shares have been purchased by the company they are treated as cancelled and the company's issued share capital is reduced accordingly (s. 706(b)).

However, the option exists for all companies to hold shares they have repurchased in treasury, so long as capital has not been used to fund the buy-back (s. 724). (The use of capital is only available to private companies—see **11.3.5.5**.) Effectively this allows such shares to be reallotted by the company without the need for shareholder approval.

Within 28 days after the shares have been purchased a return must be made to the Registrar of Companies (on form SH03) stating the number and nominal value of the shares purchased and the date of purchase (s. 707). This return will have to bear stamp duty at the rate of 0.5% of the consideration paid. In addition, s. 708 requires notice of cancellation of any shares, together with a statement of capital, which sets out details of the company's share capital after the cancellation to be provided on form SH06.

11.3.5.5 Financing buy-back or redemption

When shares are redeemed or purchased by the company, the money used to pay for them (including any payment representing a premium over the nominal value) must generally come out of distributable profits or the proceeds of a fresh issue of shares (s. 692(2), although the ability exists for private companies to use an annual cash amount not exceeding the lower of £15,000 or the cash equivalent of 5% of issued share capital to fund a buy-back of shares without reference to distributable reserves, so long as this is authorised by the articles (s. 692(1)(b)). Where the shares are purchased or redeemed with assets representing profits, the legislation requires the capital of the company to be maintained. Thus, s. 733 CA 2006 requires the company to open a 'capital redemption reserve' equal to the reduction in the share capital (assuming shares are not held in treasury). This reserve is treated in the same way as share capital or the share premium account; that is, it is shown in the balance sheet as a liability due to shareholders which has to be maintained until the company goes into liquidation.

EXAMPLE: Buy-back using distributable profits

BALANCE SHEET OF JCT LIMITED PRIOR TO BUY-BACK

FIXED ASSETS		
Premises		200,000
Fixtures		20,000
		220,000
CURRENT ASSETS		
Stock	30,000	
Debtors	40,000	
Cash	70,000	
	140,000	
CURRENT LIABILITIES		
Creditors	40,000	
		100,000
		320,000
CAPITAL		
Share capital		250,000
Share premium		10,000
Profit & loss		60,000
		320,000

JCT buys back 10,000 ordinary shares of £1 each at a price of £20,000. The purchase is made wholly out of profits (using available cash). The amendments to the balance sheet are:

(a) reduce assests (cash) by £20,000;

(b) reduce share capital by £10,000 (i.e., the nominal value of the shares);

(c) reduce profit and loss by £20,000 (to reflect the use of profits to buy back the shares);

(d) create capital redemption reserve of £10,000 (equivalent to the reduction in capital).

BALANCE SHEET OF JCT LIMITED FOLLOWING BUY-BACK

FIXED ASSETS		
Premises		200,000
Fixtures		20,000
		220,000
CURRENT ASSETS		
Stock	30,000	
Debtors	40,000	
Cash	50,000	
	120,000	

CURRENT LIABILITIES		
Creditors	40,000	
		80,000
		300,000
CAPITAL		
Share capital		240,000
Share premium		10,000
Capital redemption reserve		10,000
Profit and loss		40,000
		300,000

In the case of a *private* company, payment out of assets representing capital is permitted both in respect of a buy-back and a redemption (s. 709). The use of capital in this way (the 'permissible capital payment') is only possible once distributable profits and the proceeds of any fresh issue of shares made for the purpose have been used up (s. 710).

In order to protect the interests of members and creditors, the following detailed procedural requirements must be satisfied:

(a) The articles must not expressly restrict or prohibit the use of capital assets for this purpose.

(b) The directors must make a statement that the company will remain solvent and will, in their view, be able to carry on business as a going concern for at least a year (s. 714). The directors' certificate must be supported by an auditors' report in which the auditors certify that they are not aware of anything which would indicate that the directors' view of the situation is unreasonable. (The directors will commit a criminal offence if they have no reasonable grounds for the opinion expressed in their statement (s. 715).)

(c) Not later than one week after the date of the directors' statement, a special resolution approving the payment must be passed. The members whose shares are to be purchased may not use the votes on those shares on this resolution. In addition, both a copy of the statement and the auditors' report must be made available at any general meeting held for the purpose or must be sent out with any written resolution (s. 718).

(d) Within a week of the above resolution, the company must have published details of the proposed buy-back in the *London Gazette*. It should also notify its creditors directly or through a notice in a national newspaper (s. 719). This is to put all interested creditors on notice, as they have the right to object to the use of capital by applying to court for an order cancelling the resolution (s. 721). (Dissenting members also have this right.)

(e) The payment for the shares must be made by the company not less than five nor more than seven weeks after the date on which the resolution is passed (s. 723). This period is laid down so that members or creditors who object to the purchase have time to challenge the purchase in court.

In addition, where a payment is made out of capital, the company's accounts must reflect this. Under s. 734 CA 2006, where the permissible capital payment is less than the nominal value of the shares redeemed, the amount of the difference must be transferred to a capital redemption reserve. Where the permissible capital payment is greater than the nominal value of the shares redeemed, the situation is different. The company may then reduce the amount of any share premium account, fully-paid share capital, or unrealised profits of the company standing in any reserve by a sum not exceeding the amount by which the permissible capital payment exceeds the nominal amount of the shares.

EXAMPLE: Buy-back using capital

BALANCE SHEET OF BHW LIMITED PRIOR TO BUY-BACKS V.1 AND V.2

FIXED ASSETS		
Premises		100,000
Fixtures		20,000
		120,000
CURRENT ASSETS		
Stock	30,000	
Debtors	40,000	
Cash	70,000	
	140,000	
CURRENT LIABILITIES		
Creditors	40,000	
		100,000
		220,000
CAPITAL		
Share capital		150,000
Share premium		50,000
Profit and loss		20,000
		220,000

Buy-back V.1

BHW buys back 20,000 ordinary shares of £1 each at a price of £30,000. The purchase is made from a combination of available profits (£20,000) and a permissible capital payment of £10,000. The amendments to the balance sheet are:

(a) reduce assests (cash) by £30,000;

(b) reduce share capital by £20,000 (i.e., the nominal value of the shares);

(c) reduce profit and loss by £20,000 (to reflect the use of profits to buy back the shares);

(d) create capital redemption reserve of £10,000 (equivalent to the amount by which the permissible capital payment is less than the nominal value of shares redeemed).

BALANCE SHEET OF BHW LIMITED FOLLOWING BUY-BACK V.1
(Permissible capital payment is *less than* nominal value of shares redeemed)

FIXED ASSETS		
Premises		100,000
Fixtures		20,000
		120,000
CURRENT ASSETS		
Stock	30,000	
Debtors	40,000	
Cash	40,000	
	110,000	
CURRENT LIABILITIES		
Creditors	40,000	
		70,000
		190,000
CAPITAL		
Share capital		130,000
Share premium		50,000
Capital redemption reserve		10,000
Profit and loss		(Nil)
		190,000

Buy-back V.2

If BHW had bought the 20,000 ordinary shares of £1 each at a price of £50,000, then the accounting treatment would be different. In this case, the purchase was made from a combination of available profits (£20,000) and a permissible capital payment of £30,000. The amendments to the balance sheet are:

(a) reduce assets (cash) by £50,000;

(b) reduce share capital by £20,000 (i.e., the nominal value of the shares);

(c) reduce profit and loss by £20,000 (to reflect the use of profits to buy back the shares);

(d) reduce share premium account by £10,000 (equivalent to the amount by which the permissible capital payment *exceeds* the nominal value of shares redeemed).

BALANCE SHEET OF BHW LIMITED FOLLOWING BUY-BACK V.2
(Permissible capital payment *exceeds* the nominal value of shares redeemed)

FIXED ASSETS		
Premises		100,000
Fixtures		20,000
		120,000
CURRENT ASSETS		
Stock	30,000	
Debtors	40,000	
Cash	20,000	
	90,000	
CURRENT LIABILITIES		
Creditors	40,000	
		50,000
		170,000
CAPITAL		
Share capital		130,000
Share premium		40,000
Profit and loss		(Nil)
		170,000

11.4 Financial assistance by company for purchase of shares

Section 678 CA 2006 makes it illegal for any public company to give financial assistance directly or indirectly to assist someone to purchase shares in that company (or its holding company). (This issue in discussed in greater detail in **Chapter 12**.)

11.5 Classes of shares

11.5.1 Introduction

In most companies, all the shares issued have the same rights attached to them. It is possible, however, for a company to issue shares with different rights. The reasons for this are many, but the main driver will be that shares can be considered as both a mechanism for control (because of the possible voting rights they may carry) and investment (either because of dividends which are paid out by the company or the fact that they increase in value as the company increases in value). Some shareholders will be more concerned with the latter than the former, and vice versa. Therefore, more than one type of share will be necessary to satisfy this demand. The shares are then said to belong to different classes. For example, a company may issue preference shares, that is, shares which have a better right to receive a dividend than ordinary shares. It is also possible to give some shareholders a greater measure of control over the affairs of the company either by creating voting and non-voting shares or by providing that all shares are to carry a right to vote but that some will have more votes than others.

It is not intended to provide an exhaustive explanation of all possible share rights. However, it is important to distinguish between the two most common types of share in issue—ordinary and preference shares.

11.5.2 Ordinary shares

By far the most common type of share in issue is the ordinary share. Ordinary shares entitle the holder to dividends, should such be declared (see **10.10** and **10.11**). They also normally entitle the holder to voting rights.

11.5.3 Preference shares

Preference shares are a more sophisticated investment mechanism than ordinary shares. They may be 'preferred' in two particular ways.

First, they may carry the automatic right to a fixed, annual dividend, normally calculated as a percentage of the nominal value of the shares. This right may, in addition, be cumulative, which means that should funds not be available to satisfy a dividend payment in a particular year, the preferred shareholder's entitlement is carried forward until funds are available. Secondly, on a winding up, they may stand ahead of other shareholders in having their capital contribution to the company repaid to them. (Each of these rights is independent of the other, so some preference shares may carry one but not both entitlements.)

Thus, preference shares appear to have clear advantages over ordinary shares. However, they tend not to carry voting rights, and the preferred rights themselves are normally restricted to a fixed amount. This can mean, for example, that in certain situations ordinary shareholders may receive better dividends than preferred shareholders. As a way of redressing the balance, preference shares may also carry with them rights of participation, which effectively means that as well as enjoying preferred rights, they may also enjoy the rights which ordinary shares carry.

Rights of participation are not compulsory and must be negotiated between the company and the potential shareholder, along with all other preferential rights.

EXAMPLE

Dividend

Tony has 50 ordinary shares of £1 each and Nick has 100 5% preference shares of £1 each in Lineout Limited. Should Lineout have £5 with which it can pay out a dividend, Nick will be paid first, which will use up the full amount, so none will go to Tony. However, should Lineout have £50 with which it can pay out a dividend, Nick will be paid first, but will still only receive £5, allowing Tony to receive £45.

If, however, all Nick's shares were participating, the balance of £45 would have to be divided between Nick and Tony, resulting in Nick receiving two-thirds of this amount and Tony one-third.

Winding up

If Nick's shares also carry preferential rights on a winding up and the amount available for distribution to shareholders is £100, Nick will have his capital contribution returned first, resulting in nothing being available for Tony. However, should the amount left be £1,000, Nick will still receive his £100 first, but Tony will receive both his capital contribution, plus the remainder, that is, the full £900.

Instead, if Nick also had rights of participation on a winding up, the order of pay-out would be:

1. Nick £100;
2. Balance of £900, split one-third Tony; two-thirds Nick.

11.5.4 Rights of redemption

Redeemable shares have already been mentioned earlier in this chapter. Strictly speaking they are not a class of shares separate from ordinary or preference shares; instead, rights of redemption can be attached to either of these types of shares. (It is suggested, however, that redeemable preference shares are more likely to be created than redeemable ordinary shares, on the basis that redeemable preferred shares are a way of providing for a finite and certain investment in a company.)

11.6 Finance through borrowing

11.6.1 Types of debt finance

For many small and medium-sized companies, bank finance will be the standard source of debt finance. Normally this will take two forms, either:

(a) an overdraft facility; or

(b) a term loan.

The detail of banking arrangements is beyond the scope of this book. However, in simple terms:

(a) An overdraft is a source of finance which a company can draw upon, as it sees fit, normally subject to an overall limit. This is a relatively convenient form of finance, but also expensive, as a bank is likely to charge daily interest on the amount outstanding and a proportionately high fee for setting up and maintaining such a facility.

(b) A term loan is a fixed amount, normally provided in one go, which must be repaid according to the terms of the loan agreement (usually, but not always, by instalments of equal amounts). Interest will be charged on the amount outstanding and an arrangement fee will normally be charged at the outset.

Companies may simply rely upon one method of debt finance or a combination, depending on their needs for working and investment capital.

11.6.2 Express and implied power

A trading company has an implied power to borrow for the purpose of its trade. This is because the trade will be authorised by its objects and the borrowing will be reasonably incidental to the power to carry on the trade.

A company with power to borrow also has an implied power to give security for the loan. It is preferable to include express powers if a full objects clause is adopted rather than to rely on implied ones. In practice, banks (and other professional lenders) would probably continue to check the company's express powers despite the abolition of the consequences of the *ultra vires* rule referred to in **11.6.3**.

11.6.3 *Ultra vires* borrowing

Section 39 CA 2006 provides that 'the validity of an act done by a company shall not be called into question on the ground of lack of capacity by reason of anything in the company's constitution'. At face value, therefore, a prospective lender need not concern itself with any limitations on a company's activities. However, there is still an ancillary issue in respect of the requirement for directors to observe any restrictions which the articles may place on the powers of a company. Any lender which is aware of such a situation or which deliberately ignores such an issue may find the validity of the loan and, more particularly, any supporting security, open to challenge. This is a powerful incentive, therefore, for banks to satisfy themselves of the *vires* of a company before lending to it.

11.6.4 Exercise of borrowing powers

The power to borrow must be exercised in accordance with the company's articles of association. If the company has adopted Table A or similar, the directors will have power to borrow in circumstances where the loan is to be used for the purposes of the business (article 70). (See also article 3 of the Model Articles for Private Companies.)

11.7 Secured loans

11.7.1 Types of security

A prudent lender will usually require security for a loan made to a company. Any assets of the company may be charged by way of security. Usually security will be in the form of a mortgage, a fixed charge, a floating charge, or all three. The essential benefit of such security is that it allows the lender the possibility of selling the assets of the borrower should the borrower default on repayments of the loan. The proceeds of sale can then be used by the lender to recoup some or all of the outstanding loan. Therefore, a key issue for any lender taking security is that the company in question actually owns the assets which will be charged. Also a lender will want to know if there are other charges already attaching to such assets. Such investigations are commonly referred to as 'due diligence' and one of the key responsibilities of a lawyer acting for a lender will be to carry out due diligence on the client's behalf. (See further **11.13** for some of the usual investigations made.)

In addition to charges over the assets of the company, a lender may frequently require personal guarantees from the directors. Where a personal guarantee is given by a director who is also a shareholder, the benefit of limited liability is effectively lost to the extent of the guarantee.

When companies borrow money, they will more often than not enter into a 'debenture' with the lender. (For a discussion of the contents of this document, see **Chapter 3[illegible]**.) Unfortunately, the term 'debenture' covers a variety of loan instruments and has no one specific usage. In its simplest form, it means a document issued by a company acknowledging debt of that company. This will clearly cover unsecured loan agreements. However, in commercial circles the term very often implies that the debt is backed up by some form of security. (In fact, such documentation may be called a 'mortgage debenture'.) It is quite common to find a debenture document providing a lender with a variety of different security rights and interests, backing up a loan made to a company. The loan itself will usually be the subject of a separate legal document, in which will be set out the terms of lending and repayment.

To complicate matters further, companies may issue 'loan stock' or 'debenture stock' which consists of transferable *securities* in a company, carrying with them a contractual right to interest and repayment of the sum paid for them. These can also be classed as debentures (s. 738 CA 2006). Therefore, care should always be exercised in both the use and interpretation of the term and the actual documentation in question should be inspected to establish the nature of a company's indebtedness.

Finally it is equally important to distinguish between the terms 'security' and 'securities'. The former is a generic term for charges over property; the latter covers all forms of transferable instruments in a company, most commonly shares and loan stock.

11.7.2 Mortgages and fixed charges

A lender may take security in the form of a mortgage or a fixed charge. The essential difference between the two is that a mortgage requires the formal transfer of title in the asset to the mortgagee, subject to an automatic right for title to be transferred back to the mortgagor once the debt is repaid—the so-called 'equity of redemption'. There are no such formalities required to create a fixed charge, merely an intention by the parties that the asset in question can be appropriated by the charge-holder and sold by it. However, in most security documentation, it will be clear from the wording that a fixed charge is intended. Both types of security must attach to specific, identifiable assets or assets which can be ascertained and defined.

In the case of a mortgage, the mortgagee actually owns title to the asset and can, thus, sell it without reference to the mortgagor, provided that the mortgagor is in default under the loan. In the case of a fixed charge, title remains with the chargor, but the chargor is not entitled to sell the asset without the consent of the charge-holder.

Mortgages can either be equitable or legal. Legal mortgages require specific formalities to be fulfilled, in particular the transfer of title in the property according to the law. An equitable mortgage is created where there is evidence of a desire to create a mortgage without fulfilling all such formalities.

It is important to note that mortgages specifically of freehold and leasehold property are somewhat different and are governed, inter alia, by Pt III of the Law of Property Act (LPA) 1925. In particular, the creation of a mortgage over land is not possible by the transfer of the legal estate (s. 85 LPA 1925). Instead it must be created by way of a charge by deed expressed to be by way of legal mortgage.

An equitable mortgage is weaker than a legal one, in that a bona fide purchaser for value without notice of the equitable mortgage takes the property free from it. However, there are in place specific registration requirements which make it more difficult for such a purchaser to claim ignorance of such a fact, particularly in relation to registered and unregistered land. Also, the circumstances of the equitable mortgage may mean that the owner cannot sell the property in any event. For example, if A gives B possession of a share certificate as security for a loan made by B to A, this may constitute an equitable mortgage. (It cannot constitute a legal mortgage as no effective transfer of title in the shares from A to B has taken place; see **12.2.3**.) Without possession of the share certificate, A cannot effectively transfer title in the shares to anybody else.

All fixed charges are equitable. Confusingly, they may sometimes be referred to as equitable mortgages. In fact, commentators and judges often use the terminology loosely. Rather than worry about specific labels, the main distinction mentioned above should be borne in mind; that is, a mortgage either grants or purports to grant a proprietary interest in property, whereas a fixed charge grants an immediate right over property which can be exercised in certain situations.

A further important distinction is that between fixed and floating charges, which is discussed next.

11.7.3 Floating charges

A floating charge is an equitable charge over assets of a particular description owned by the company from time to time. A floating charge can be given over assets which are repeatedly dealt with by the company. Perhaps stock-in-trade is the clearest example. A company cannot give a fixed charge over its stock since to do so would prevent it from selling that stock without first obtaining the consent of the mortgagee. This would obviously hinder the ability of the company to carry on its business. However, if it gives a floating charge over the stock, the charge will 'float' over whatever stock the company owns from time to time—it can therefore sell the stock free from the charge and buy new stock to which the charge will automatically attach.

The nature of a floating charge was defined by Romer LJ in *Re Yorkshire Woolcombers' Association Ltd* [1903] 2 Ch 284, in the following way:

> . . . if a charge has the three characteristics I am about to mention it is a floating charge:
>
> (a) if it is a charge on a class of assets of a company present and future;
>
> (b) if that class is one which, in the ordinary course of business of the company, would be changing from time to time; and
>
> (c) if you find that by the charge it is contemplated that, until some future step is taken by or on behalf of those interested in the charge, the company may carry on its business in the ordinary way as far as concerns the particular class of asset I am dealing with.

In the case of *Re Spectrum Plus Ltd* [2005] 2 BCLC 269, the House of Lords considered this dictum once again and provided fresh insight into its significance. Lord Scott proffered an analysis of the history of the case law surrounding this issue. As part of this analysis, he pointed out two key things:

1. that Romer LJ's dictum was never intended to be definitive, nor would a charge always have to demonstrate all three characteristics to be classed a floating charge;
2. that the first two characteristics were not, in any event, distinctive of a floating charge, albeit they may be quite typical. It was the third characteristic which distinguished a floating charge from a fixed.

As regards this second point, Lord Scott expressed a view that '. . . if a security has Romer LJ's third characteristic . . . it qualifies as a floating charge, and cannot be a fixed charge, whatever may be its other characteristics'. For this reason he held that:

> . . . the essential characteristic of a floating charge, the characteristic which distinguishes it from a fixed charge, is that the asset subject to the charge is not finally appropriated as a security for the payment of the debt until the occurrence of some future event.

At first sight a floating charge would seem to give no security at all to the lender since the company can continue to deal with the assets which are charged. However, a floating charge 'fixes' on the charged assets owned by the company at the time when the charge 'crystallises'. A floating charge crystallises when:

(a) The winding up of the company commences (in the case of a winding up by the court this is usually when the winding-up petition is presented (s. 129(2) Insolvency Act (IA) 1986); in the case of voluntary winding up it is when the winding-up resolution is passed (s. 86 IA 1986)).

(b) A receiver is appointed by the court.

(c) A receiver is appointed by the lender under a power given by the debenture.

(d) Any other event occurs which the debenture specifies will cause crystallisation.

Due to some very technical issues arising out of the Bills of Sales Act, individuals and partnerships are effectively prevented from creating floating charges. By analogy, it is believed that limited liability partnerships can also grant these charges, on the basis that they are a legal personality akin to a company. (See **Chapter 29** for discussion of limited liability partnerships.)

11.7.4 Advantages and disadvantages of floating charges

As far as the borrowing company is concerned a floating charge has one great advantage over a fixed charge; that is, until crystallisation, it can deal freely with the charged assets without the permission of the lender.

From the lender's point of view a floating charge suffers from a number of disadvantages when compared with a fixed charge. In particular:

(a) Its value as a security is uncertain until crystallisation.

(b) It is postponed to execution and distress for rent completed before crystallisation.

(c) It is postponed to preferential creditors on the liquidation of the borrowing company (see **26.8.4** and **26.8.5**).

(d) It is postponed to later fixed charges in certain cases (see **11.9.1**).

(e) A percentage of monies realised under the floating charge must be set aside for the benefit of unsecured creditors in a liquidation (see **26.8.5**).

(f) It may be invalid as a security if the company goes into liquidation within a year (see **27.4**).

Historically, the great advantage of a floating charge over the whole of the assets and undertaking of a company was that it allowed the chargee the ability to take control of the company in certain circumstances by appointing an administrative receiver, who would then realise the charged assets of the company on the chargee's behalf. This possibility was removed in all but a few well-defined circumstances by the changes which the Enterprise Act 2002 made to the Insolvency Act 1986. However, it may, instead, be possible for a floating charge-holder to appoint an administrator over such a company. (See **26.4** for further discussion.)

11.8 Registration of charges

11.8.1 Introduction

Many types of security granted by companies must be registered at Companies House. In this way, they are said to be 'perfected', that is, they are effective against third parties. The current relevant provisions are contained within Pt 25 CA 2006.

Part 25 CA 2006 was amended in April 2013 by the Companies Act 2006 (Amendment of Part 25) Regulations 2013. Under the previous regime, there was always some doubt about the registrability of certain company charges. Further, the process of registration was cumbersome, in that the original charge document had to be submitted as part of the registration process and substantial parts of it had either to be reproduced or paraphrased in the registration form. Finally, the process did not allow for a more streamlined system of electronic registration. The changes to Pt 25, therefore, aim to meet these concerns.

11.8.2 Sections 859A–Q CA 2006

11.8.2.1 Requirement to register charges

Section 859A requires registration with the Registrar of Companies of nearly all types of charge and mortgage created by a UK-registered company. As such, registration is required of all floating charges and other charges over a company's land, goodwill, book debts, and most other types of property. Certain types of charge are excluded from registration by the effect of s. 859A(6), for example, security interests over shares in another company owned by the borrowing company (as they are excluded from registration by the Financial Collateral Arrangements (No. 2) Regulations 2003), nor is any security interest which relies upon possession of the property in question registrable, i.e., a pledge or lien (although these are extremely rare in a corporate finance context).

11.8.2.2 Method of registration

Registration must be made by delivering to the Registrar:

(a) prescribed particulars of the charge on form MR01 (ss. 859A(2) and 859D);
(b) a certified copy of the original instrument creating the charge (s. 859A(3)); and
(c) a fee of £10 or £13 (depending upon the method of registration adopted).

Registration must occur within the period of 21 days beginning with the day after the date of creation of the charge (s. 859A(4)). In turn, s. 859E sets out how this rule is to be applied. The following, non-exhaustive table sets out what are considered to be the most likely instances:

Form of charge	Date of creation of charge
A deed which is effective on execution and delivery	On delivery of the deed (subsequent to its execution)
A written instrument which is not a deed and which is expressed to be effective on its execution	On execution of the instrument
A written instrument which is not a deed and whose effectiveness is determined by something other than its execution	On the instrument taking effect

The ability to register is afforded to the relevant company or any person interested in the charge (s. 859A(2)). (As we shall see below, it is very much in the interests of the lender to make sure that the charge is registered.)

11.8.2.3 Register of charges at Companies House

The Registrar keeps a register of the charges created by each company (s. 859I), on which are placed both the registered particulars and the certified copy of the charge document. As this document is open to inspection by the public, the system allows for certain sensitive information to be redacted from it prior to its registration (s. 859G).

11.8.2.4 Certificate of registration

Once a charge has been registered, the Registrar gives a certificate of registration to the person who registered the charge (s. 859I(3)). The certificate is conclusive evidence that the necessary documents were delivered in time (s. 859I(6)). The certificate will bear a unique 12-digit reference code which will match the one on the Companies House register.

11.8.2.5 Extension of time limit for registration (s. 859G)

If the charge is not registered within 21 days the court may extend the time limit, provided that it is satisfied that the failure to register was:

> . . . accidental, or due to inadvertence or to some other sufficient cause, or is not of a nature to prejudice the position of creditors or shareholders of the company, or that on other grounds it is just and equitable to grant relief . . .

The court may impose terms and will, in practice, always impose a condition that the registration is not to prejudice rights acquired by other persons before registration finally takes place.

11.8.3 Effect of non-registration

Section 859H(3) provides that failure to register a registrable charge shall result in the relevant security being void against a liquidator, an administrator, and any creditor of the company. The importance of this provision is that if the company goes into liquidation before the loan has been repaid, the unregistered chargee loses his security. This is so even if a later secured creditor had actual notice of the charge when he took his security (*Re Monolithic Building Co* [1915] 1 Ch 643). It should be noted that non-registration makes the security void against the liquidator or creditor but not against the company. The lender is, therefore, entitled to enforce his security against the company up to the time when winding up commences (but not after that time, since the security is then void against the liquidator).

Furthermore, s. 859H(3) is stated to be:

> . . . without prejudice to any contract or obligation for repayment of the money secured . . . and when a charge becomes void under this section, the money secured by it immediately becomes payable. (s. 859H(4)).

The chargee can, therefore, demand payment immediately if the charge is not registered even if the instrument creating the charge provided for repayment at a later date.

The practical problem is that, although the secured debt is not extinguished by non-registration of the charge, the chargee will only rank as an ordinary creditor in a liquidation of the company. This means that the chargee will have to wait until those with valid, registered fixed and floating charges (and preferential creditors) have been paid out of the company's assets. The chargee ranks with all the other ordinary creditors and, if there are insufficient assets to pay all the ordinary creditors, may only receive a fraction (or none) of the money due to it (see **26.8** for a more detailed discussion of the order of entitlement to assets on a liquidation).

11.8.4 Company's charges information

Section 859P requires the company to keep copies of all registrable charges at its registered office where they must be open to inspection free of charge by members and creditors and open to inspection by anybody else on payment of the prescribed fee. A person lending money to the company should check these copies carefully so that he can see what charges, if any, the company has created over the property which is to be charged to him.

11.8.5 Other types of registration: charges over land

In addition to registration under the Companies Act, mortgages of, and charges on, land by a company may have to be registered at HM Land Registry or at the Land Charges Department (depending on whether the land is registered or unregistered, respectively).

11.8.6 Constructive notice

Any prospective lender to a company should always make a charges search at Companies House against the company. This will provide information as to the security granted to date by that company. (The rules on priority of charges—see below—mean that such knowledge is important to lenders.) However, it should be noted that any person intending to take security from a company is deemed to know the contents of the register at Companies House, even if they have not made a search. Further, it is also arguable that any person who ought to have searched the register (for any reason) but failed to do so, is fixed with knowledge of the contents of the register.

11.9 Priority of charges

11.9.1 Fixed charges

A company which creates a floating charge retains the right to deal with the assets which are subject to the charge. As we have already seen, this means that the value of the security may be reduced by the sale of the assets over which the charge floats. Furthermore, unless it contractually agrees not to do so (see below), the company is free to deal with the assets by charging them further, in particular, by granting fixed charges over certain assets to support further borrowing. A floating charge, even though properly registered, is normally postponed to a later fixed charge, such that the fixed chargeholder has a first entitlement to the proceeds of the asset in question. In turn, this means that the value of the floating charge will be eroded.

The floating charge will usually only have priority over later fixed charges if:

(a) the instrument creating the charge prohibits the creation of later fixed charges ranking in priority to or *pari passu* (i.e., equal) with the floating charge (such a provision is usually in the form of a 'negative pledge'); *and*

(b) the later fixed chargee has *notice of this prohibition* at the time when he takes his charge.

11.9.2 Floating charges

As between several floating charges, the *first in time* will have priority provided that it is properly registered. However, a later floating charge over some particular type of asset will probably take priority over an earlier floating charge over the whole of a company's property (*English and Scottish Mercantile Investment Co v Brunton* [1892] 2 QB 700).

11.9.3 Avoidance of charges

In certain circumstances charges may be avoided, other than for non-registration, if made within a short period before the commencement of insolvency proceedings. This topic is dealt with in **Chapter 27**.

11.10 Remedies of debenture-holders

11.10.1 Express and implied powers

If the company fails to pay interest or principal money (i.e., the debt itself) the lender may sue as a creditor or petition for winding up. In addition, the debenture may contain an express power of sale and a power to appoint a receiver (see below). The debenture will state the circumstances in which these powers are to arise. It may, for example, give such powers to the lender when his interest is in arrears for a specified period, when the company breaks any term of the debenture, when any other creditor of the company appoints a receiver, and when the company suffers execution by a judgment creditor.

Section 101 LPA 1925 gives the lender implied power to sell and to appoint a receiver if the debenture is made under seal and interest is two months in arrears or principal money has not been paid three months after it becomes due. In drafting a debenture, express powers should be given since they can be made wider than the implied powers; if the debenture is not executed as a deed, express powers are essential.

11.10.2 Application to the court

In the absence of express powers an application may be made to the court for sale or appointment of a receiver or manager if:

(a) liquidation of the company has commenced; or

(b) the company is in arrears with payment of principal or interest; or

(c) the lender's security is in jeopardy.

If the court orders sale the chargee will be paid the principal money and interest and any balance will be paid to the company. The assets will be treated as disposed of by the company so that a chargeable gain or allowable loss may result—thus affecting the company's corporation tax position (see **Chapter 18**).

11.11 Receivers

A receiver is appointed to realise the security of a debenture-holder. His position is, therefore different from that of a liquidator, whose function is to wind up the company entirely. Once the receiver has paid the debenture-holder he will return any surplus to the company, which may then continue to trade. In fact, very often the appointment of a receiver by a debenture-holder will lead to the liquidation of the company, for example, because, after his appointment, the receiver finds that he can only obtain payment by winding up the company or because other creditors petition for winding up.

It is important to distinguish between a receiver and an administrative receiver. For the effect of an appointment of an administrative receiver see **Chapter 26**. Note, however, that the possibility of appointment of an administrative receiver is now considerably reduced.

11.12 Position of lenders and debenture-holders

Many debentures are short-term loans to a company (typically by a bank) on which interest will be paid by the company at a fixed or variable rate. The lender will consider the interest part of its general profits rather than as a source of investment income.

Some types of debenture are issued to people who have lent money to the company on a long-term basis and who may, therefore, be regarded as investors in the business. The nature of their investment is quite different from the investment made by shareholders. As we shall see in **Chapter 20**, the tax treatment of debenture interest is usually different from the treatment of dividends paid to shareholders. There are a number of other important differences between the two types of investment, which may be summarised as follows:

(a) Debenture-holders are not members and so do not have the right usually given to the members of voting at meetings.

(b) Debenture interest is payable out of capital if the company fails to make profits, so that a debenture is a safer investment (although if the company makes large profits the debenture-holders will not usually benefit).

(c) Debenture-holders are creditors on a winding up and will usually have a charge over some or all of the company's assets, whereas shareholders are repaid their investment only if the company is solvent.

(d) Debenture-holders, unlike shareholders, may be repaid while the company is a going concern (usually at a fixed date or at the option of the company). Shareholders may only be repaid where capital is reduced or where the company redeems or purchases its own shares.

11.13 Steps to be taken by a lender to a company

A person who wishes to lend money to a company should take the following steps either personally or through his advisers. Some of them are dictated by common sense, others by legal requirements:

(a) Investigate the financial standing and management of the company.

(b) Search at the Companies' Registry to see the company's last few sets of accounts and what charge particulars have been registered.

(c) Search at the company's registered office—inspect copies of charges and obtain evidence of discharge of any registered charges.

(d) Search at the Land Registry or Land Charges Department (as appropriate) if a charge is to be taken over land.

(e) If there are any floating charges, make sure that they have not crystallised. (Until regulations requiring registration of crystallisation are made there is no machinery for ensuring this, but the directors of the company should be asked to certify that no events leading to crystallisation have occurred and, if possible, confirmation should be obtained from the chargees.)

(f) Include in the debenture power to appoint a receiver and a power of sale. If the charge is a floating charge, provide for its crystallisation.

(g) Ensure that the charge is registered within 21 days.

online resource centre

For further resources and online chapters please visit the Online Resource Centre at www.oxfordtextbooks.co.uk/orc/business13_14/.

12

Disposal of shares

This chapter covers the following topics:

12.1 Introduction

In this chapter we shall consider the various ways in which a shareholder in a company may dispose of his interest in the company either during his lifetime or on death.

On disposal of shares tax will often become payable, although there are a number of reliefs available; this topic is dealt with in **Chapter 22**.

A disposal of shares by a substantial shareholder will alter the control of the company and possibly affect the rights of the remaining shareholders. The interests of the incoming shareholder and the remaining shareholders have to be balanced against each other. Arrangements for achieving a balance between those interests have to be anticipated and made in advance (usually by drafting suitable articles when the company is formed). It is, therefore essential that potential problems should be foreseen and suitable arrangements made for the particular circumstances of each company.

We shall also consider financial involvement by a company in providing financial assistance for the purchase of its own shares or those of a holding company.

12.2 Transfer of shares

12.2.1 Introduction

A transfer of shares may be made by means of a sale or a gift *inter vivos*. The death or bankruptcy of a shareholder gives rise to an automatic transmission of shares (which will be followed by a transfer) and the special rules for transmission are dealt with later in the chapter.

A transfer of shares is likely to involve consideration of each of the Companies Act 2006, the Stock Transfer Act 1963, and the relevant company's articles of association.

12.2.2 Contract for sale

A shareholder who wishes to sell his shares may make a contract in any form that he wishes. The contract for sale is sufficient to give the purchaser an equitable interest in the shares. As between vendor and purchaser, the vendor will be liable to account to the purchaser for any dividends received and to vote as directed by the purchaser. However, *membership of the company* does not begin until the purchaser is registered as a member in the register of members which the company is required to keep. An entry cannot be made in the register of members until the company has received a 'proper instrument of transfer' (s. 770(1) CA 2006): this will take the form of a stock transfer form.

12.2.3 Procedure for transfer

Section 1 of the Stock Transfer Act 1963 provides that a transfer of fully paid shares may be made on a stock transfer form signed by the transferor and specifying:

(a) particulars of the consideration;

(b) description of the number or amount of the shares;

(c) particulars of the person by whom the transfer is made; and

(d) the full name and address of the transferee.

Once the sale of the shares has been agreed the vendor should execute a stock transfer form and send it together with the share certificate to the purchaser, who pays the stamp duty (see **12.2.4** below). The purchaser will apply to the company for registration by sending the stamped transfer and share certificate to the company. The transfer must be registered within two months of the application (s. 771(1) CA 2006) (unless refused; see below) and the company must send the purchaser a share certificate within the same period (s. 776(1) CA 2006). The procedure explained above applies on a gift of shares as well as on a sale (save that no stamp duty is payable).

The process of registration is effectively controlled by the board and the way in which it can and should respond to any proposed transfer will be determined by the articles. (See **12.2.5** for more detailed discussion.) However, any potential transferee should recognise that registration may not always be an automatic right and may in some circumstances be refused.

Section 771(1)(b) CA 2006 requires that any notice of refusal to register must be sent to the transferee within two months of the application, accompanied by reasons for the same. Section 771(2) also permits the transferee to request information on the reasons for refusal in addition to that supplied by the company in the first instance. However, the Act provides no guidance about these issues, especially the extent or the detail of the information in question. This may, therefore, prove to be an area which is ripe for dispute in the future.

(It should be noted that shares of publicly quoted companies may be transferred electronically under the CREST system. Such shares are said to exist in uncertificated form. The details of this system are beyond the scope of this book. Useful information on CREST can be found on its website www.euroclear.com.)

12.2.4 Stamp duty on transfer of shares

Stamp duty on a transfer of shares is charged at a rate of 0.5% of the consideration payable with the resulting figure being rounded up to the nearest £5. The purchaser of the shares pays the relevant amount of duty.

In any circumstances where the amount of stamp duty is calculated at £5, that is, where the consideration is £1,000 or less, no actual duty is payable.

EXAMPLE

Consideration payable	*Stamp duty charged*
£1	£nil*
£70	£nil*
£830	£nil*
£1,620	£10
£45,763	£230

* In each instance, the stamp duty calculation results in an amount of £5, hence the fact that no duty is payable.

Certain transfers of shares are exempt from stamp duty. One of the most common types is a gift of shares, i.e., a transfer for no consideration in money or money's worth.

12.2.5 Restrictions on right to transfer

Unless the articles provide to the contrary, every shareholder has a *right* to transfer his shares (which in effect means that the transferee has a right to be registered). However, the articles of the company can impose a restriction on the right to transfer shares. In the case of private companies a restriction is extremely common. At one time a company could not be a private company unless there was a restriction in its articles on the right to transfer shares. (This requirement was removed by the Companies Act 1980 (CA 1980), which was consolidated into the Companies Act 1985 (CA 1985).) Whilst the historical premise for such a restriction has disappeared, a restriction is still thought to be desirable, since it enables the company (usually through the directors) to control the identity of the shareholders.

Where there are restrictions on the right to transfer shares, the company must decide within two months of application for registration whether or not to permit the transfer. If within that time the company has not given notice of refusal of registration to the transferee together with its reasons, the company and its officers who are in default are liable to a fine (s. 771(3) and (4) CA 2006) and the transferee becomes *entitled* to be registered.

It is not possible to consider all the possible types of restriction on the right to register but some of the more common restrictions will now be considered.

12.2.5.1 'The directors may in their absolute discretion decline to register any transfer of any share, whether or not it is a fully paid share'

As with most restrictions on transfer, it is the directors who have power to refuse registration. The power is a negative one, that is, the directors have power to *refuse* registration—their positive approval is not required. This may seem an unimportant distinction but it means that a resolution of the directors is required to refuse registration, and since a resolution requires a majority in favour, an equality of votes will not be sufficient (unless, of course, the chairman has a casting vote and is against registration). This should be borne in mind in the case of 'two-man' companies, since either director will be able to ensure a transfer of his own shares merely by voting *against* the resolution to refuse registration. The directors' power to refuse registration must be exercised in good faith but it is very difficult to prove bad faith. The directors do not need to give reasons for refusal even if the article does not specifically excuse them from doing so.

It should be noted that this restriction is a restriction on the right to *transfer* shares, it is not a restriction on the right to *sell* them. If shares are sold but the purchaser is not registered, the vendor will hold the shares on trust for the purchaser. The purchaser will not be able to sue the vendor for damages (or his money back) unless the vendor guaranteed that registration would take place.

12.2.5.2 'The directors may refuse to register the transfer of a share, and if they do so, the instrument of transfer must be returned to the transferee with notice of refusal unless they suspect that the proposed transfer may be fraudulent'

This wording is found in article 26(5) of the Model Articles for Private Companies. It is not dissimilar to the one above. Note that it expressly recognises the obligation under s. 771(1) CA 2006 to provide the transferee with a notice of refusal to register.

12.2.5.3 'The directors may decline to register a transfer of any share in favour of a person of whom they disapprove or of a share over which the company has a lien'

This restriction gives the directors two grounds for refusing registration. One is clearly subjective, whilst the other is objective. A company may wish to restrict the transfer of a share over which it has a lien as a way of protecting its security over the asset. In terms of an 'undesirable' shareholder, the provisions of s. 771 CA 2006, which require the company to give reasons for any refusal, will be particularly relevant. Moreover, the transferee is entitled to ask for further reasonable information about the reasons for the refusal (s. 771(2)). This could be fertile ground for dispute.

12.2.5.4 'The directors may decline to register a transfer of any share except a transfer to [a member of the company or to a member of the family of the transferor]'

This type of restriction may be appropriate to restrict a shareholder in his right to bring in outsiders against the wishes of other members of the company; it leaves him free to transfer to insiders (i.e., the existing members of the company) or his own family. The words in square brackets could be adapted to include various other groups of permitted transferees, e.g., named persons or employees of the company. The term 'family' must, of course, be defined by the articles.

12.2.6 Pre-emption rights

The object of restrictions on the right to transfer shares is to keep a private company private. However, the restrictions referred to above are not entirely sufficient for that purpose since they are merely restrictions on *transfer* and do not prevent sale or gift of the equitable title to the shares. If it is decided that the company should be kept completely private, the articles should include pre-emption rights. The usual provision is that a member who wishes to transfer shares must first offer them to the existing members of the company. In drafting an article providing for pre-emption rights the following points should be considered:

(a) Should the transferring member be free to transfer to *any* existing member of the company or should he be obliged to offer his shares to *all* the existing members in proportion to their present holdings?

(b) Should the transferring member be obliged to transfer part of his holding to the existing members if they do not wish to take all the shares which he proposes to transfer?

(c) Should any exceptions be made to the pre-emption rights? For example, the articles may provide that the pre-emption rights do not apply on a transfer to a member's family as defined by the article.

(d) How is the price payable to be fixed? It is quite common for the price to be fixed by agreement or by the auditors if no price can be agreed between vendor and purchaser.

(e) How long are the other members to be given to make up their minds? A period should be specified for the avoidance of doubt.

(f) How is the transferring member to give notice of his intention to sell? It is quite common for the article to require notice to be given to the company. The secretary will then inform the other members of the offer.

A pre-emption right is a right given to the other members of the company. It is also possible for the articles to provide that a member who wishes to transfer shares shall have a right to *require* the other members to buy his shares.

It is always important to preserve the distinction between pre-emption rights on transfer and those on allotment (see **11.2.4**). The former are not compulsory and can only be imposed by inclusion in the articles; the latter are and are imposed by statute.

12.3 Transmission by operation of law

When a member of a company dies, his shares vest automatically in his personal representative, who is entitled to any dividend paid by the company but may not vote at general meetings. The personal representative does not, however, automatically become a member of the company since membership begins only with an entry in the register of members. A personal representative will have to prove his title to the shares, by production of the grant of representation. Having done so, he has two courses of action open to him:

(a) The personal representative can apply, by means of a letter of request, for registration by the company as a member (the entry in the register of members will not refer to his representative capacity). The articles of the company will usually contain a provision (such as Table A, article 30 or article 27 of the Model Articles) permitting the personal representative to be registered as a member. If he is registered as a member, a subsequent transfer to a beneficiary will require a stock transfer form to be completed.

(b) Alternatively, if the personal representative wishes to sell the shares so as to raise cash for the purposes of the deceased's estate or when he wishes to vest the shares in the deceased's beneficiary, he can do so without himself being registered, by means of a stock transfer form.

A restriction on the right to transfer shares does not apply to a transmission on death unless the articles specifically so provide.

12.4 Buy-back and redemption by a company

As we have already seen (**11.3.5**), a company can issue redeemable shares or buy its own shares in certain circumstances. Effectively, this is a form of transfer, which allows a shareholder a method of exit from the company (or, at least, a reduction in their shareholding). In contrast to other forms of transfer, however, the shares bought back or redeemed are cancelled.

12.5 Financial assistance

12.5.1 Introduction and rationale

One of the fundamental principles of company law is the concept of maintenance of capital. That is, the capital of a company, as represented by its assets, should be maintained for the benefit of the company, its shareholders, and its creditors. Companies should not generally return capital invested by shareholders, save on a winding up. Any derogation from this principle should be regulated to prevent abuse. This principle lies at the core of the regulation of financial assistance for the purchase of shares.

The general prohibition on financial assistance (see **12.5.2**) is designed, therefore, to maintain the capital of a company. In practical terms, it aims to prevent individuals acquiring a company's shares where that company's assets are used or put at risk by helping to finance the acquisition.

Until recently, the statutory prohibition on financial assistance has been fairly extensive in its scope. Given the consequences of breaching this prohibition, there has been great sensitivity in practice about its application, such that the spectre of financial assistance arises in many transactions, along with all its concomitant complications. This led to a belief that the provisions on financial assistance may result in greater inconvenience and cost than the harm they are designed to prevent. As such, the Companies Act 2006 has introduced a substantially altered regime, which is only of relevance to public companies.

12.5.2 General prohibitions on financial assistance

Unlawful financial assistance can occur in four defined situations:

(a) Where a *public* company gives financial assistance directly or indirectly to any person for the purchase of its shares or any subsidiary thereof (either public or private) does the same (s. 678(1) CA 2006).

(b) Where a public company subsidiary gives financial assistance directly or indirectly to any person for the purchase of shares in its private parent company (s. 679(1) CA 2006).

(c) Where a public company (or any subsidiary thereof) gives financial assistance directly or indirectly for the purpose of reducing or discharging any liability incurred by a person in buying shares in that public company (s. 678(3) CA 2006).

(d) Where a public company subsidiary gives financial assistance directly or indirectly for the purpose of reducing or discharging any liability incurred by a person in buying shares in that company's private parent company (s. 679(3) CA 2006).

Hence, assistance can be given before, at the same time as, or following, the time of the acquisition of the shares in question and may be given directly or indirectly. It should be noted that the prohibition is also operative not only where a person is acquiring shares in a company but also where such person is proposing to acquire shares.

12.5.3 Types of financial assistance

These are defined in s. 677 CA 2006 and examples are provided below. The examples are by no means exhaustive and lawyers need to consider the full financial ramifications of the acts of relevant companies before, during, and after acquisitions of shares in such companies or any of their parent companies.

12.5.3.1 Financial assistance by way of gift

A simple example would be the provision by a company of funds to an individual to buy shares in that company or any parent company. Another example would be a sale or transfer at an undervalue. Note that this could be a sale or transfer of the shares themselves, or a sale by a company to an individual of an asset at an undervalue, which the individual then sold at full value in order to apply the realised funds in buying shares in the company.

12.5.3.2 Financial assistance given by way of guarantee, security, or indemnity

These are forms of financial assistance which are provided indirectly. An example of each form is set out below.

Guarantee

A Limited gives a guarantee to a bank in respect of the obligations of C, who has borrowed from the bank in order to buy shares in B plc, the parent company of A Limited.

Security

E Limited is acquiring F plc, a subsidiary of G Limited. To finance the purchase, E Limited is borrowing from a bank. The bank requires security for the loan in the form of charges over the assets of both E Limited and F plc. The latter is therefore providing financial assistance by way of security for the purchase of its shares by E Limited.

Indemnity

H plc offers its shares as consideration to buy the shares in T plc which H plc wishes to take over. It offers to the shareholders of T plc, in return for their agreement to sell their shares to H plc, an indemnity against any losses suffered as a result of their receipt of shares in H plc (due to, for example, fluctuations in their market value). Here, H plc is providing financial assistance by way of indemnity for the purchase of its shares by the shareholders of T plc.

12.5.3.3 Financial assistance given by way of loan

A public company providing a loan to one of its directors to allow him to buy shares in that company or its parent company is a simple example of this form of financial assistance. (Note also that the provisions of ss. 197 CA 2006 et seq. would also have to be considered.) However, s. 677(c)(i) also refers to assistance:

> by way of any . . . agreement under which any obligations of the person giving the assistance are to be fulfilled at a time when in accordance with the agreement any obligation of another party to the agreement remains unfulfilled.

This part of the section exists to extend its ambit beyond loans to other types of credit or deferred payment transactions. An example of this would be where K plc sells assets to M Limited and allows deferred payment for those assets, in the knowledge that M Limited is about to buy shares in K plc. By deferring payment, K plc has provided assistance to M Limited for the purchase of shares in K plc.

12.5.3.4 Financial assistance reducing to a material extent a company's net assets

This provision covers any form of financial assistance, other than those described in **12.5.3.1** to **12.5.3.3**, where the effect of providing the assistance is to reduce to a material extent a company's net assets. The latter are taken as being the aggregate of the company's assets less the aggregate of its liabilities, using the actual market value of the assets (as opposed to the book value) at the time of the provision of the assistance. There is no definition in the Companies Act of what is a material reduction: it is a matter to be assessed by reference to the individual circumstances of each case.

An example of this form of financial assistance is where a private company subsidiary pays the professional fees of those involved in the purchase of shares in its public parent company, provided that the purpose of this was to assist the acquisition of the company's shares, and the amount involved reduced the subsidiary company's net assets to a material extent.

12.5.4 Consequences of providing unlawful financial assistance

A company which provides unlawful financial assistance is liable to a fine and directors may be liable to imprisonment or a fine, or both. Any contract to provide financial assistance is illegal and therefore the obligations of the providing company cannot be enforced.

12.5.5 General exceptions

12.5.5.1 Principal and larger purpose exceptions

A number of exceptions exist to the general prohibitions described above, viz:

(a) if the company's principal purpose in giving the assistance is not to give it for the purpose of any such acquisition, or the giving of assistance for that purpose is but an incidental part of some larger purpose of the company and in either instance the assistance is given in good faith in the interests of the company (ss. 678(2) and 679(2) CA 2006);

(b) if the company's principal purpose in giving the assistance is not to reduce or discharge any liability incurred by a person for the purpose of the acquisition of shares in the company or its holding company, or the reduction or discharge of any such liability is but an incidental part of some larger purpose of the company and in either instance the assistance is given in good faith in the interests of the company (ss. 678(4) and 679(4) CA 2006).

Whether or not the principal or larger purpose exceptions can be relied upon will depend on the facts of each case. The burden of proof is on the company providing the assistance to convince the court that an exception applies.

The leading case on this matter is *Brady v Brady* [1989] AC 755, which considered s. 153 CA 1985, the forerunner to the above provisions. The financial assistance given in this case was part of a scheme to assist some shareholders in buying out others to resolve a management deadlock. The court drew a distinction between the purpose of providing financial assistance and the reason for so doing. The former was held as being to allow shareholders to acquire shares in the company, whilst the latter was held as being the resolution of the deadlock. The court found, on the facts, that there was no evidence of any principal purpose to which the assistance was subsidiary or any larger purpose.

The result of *Brady v Brady* is that 'purpose' has a narrow interpretation. For a company to rely on the exceptions in s. 153, there had to be clear evidence of either:

(a) a principal purpose other than the acquisition of shares for which financial assistance is given to an individual; or

(b) a larger purpose for the company (as opposed to individual shareholders, directors, or prospective purchasers of shares) in providing financial assistance to an individual other than the acquisition of shares.

In addition, the company had to satisfy the court that it acted in good faith in the interests of the company. Given the narrow interpretation that was given to the exceptions in s. 153, and the requirement of good faith, it is difficult to be confident as to the circumstances in which the equivalent exceptions in the 2006 Act can be relied on.

12.5.5.2 Other exceptions

Section 681 provides that certain events will not amount to financial assistance. These include:

(a) a distribution by way of dividend or in the course of a company's winding up;

(b) an allotment of bonus shares;

(c) a reduction of capital;

(d) a redemption or buy-back of shares; and

(e) anything done under an order sanctioning a compromise or arrangement with members or creditors of the company.

Given that the exceptions described above are specific events, these may be relied on with more confidence than the exceptions in **12.5.5.1**.

Finally, there are some very specialised exceptions in s. 682 which relate mainly to issues concerning the provision of assistance to employees to partake in employee share schemes. The details of these are beyond the scope of this book.

12.5.6 Private companies and financial assistance

The new 2006 Act regime obviously benefits many transactions involving private companies. However, it is suggested that even where the prohibitions in ss. 678 and 679 are irrelevant, an instance of financial assistance may still need careful legal analysis, particularly from the perspective of directors' duties. An ill-conceived or irresponsible method of financial assistance which results in subsequent financial harm to the company providing it could leave directors exposed to claims that they neither promoted the success of the company nor acted with reasonable care and diligence. The practice may develop, therefore, of seeking prior approval of shareholders, and directors may be well served to obtain appropriate accountancy advice about the financial repercussions of any proposed financial assistance, in any event.

online resource centre

For further resources and online chapters please visit the Online Resource Centre at www.oxfordtextbooks.co.uk/orc/business13_14/.

13 Company meetings and resolutions

This chapter covers the following topics:

13.1 Types of general meeting

In this chapter, we shall look at meetings of shareholders and the resolutions which are passed at such meetings. In **Chapter 10**, we saw that certain transactions and activities within a company are subject to shareholder control. In this chapter, we are concerned with how that control must be exercised. The rules about these matters are sometimes quite technical but their importance cannot be overestimated. A solicitor advising a company or a shareholder must be able to recognise situations where shareholder decisions are necessary and, as such, may be called upon to see that the correct procedures are adopted to achieve those decisions. Moreover, those procedures will have to be reflected in correctly drafted documentation, such as notices of meetings or minutes of meetings, which the solicitor will normally produce on behalf of the client.

It is important to recognise that these meeting procedures will be governed by a combination of statute and the relevant company's articles. In some instances, statute will be prescriptive; in others its effect can be displaced or modified by the articles.

We are not concerned in this chapter with directors' meetings (which were dealt with in **Chapter 9**); we are only concerned with meetings of shareholders. Shareholders' meetings are also called 'company meetings' or 'general meetings'. Company meetings are of two types: annual general meetings and general meetings.

13.1.1 Background

The position under the Companies Act 1985 was relatively complicated. Much of what the 2006 Act has attempted to do is to streamline the governance of shareholders' meetings, particularly for private companies, which is in line with the Government's 'think small first' policy. The main contrasts between the new system and the one it replaced are:

(a) Under the 1985 Act, there were four possible resolutions which shareholders might pass: ordinary, special, extraordinary, and elective (the last being in respect of private companies only). Under the 2006 Act, only two shareholders' resolutions are recognised: ordinary and special.

(b) Under the previous regime, the type of resolution to be proposed at a shareholders' meeting determined the length of notice required, which was either 14 or 21 days. The 2006 Act only requires 14 days' notice in every circumstance except the annual general meeting of a public company, where 21 days' notice is required. (A company's articles may, however, require longer notice in certain situations; see discussion at **13.4.2**.)

(c) Previously all companies were required to hold an annual general meeting, although the shareholders of a private company could dispense with this requirement through an elective resolution passed to this effect. (Elective resolutions generally were a way of allowing private companies a limited form of deregulation from the requirements of the 1985 Act, if shareholders so wished.) Under the new regime, only public companies must hold annual general meetings.

(d) The 1985 Act recognised the concept of a written resolution of the shareholders of a company as an alternative to a formal meeting and vote. However, the consent of all shareholders of a company to a resolution in such form was required for it to be passed. (This is in contrast to a resolution passed at an actual meeting where the votes of only those shareholders present are relevant for determining whether or not a resolution is passed.) This meant that written resolutions could only effectively be used where there was unanimity amongst all the shareholders of a company. The 2006 Act has liberalised the use of written resolutions by allowing them to be passed by the same majority as is required in a general meeting.

13.1.2 Annual general meetings

Only public companies are now required to hold annual general meetings (AGMs) (s. 336 CA 2006). An AGM must be held in each period of six months beginning with the day following the company's accounting reference date. Normally companies use the AGM as an opportunity to fulfil certain statutory or regulatory requirements, for example, that they lay before the company in general meeting copies of their annual accounts. (This requirement used to apply to all companies, public or private (s. 241 CA 1985). As from 6 April 2008, only public companies are obliged to present accounts to a general meeting (s. 437 CA 2006).)

13.1.3 General meetings

Any meeting which is not an AGM is a general meeting (GM). As a consequence, both public and private companies may hold GMs. A GM is held as and when necessary.

Previously, this type of meeting was often referred to as an Extraordinary General Meeting and the articles of some companies would state this fact explicitly. It is arguable, therefore, that if a company's articles insist on the use of such terminology, then it is necessary to use the epithet 'Extraordinary'.

The procedure for calling GMs will be considered shortly, but first it is necessary to consider the types of resolution needed to transact business at general meetings.

13.2 Resolutions

A company in general meeting can only transact business by passing the appropriate type of resolution. There are two types of shareholder resolution: ordinary and special.

13.2.1 Ordinary resolutions

An ordinary resolution is one which requires a simple majority of votes in favour if it is to be passed (a simple majority means more votes in favour than against—an equality of votes is not sufficient—s. 282(1) CA 2006). An ordinary resolution is sufficient to transact any business at a general meeting save in those cases where the Companies Act requires a special resolution or where the articles require a special resolution or unanimity of the members.

Where there is equality an ordinary resolution may be passed on the chairman's casting vote, if the articles so provide. In the case of a small company, the decision as to whether to allow an article giving a casting vote may be crucial. The presence of a casting vote resolves the problem of deadlock but may in some cases be considered to give the chairman too much power or may, in fact, no longer be possible. (See **14.3.5** for further discussion of this issue.)

13.2.2 Special resolutions

A special resolution requires a 75% majority—that is, at least three votes must be cast in favour of the resolution for every one cast against it (s. 283(1) CA 2006).

13.2.3 Which type of resolution is required?

The Companies Act sets out a number of circumstances in which shareholders' resolutions are required, either to cause something to happen or, more commonly, to allow the company to commit to a course of action. A company's articles may also impose further requirements for a decision of the shareholders, however, instances of these tend to be relatively rare.

As a basic rule, special resolutions are required where the deemed prejudice to shareholders could be considerable. Therefore, a proposed change to the articles requires such a resolution to bring it into effect (s. 21 CA 2006). By contrast, ordinary resolutions normally act as shareholder permission for a transaction. For example, a proposed substantial property transaction between a director and a company needs the prior consent of the shareholders by ordinary resolution (s. 190 CA 2006), but the directors must still decide to commit the company to the transaction.

It is not the intention of this chapter to set out all possible instances of special and ordinary resolutions. Reference to the necessary resolution is made, as appropriate, in the other chapters dealing with company law issues. However, the following instances of shareholders' resolutions are possibly the most common:

Special Resolutions

(a) To alter the articles of association.

(b) To change the company's name (subject to any alternative mechanism in the articles).

(c) To approve the buy-back of shares in a private company.

(d) To disapply statutory pre-emption rights on an allotment of shares.

Ordinary Resolutions

(a) To approve a substantial property transaction with a director.

(b) To approve the duration of a service contract of a director, where the guaranteed term of the contract exceeds two years.

(c) To provide directors with authority to allot shares (where so required).

13.3 Calling a general meeting

Once the need for shareholder consent has been identified, it is necessary to seek this either in a meeting of the shareholders or by written resolution (if the latter is permitted). Written resolutions are considered at **13.7**. In this next section we will look at calling a general meeting.

As with so many aspects of company law, the rules are partly statutory and partly depend on the provisions of the company's own articles. Most of the statutory rules are designed to protect the shareholders, whose voting rights would be worthless if they were not backed up by rights to be notified of meetings or to call meetings themselves.

13.3.1 Call by directors

Section 302 CA 2006 gives the directors power to call general meetings of a company. In any event, the articles of many companies are likely to contain a provision granting directors the authority to call shareholders' meetings. Either way, therefore, general meetings of a company will normally be called by the directors, so a board meeting is the usual starting point in the process.

13.3.2 Shareholders' right to requisition meeting

13.3.2.1 Requisition to directors

Section 303(1) CA 2006 permits a specified percentage of shareholders to request the directors to call a meeting. This can be a valuable right in circumstances where the shareholders disagree with the approach of the board and want to air their views in a formal environment.

Such a request can be in paper or electronic form (s. 303(6)) and must state the general nature of the business the shareholders want dealing with at the proposed meeting. It can include the text of any specific resolution to be proposed to the meeting (s. 303(4)).

The specified percentage is sufficient members of the company to represent at least 5% of the paid-up share capital of the company as carries the right to vote at general meetings (s. 303(2) and (3)).

Once such a requirement is made of the directors, they must call a meeting within 21 days, which must be held on not more than 28 days' notice (s. 304(1)). Such notice must include a copy of any proposed resolution received from the requisitionists (s. 304(2)) and if that resolution is actually a special resolution, the specific requirements for special resolutions contained within s. 283 of the Act must be complied with in the notice, otherwise the directors are deemed not to have fulfilled their obligation under this section (s. 304(4)).

13.3.2.2 Power of shareholders to call meeting in default

If the directors of a company fail to comply properly with a s. 303 request, s. 305 CA 2006 permits the requisitionists (or any of them representing more than one half of the total voting rights of all of them) to call a meeting instead. In doing so, the meeting must be called as much as possible in the same manner as that in which meetings are required to be called by the directors (s. 305(4)) (presumably under both the Act and the articles, as is relevant). The date of such a meeting must be no later than three months from the date on which the directors' obligation under s. 304 arose (s. 305(3)).

13.3.2.3 Court power to order meeting

Section 306(1) CA 2006 gives the court power to order meetings if for any reason it is impracticable either:

(a) to call a meeting of a company in any manner in which meetings of that company may be called; or

(b) to conduct a meeting in the manner prescribed either by the Act or by the company's articles.

An application to court for such an order can be made by either a director or shareholder (s. 306(2)). The predecessor to this section, s. 371 CA 1985, was often used to get round either practical problems to do with calling meetings or to resolve issues of deadlock in 'two-man' companies, where a dissenting shareholder refused to attend a general meeting, thus rendering it inquorate. See, for example, *Re Opera Phonographic Ltd* [1989]. (See discussion of quorum issues below at **13.5.1**.)

13.4 Notice of meetings

13.4.1 Service of notice

Section 301 CA 2006 makes it a pre-condition of the validity of any resolution of the shareholders that notice of the meeting and the resolution is given in accordance with the Act and the company's articles. Subject to any provision in the articles, every member and every director of a company must receive notice of a general meeting (s. 310). It is common practice for the board of directors to approve the content of any such notice and agree that it should be distributed to all relevant persons.

The following explanation will look at the statutory requirements which will have universal application. It will also be important to consider the articles in every instance to ascertain any specific further requirements which must be fulfilled.

Section 308 CA 2006 permits a notice of a general meeting to be given either:

(a) in hard copy form; or

(b) in electronic form (most commonly by e-mail or possibly by text message); or

(c) via a website; or

(d) by a combination of any or all of the above.

Schedule 5 to the 2006 Act sets out rules for any communications sent out by a company, including those in electronic form or via a website. Communication in either of these two forms requires the prior consent of a shareholder.

Additionally, in respect of website communications:

(a) Shareholders must still be notified of the presence of the information or notification on the website and that it is in respect of a general meeting, stating the time, date, and place of the meeting (s. 309).

(b) As an alternative to seeking the consent of every member in every circumstance, a company may by a provision in its articles or by a shareholder resolution provide for website communication, after which shareholders must be asked to agree to the supply of information via a website and will be deemed to do so unless they specifically object within 28 days of such a request.

In respect of closely-held companies, the use of a website is probably academic, because e-mail or paper notification is likely to be the most appropriate method. However, the website method may have more attraction to companies with a large number of shareholders.

13.4.2 Length of notice

13.4.2.1 Full notice

The length of notice required depends on the nature of the meeting and the company. For private companies all general meetings must be called on at least 14 days' notice (s. 307(1) CA 2006). For public companies all general meetings must be held on at least 14 days' notice, except AGMs where 21 days' notice is required (s. 307(2) CA 2006).

The calculation of what the notice period should be is always something which should be treated with care. Section 360 of the 2006 Act clarifies the issue by excluding from the notice period both the day of giving the notice and the day of the meeting itself.

The above notice periods are minima, laid down by the Companies Act. Each company must decide upon the notice periods it wants and state them in its articles of association. Clearly most companies will elect to follow the Companies Act, but companies can provide for different notice periods provided that they do not fall below the statutory minima. Note that it is quite common for articles to provide for 'clear days' of notice, that is, *exclusive* of the date of service and the date of the meeting, which echoes the effect of s. 360 above. Moreover the articles may also deem a date of receipt of any notice, so this needs to be factored into the calculation of the necessary notice period. The golden rule is always to err on the side of caution.

13.4.2.2 Short notice procedure

For many companies, it is often unnecessarily burdensome to wait for full notice periods to elapse. The Companies Act, therefore, provides a mechanism for 'short-circuiting' the process by allowing for shorter notice than already mentioned.

For private companies, s. 307(5) provides that shorter notice than that normally required may validly be given in respect of all general meetings of such a company if a majority in number of members owning not less than 90% of the shares that carry an entitlement to attend and vote at the meeting agree to such shorter notice. Note that a private company may demand a higher percentage than 90%, but this must not exceed 95% (s. 307(6)(a)). It is quite unlikely for a company to avail itself of such a possibility and in the case of a company with small numbers of shareholders and relatively similar-sized shareholdings, the difference between 90% and 95% acceptances is usually academic, as agreement of most, if not all, shareholders will be needed to meet this threshold.

EXAMPLE

Scenario one

Random Limited has three shareholders, A, B, and C, who each own 30%, 30%, and 40% of the voting share capital in the company. Consent to short notice of a general meeting of Random Limited can only effectively be given by all the members of the company.

Scenario two

Colston Limited has four shareholders, A, B, C, and D, who each own 45%, 45%, 5%, and 5% of the voting share capital in the company

(a) If A and B only consent to short notice, this is not effective consent, as they do not constitute a majority in number, despite owning between them 90% of the voting share capital.

(b) If A, C, and D only consent to short notice, this is not effective consent, as, whilst they constitute a majority in number, they only own between them 55% of the voting share capital.

(c) If A, B, and either C or D consent, this is effective consent.

Therefore, it does not matter if the required percentage is 90% or set at 95% in Colston's articles; shareholders owning at least 95% of the voting capital must consent in any event.

For *public* companies shorter notice than that normally required may validly be given if:

(a) in the case of an AGM all the members entitled to attend and vote at the meeting agree to short notice (ss. 307(7) and 337(2)); and

(b) in the case of any other general meeting a majority in number of members owning not less than 95% of the voting shares and entitled to attend and vote at the meeting agree to short notice.

For many private companies (especially family companies or companies where the members are all directors), the possibility of short notice allows a meeting to be held at very short notice—normally by informally gathering together all the relevant shareholders and then obtaining their consent to formal notice of the general meeting. However, for companies with large numbers of shareholders, it is not normally a practical alternative to the giving of proper notice.

13.4.3 Contents of notice

The notice of a meeting must state the date, time, and place of a meeting (s. 311(1) CA 2006). It must also sufficiently describe the business which is to be transacted for members to be able to decide whether they wish to attend (s. 311(2) CA 2006). If a special resolution is to be proposed, its wording must be set out verbatim in the notice and must be expressed to be proposed as a special resolution (s. 283(6) CA 2006).

It is a question of judgement in each case how much detail of the business needs to be stated. However, in drawing up a notice it is better to err on the side of inclusion rather than exclusion. A company's articles can demand fuller information than that required by s. 311(2), in any event. For both of these reasons, there is normally no distinction drawn between ordinary and special resolutions and full wording of either type of resolution will usually be set out in the notice.

Section 325 CA 2006 requires that any notice of a general meeting should always tell a member of his right under s. 324 to send a proxy (who need not be a member) to attend and speak and vote on his behalf. If any additional rights in this regard are afforded by the company's articles, these rights should also be stated.

13.5 Proceedings at meetings

13.5.1 Quorum

A meeting cannot consider business unless a quorum is present at the time when the meeting proceeds to business. Unless the articles otherwise provide or the company has only one member, two members personally present or their proxies or their representatives (in the case of a corporate shareholder) are a quorum (s. 318).

The appointment of a representative of a corporate shareholder is governed by s. 323 CA 2006 and ss. 324 to 331 contain provisions about proxies. (A company may, if it chooses, provide for further rights for proxies over and above those provided by the Act—s. 323.)

13.5.2 Voting

13.5.2.1 Show of hands

A vote on a resolution will normally be decided on a show of hands, that is, one shareholder, one vote (s. 284(2) CA 2006). However, the inequities of this when there are diverse shareholdings are obvious. Therefore, a vote may, instead, be taken on a poll, that is, one vote per share (s. 284(3)).

13.5.2.2 Poll

A poll must be demanded at the relevant meeting and a company's articles will make provision for how this is done. The only stipulation the Companies Act 2006 makes is that a provision in the articles is void if it renders ineffective a call from a poll from either at least five members or members holding more than 10% of the voting rights or any member or members with 10% of the paid-up capital with a right to vote (s. 321(2)).

It is quite normal for articles to provide for more extensive rights by allowing any two members (instead of five) or the chairman to call for a poll as well.

Proxies have the same right to call for a poll as the member or members they represent.

The following examples demonstrate the difference between voting on a show of hands and voting on a poll.

EXAMPLE

Cotton Limited has four shareholders, A, B, C, and D, who each own respectively 45%, 40%, 10%, and 5% of the voting share capital in the company.

Assume that in each of the scenarios which follow all of the shareholders in Cotton attend the meeting in question and that there are no abstentions.

Scenario one—ordinary resolution: vote on a show of hands
At least three of the four shareholders must vote in favour for the resolution to be passed.

Scenario two—ordinary resolution: vote on a poll
Any permutation of at least three shareholders voting in favour will be sufficient for the resolution to be passed.

If only two shareholders vote in favour, it must either be A and B or A and C. (Neither A and D nor B and C, for example, constitute a majority.)

Scenario three—special resolution: vote on a show of hands
Any permutation of at least three shareholders voting in favour will be sufficient for the resolution to be passed.

Scenario four—special resolution: vote on a poll
Irrespective of how C and D vote, A and B must vote in favour.

13.6 Minutes and returns

Minutes must be kept of all decisions taken at general meetings and must be available for inspection by the members at the registered office (ss. 355 and 358 CA 2006). Copies of special resolutions must be sent to the Registrar of Companies within 15 days of being passed (s. 30 CA 2006), as must any ordinary resolution authorising directors to allot shares under s. 551 CA 2006 (s. 551(9)).

13.7 Written resolutions

13.7.1 Validity

A *private* company may pass resolutions in writing under s. 288 CA 2006 without a meeting or any previous notice being given. Such a company may pass any type of resolution—ordinary or special—using this procedure, save for two exceptions. These are the removal of a director under s. 168 CA 2006 or the removal of an auditor under s. 510 CA 2006. (There were similar provisions in the 1985 Act.)

For a written resolution to be effective, a required majority of the members of the company entitled to vote on the resolution must consent to it as follows:

(a) For ordinary resolutions, members representing a simple majority of the *total* voting rights of the members entitled to vote on the resolution (s. 282(2)).

(b) For special resolutions, members representing at least 75% of the *total* voting rights of the members entitled to vote on the resolution (s. 283(2)).

Section 284C(1) stipulates that in respect of a written resolution each member has one vote in respect of each share held.

Therefore, whilst the validity of resolutions at general meetings is based on a count of the votes cast by the members actually present, by contrast, the effectiveness of a written resolution is based upon all the votes which could be cast.

The date of any written resolution is determined by the time at which the required majority has signified its agreement to it (s. 296(4)). A member signifies his agreement when the company receives from him, either in hard copy or electronic form, an authenticated document indicating his agreement to the resolution (s. 296(1)).

EXAMPLE

Random Limited has three shareholders, A, B, and C, who each own 30%, 30%, and 40% respectively of the voting share capital in the company.

In respect of a proposed special resolution:

(a) if A and B only attend a general meeting and vote in its favour (either on a show of hands or a poll), this will be a unanimous vote and the resolution will be passed;

(b) instead, if A and B only consent to the resolution in the form of a written resolution, the resolution will not be passed, as A and B only hold 60% of the voting capital in the company, not the minimum of 75% required.

(Note that in respect of (b), the position would be different if an ordinary resolution was proposed.)

Under s. 300 CA 2006, any provision in a private company's articles which prevents it from passing written resolutions using the statutory procedure is void.

For many private companies, written resolutions are quite often a preferred alternative to the holding of a general meeting.

13.7.2 Documentation

As with the calling of general meetings, a request for a written resolution will normally be prompted by the board of a company. In this instance, s. 291 CA 2006 must be complied with, otherwise all officers of the company in default will commit an offence, although such default will not affect the validity of the resolution itself. The requirements of s. 291 are:

(a) The resolution must go out to all members entitled to vote on the resolution.

(b) This may be done either in hard copy, electronic form, or through a website (or a combination of any or all of these methods).

(c) The resolution must be accompanied by a statement explaining how a member may consent to the resolution and the date by which the resolution must be passed. (A written resolution will lapse if not passed by either the period set out in the articles or, if there is none, by the end of the 28th day after the circulation of the resolution—s. 297(1).)

Section 291 envisages either individual copies of the resolution for each member or a single copy to be submitted in turn to each member. Consent to a resolution is normally achieved by a member signing and dating a document which includes the full text of the resolution.

In the same way that members of a company can requisition the board to call a general meeting, so s. 292 of the 2006 Act provides that members representing at least 5% of the total voting rights of all members can require a written resolution to be distributed at their instance. (The articles can provide for a lower percentage.)

In many instances of closely-held companies, if possible, arrangements will be made for all relevant shareholders to be present to receive and agree to the written resolution simultaneously. This will provide certainty that the resolution has been received by all relevant shareholders and that it has been consented to at a particular moment in time. Posting out or e-mailing written resolutions to shareholders and waiting for their responses is much less satisfactory.

13.7.3 Effect on requirements for specific resolutions

There are a number of resolutions which require specific documents to be available for inspection at the registered office in advance of the relevant general meeting and at the meeting itself for the resolution to be effective (normally for the purpose of informing shareholders), for example:

(a) authority for purchase of own shares—the relevant contract for the purchase or a memorandum thereof must be available (required by s. 696 CA 2006);

(b) reduction of share capital by a private company—the supporting solvency statement of the directors must be available (required by s. 642 CA 2006);

(c) approval of the term of a director's service contract—a memorandum of the contract, including details of the relevant term, must be available (required by s. 188 CA 2006);

(d) approval of loans, etc., to directors—a memorandum setting out prescribed details of the loan, etc., must be available (required by ss. 197, 198, or 201 CA 2006, depending upon the particular type of transaction).

If the written resolution method is chosen instead, the above requirement must be varied. The basic, alternative requirement in each case is the supply or disclosure of specific information or documentation to all members at or before the time at which the written resolution is supplied.

13.7.4 Recording

Copies of all written resolutions passed must be maintained in the same way as minutes of a general meeting (s. 355 CA 2006).

13.8 General conclusions

Some general conclusions can be reached about decision-making in a company.

(a) Whenever a shareholders' decision is required in a *private* company, there is usually a choice between achieving this decision at a general meeting or by written resolution.

(b) Two exceptions to the rule at (a) are the removal of a director and the removal of an auditor, both of which must occur at a general meeting.

(c) The relevant procedure is likely to be governed by a combination of statute and the articles; as such, both must be considered.

(d) There are possibly three material factors which will influence the method adopted for reaching a decision of the shareholders: the number of shareholders in the company, which of those shareholders are known to support the proposal, and the speed at which it is desired to happen.

(e) Shareholders may be asked to pass an ordinary resolution or a special resolution. The former is passed by a simple majority; the latter by a majority of at least 75%.

(f) The starting point for either a general meeting or a written resolution is a resolution of the board of directors either to distribute a notice of the general meeting or to circulate a copy of the written resolution.

(g) General meetings must be called by appropriate notice, which for private companies is normally 14 clear days, although there may be specific exceptions to this stated in a company's articles. Shareholders can consent to much shorter notice. This consent must be given by shareholders who constitute a majority in number and who, between them, hold at least 90% of the nominal voting share capital. (There may be instances where a company's articles demand a higher percentage, i.e., 95%.)

(h) For any meeting of the directors or shareholders, the quorum requirement must be satisfied.

(i) Voting at a directors' meeting is usually taken by majority decision, on the basis of one vote per director.

(j) Voting at a general meeting can be taken either by a show of hands, on the basis of one vote per shareholder, or on a poll, that is, one vote for every share held. Only the votes cast at the meeting are relevant.

(k) Agreement to a written resolution must be given by the relevant majority of eligible members, which effectively means those shareholders who are entitled to attend and vote at general meetings. For an ordinary resolution, a simple majority of all the voting shareholders of the company must agree; for a special resolution, at least three-quarters of all the voting shareholders should consent.

(l) Quite often a shareholder resolution will be enabling. As such, there will often be the need for the board to approve formally a transaction or document once the shareholders' permission has been obtained. For example, if shareholders' authority to a proposed allotment of shares has been necessary, the board must then formally resolve to make the allotment.

(m) One major exception to (l) is that any decision to alter the articles is purely within the power of the shareholders. The only follow-up for the board would be to resolve to meet the registration/filing responsibilities which arise from such a decision, e.g., to register both a copy of the revised articles and a copy of the resolution itself.

(n) Many company decisions result in filing and registration obligations. For example, the appointment of a director must be notified to Companies House within 14 days and there will have to be appropriate additions made to both the company's register of directors and register of directors' residential addresses.

(o) Minutes/records of decisions taken at board and shareholder level must be taken and kept.

online resource centre

For further resources and online chapters please visit the Online Resource Centre at www.oxfordtextbooks.co.uk/orc/business13_14/.

14 The articles of a private company

This chapter covers the following topics:

14.1 Introduction

14.1.1 Outline

In this chapter, we will look at the articles of a private company. We saw in **Chapter 8** that all companies are required to have articles of association and that these articles define and regulate the relationships within the company. We also saw that 'standard' articles are made available through regulation and that a company can either adopt these articles wholesale or have articles specifically drafted for it (often based on those standard articles).

In this chapter, we will look at some of the major issues which the articles of a private company are likely to address. We will also look at the way in which the articles of a company can be altered and any restrictions thereto.

In many ways, the articles of a company should be looked on as all other contracts—there are likely to be as many variations as there are similarities. Therefore, it is important never to assume the contents of a company's constitution and any lawyer needs to be satisfied that the articles have been accurately complied with.

As was explained at **7.3.5**, the articles of association of most companies in existence are likely to be influenced and informed by the provisions of either Table A or the Model Articles. As such, the relevant contents of each will be considered in this chapter.

14.1.2 Background to the Model Articles

As part of the changes to company law effected by the Companies Act 2006, a new set of articles for use by private companies was introduced as the standard set of 'default' articles for private companies. (Additionally, a standard set of articles for public companies was also created.) These new Model Articles have been effective since 1 October 2009 and reflect the regime under the 2006 Act. However, the new Model Articles are not compulsory for companies, nor do they automatically replace the articles of pre-existing companies.

Perhaps one of the most notable features of the Model Articles for private companies is that they are relatively brief. This has been achieved by relying much more on the 2006 Act to regulate matters and by simplifying many procedural matters.

The Model Articles have their pros and cons in various instances, so it is not expected that lawyers will advise clients to adopt them unquestioningly. Furthermore, many law firms have their own standard articles which they are likely to consider better tailored to their clients' needs. Indeed, one of the possible criticisms of the Model Articles is that they are not comprehensive in themselves and reference will often have to be made to the Companies Act itself to fill in the gaps.

14.1.3 Background to Table A

Prior to the introduction of the Model Articles, Table A contained in the Companies (Tables A to F) Regulations 1985 was the model set of articles available for adoption by both private and public companies. These articles were introduced at the same time as the Companies Act 1985 came into effect (although Table A had existed in various iterations since 1862) and the regime under that Act informed much of their content. This version of Table A was amended on a number of occasions after 1985, most recently in October 2007, so the date of incorporation of an existing company will determine which particular version of Table A is relevant to that company (assuming that Table A was adopted in whole or in part). In other words, a company which was incorporated in 1992 and which chose Table A as its articles will have articles which differ somewhat from a company which was incorporated in 2008 and also adopted Table A.

A further complication is that the amendments brought about in October 2007 also resulted in the bifurcation of Table A into one version for private and one for public companies, a split which was followed through into the subsequent Model Articles.

To put all this into context, many companies which were formed prior to the availability of the Model Articles will have Table A articles or, at least, articles based on Table A. As the 2006 Act does not normally displace or update any provisions within pre-existing articles, company lawyers will have to continue to be familiar with Table A and its effect for a number of years yet.

We will now consider some of the main issues which a company's articles are likely to address. (Note that all references to the Model Articles are to the version for private limited companies, unless otherwise indicated.)

14.2 Provisions concerning shares and membership

14.2.1 Share capital

A company needs to reserve for itself the power in its constitution to create and allot shares Accordingly, both Table A and the Model Articles contain such a power.

14.2.1.1 Table A

Articles 2 and 3 of Table A provide for the creation of different classes of shares. There are also provisions which deal with partly-paid shares and the company's lien for amounts unpaid on shares (i.e., if shares are issued without being paid for in full the company has a lien (a charge) over the shares to secure payment for them). There are relatively few cases where shares are issued by private companies without payment in full at the time of issue, so these provisions are unlikely to be of particular relevance.

14.2.1.2 Model Articles

The Model Articles contain a similar power to allot shares of differing rights (article 22). However, article 21 specifically requires all shares to be fully paid-up on issue, which reflects the rarity of partly-paid shares in private companies. As such, there are no provisions regarding a lien on partly-paid shares.

Two specific consequences of article 22 of the Model Articles should be noted:

(a) The rights of any shares issued may be determined by ordinary resolution. This may have some administrative convenience. However, it is quite often the case that specific and detailed share rights will be set out in the articles for reasons of certainty.

(b) Advantage is taken of s. 685 CA 2006 to permit the directors to determine the terms of any redeemable shares, although, again, for reasons of certainty, a company may prefer to set out these rights in the articles.

14.2.2 Issue of shares

Neither the Model Articles nor Table A give directors automatic authority to issue shares. It may be considered desirable to include such power in the articles of a company so that a meeting of members is not needed for the issue of shares when the company is newly formed and for the foreseeable future. (Remember that the effect of s. 550 CA 2006 is that directors of companies with only one class of shares are able to allot further shares of the same class without the need for authority from the shareholders, so the inclusion of such a provision is likely to anticipate allotments in wider circumstances.)

Any issue of shares wholly for cash has to be offered to the existing members pro rata their shareholdings in accordance with the statutory pre-emption rules set out in s. 561 CA 2006, unless the articles make alternative provision. Those drafting the articles should consider whether this would be appropriate. (Neither the Model Articles nor Table A make any such provision.) A number of amendments are possible and the following, in particular, might be considered:

(a) a provision which excludes or disapplies the statutory pre-emption rights so as to allow shares to be issued to non-shareholders or other than pro rata (provided the directors are authorised to issue shares, if necessary);

(b) in contrast, a provision which imposes pre-emption rights which are more extensive than those provided by statute—statutory pre-emption rights of the existing members only apply when the consideration for the proposed allotment is cash and when the shares are of a specified type. As such, a provision could be inserted providing for pre-emption rights in respect of every possible category of allotment.

14.2.3 Transfer of shares

In the case of many private companies, it can be considered appropriate that a shareholder should not be free to transfer his shares to anyone he chooses. The reason for this is that if an existing shareholder is free to transfer to anyone, he is, in effect, in a position to decide who his fellow shareholders' future associates should be.

Article 26(5) of the Model Articles grants the board absolute discretion to refuse the registration of any transfer. (This should be read in conjunction with s. 771 CA 2006, which imposes an obligation to give notice to the transferee of any refusal, together with the reason for it, within two months of the transfer being lodged with the company.)

In Table A, by contrast, very few restrictions on transfer are imposed. A shareholder is free to transfer his shares in most cases; the directors only have power to refuse if the shares are not fully-paid or if the company has a lien on them (articles 23–28). (The company will only have a lien if the shares have not been fully-paid for when requested by the company.)

Notice that, with this type of provision, a majority vote of the directors is needed to refuse to register the transfer. If the directors are equally divided, the transferee will become entitled to be registered.

The power of the directors to refuse to register a transfer does not prevent an existing shareholder from selling his shares or giving them away; it simply prevents the transferee from becoming the legal owner of the shares. If the registration is refused, then the existing shareholder holds the shares on trust for the purchaser or donee who becomes the equitable owner of the shares. Quite what the ongoing relationship between the two parties will then be is uncertain. However, this is obviously an undesirable situation for the transferee to be in (especially if a considerable amount of money has been paid for the shares). Therefore, every effort should be made in advance by the solicitor of the transferee to ascertain that there will be no such problems.

The provisions of both the Model Articles and Table A are relatively unsophisticated and a company may wish for a transfer provision which is more directed.

There is a considerable range of possibilities. We will consider a few examples.

14.2.3.1 A requirement that a member who wishes to sell should first offer the shares to the existing members pro rata

This type of right is usually called a pre-emption right. It should not be confused with the statutory pre-emption right which arises on the issue of new shares for a cash consideration. The Companies Act 2006 does not impose any pre-emption rights where a shareholder wishes to transfer shares, so, if thought desirable, it must appear in the articles (or possibly a shareholders' agreement).

In its simplest form a pre-emption right which applies on transfer will provide that if a shareholder wishes to transfer his shares, he must first offer them to some or all of the existing shareholders, either in all circumstances or in some specified circumstances. The details of such clauses vary considerably. An attempt is usually made to be fair to both the shareholder who wishes to transfer his shares and to those who may wish to buy.

In drafting such a clause, the following are among the matters which should be considered:

(a) Are all the other shareholders to be entitled to buy some of the shares? (The right could be restricted, for example to the directors or to shareholders of the same class.)

(b) Are the shares to be offered to those entitled according to the proportion of shares which they own? (This is by far the most likely arrangement.)

(c) If a shareholder does not wish to buy, then what is to happen to the proportion of the shares which he could have bought? (In such a case the article could provide for a second round of offers to those shareholders who did take up the initial offer, or it could allow the selling shareholder to sell to whoever he chooses once the initial offer has been rejected.)

(d) How is the price to be fixed? (It is important that there should be a mechanism, otherwise the shareholder who wishes to sell to an outsider could circumvent the pre-emption procedure by offering to sell at an excessive price. The article may require an independent valuation by a specially appointed accountant, it may provide for valuation by the company's own auditor, or it may fix the price in some arbitrary way.)

(e) Are there to be time limits? (There should be, otherwise the procedure will be unfair to the shareholder who wishes to sell as the others will be able to cause him delay.)

(f) Are there to be any safeguards in case the selling shareholder refuses to make the offer? (A common provision is to say that the directors are his agents and so can make the offer on his behalf.)

14.2.3.2 Variations on the above approaches

Within the range of absolute refusal of a transfer to pre-emption rights for existing members are many hybrid transfer articles. Some examples are:

(a) complete freedom to transfer, so long as to a family member or another shareholder, otherwise the directors may refuse to register the transfer;

(b) complete freedom to transfer, subject to specifically defined exceptions, such as transferees who are not based in the UK or corporate transferees.

14.3 Provisions concerning meetings of shareholders

14.3.1 Relationship with statute

The Companies Act 2006 has simplified certain aspects of shareholder decision-making. Furthermore, it contains a number of provisions, which, subject to anything contrary in the articles, determine how shareholder meetings are called. The Model Articles do not displace these provisions, so the Act is determinative, if these are the chosen articles of a company.

The original 1985 version of Table A made provision for company meetings in articles 36–63. These regulations were based upon the requirements of the Companies Act 1985. In light of the simplifications introduced by the Companies Act 2006, companies with this type of Table A articles (or similar) may find themselves complying with internal regulations which are more stringent than the minima now set out in statute.

In recognition of this issue, from 1 October 2007 until the introduction of the Model Articles, revised versions of Table A (for both public and private companies) existed, which reflected the then newly introduced provisions of the 2006 Act. Therefore, companies which adopted Table A (in whole or in part) during that time will have articles whose provisions relating to general meetings do actually dovetail with the 2006 Act.

What follows is an explanation of those provisions which commonly need specific consideration. Where appropriate, a contrast will be made between the 1985 and 2007 versions of Table A. (For ease of reference, we shall refer to these as Table A 1985 and Table A 2007.)

14.3.2 Notice of general meetings

14.3.2.1 Model Articles

No specific provision is included in the Model Articles, as s. 307(1) CA 2006 is relied upon.

14.3.2.2 Table A 1985

Article 38 of Table A 1985 stipulates that 21 clear days' notice must be given of:

(a) an annual general meeting;
(b) a general meeting at which a special resolution is to be considered; and
(c) a general meeting at which a resolution to appoint a director is to be considered.

These requirements can now be considered excessive, as s. 307 CA 2006 only requires a minimum of 14 days' notice for all general meetings of a private company. Companies which are subject to this requirement may want to make the necessary change to their articles.

14.3.2.3 Table A 2007

By contrast, Article 38 of Table A 2007 stipulates 14 days' notice for all types of resolution, in line with the 2006 Act.

14.3.3 Consent to short notice

14.3.3.1 Model Articles

No specific provision is included in the Model Articles, as ss. 307(4)–(6) CA 2006 are relied upon.

14.3.3.2 Table A 1985

Table A 1985 effectively repeated the provisions of the Companies Act 1985 regarding consent to short notice in article 38(b). In particular, the requisite percentage of consenting shareholders must be 95%. Section 307(6) CA 2006 allows for a lesser minimum percentage of 90% and a maximum of 95%. Therefore, whilst Table A 1985 still dovetails with statute, there may be some administrative convenience to be found in choosing the lesser percentage by an alteration to the articles.

14.3.3.3 Table A 2007

Article 38 of Table A 2007 follows the 2006 Act and stipulates the lower percentage of 90%.

14.3.4 Quorum of shareholders' meeting

14.3.4.1 Model Articles

Article 38 of the Model Articles stipulates that a quorum is necessary for valid business to be transacted at a general meeting, but relies upon the provisions of s. 318 CA 2006 to determine the number, which is two members present or their proxies or representatives (in the case of corporate shareholders) unless the company has a single member, in which case this figure is reduced to one.

Section 318 is subject to contrary provision in the articles, so companies may wish to include alternative quorum requirements. For example, whilst a quorum of two will be appropriate in many instances, an alternative to this may be that all current members must be present to form a quorum. This may be appropriate where the shareholders are few in number and each wants equal influence in the company. An alternative approach may be that specifically identified shareholders have to be present. Again, this would be to reflect the respective power and influence of certain shareholders.

14.3.4.2 Table A 1985 and 2007

Both versions of Table A stipulate a quorum of two, but the 2007 version also makes provision for a quorum of one in the case of a single shareholder.

14.3.5 Chairman's casting vote

A casting vote available to the chairman of a shareholders' meeting can be a useful mechanism for overcoming deadlock at shareholder level. However, the 2006 Act has effectively nullified the possibility of a casting vote at general meetings through the requirements of ss. 281–283 and any pre-existing provision granting such a casting vote (for example, article 50 of Table A 1985) is ineffective, unless the provision was in existence prior to 1 October 2007. For this reason, neither Table A 2007 nor the Model Articles provide for the possibility of a casting vote.

In any event, a casting vote can also prove to be an excessively powerful right. Shareholders, therefore, need to consider carefully the continued inclusion of a casting vote in the articles, should such a provision exist and still be effective.

14.3.6 Voting on a poll and proxy notices

14.3.6.1 Model Articles

Article 44 of the Model Articles regulates the demand for a poll, which may be demanded:

(a) in advance of the relevant meeting;

(b) at the meeting itself prior to the matter being put to the vote on a show of hands;

(c) immediately after the vote on a show of hands.

The following persons may demand a poll:

(a) the chairman of the meeting;

(b) two or more shareholders having the right to vote at the meeting;

(c) one or more shareholders holding at least one-tenth of the total voting rights.

In terms of the appointment of a proxy, articles 45 and 46 govern the form and delivery of a proxy notice. It is important to fulfil the requirements of both these articles to avoid the appointment being invalidated.

14.3.6.2 Table A 1985 and 2007

The mechanisms for calling a poll in both versions of Table A are possibly over-bureaucratic for small, closely-held companies. Simpler procedures, such as those found in the Model Articles, may, therefore, be substituted for these.

Also, the rights of proxies have been increased under the 2006 Act to allow them to vote on a show of hands (ss. 284 and 285). The absence of such a statement will not disenfranchise any proxy holder, but it may be appropriate to update the articles to reflect the new position.

14.3.7 Written resolutions

14.3.7.1 Model Articles and Table A 2007

The possibility of a written resolution as an alternative to a general meeting is on a statutory basis (chapter 2, Part 13 CA 2006). As such, neither Table A 2007 nor the Model Articles make provision for written resolutions.

14.3.7.2 Table A 1985

Table A 1985 reflects the fact that, at the time of its introduction, there was no statutorily endorsed method of making shareholder decisions by written resolution. As such, article 53 provided for this by reflecting the common law position that the unanimous consent of the shareholders could, in many circumstances, be as effective as a resolution passed at a general meeting.

14.4 Provisions concerning directors

14.4.1 Introduction

The commentary at **14.3.1** is equally applicable here. Some of the more complex and undesirable provisions concerning directors which existed in Table A 1985, no longer feature in the Model Articles. This is mainly because they were tied into a company's annual general meeting, which for private companies is no longer a legal requirement.

More generally, however, legislation governing directors' proceedings is minimal, so there is not the same option for the Model Articles to rely upon the 2006 Act, as is the case with general meetings.

14.4.2 Number of directors

As the minimum number of directors is determined by statute (one for private and two for public) and as a company is unlikely to find any material benefit in a ceiling limit on the number of directors, it is usually unnecessary for a company to deal with such matters in its articles. It is likely that for this reason the Model Articles are silent on both points. By contrast, both versions of Table A stipulate a minimum number of two directors (article 64), but no maximum. This is subject to any contrary stipulation by ordinary resolution.

14.4.3 Appointment of directors

14.4.3.1 Model Articles

The appointment of directors is purely a constitutional matter for a company. The position under the Model Articles is straightforward. A director may be permanently appointed either by ordinary resolution or a decision of the directors (article 17).

14.4.3.2 Table A 1985 and 2007

Both versions of Table A contain two methods for appointing directors, i.e., either by ordinary resolution or by a board decision (articles 76–79). Whilst appointment by the shareholders results in a permanent appointment, appointment by the board is only temporary under Table A 1985 (but not Table A 2007), requiring confirmation by ordinary resolution of the shareholders at the next available AGM. In a closely-held company, such reference of a board decision to the shareholders is inappropriate. Moreover, there is no longer a requirement on private companies to hold an AGM, so the mechanism for confirmation has become inappropriate. (This is reflected in the 2007 version of Table A, where any appointment by directors is permanent.)

Finally, there are complex notice provisions contained in both versions of Table A which relate to these methods of appointment. Generally the worth of these notice provisions must be questioned in a closely-held company.

14.4.4 Retirement by rotation

14.4.4.1 Introduction

Retirement by rotation is effectively a corporate governance device. If members of the board come up for reappointment by ordinary resolution on an annual basis, shareholders are given influence and control over poor or unpopular management. If such provisions are absent, this can make investment in that company unattractive. However, such issues are only really germane to companies in which there is considerable trade in their shares, i.e., listed companies. For closely-held, private companies, retirement by rotation is likely to be nothing more than an administrative nuisance, especially now that the need for private companies to hold annual general meetings has disappeared.

14.4.4.2 Model Articles and Table A 2007

Neither Table A 2007 nor the Model Articles contain provision for retirement by rotation of directors, reflecting the position mentioned above.

14.4.4.3 Table A 1985

Table A 1985 (articles 73 et seq.) makes elaborate provision for directors to retire by rotation (one-third of the board retires each year in most circumstances and is presented for re-election at the relevant AGM). Note, however, that article 84 ameliorates the position, by excluding the managing director and any other executive director from the need to retire by rotation

14.4.5 Removal of directors

The members of the company have power to remove a director from office by ordinary resolution (see s. 168 CA 2006.) It may be considered appropriate to include in the articles a *Bushell v Faith* clause which will grant a director who is a shareholder weighted voting rights which effectively give him the power to defeat the resolution for his removal. (No such clause exists in either the Model Articles or Table A.)

Whilst a *Bushell v Faith* clause is acceptable to protect a director, any attempt to deprive the shareholders of their rights under s. 168 is not, so any attempts to provide the shareholders with 'alternative' methods of removal in the articles must be treated with caution. However, it is also acceptable to allow the board to decide on the removal of a director. The mechanism commonly employed is to state that a director must resign if requested by all other directors to do so.

14.4.6 Directors' decision-making

14.4.6.1 Model Articles

Articles 7 to 16 of the Model Articles govern board decisions. Article 7 provides for two methods of decision-making by the directors:

(a) by majority decision at a board meeting;

(b) by the method provided for in article 8.

Discussion of both these methods follows.

Any director can call a board meeting by giving appropriate notice to every other director (article 9(1)). The notice must contain details of when and where the meeting is to take place. Notice need not be in writing, which presumably allows notice by e-mail, text or other electronic method which the directors may find suitable.

Article 10 allows for the fact that directors need not be in the same place to hold a board meeting so long as they can communicate to each other any relevant information or opinions (thus recognising the impact which technology can have on how meetings are conducted). This is supported by a requirement in article 9(2)(c) that the content of the notice must indicate how it is proposed that the directors should communicate with each other if they are not to be in the same place during the meeting.

Article 8 allows directors to make decisions unanimously outside the forum of the board meeting if they all indicate to each other *by any means* that they share a common view on a matter (article 8(1)). One possible method of doing so is by a written resolution of all directors (article 8(2)). However, other possibilities might be e-mail exchange or simply informal discussions outside a specific board meeting.

Whilst such concepts may mirror practice in some small, closely-held companies, it is suggested that possible dangers lurk with such practice being seen as generally appropriate, namely evidential problems with recording such decisions. Also, in those instances where the directors' duty to promote the success of the company is germane, the absence of a properly recorded discussion and decision in a board meeting may make it harder for the board to defend its position at a future date.

14.4.6.2 Table A 1985 and 2007

Regulation 88 of both versions of Table A governs directors' proceedings in the following ways:

(a) Any director may call a board meeting, as may any secretary at the request of a director. There are no specific requirements about the form or content of any notice. Also, the common law implication is that any notice must be reasonable in length.

(b) It is not necessary to notify any director who is absent from the UK of a board meeting.

(c) All board decisions are carried by a majority of votes.

This, and other related provisions of Table A, assume that the board meeting is the appropriate forum for decisions of the directors. However, article 93 alternatively permits decisions to be made by a unanimous written resolution of the directors (which is not as wide as article 8 of the Model Articles).

14.4.7 Quorum of directors' meeting

14.4.7.1 Model Articles

Article 11(2) permits the board to determine the necessary quorum but:

(a) if no such determination is made, the default provision is two directors;

(b) the quorum cannot be set at less than two.

Additionally, if the number of directors falls below the number required for a quorum, those directors or director remaining may only act either to fill the vacancies on the board or to call a general meeting for that purpose.

It may seem unusual to stipulate a minimum quorum of two directors when a private company need only have one director. However, article 7(2) of the Model Articles contains a carve-out in respect of companies with only one director, such that none of the provisions regarding directors' meetings applies and the sole director may take decisions in whatever way is thought suitable.

As with the quorum provision for general meetings issues arise on the setting of a quorum for board meetings. For example, in a company with several directors, a stipulated quorum of only two may be regarded as too few. Also, the presence of particular directors may be regarded as essential to the quorum, so these persons could be specified as a necessary part of the quorum.

14.4.7.2 Table A 1985 and 2007

Both versions of Table A allow the board to determine the quorum but the default provision is two directors. Additionally, if the number of directors falls below the number required for a quorum, those directors or director remaining may only act either to fill the vacancies on the board or to call a general meeting.

14.4.8 Chairman's casting vote

As a way of avoiding deadlock at board level, the chairman of the board of directors may be provided with a casting vote. This concept was unaffected by the changes brought about by the 2006 Act, which prevent a casting vote at shareholder meetings. As such, the Model Articles contain a casting vote provision (article 13). Both versions of Table A also provide the chairman of the board of directors with a casting vote.

The inclusion of such a provision needs careful consideration to ensure that one director is not given disproportionate power at board level.

14.4.9 Restrictions on voting

See 9.9.2.5 for discussion of this issue.

14.4.10 Secretary

Private companies are no longer required to have a secretary, but may continue to appoint somebody to this role (s. 270 CA 2006). The Model Articles contain no such mechanism for doing so, but it is presumed that any desired appointment will fall to the directors to confirm. To reflect the previous situation, where all companies had to appoint a secretary, both versions of Table A allow for this event by authorising the board to make any such appointment on such terms as it thinks fit.

14.5 Single member companies

Much of the previous discussion assumes that companies will have at least two directors and/or shareholders. It is possible to create a private company with only one director and one shareholder. This situation will normally arise when either a sole trader is looking for the benefit of limited liability or where a company is a wholly-owned subsidiary of another.

In such a situation, specific thought needs to be given to articles which reflect the reality of the situation, particularly in relation to meetings of both the board and shareholders. It will be equally important to remember that such specific articles will need amendment if the number of directors or shareholders increases above one. If there is a high possibility of this at some time in the future, the articles should perhaps be drafted to anticipate this change in circumstances.

14.6 Alteration of articles

14.6.1 Power to alter

Section 21 CA 2006 gives a company power to alter its articles by special resolution.

The articles of a company may not be made unalterable. A clause in the articles which purports to prevent the shareholders from altering the articles is invalid. However, a contract between shareholders as to how they will vote on a resolution to alter the articles is not void (*Russell v Northern Bank Development Corporation* [1992] 1 WLR 588). In addition, s. 22 CA 2006 provides for the entrenchment of specified provisions of the articles. The method for entrenchment can be any mechanism for amendment or removal of the specified provisions which is more restrictive than the passing of a special resolution. It is important to recognise that entrenchment does not mean that the specified provisions can never be altered, but the mechanism chosen may make the possibility of any subsequent change extremely remote. Note that s. 22(2) is not yet in force, so it would seem that entrenchment provisions can be included by an amendment to the articles by special resolution, rather than unanimous consent of the shareholders being necessary.

14.6.2 Registration

Once the special resolution altering the articles has been passed, the resolution and a printed copy of the amended articles must be sent to the Registrar within 15 days. The Registrar officially notifies his receipt of these documents and the company cannot rely on the changes as against other persons who did not know of such changes until he has done so under the same rules as for change of name and alteration of objects. The company must ensure that copies of the altered articles are available, so that the directors and secretary may consult them and in case any member exercises his statutory right to a copy of the articles (s. 32 CA 2006).

14.6.3 Alteration to be for the benefit of the company

14.6.3.1 Shareholders may decide for themselves

There are no provisions in the Companies Act giving shareholders, or any particular proportion of the shareholders, power to challenge the validity of an alteration to the articles. However, the courts have held that an alteration is invalid if it is not 'bona fide in the interests of the company as a whole' (per Lord Lindley MR in *Allen v Gold Reefs of West Africa Ltd* [1900] 1 Ch 656). The test is very much easier to state than to apply to the facts of particular cases. As we have already seen in relation to derivative actions (see **10.6**), the court is very reluctant to interfere with decisions made by the majority in a company.

The court will normally regard an alteration as being in the interests of the company if the majority of the shareholders are in favour of the alteration (as they must be since a special resolution will have been passed before any question as to the validity of the alteration can arise). Thus, in *Allen v Gold Reefs of West Africa Ltd,* the articles contained a provision imposing a lien on partly-paid shares. One shareholder owed money to the company and the articles were altered to impose a lien on fully-paid shares as well as on partly-paid shares. The court regarded the fact that one (and only one) shareholder was indebted to the company at the time of alteration as something exciting suspicion as to the bona fides of the company, but nevertheless came to the conclusion that the alteration was in the interests of the company as a whole. Clearly it is in the interests of a company that it should have security for money due to it and no discrimination against particular members was expressed in the altered articles.

Shuttleworth v Cox Brothers and Co (Maidenhead) Ltd [1927] 2 KB 9, is perhaps a stronger illustration. The majority of the directors suspected that one of the board had been guilty of misconduct but they had insufficient proof of any grounds giving a right to dismiss him. They therefore altered the articles to say that any director would cease to hold office if requested to resign by the majority of the directors. The test applied by the court was whether any reasonable man could come to the conclusion that the alteration was in the interests of the company. If it was open to a reasonable man to come to that conclusion, the alteration would only be invalid on proof of actual bad faith. The court was satisfied that a reasonable man could come to the conclusion that the alteration was in the interests of the company and so, since the plaintiff could not prove actual bad faith, the alteration was held to be valid.

14.6.3.2 Discrimination

The courts have recognised that an alteration to the articles cannot be in the interests of the company as a whole if it discriminates against some members, however few. At first sight this seems strange in view of the two cases mentioned above, both of which appear to involve actual discrimination against a particular shareholder. However, on closer analysis neither of those cases involved any discrimination. In *Allen v Gold Reefs of West Africa*, the lien applied, potentially, to all the fully-paid shares whoever owned them, so that it might apply to any shareholder at some time. Similarly in *Shuttleworth v Cox*, the new article potentially applied to any shareholder who became a director and who fell into disfavour with the rest of the board. A good illustration of the type of case where an alteration *is* discriminatory and so void is given by the Australian case, *Australian Fixed Trust Proprietary Ltd v Clyde Industries Ltd* (1959) SR (NSW) 33. In that case the articles were altered so as to require shareholders who were unit trust managers to obtain the approval of the majority of their unit-holders before exercising the voting rights attached to their shares. This clearly discriminated against shareholders who happened to be unit trust managers and so was void.

The narrowness of the distinction between cases which are, and cases which are not, discriminatory is well illustrated by the cases of *Sidebottom v Kershaw, Leese and Co Ltd* [1920] 1 Ch 154, and *Brown v Abrasive Wheel Co* [1919] 1 Ch 290. In *Sidebottom v Kershaw, Leese,* the articles were altered so as to give the directors power to direct a shareholder who was concerned with a competing business to transfer his shares. This was held to be a valid alteration. The company could properly come to the conclusion that it was in its interests that competitors be excluded from membership and there was no discrimination based on the number of shares owned. In *Brown v Abrasive Wheel Co,* the articles were altered to give 90% of the shareholders power to require the minority shareholders to sell their shares. In fact, the majority shareholders (who owned 98% of the shares) had good commercial reasons for wanting the alteration, but nevertheless the court held that the alteration was invalid. Although it was bona fide in the interests of 98% of the present shareholders it was not in the interests of the other 2%, nor was it necessarily in the interests of future shareholders and so it was discriminatory.

14.6.3.3 Conclusion in the common law

The two basic rules which seem to have evolved from the cases are:

(a) The members may generally decide themselves whether an alteration is bona fide in the interests of the company as a whole.

(b) The court will interfere with their decision where the members could not properly come to that decision because it discriminates between groups of members.

14.6.3.4 Section 994 CA 2006

It should be noted that much of the usefulness of the common law has been superseded by the above section (formerly s. 459 CA 1985). The alteration of articles to the prejudice of some part of the members will be good grounds under which to bring an action under s. 994. However, if the alteration affects directors as opposed to shareholders (as in the *Shuttleworth* case), the common law is still of relevance. (See **10.7** for further discussion of unfair prejudice.)

14.6.3.5 Class rights

Section 630 CA 2006 deals with class rights, i.e., different rights attaching to different shares. The basic rule is that any proposed amendment to any class rights must be approved either:

(a) in writing by three-quarters of the shareholders in the relevant class; or

(b) by a resolution passed by three-quarters of the shareholders in the relevant class at a separate meeting of the class of shareholders in question.

Alternatively, the articles themselves may set out rules covering this issue which may require a greater or lower level of consent than above.

Any proposed amendment to the articles which affects any class rights must first receive such approval as well as be approved itself by special resolution of the company as a whole.

online resource centre

For further resources and online chapters please visit the Online Resource Centre at www.oxfordtextbooks.co.uk/orc/business13_14/.

15

Disclosure obligations of companies and company accounts

This chapter covers the following topics:

15.1 Introduction

One of the core concepts of company law is that information about a company, its 'constitution', and financial status should be made available to the public. (This is one of the 'trade-offs' for limited liability.) The purpose of this policy of 'openness' is to enable anyone interested in the affairs of a company (whether they are current or prospective shareholders in the company or its creditors) to have access to the information they need to make an informed judgement on the company's financial affairs and the abilities of the company's management. They will also be able to determine whether the company and its directors have the necessary authority and powers to enter into the transaction which, for example, a third-party creditor may be considering. In any transaction involving a company, it is prudent to carry out relevant searches to obtain all necessary information *and* to obtain confirmation from the company that such information is up to date and correct.

Information is made available by the company:

(a) keeping at its registered office records and registers available for inspection by its members and the public (see **8.10**);

(b) disclosing financial information to its members through the annual directors' report and annual audited accounts;

(c) delivering to the Registrar of Companies documents which the Registrar in turn makes available to the public for inspection; and

(d) the publication of certain information about the company in the *London Gazette*.

In this chapter, we will look at the information about companies which is publicly available, paying particular attention to the rules with which the company must comply in relation to its accounts, as well as giving some guidance on how to interpret the published accounts of a company.

15.2 Company searches

15.2.1 General

While information about a company can be obtained from advertisements placed by the Registrar of Companies in the *London Gazette* or from inspecting the records and registers maintained by the company at its registered office, the most common method of acquiring information on a company is by making a search at the Companies' Registry. The Registrar of Companies keeps copies of the information supplied to him by the company and this is available for public inspection. In this section of the chapter, we will look at the information which a company must supply to the Registrar and then look at the procedure for making a company search.

15.2.2 The information available for inspection

The information available for inspection at the Companies' Registry includes the following:

(a) the company's memorandum and articles of association;
(b) particulars of directors and secretary (giving details both of the original directors and secretary as well as subsequent changes);
(c) particulars of the issue of shares;
(d) particulars of (most) charges;
(e) particulars of all special resolutions (and any elective and extraordinary resolutions passed under the 1985 Act regime);
(f) notice of the accounting reference date;
(g) notice of any increase of capital;
(h) particulars of resolutions granting directors authority to allot shares;
(i) particulars of the address of the registered office (both the first address and subsequent changes);
(j) the annual return; and
(k) the accounts.

Of this list, the last two items merit further consideration (see **15.3** for the rules relating to the accounts which the company must file). So far as the 'annual return' is concerned, currently s. 854 CA 2006 requires every company to make an annual return to the Registrar on Form AR01 once in every year (a fee of £14 is payable for electronic filings; £40 for paper ones). The company is required to file returns signed by a director or the secretary made up to the company's return date which must be within 12 months of the date of the previous return or, in the case of a new company, of the date of incorporation. The return must be filed with the Registrar within 28 days of the return date.

The contents of the return are determined by statute/regulation. The details which it will contain are:

(a) the address of the registered office of the company;
(b) the company's principal business activities;
(c) the location of the register of members if it is not kept at the registered office;
(d) the location of the company's register of debenture holders if it is not kept at the company's registered office;
(e) the company's type (that is to say, public limited company, private company limited by shares, or whatever);
(f) details of the company secretary (if any);
(g) details of every director plus nationality, date of birth, business occupation, and the particulars required for the register of directors;

(h) details of the company's issued share capital;

(i) details of the members of the company on the date on which the return is made up plus the persons who have ceased to be members since the last return;

(j) details of the shares held by members.

15.2.3 Failure to file annual returns

In addition to accounts, the annual return is one filing which Companies House expects to receive every year from a company. As such, policing default is very easy. Failure to submit an annual return in the due time period is a criminal offence and both the company and all officers thereof are liable to a fine (s. 858 CA 2006). Additionally, persistent failure to comply with filing obligations can be grounds for a disqualification order being made against a director (s. 3 Company Directors Disqualification Act 1986).

15.2.4 The procedure for making a company search

The wide range of information which companies are required to file with the Registrar of Companies is filed by the Registrar by reference to each company's unique company number. With the company's current name or registration number (and on payment of the relevant fee), it is possible to obtain a copy of the company's file. To do this, a company search can be carried out in person, by post, telephone or via Companies House Direct, a web-based online service. Full details of the latter, together with information on all Companies House services, can be obtained at www.companieshouse.gov.uk. The online service provides free access to certain general company information, including an index of all registered companies. More specific information and company documents can be downloaded on payment of the relevant fees. Companies House can also supply copies of company documentation on request by post, fax or email. Company information up to 31 December 2002 can be supplied via a set of microfiches.

15.3 The duty to submit accounts

15.3.1 What is meant by 'accounts'?

As a general rule (although see discussion at **15.4** below) limited companies are required by the Companies Act 2006 to prepare a set of 'individual accounts' for each financial year of the company (s. 394 CA 2006). These consist of a profit and loss account and a balance sheet (s. 396 CA 2006). Any accounts prepared must give a true and fair view of the financial status of the company (s. 393 CA 2006). They must also comply with specific rules on format and content (see both The Small Companies and Groups (Accounts and Directors' Report) Regulations 2008 and The Large and Medium-sized Companies and Groups (Accounts and Reports) Regulations 2008).

Where a company is a parent company (and is not a 'small' company; see **15.4** below) it must also prepare group accounts (s. 399 CA 2006), which must comprise a consolidated balance sheet and a consolidated profit and loss account setting out financial details of the parent and all its subsidiaries (s. 404 CA 2006).

Additionally, a directors' report must accompany the accounts (s. 415 CA 2006). This report must contain details of all directors during the relevant financial year, the principal activities of the company throughout the year and the amount of any dividend recommended by the directors. Also, unless the company is 'small' (see discussion below at **15.4**), this report should contain a 'business review', which effectively is an analysis of the company's performance and the risks it may be facing (s. 417 CA 2006). This review is designed to give shareholders the opportunity to assess how well directors have fulfilled their duty to promote the success of the company.

Subject to certain exceptions, there is a duty for all accounts to be audited (s. 475 CA 2006). As a consequence, companies must normally appoint auditors annually, who are required to produce a report on the accounts. This report effectively benchmarks the contents of the accounts against certain established accounting standards. (In reality, auditors prepare both the accounts and their report—it is unlikely that a company will prepare accounts independently of the auditors and then submit them for audit.)

15.3.2 Provision of accounts to members

Annual accounts must be approved by the board and signed off on its behalf. Once this has been done, the company must send copies of the accounts to the shareholders (s. 423 CA 2006). For private companies this must be no later than the deadline for submission of the accounts to Companies House, which is nine months from the end of the relevant accounting period.

For public companies, there is a different procedure, which allows shareholders greater influence. Once they have been prepared, the final accounts must be laid before the company in general meeting (s. 437(1) CA 2006). This meeting is called the accounts meeting (s. 437(3) CA 2006) and in most circumstances this will be the annual general meeting of the company. The relevant accounts must be sent out to shareholders no later than 21 days before the accounts meeting (s. 424(3) CA 2006).

15.3.3 Filing of accounts

Subject to what is said below about small and medium-sized companies, all companies must send copies of their accounts to the Registrar of Companies. In the case of private companies, this must be no later than nine months after the end of the relevant accounting period (s. 442(2)(a) CA 2006) and for public companies this must be no later than six months after the end of the relevant accounting period (s. 442(2)(b) CA 2006). These accounts are then a matter of public record and anyone who pays to do a company search will be able to get a copy of the accounts of most companies.

Failure to deliver accounts on time has a number of consequences, namely:

(a) Automatic civil penalties on a scale which is linked to the length of the delay (s. 453 CA 2006). (Note that the penalties are higher for public than private companies.)

(b) Criminal penalties (by way of fine) for every relevant director.

(c) The failure may amount to grounds for disqualification proceedings against the directors concerned under the Company Directors Disqualification Act 1986.

15.4 Small and medium-sized companies

15.4.1 Small companies

If a private company comes within the definition of a small company for a particular financial year, its duty to deliver accounts to the Registrar of Companies is modified by ss. 444 and 444A CA 2006. (Note that public companies can never be small for these purposes.) Effectively this means that it can submit fewer elements of its accounts/reports than normal and, if it prefers, abbreviated accounts, instead of the ones actually prepared for statutory purposes. Additionally, certain information can be omitted from the accounts and reports. The combined effect of these provisions is that a small company can maintain a greater degree of privacy about its financial status. (There is an additional exemption for small groups of companies from the duty to produce consolidated accounts. The detail of this is not considered.)

A private company is small if at least two of the following criteria are satisfied:

(a) the company's turnover does not exceed £6.5 million;

(b) its balance sheet total does not exceed £3.26 million;

(c) the average number of employees does not exceed 50 people.

In the above definitions 'turnover' effectively means the sums earned by the company in selling goods or services before deducting expenses. The balance sheet total is, broadly speaking, the value of the company's assets without deducting any liabilities. The number of employees should be calculated as an average over the relevant financial year.

The status of a small company is not permanent, nor is it safe to assume that a company will benefit from the regime simply because it fulfils the conditions for a small company in a particular financial year. Put simply, a company must either acquire small company status at the outset of its existence and then lose that status by ceasing to be a small company for two consecutive years or, if it does not start out as small, it must acquire small company status by being small for at least two consecutive years. This rather confusing rule is best explained by an example.

EXAMPLE

Scenario A

Assume that Lazlo Limited is a small company for its first financial year. If Lazlo ceases to fulfil the relevant conditions in its second financial year, it will still be a small company for that financial year. However, if this situation continues for the third financial year after incorporation, it will at this point lose its small company status.

Scenario B

Assume that Lazlo Limited is not a small company for its first financial year, but that it fulfils the relevant conditions in its second financial year. It will still not be a small company for this second year. However, if it fulfils the relevant conditions in its third financial year after incorporation, it will at this point acquire small company status.

Scenario C

Assume that Lazlo Limited has fulfilled the relevant conditions for small company status for the previous two financial years. For the most recent financial year, however, it does not fulfil those conditions. Nevertheless, it will continue to be a small company for the purposes of the current financial year.

In addition to revised filing requirements, small companies may benefit from an exemption from audit (s. 477 CA 2006). The benefit of this is that audit is a relatively expensive process, so the exemption can result in a cost saving for a company. However, even if the board of directors decide to dispense with an audit, members holding at least 10% in nominal value of the company's issued share capital have the right to demand an audit (s. 476 CA 2006).

As well as being a small company for the financial year in question, a company must also have a turnover which is not more than £6.5 million and a balance sheet total which is not more than £3.26 million. (As we have seen, companies may qualify as small in respect of their status for the previous financial year, so this rule ensures that companies are actually small for the financial year in question.)

15.4.2 Medium-sized companies

The exemptions from reporting and filing available to small companies are available to a lesser degree for medium-sized companies, although medium-sized companies can never benefit from the exemption from audit. (As with small companies, medium-sized companies are not exempt from the requirement to produce full accounts nor from the requirement to provide accounts to their own shareholders.)

A medium-sized company is one which satisfies at least two of the following criteria:

(a) its turnover does not exceed £25.9 million;

(b) its balance sheet total does not exceed £12.9 million;

(c) the average number of employees does not exceed 250.

These conditions should be applied in the same way as for the calculation for small companies. Additionally, medium-sized company status is acquired and lost in the same way as for small companies.

15.5 Appointment of auditors

Where auditors are required, their appointment is regulated by the Companies Act 2006. Both the board of directors and the shareholders (by ordinary resolution) have the power to appoint auditors in defined circumstances (s. 485 for private companies and s. 489 for public companies). In simple terms, the very first appointment of auditors is made by the board and thereafter the shareholders make the appointment. The appointment of auditors should happen annually. For public companies, therefore, the annual accounts meeting, i.e., the AGM, is the most appropriate forum; for private companies, a specific general meeting could be called for this purpose or it could be effected by written resolution. However, to reduce the administrative burden on private companies, s. 487(2) provides for automatic reappointment of incumbent auditors (appointed by the shareholders), unless:

(a) the company's articles require annual appointment;

(b) the shareholders have either resolved by ordinary resolution to block the reappointment or an objection to the reappointment has been received by the company from at least 5% of the shareholders who would be entitled to vote on such a resolution;

(c) the board has resolved that an audit is unnecessary for the financial year in question.

15.6 Profit and loss account

A profit and loss account is an account which shows what income the company has received in a particular period of time and what expenses have been incurred by the company in producing that income. Once the expenses are deducted from the income the resulting figure is a profit (or a loss if the expenses are more than the income). The profit and loss account is strictly speaking only designed to show income profits. If a company makes a capital profit (for example, if it sells its factory for a profit) this may be shown as an addition to the profit and loss account. It will then usually be labelled as an 'exceptional item' as opposed to the ordinary income profit.

Profit and loss accounts are almost always prepared for 12-month periods (the company may wish to produce forecasts or full accounts for its own internal purposes on a more regular basis). The period covered by the accounts ends with the accounting reference date which the company can choose for itself (see **8.13**). Companies are not required to prepare accounts for a calendar year (although some companies do choose 31 December as their accounting reference date, in which case the accounts will be for a calendar year).

A very simple traditional profit and loss account might look like the following:

EXAMPLE

XYZ Ltd
Profit and loss account
Year ending 31 March 2000

	£	£
INCOME		
Sales		200,000
Opening stock	80,000	
Purchases	90,000	
	170,000	
Less closing stock	70,000	
		100,000

Gross profit from sales		100,000
Interest received		8,000
		108,000
EXPENDITURE		
Wages	55,000	
Miscellaneous	10,000	
		65,000
PROFIT BEFORE TAX		43,000
DEDUCT TAX		12,000
TRANSFERRED TO RESERVE		31,000

Notice the following points in relation to it:

(a) The account is divided into three parts. The first shows the income of the business. The second shows the expenditure which is incurred in earning that income and the third shows what has happened to the income. (This third part is strictly speaking the appropriation section rather than part of the profit and loss account itself. If any dividends were paid they would be shown as a deduction in this section.)

(b) In the income section the opening and closing stock are shown. Unless stock is taken into account it is impossible to work out the profit. If a company has a storeroom full of goods left over from last year which it sells this year, it cannot calculate its profit unless it takes into account the fact that it paid for that stock.

(c) The figure which is labelled 'transferred to reserve' is what is left of the profit after the tax has been paid. It is in effect profit which has been retained in the business. An explanation of the term 'reserve' in this context is given in **15.7**.

15.7 Balance sheet

A balance sheet shows the assets and liabilities of the company. An asset is something of value or potential value. The factory which a company owns is an asset, so is any money which it has in the bank. Sometimes the balance sheet will also show much more intangible things such as goodwill. Goodwill is the difference between the real assets of a company and its overall value to a purchaser. For example, a company running a business in a shop might own the following assets:

	£
The shop	100,000
Fixtures (shelves, etc.)	10,000
Stock (the goods for sale)	5,000
Cash	2,000

If the company decided to sell the business it would be likely to want more than £117,000 for it. The real value of the business includes the fact that it has a loyal group of customers, or it is situated in a good location for running this type of business (or both). The difference between the assets value and what the shop could be sold for is the goodwill of the business.

The liabilities part of the balance sheet includes liabilities due to outsiders (such as bills owed by the shop) or money owed to the bank or other lenders. The money which would be paid to the shareholders if the company were wound up is also shown as a liability because, at least in theory, it will be paid out to the shareholders one day.

A simple traditional balance sheet might look like this:

EXAMPLE

Balance sheet of XYZ Ltd
31 March 2000

	£	£
FIXED ASSETS		
Premises		400,000
Fixtures		10,000
		410,000
CURRENT ASSETS		
Stock (goods for sale and/or materials)	5,000	
Cash	2,000	
	7,000	
LESS CURRENT LIABILITIES		
Electricity bill	4,500	
		2,500
		412,500
CAPITAL		
Share capital		200,000
Share premium account		160,000
Bank loan		10,000
Reserves		42,500
		412,500

Notice the following points in relation to it:

(a) The totals balance, i.e., the net assets of the company equal its capital. This happens because of the 'double entry' system used to record transactions in the company's books. A simple example of this is where share capital is contributed to a company. If someone buys shares for £100 at par value, this would be represented in a balance sheet by two entries. The company would have £100 in cash, a current asset; and it would have capital of £100 (a liability to the shareholder). Extrapolating this, a company's net assets will always reflect its capital, as is seen here. They can effectively be seen as the way in which a company has employed its capital in its business.

(b) A distinction is made between fixed assets and current assets. Fixed assets are assets which are likely to be held by the company for a considerable period of time. Current assets are those which are likely to be used up by the company in the course of its business.

(c) Current liabilities (that is sums owed by the company which are likely to be paid within a year) are shown as a deduction from current assets. They are accordingly not in the same part of the account as the long-term liabilities.

(d) The second half of the balance sheet is labelled 'capital'. Although in common parlance the word capital often means money or wealth, to an accountant it is a liability which is owed to someone with a proprietary or other long-term interest in the business. The money owed to the bank is included in capital on the assumption that it is a long-term loan and so is something like an investment in the business. If the same money was owed to the bank on an overdraft it would be shown as a short-term liability like the electricity bill.

(e) The other sums shown under the heading of capital are all sums due to the shareholders of the company. The share capital is the liability which arises from the fact that the shareholders paid the nominal value of their shares to the company at some time in the past. The share premium is the liability which arises from the fact that when the shares were issued the shareholders paid more than the nominal value for them. The difference between these two sums is theoretical only. Remember that a company cannot generally return the sums invested by the shareholders until the company is wound up.

(f) The item referred to as reserves is in a way a balancing item. If the company was wound up its assets would realise £417,000. This would be used to pay the bank and the outstanding bill. This would then leave £402,500 for the shareholders. They would be repaid their original investment of £360,000 (shown in share capital and share premium). This would then leave £42,500. The reserve is in effect a liability owed to shareholders which results from the fact that the company has made profits over the years.

(g) The balance sheet is dated 31 March. Businesses constantly acquire and dispose of assets, pay bills and incur new liabilities. A balance sheet is, therefore, always relevant to a particular moment in time, not to the whole of a period of time (in which respect contrast the profit and loss account).

(h) The company has a surplus of short-term assets over short-term liabilities. The resulting surplus is called net current assets (confusingly it is also often called 'working capital' even though it is an asset). This figure is particularly important as it is a strong indication of the solvency of the company.

15.8 Format of accounts

Formats for both profit and loss accounts and balance sheets are set out in Regulations (see **15.3.1**). These are templates which all companies must choose from in presenting their accounts for each financial year. They set out the order in which all the different items in the accounts must appear. For the purposes of illustration we have not adhered exactly to any of the formats in the very brief examples given above.

Companies' published accounts are often difficult for beginners to follow because much of the information is given in the form of notes. Indeed the published profit and loss account is likely to contain very little information about the company's income and expenditure unless close attention is paid to the notes as well as to the account itself.

15.9 Interpretation of accounts

15.9.1 Introduction

In this section, we will look at some ideas about interpretation of accounts. Interpretation is a process whereby information is extracted from the accounts for two main purposes:

(a) to assess the company's present financial position in relation to profitability and solvency;

(b) to predict the future prospects of the company

Neither of these processes is an exact science. Interpretation of accounts will not always produce a 'right answer' but rather an opinion about the company.

15.9.2 Reasons for interpretation and sources of information

Interpretation of accounts is likely to be undertaken by or for a variety of people for a variety of reasons. In particular the management of the company may wish to know how efficient the business is. Investors or potential investors in a quoted company will want to know whether the company is over- or undervalued (in their opinion) at the present price of the shares. Creditors will be particularly concerned to investigate the company's solvency.

The most obvious source of information about the accounts of the company is the published accounts of the company. It should be noted, however, that these accounts will not provide as much information as the interpreter might ideally like. The management of the company will have more detailed accounts than the published accounts in the form of what are usually called management accounts. These are not available to the public (not even to the shareholders) as a matter of right, but sometimes the management may be willing to show them to others such as potential lenders or purchasers of the business.

If the information which is available to the particular investigator is limited to published accounts, then he will usually do well to look at the accounts for several years. In interpreting the performance of a business the trend over a period of time is very important. Past results are not necessarily a guide to the future, but nevertheless they may give some indication of the likely progress of the company in the future. An investor, for example, is likely to be more interested in a company which shows a long record of growth than one which has been merely holding its own.

15.9.3 What are the limits inherent in accounts?

The most obvious limit is the possibility of outright fraud. If the accounts are a work of fiction they will tell you nothing useful. The process of auditing accounts ensures that fraud is unusual.

Published accounts are produced once a year and, as we have seen, may be submitted to the Registrar up to six months after the end of the accounting period (nine months if the company is private). This means that the accounts may be quite considerably out of date. The balance sheet date should be checked both to see how out of date the accounts are and also to see how typical that date might be. The balance sheet of a resort hotel business may tell a very different story if it is drawn up just after the end of the season (when there will be an unusually large amount of cash or an unusually small overdraft), than if it is produced at the end of the winter.

The notes to the accounts should be examined carefully to see what the company's policy is in relation to valuation of assets. In particular, have the fixed assets been revalued recently so that the figures approximate to market value? If not, then the fixed assets may be shown at historic cost (i.e., what was paid for them) in which case the accounts will not show the true increase or decrease in the value of those assets.

Another important factor to look for is how debtors have been dealt with in the accounts. The figure described as debtors shows the amount of money owed to the company. Almost all businesses suffer some degree of bad debts. That is, some of the people who owe them money cannot or will not pay what they owe to the company. Bad debts and an estimate of potential bad debts ('provision for bad debts') should be deducted in computing the profits, and from the current assets of the company, otherwise the accounts will be misleading.

Often the accounts will include some special feature which is relevant to the accounts in a particular year only. These are usually called exceptional items. For example, in a particular year a company may have sold a fixed asset or issued shares. In both of these cases it will have received a large amount of cash. If it has not yet spent the cash then the net current assets figure may be unusually high. Will the company still have enough cash to pay its creditors if it replaces the fixed asset which it sold?

15.10 Solvency

15.10.1 Introduction

A company is solvent if it is able to pay its debts as they fall due. It is important to realise that solvency is not the same thing as profitability. A company may make profits and yet be insolvent. For example, the profits may arise from the fact that the company has supplied goods or services for which it has not yet been paid. This company will be insolvent if it has to pay its own creditors before it collects from its debtors. Similarly a company may be unprofitable and yet solvent for a very long time. For example, a company may be making losses and yet can keep itself going by selling fixed assets.

In judging the solvency of a company it is desirable to work out certain solvency ratios. These are calculations made from the information given in the accounts.

15.10.2 Current ratio

The first of the ratios is the 'current ratio': this is a test of the company's liquidity. Liquidity is the ability of a company to pay its debts in the short term. The current ratio is the ratio of current assets to current liabilities.

In the example in **15.7**, the current assets were £7,000 and the current liabilities were £4,500. This gives a ratio of 7:4.5 or 1.55:1. This would generally be regarded as a satisfactory figure as it means that for every pound which the company will have to pay in the short term, it has, or will soon receive, £1.55. However, this does assume that the stock will be easy to sell at the value shown in the balance sheet (in the case of stock the value will normally be the lower of purchase price or current value).

15.10.3 Acid Test

Because stock cannot always be sold in a hurry, the liquidity ratio (also known as the 'acid test') is often preferred to the current ratio. This compares liquid assets (i.e., cash and things as good as cash) with current liabilities. Applying this ratio to our figures of current assets of £7,000 and current liabilities of £4,500, we get a ratio of 2:4.5 or 0.44:1. This is much less satisfactory. It means that for every pound that the company will have to pay, it only has ready access to 44p. This is not necessarily as dangerous as it may seem at first sight, however. If the company can rely on selling a lot of stock quickly it will be able to pay the electricity bill. Similarly the company may have an arrangement with its bank for an overdraft which will see it through the temporary crisis of the payment of the electricity bill.

A company which is in the position of the one illustrated here is in danger of overtrading. This occurs where a company has insufficient working capital (i.e., net current assets). As it pays its bills it may be unable to replace its stock which obviously means that it cannot continue to be profitable and solvent in the future. The solution to this problem may be for the company to acquire more working capital, either by retaining more profits in the business, by acquiring further investment or by increasing the size of its long-term borrowing. (In our example the last of these is likely to be a real possibility in view of the large amount of fixed assets and the small amount of borrowing.) The fact that not all companies can in practice do any of these things is the reason for a very high proportion of business failures.

15.11 Profitability

The bottom line profit figure is found in the profit and loss account. In our example above, the profit is £43,000 before tax and £31,000 after. The proprietor of the business will want to know whether this figure is satisfactory or not. There is no simple answer to this, not least because different people have different expectations and so are more or less easily satisfied. The most important step to take may be to compare with previous years and to compare with other similar business (this is more easily done with large companies as the published accounts of small and medium-sized companies give much less information). However, ratios can help here as with solvency.

15.11.1 Investment

An investor or potential investor will be interested in the whole of the company's financial situation. He will be particularly interested in what return on capital he can expect (i.e., in how much income will be generated by his investment). One simple calculation which may assist in judging this is the 'return on capital employed'. This is the net profit (before tax, dividends and any interest paid) expressed as a percentage of the company capital (including debentures and other long-term loans); in our example this is 43,000/412,500 × 100 = 10.42%. This figure should be judged against previous years' profits and if possible against other similar companies. If the shareholders are also directors of the company, they might wish to treat any directors' fees as part of the return on capital if they exceed what the directors regard as a fair return for their labour.

An alternative to the return on capital calculation is to calculate earnings per share. In our example assume that there are 10,000 shares, the earnings per share would then be 31,000/10,000 = £3.1 per share (it is usual to deduct tax in this calculation). This information is often given in relation to companies quoted on the stock exchange. Similarly in relation to such companies a price/earnings (or P/E) ratio can be calculated. This compares the market price of the share (on the Stock Exchange) with the earnings per share. A high P/E ratio shows that the stock market has confidence in the company as its shares are valuable despite low earnings. It is not possible to calculate a P/E ratio for a private or unquoted public company as there is no market price for their shares.

15.11.2 Efficiency ratios

These are ratios which are mainly calculated so that the management of the company and other interested parties can calculate how efficient the profit-making process of the company is. The return on capital employed (see **15.11.1**) is a good indicator of the company's general efficiency in making money.

Another useful ratio is the net profit percentage. This expresses trading profit (before deduction of tax and interest payments) as a percentage of sales. In our example this is 43,000/200,000 × 100 = 21.5%. This should be compared with other businesses and with previous years. Whether 21.5% is a good profit margin depends on the nature of the business in question.

online resource centre

For further resources and online chapters please visit the Online Resource Centre at www.oxfordtextbooks.co.uk/orc/business13_14/.

16

Public companies

This chapter covers the following topics:

16.1 Introduction

As we have seen from **Chapter 7**, it is possible to create three different types of company:

(a) a company limited by shares;

(b) a company limited by guarantee; and

(c) an unlimited company.

We considered the key elements of these three different types of company in **Chapter 7**. It is possible to incorporate all three types of company as a 'private company' but only companies limited by shares can be 'public companies'.

The differences between the two types of company are important and we will consider them briefly in this chapter. In addition, we will look at the rules for re-registering a private company as a public company and vice versa.

We will also briefly consider the concept of listing of shares of a public company with the United Kingdom Listing Authority (UKLA) and the admission of shares to trading on the Stock Exchange.

Although the most well-known companies in the country will (with a few exceptions) be public listed companies they represent a tiny minority of the total number of companies registered at the Companies' Registry. In very simple terms, there are over 2.5 million companies registered in Great Britain, of which around 12,000 are public. Also, being a public company does not automatically mean the company is listed. This is a common misconception. Only a public company which has been successful in gaining a listing and whose shares have been admitted to trading is referred to in practice as a 'listed company'.

16.2 The distinguishing features of a public company

16.2.1 Definition

A public company is defined by s. 4(2) CA 2006 as a company whose certificate of incorporation states that it is public (see **16.2.2.2** below for further discussion).

16.2.2 The differences between public and private companies

The following is a non-exhaustive list of some of the differences between public and private companies.

16.2.2.1 Name

The name of a public company must end with the words 'Public Limited Company' or its equivalent. Equivalent for this purpose includes 'PLC' (although there is no requirement that these letters be capitalised) and, for Welsh companies, Cwmni Cyfyngedig Cyhoeddus (or CCC). The company will be a Welsh company if the company states in its memorandum that its registered office is to be in Wales.

16.2.2.2 The company's memorandum

As the memorandum is simply a registration document, expressing the wish of those setting up the company to be formed as one (s. 8 CA 2006), there is no difference between the memorandum of a public and private company. Instead, the registration document submitted pursuant to s. 9 will have to include a statement that the company should be public. If registration is successful, the fact that the certificate of incorporation states that the company is public will be sufficient evidence of the fact (s. 4(2) CA 2006). (This is in contrast to the situation under the 1985 Act where the memorandum had to include an additional clause stating that the company was to be a public company.)

16.2.2.3 The nominal value of the share capital

The nominal value of the public company's issued share capital must not be less than the 'authorised minimum' which is currently £50,000 (s. 763(1) CA 2006). When a public company allots shares, it is under an obligation to ensure that at least 25% of the nominal value of each of the shares issued (plus the whole amount of any premium on the shares) is paid on allotment (s. 586 CA 2006).

16.2.2.4 Number of members and officers

The 2006 Act permits single-member public companies (s. 7(1) CA 2006). (Previously, under the 1985 Act, all public companies had to have a minimum of two members.) However, in contrast to private companies, public companies must appoint at least two directors (s. 154(2) CA 2006). Also, public companies must have a suitably qualified secretary appointed (ss. 271 and 273 CA 2006).

16.2.2.5 The issue of shares or debentures

The principal advantage which a public company has over a private company is its ability to raise capital by offering shares or debentures to the public for cash or other consideration; private companies are prohibited from doing so (s. 755 CA 2006). Therefore, if a private company is proposing to make an offer to the public, a shareholder, creditor, or the Secretary of State may apply to the court for an order restraining it from such action (s. 757 CA 2006). However, if the offer has already been made, a shareholder, creditor, or the Secretary of State may apply to the court for an order that the company be re-registered as a plc or, if this would be impractical, that the company be wound up (s. 758 CA 2006). Alternatively, the court may make a remedial order, which may involve the directors or the company (or both) having to buy back the shares issued (s. 759 CA 2006).

(Note that offers of shares to the public are governed by Pt VI of the Financial Services and Markets Act 2000. These require the publication of a prospectus approved by the Financial Conduct Authority (FCA) in any case where shares are to be 'offered to the public' within the terms of the legislation.)

16.2.2.6 Registration requirements

The procedure to be followed and the documents required to register a public company from scratch are the same as for a private company. Once the Registrar of Companies is satisfied that the documents comply with the registration requirements, a certificate of incorporation will be issued.

However, before the public company can do business or borrow money, the company must obtain from the Registrar a further certificate which will only be issued if the Registrar is satisfied that the company's share capital is adequate (a 'trading certificate') (s. 761 CA 2006). The procedure which the company must go through to get this trading certificate involves a director or the company secretary filing a statement of compliance with the Registrar. The declaration will state that the nominal value of the company's allotted share capital is at least equal to the authorised minimum (of £50,000). The company must also supply details of:

(a) the amount paid up on the allotted share capital;
(b) the amount of the preliminary expenses and details of who will meet them; and
(c) any amount or benefit paid to the company's promoters.

A company which does not obtain a trading certificate before it commences business can face some severe consequences (s. 767 CA 2006). If the company fails to meet its obligations in connection with a transaction entered into at a time when it does not have the additional certificate, the directors will be jointly and severally liable to indemnify the other parties to the transaction for any loss. Furthermore, both the company and its officers will be liable to a fine and if the company fails to obtain this certificate within one year of its registration, the court can wind the company up (s. 122 Insolvency Act 1986).

16.2.3 Special rules applicable to public companies

We saw in **16.2.2.5** that a public company can raise capital by offering shares to the public. This can give the company a much wider source of potential investors than is the case with a private company. The price of this is that to protect the public, public companies are subject to a number of restrictions which do not apply to private companies.

16.2.3.1 Payment for share capital

(a) The original subscribers to a public company's memorandum are required to pay cash for their shares.
(b) At least 25% of the nominal value and the whole of any premium on shares in a public company must be paid on allotment.
(c) A public company cannot accept an undertaking to do work or perform services as consideration for the allotment of shares. (In any event, it is unusual for a private company to seek such consideration for any allotment it may make.)
(d) A public company can accept the transfer of assets to the company as full or part payment for the allotment of shares but any undertaking to transfer those assets to the company must be performed within five years of the allotment. In addition, the company must take steps to satisfy itself that the value of the assets transferred to the company is accurate by obtaining an expert's valuation and report.

16.2.3.2 Pre-emption rights on the allotment of shares

A public company, unlike a private company, cannot make a general exclusion of the statutory pre-emption rights set out in s. 561 CA 2006 by a provision in its articles. However, in respect of specified allotments where the directors are authorised to make those allotments, a public company (like a private company) can disapply these pre-emption rights by passing a special resolution or through a provision in its articles (ss. 570 and 571 CA 2006).

16.2.3.3 Serious loss of capital

The directors of a public company are under an obligation to convene an extraordinary general meeting (EGM) if the company's net assets are 50% or less of its called-up share capital. The meeting must be convened within 28 days of one of the directors becoming aware of this fact and it must be held within 56 days. Obviously, the purpose of the meeting is for the problem to be considered, but the governing provision (s. 656 CA 2006) does not require the directors to take any definite steps to remedy the position.

16.2.3.4 Purchase by a public company of its own shares

Public companies, like private companies, can buy back their own shares and issue redeemable shares. However, only private companies can use capital to purchase or redeem shares (s. 709 CA 2006).

(In addition, the tax rules which allow a shareholder whose shares have been bought by the company to treat the purchase as a disposal for capital gains tax purposes, rather than the receipt of a distribution attracting income tax, only apply to the shares in unquoted companies. It should, however, be remembered that a public company will not necessarily have a listing on the Stock Exchange.)

16.2.3.5 Financial assistance for the acquisition of shares and loans to directors

The rules prohibiting companies from providing financial assistance for the purchase of their own shares now only apply to public companies (s. 678 CA 2006). As has been the case in the past, if this situation could impede a proposed transaction, the answer may be to re-register the company as private to avoid the prohibition (see **16.2.4**).

16.2.3.6 Loans to directors

Whilst loans to directors by all types of company will require shareholders' approval by ordinary resolution (subject to a number of exceptions), only quasi-loans to, and credit transactions with, directors of public companies need similar shareholders' approval (ss. 197–214 CA 2006).

16.2.3.7 Distribution of profits

In addition to the general rules restricting the funds from which companies can make distributions, s. 831 CA 2006 imposes an extra condition on a public company before it can make a distribution as follows:

(a) Its net assets must not be less than the aggregate of its called-up share capital and undistributable reserves.

(b) The distribution itself must not reduce the net assets to less than the above aggregate.

The undistributable reserves are:

(a) Its share premium account (which will reflect any premium paid to the company by shareholders for their shares).

(b) Its capital redemption reserve (which will have been created if any buy-back of shares has occurred).

(c) The amount by which its accumulated, unrealised profits exceed its accumulated, unrealised losses (on the basis that only realised sums are relevant in the context of distributions).

(d) Any other reserve it is prevented from distributing, either by statute or its articles.

If this prohibition applies and the company wishes to continue to make a distribution, the usual approach is to reduce the share capital, such that the aggregate is then less than the net assets.

16.2.3.8 Accounting requirements

The provisions which permit 'small' and 'medium-sized' companies to prepare and file less detailed accounts with the Registrar of Companies do not apply to public companies. (See **Chapter 15** for further details.)

16.2.3.9 Written resolutions

The ability of the members of private companies to take decisions by written resolutions rather than passing resolutions at general meetings does not extend to public companies (s. 288 CA 2006).

16.2.3.10 Annual general meetings

In contrast to private companies, the Companies Act 2006 continues to require public companies to hold AGMs (s. 336 CA 2006) and public companies are likely to continue to use these as an opportunity to fulfil their statutory obligations to lay audited accounts before a general meeting (s. 437 CA 2006) and to re-appoint auditors annually (s. 489 CA 2006).

16.2.4 Re-registration of a private company to a public company and vice versa

Given the various special rules to which public companies are subject, promoters of a company are unlikely to want to incorporate their company as a public company unless they intend to issue securities in the company to the public within the foreseeable future. However, many companies start life as private companies and are then converted into public companies so that they can be listed and have their shares traded on the Stock Exchange. The reasons why a company might do this are explained in 16.3.2. Equally, although perhaps less frequently, the shareholders and/or directors of a public company may decide to convert the company into a private company. They may do so for a variety of reasons, for example:

(a) To avoid the prohibition on financial assistance by public companies.

(b) Where the board has decided that the company's securities should no longer be in public hands. (Normally because of the wish to assume a greater control over the company without reference to external investors. This is often referred to as a 'public to private' deal.)

(c) After a successful takeover, where the purchaser of the shares in the takeover target wants the target to continue to operate as a wholly-owned private subsidiary.

16.2.4.1 Re-registration of a private company as a public company

The procedure which the private company will have to go through in order to re-register as a public company is set out in ss. 90–96 CA 2006. The company cannot be re-registered unless it satisfies the various requirements in relation to share capital to which public companies are subject (as explained above).

Provided the requirements with regard to share capital are satisfied, the company must pass a special resolution which:

(a) states that the company should be re-registered as a public company;

and

(b) alters the company's articles to meet the company's new circumstances (by, for example, removing restrictions on transferability).

Once the resolution has been passed an application for re-registration has to be submitted to the Registrar of Companies with:

(a) a printed copy of the company's articles in their altered form;

(b) a copy of the special resolution;

(c) a copy of a statement in writing by the company's auditors confirming that the company's net assets are not less than the combined total of its called-up share capital and distributable reserves (this written statement should relate to a balance sheet prepared for a date not more than seven months before the date the company has made its application for re-registration);

(d) a copy of the balance sheet on which the auditors based their written statement referred to in (c) above together with an unqualified report on the balance sheet by the company's auditors;

(e) certain reports and statutory declarations where shares have been allotted for non-cash consideration since the date of the balance sheet;

(f) confirmation of the details of the proposed secretary where the company does not have a secretary at the time (s. 94(1)(b) CA 2006);

and

(g) a fee of £20 (or £50 if same-day registration is required).

Once the Registrar of Companies is satisfied with these papers, a certificate will be issued confirming that the company has been re-registered as a public limited company (s. 96 CA 2006). The change to the company's articles and name also take effect as a result.

16.2.4.2 Re-registration of a public company as a private company

It is easier for a public company to be re-registered as a private company than the other way round for the reason that there are no specific criteria for private companies to fulfil (with the exception of having at least one director and one shareholder). Section 97 CA 2006 stipulates that a company must pass a special resolution by which it:

(a) resolves to re-register as a private company;

(b) removes the words 'public limited company' (or their equivalent) from its name and replaces them with 'limited'; and

(c) makes any other alterations to the articles of the company to suit its new circumstances.

An application to re-register pursuant to s. 100 CA 2006 must be delivered to the Registrar, together with the special resolution and a printed copy of the altered articles.

Once the Registrar of Companies is satisfied with these papers, a certificate will be issued confirming that the company has been re-registered as a private limited company (s. 101 CA 2006). The change to the company's articles and name also take effect as a result.

One consequence of a public company re-registering as a private company is that its securities may be less easily transferred. Therefore, protection is given to minority shareholders by s. 98 in case they object to this change in the status of the company. Minority shareholders have the right to apply to the court within 28 days of the special resolution being passed to have the resolution cancelled. Such an application for cancellation can only be made by:

(a) shareholders holding not less than 5% of the nominal value of the company's issued share capital (or for any class of the share capital, if there is more than one); or

(b) not less than 50 of the company's members.

The application for cancellation can only be made by a person who has not consented to or voted in favour of the resolution and the court can make an order either cancelling or confirming the resolution on such terms and conditions as it thinks fit (which could, for example, include ordering that the company should buy the shares of the dissentient member or members).

Re-registering a private company as a public company is always a voluntary act. However, in two circumstances, a public company can be compulsorily re-registered as a private company:

(a) If the court makes an order confirming a reduction of capital of a public company which results in the nominal value of the company's allotted share capital falling below the authorised minimum, the company ceases to be a public company. In these circumstances, the court can make an order to the effect that the company will be re-registered as a private company (making consequential amendments to the memorandum and articles of the company) which will avoid the necessity for the company to pass a special resolution to re-register.

(b) The cancellation by a public company of shares (in very specific circumstances) will lead to the company having to apply to be re-registered as a private company if the cancellation reduces the company's allotted share capital below the authorised minimum.

16.3 Seeking and maintaining a listing

16.3.1 Introduction

In this section, we will look very briefly at the advantages and disadvantages of obtaining a listing and the requirements for seeking and maintaining that listing. It is not our intention to go into this area in detail but merely to outline the key issues. We have used the expression 'a listing' as a generic expression for obtaining a listing of a company with the UK Listing Authority (UKLA) and having its shares admitted to trading on the Stock Exchange. When its shares have been admitted to the Stock Exchange, which is an international market for buying and selling shares, those who trade shares ('brokers') will quote prices at which they will buy and sell shares of that company. Thus, a listed company may also be referred to as a 'quoted' company, i.e., it is 'quoted' on the Stock Exchange. Also, 'quoted company' has a specific meaning for the purposes of the 2006 Act; see s. 385.

Readers who wish to consider the issue of listing in greater detail may wish to start by accessing the FCA's website (www.fca.org.uk), where pages relevant to the UKLA can be found.

16.3.2 The advantages and disadvantages of a listing

It will take a great deal of time for the officers of the company (and their advisers) to seek and maintain a listing. It is, therefore, an expensive exercise. While there may be a number of advantages to the company being listed, the company will have to accept the imposition of restrictions over and above those imposed on it by the Companies Acts and other legislation which affects every company. The key to understanding the need for these restrictions to be imposed is to appreciate that the principal advantage to a company of being listed is that its shares are more easily marketed and that it therefore has greater access to capital, part of which usually involves an increase in the number of shareholders. Therefore, the company has the obligation to make public information relating to its current performance and future prospects so as to give the company's current and potential future shareholders adequate information on which to base their decisions on how to deal in the company's shares.

While improved marketability (in the sense that all the shares, including minority holdings, will be freely tradable on a market which is open to a wide range of potential investors) is the principal advantage of the company being listed, it is not the only advantage. The mere fact of being a listed company may improve the status of the company within the market in which it operates. Having its shares quoted on the Stock Exchange may provide a company with a future source of finance as it can issue new shares to raise additional funds rather than borrow money from a bank. Should the company wish to grow by means of acquisitions, it may find that its ability to offer its quoted shares as full or part payment of the purchase price for the company it is acquiring is an attractive and cost-efficient alternative to borrowing money or using its own cash reserves.

While a listing can be attractive to an acquisitive company, it can also create problems for a company which could be the target of a takeover itself. Such a company could find that a potential bidder is able to acquire a stake in it through the open market, although there are a number of mechanisms in place to ensure that a company is aware if it is the target for a potential bid. Another potential disadvantage, particularly if the company seeking the listing has traditionally been run by a small group of directors/shareholders, is that they will find their activities become the subject of much closer scrutiny by both their shareholders and other interested parties (both potential investors and the press) following the listing. Since the price of a company's shares will depend on the market's view of their value, the price can fluctuate, sometimes dramatically, in response to both good and bad news about the company. To prevent people with inside information about the company's activities taking advantage of that knowledge, there are various prohibitions in place to prevent 'insiders' using information for their own benefit which is not freely available.

16.3.3 Regulations governing an application for a listing

When a company wishes to seek a listing, it must follow an application procedure and satisfy admission requirements set out in the Listing Rules. These Rules are published by the Financial Conduct Authority (acting as the UKLA). The Listing Rules set out the conditions which a company must meet if it is to be considered for listing. They also require the publication of a prospectus, which document must comply with the Prospectus Rules. In parallel with this process, the company also has to seek admission for its shares to be admitted to trading on the London Stock Exchange, and must comply with the latter's Admission and Disclosure Standards. If the company is able to satisfy all these requirements, it can be admitted to the Senior Equity Market in London, which is known as the Official List.

(There is a secondary market, open to smaller companies, called the Alternative Investment Market. We shall not look further at the rules relating to companies quoted on this market.)

To be admitted to listing, the company must be registered as a public company and, normally, it must intend to place on the market shares which are expected to have a market value of £700,000 or more. The company will not be admitted (save in exceptional circumstances) if it has not published or filed accounts covering the three years preceding the application for listing, and the company must have produced by independent accountants a report covering the three preceding years.

As the intention behind a listing is to create a market in shares in the company, any restrictions on transfer which are contained within the company's articles must be removed.

The directors must obviously consider that the company is financially viable and therefore a further condition for admission is that they must be satisfied that the company's working capital is sufficient. This admission requirement is satisfied by the sponsor sending a letter to the UKLA stating that the directors have made careful enquiries to satisfy themselves and the sponsor that the working capital is indeed adequate. The final principal admission requirement is that it must be intended that at least 25% of any class of shares will be in the hands of the public as defined by the Listing Rules.

The Prospectus Rules require a range of information to be published in a prospectus which is made available to potential investors. The purpose of this document is to provide potential investors with comprehensive information on the company seeking to be listed, to allow them to make an informed decision on whether or not to invest. Should information in the prospectus prove to be misleading, false, or deceptive, both civil and criminal liability can arise under the Financial Services and Markets Act 2000, as well as liability in contract and tort. The detail of this liability is beyond the scope of this book.

16.3.4 Methods of listing

If the securities do not need to be marketed to new investors (i.e., the company's shares are already sufficiently within the hands of the public and it does not want, as part of the listing, to issue new shares to new investors), the company can become listed by way of an 'introduction'. Effectively, its existing share capital is 'introduced' to the market by the sponsor. However, if the shares need to be marketed, admission can be achieved by any of the methods set out below.

(a) An *offer for sale* under which securities already in issue or allotted are offered to the public at large. This will entail making application forms available to the public who will complete and return them, paying the specified fixed price for the shares.

(b) An *offer for subscription* under which securities not yet in issue or allotted are offered to the public at large. The same procedures as in (a) will be followed.

(c) A *placing*. In this case, the company's shares will not be offered to the public generally; rather they will be offered to clients of the sponsor.

(d) An *intermediaries offer*. This involves securities being allocated to 'intermediaries' (for example, Stock Exchange member firms) who will in turn allocate the securities to their own clients.

16.3.5 Continuing obligations after a listing has been achieved

A company, once listed, is subject to a range of continuing obligations. These continuing obligations are imposed on listed companies primarily by the Listing Rules and the Disclosure and Transparency Rules. It is beyond the scope of this text to consider the detail of these, however, their purpose is simply understood—to maintain a flow of relevant and up-to-date information to shareholders and the market. This is intended to ensure a fair and orderly market in the listed company's shares.

Companies considering a listing should recognise that after the listing there will be a far greater flow of information about the company into the public domain. In turn, the company must set up systems to enable it to meet its continuing obligations. Finally, it may find itself consulting its professional advisers on a regular basis about what it should do to meet these obligations.

online resource centre

For further resources and online chapters please visit the Online Resource Centre at www.oxfordtextbooks.co.uk/orc/business13_14/.

Taxation

17

Income tax: sole traders and partnerships

This chapter covers the following topics:

17.1 Basic system

17.1.1 Introduction

The basic provisions of income tax are set out in the Income Tax Act (ITA) 2007. Individual taxpayers pay tax on their total taxable income for a particular tax year, that is, the total income received in that year less any relevant allowances, deductions, and reliefs, as provided for by legislation. The tax year runs from 6 April to the following 5 April and liability for income tax will attach to a particular tax year.

EXAMPLE

Income earned in September 2012 falls within the tax year 2012–2013 (i.e., 6 April 2012–5 April 2013), so will form part of the taxpayer's income tax liability for that tax year. Income earned in May 2013, by contrast, falls in the next following tax year, so will fall into the 2013 –2014 year of assessment for income tax purposes.

Income can come from a variety of sources. However, perhaps the most common are:

(a) Income from employment, i.e., a salary.
(b) Income from a trade or profession.
(c) Interest on deposits or savings.
(d) Dividend payments on shareholdings.
(e) Rental income.

As such, all sources of income earned in a relevant tax year need to be aggregated to form an accurate picture of a taxpayer's income tax liability for that year. To this end taxpayers are required to provide Her Majesty's Revenue and Customs (HMRC) with details of all income and expenditure in a relevant tax year, and hence their total taxable income, by completing a tax return following the end of that tax year.

EXAMPLE

Clive is an architect. His main source of income is his drawings as a partner in an architects' practice. His other sources of income are:

(a) Rent he receives from two properties he leases out.

(b) Interest on various savings accounts he holds.

(c) Dividends from shareholdings he has in a number of companies.

Therefore, in any particular tax year, Clive's income tax liability will be based upon the aggregate income from all these sources, which falls within that tax year.

In this chapter, however, we are specifically concerned with income earned from a trade or profession.

17.1.2 Income tax rates

Tax is payable at rates set in the annual Budget. For 2013/14, income tax rates are:

Basic — 20% (payable on *the first* £32,010 of taxable income).

Higher — 40% (payable on amounts *in excess of* £32,010 and *up to* £150,000 of taxable income).

Additional — 45% (payable on amounts in excess of £150,000 of taxable income).

Most individuals receive a personal allowance, that is, an income threshold which must be exceeded before income tax is payable, which is also set in the annual Budget. For the current tax year , this is £9,440 . The personal allowance for those earning over £100,000 is reduced by £1 for every £2 earned above £100,000.

EXAMPLE

Chris; Tax Year 2013/14:	£
Income	92,000
Less Personal allowance	9,440
Taxable income	82,560
Tax payable:	
£32,010 @ 20%	6,402
£50,550 (£82,560 –£32,010) @ 40%	20,220
Total income tax:	26,622

17.2 Taxable profits from a business

17.2.1 Introduction

The owner(s) of an unincorporated business are taxed on the profits made by their business, which will form part of their individual taxable income. Thus, money earned by the business is treated as money earned by the relevant sole trader or partners. (Compare this to the tax treatment of a company, where the company is a separate taxable person from those who own and manage it. See **Chapter 18** for more details.)

Taxable profits are income receipts generated from trading activities *less* deductible expenditure incurred by the business plus any other sums deductible under tax legislation (e.g., capital allowances—see **Chapter 21**).

EXAMPLE

	£	£
Income receipts		375,000
less		
Deductible expenditure	220,000	
Capital allowances	15,000	
		235,000
Taxable profits		140,000

Where total deductions exceed income, this creates a loss for tax purposes (see **17.4**).

EXAMPLE

	£
Income receipts	128,000
Deductible expenditure	163,000
Loss	(35,000)

17.2.2 Income receipts

Income receipts are usually recurrent or capable of recurrence, and must be distinguished from capital receipts, which do not attract income tax. In general, receipts from the sale of stock are income; receipts from the sale of fixed assets are capital. Also, receipts in respect of labour costs, time spent, or professional advice would be treated as income.

Take a bathroom fittings shop as an example. The fittings that are sold are stock, whilst the shop and delivery vehicles are fixed, capital assets. Sales of fittings will create income receipts; a sale of the shop or a delivery vehicle would create a capital receipt. Contrast this with a car dealership where the vehicles for sale are its stock-in-trade and money received from their sale will be treated as income for tax purposes.

The specific rules by which trading income is ascertained and charged to income tax are contained in the Income Tax (Trading and Other Income) Act (ITTOIA) 2005.

17.2.3 Deductible expenditure

17.2.3.1 Nature of deductible expenditure

To be deductible for income tax purposes, expenditure must be:

—of an income rather than a capital nature; and

—wholly and exclusively laid out or expended for the purposes of the business (s. 34 ITTOIA 2005).

Some common examples of deductible expenditure are:

(a) rent for leasehold premises;

(b) salaries paid to employees;

(c) utilities (electricity, gas, telecommunications, etc.);

(d) rates/council tax;

(e) purchases of stock for re-sale;

(f) advertising costs;

(g) business stationery.

17.2.3.2 Nature of non-deductible expenditure

If a business expense is excessively large and so also partly represents a gift, it will not be deductible as it is not wholly for the purposes of the business. Similarly, expenditure on something partly connected with the business and partly not so connected (e.g., there is an element of personal enjoyment) will not be deductible, as it is not exclusively for the purposes of the business.

Part 2, Chapter 4 ITTOIA lists specific types of non-deductible expenditure. Many of these would be non-deductible anyway because they are not of an income nature, or not wholly and exclusively incurred for the purposes of the business. Among other things, s. 35 ITTOIA prohibits the deduction of provisions for bad debts; and most business entertainment expenses are non-deductible under s.45 ITTOIA.

17.2.3.3 Capital allowances

Where a business buys certain types of capital assets, capital allowances may also be available to deduct from income receipts. The cost of the capital asset is not deductible, as it is not expenditure of an income nature. However, a designated percentage of the purchase price—effectively deemed depreciation—may be deductible annually from income receipts. (See **Chapter 21** for further details and examples.)

17.2.4 Accounting bases

In calculating profits, a business must be consistent in allocating receipts and expenses to one accounting period or to a later period. If it fails to do so, its accounts are useless to the business for the purposes of comparison. In addition, the business could manipulate its receipts and expenses to avoid tax.

Almost all businesses produce annual final accounts. These show its profits—calculated according to normal accountancy practice—and how they are allocated to the proprietor(s). These accounts may not, however, be wholly suitable for tax purposes as often there are special tax rules which define what is taxable as income and what is deductible as an expense. (See s. 25 ITTOIA for a statement to this effect.)

For tax purposes, accounts have to be agreed with the Inland Revenue and must give a true and fair view of profits. These accounts do not have to be fully audited. However, certain fundamentals such as creditors, debtors, work-in-progress, and stock must feature in them.

17.3 The basis of assessment: the tax year

Liability to tax is calculated by reference to income and expenditure in a tax year. We have already seen that the tax year runs from 6 April to the following 5 April. Most businesses work on a 12-month accounting period, which need not, however, correspond with the tax year. Because accounting periods and tax years may not correspond, there are rules for allocating the profits of accounting periods to tax years. This system is known as the current year basis and is discussed below. (The legislative basis for these rules is found in Pt 2, Chapter 15 ITTOIA).

17.3.1 Current year basis

In calculating the taxable income for a specific tax year, HMRC treats profits of an unincorporated business for the accounting period *ending* in that tax year as the income for that tax year.

The dates for payment of tax under the system are 31 January in the year of assessment, 31 July following the year of assessment and 31 January following the year of assessment. The first two instalments are estimated (in effect, payments on account based on the previous year's tax liability). The third will either be a balancing payment or rebate, depending whether tax had been over- or under-estimated, calculated once full details of actual profits have been received by HMRC. (It should be remembered that tax returns received by HMRC are always historical; either a paper return is submitted by 31 October after the end of the tax year in question or the following 31 January, if submission is made online.)

EXAMPLES

Jones & Co (a partnership)

Accounting period:	1 January to 31 December
Tax year 2011/12:	6 April 2011 to 5 April 2012
Accounting period *ending* in the tax year 2011/12:	1 January 2011 to 31 December 2011

The tax liability of the partners for the tax year 2011/12 will be based on profits to the year-end 31 December 2011.

James Currie (a sole trader)

Accounting period:	1 May to 30 April
Tax year 2011/12:	6 April 2011 to 5 April 2012
Accounting period *ending* in the tax year 2011/12:	1 May 2010 to 30 April 2011

The tax liability of James for the tax year 2011/12 will be based on profits to the year-end 30 April 2011.

In both examples, tax will be payable on 31 January 2012 and 31 July 2012 (estimated according to previous year's profits) and any adjustment will be due on 31 January 2013 once actual profits are known by HMRC (as well as an estimated payment on account being made in respect of the next tax year).

17.3.2 Opening and closing year rules

17.3.2.1 Introduction

The current year basis above is modified when a business begins trading or ceases to trade. Then, the opening and the closing year rules apply.

17.3.2.2 Opening year rules

The opening year rules apply to the first two tax years of the business. They are as follows:

Year of commencement	Profits from date business commenced to following 5 April (i.e., the end of the first tax year of the business).
Second year	Profits of first 12 months of trade *or* the current year basis when an accounting period of at least 12 months ends in the tax year.
Third and subsequent years	Current year basis.

EXAMPLE

R Najran—Electrician

Date business commenced:	1 June 2009
First tax year for assessment:	2009/10
Accounting year end:	30 September
Relevant periods for assessment:	
First year (2009/10)	Profits from 1 June 2009 to 5 April 2010
Second year (2010/11)	Current year basis, i.e., profits from 1 October 2009 to 30 September 2010
Third year (2011/12)	Current year basis, i.e., profits from 1 October 2010 to 30 September 2011

If R Najran had chosen an accounting year end of 30 April, the relevant periods for assessment would have been:

First year (2009/10)	Profits from 1 June 2009 to 5 April 2010
Second year (2010/11)	First 12 months trading, i.e., profits from 1 June 2009 to 31 May 2010

Third year (2011/12)	Current year basis, i.e., profits from 1 May 2010 to 30 April 2011

Here, the relevant profit for the second year is the first 12 months of trading because the accounting date within that year of assessment (30 April 2010) is less than 12 months from the commencement of business.

The above example also shows that, unless an accounting period corresponds exactly with the tax year, some profits will be assessed twice in the first and second years of assessment. Overlap relief operates in such circumstances (see ss. 204–207 ITTOIA), providing a credit to take account of such double assessment.

17.3.2.3 Closing year rules

When a business ceases there is a notional accounting period from the day after the end of the last accounting period to the date of cessation.

EXAMPLE

W Morrison—Consultancy

Date business ended:	31 December 2010
Final tax year for assessment:	2010/11
Accounting year end:	30 April
Relevant periods for assessment:	
2008/09	1 May 2007 to 30 April 2008
2009/10	1 May 2008 to 30 April 2009
2010/11	1 May 2009 to 31 December 2010

17.4 Losses under the income tax system

If a trader makes a trading loss (i.e., deductible expenses exceed income profits) during an accounting period, the tax assessment will be a 'nil' liability. In addition, tax relief will be available in respect of the loss as follows. (Note: the ITA is the relevant legislation; the ITTOIA does not deal with losses.)

17.4.1 Set-off against same year income

Under s. 64 ITA 2007, the taxpayer may elect to deduct the loss from any other taxable income in the year of assessment in which the loss was made. Where, as is usual, the loss-making period is partly in one tax year and partly in another, HMRC will, in practice, allow the whole of the loss to be set off against the income of the tax year in which that period ends.

If a loss is not fully relieved because (a) the other income of the year of the loss was insufficient; or (b) the taxpayer did not elect to take the relief, a similar election may be made in respect of the immediately preceding tax year, provided the taxpayer is still carrying on the same trade on a commercial basis.

Note that in both cases the loss may be set off against *any* of the taxpayer's income from whatever source. Any claim must be made in writing within 12 months of 31 January immediately following the year of assessment in which the loss arose.

Special rules apply to prevent relief under s. 64 being given where the trade is not being carried on with a view to profit.

Trading losses can, in limited circumstances, be set against the taxpayer's capital gains in the tax year when the loss arises and in one following tax year under ss. 261B and 261C

Taxation of Chargeable Gains Act 1992. The relief only applies to such losses as have not been used up following a claim under s. 64.

17.4.2 Set-off against future income

Under s. 83 ITA 2007, a loss may be set against income from the same trade (but not from any other source) in future years (without time limit) to the extent that it has not been completely relieved under s. 64, either because no relief was claimed or because the income was insufficient. Relief is given by a deduction from the income of the next tax year in which there are profits, and then the year after that, and so on until the loss is completely relieved.

The following example demonstrates the operation of ss. 64 and 83.

EXAMPLE

Profits and losses of a trade made during accounting periods ending on 31 December:

2009	£50,000	profit
2010	£200,000	loss
2011	£60,000	profit
2012	£70,000	profit

In addition to his trade, the taxpayer has a part-time employment producing an income of £20,000 per annum throughout the period. If claims for relief under ss. 64 and 83 are made, the income tax position is as follows (personal allowances or other reliefs have been ignored for the purpose of the example):

	2009/10	2010/11	2011/12	2012/13
Trading income	50,000	nil	60,000	70,000
Employment income	20,000	20,000	20,000	20,000
	70,000	20,000	80,000	90,000
Losses available		200,000	110,000	50,000
Loss relief	70,000*	20,000*	60,000**	50,000**
Final income	nil	nil	20,000	40,000
	*s. 64	*s. 64	**s. 83	**s. 83

Note:

(a) The loss in the tax year 2010/11 was available to be set off against other profits being taxed in that year, or against the previous year's profits, under s. 64 ITA 2007. As there were unrelieved losses once this was done, the balance was carried forward and relief sought against later profits under s. 83.

(b) Full relief was not obtained until 2012/13 even though the loss was made in 2010.

(c) The deduction in 2011/12 was only £60,000 because s. 83 does not allow relief against income from other sources (NB, s. 83 ITA 2007).

17.4.3 Carry back of terminal losses

Section 89 ITA 2007 allows losses from the last year of a trade to be deducted from income from the same trade in the three years of assessment before the discontinuance, taking later years before earlier years. Relief under s. 64 will be available for the year of discontinuance.

If a business makes losses for a number of years before discontinuance there will be no loss relief unless the trader has other sources of income. Section 83 relief is unavailable since there will be no future profits. Section 89 will not operate in these circumstances, since the loss can only be carried back three years and those years will have had nil assessments because of the earlier losses.

17.4.4 Losses in early years of trade

Section 72 ITA 2007 allows losses made during the first four years of a trade to be set off against income of the three tax years before the loss, taking earlier years before later years. The loss can be deducted from all the income of those years from whatever source. If there is more than one income source, rules in s. 64 will be applied to deal with the order in which relief is given. The principal effect of s. 72 is to allow a sole trader who starts a trade to set losses off against income received before the business started. This provides an increased ability for start-up businesses to set off losses in their early years.

17.4.5 General

Where loss relief is obtained, the saving for the taxpayer is the amount of tax on the amount of the relief: a basic rate taxpayer would save £200 in tax on relieved losses of £1,000. Naturally, all the sections giving relief prevent double relief being claimed in respect of the same sum, e.g., if relief is claimed under s. 72 only the unrelieved balance, if any, may be carried forward under s. 83. Where relief is given by setting a loss off against income that has already been taxed (i.e., carry back), the relief is provided by a tax repayment by HMRC.

17.5 Income tax liability of partnerships

17.5.1 General

Discussion thus far has focused on the general income tax treatment of trading income. Some specific issues relating to partnerships now need to be considered (although the rules applicable if a partner dies or retires or joins the firm are considered instead in **Chapter 23**).

A partnership is not a separate legal person: it is a group of individuals. Each partner is taxed on his share of the total partnership profits or losses taking into account his personal reliefs and other sources of income. Thus, for *assessment* and *collection* of tax, each partner is treated as a notional sole trader. The relevant legislation is in Pt 9 ITTOIA.

17.5.2 Business expense or profit share?

Normal income tax principles are used to calculate the total partnership profits by ascertaining taxable receipts and deductible expenses. However, for a partnership, any payment made by the business *to a partner* is examined to determine whether it is a deductible expense or an allocation of taxable profit. The latter *cannot* reduce the taxable profit of the partnership.

The following items merit special attention:

(a) *Salary*

The tax treatment of a 'salary' payable to a 'partner' depends on whether HMRC regards the recipient as a true partner sharing in the profits in a particular, agreed way (this method of allocating profits is usually used to provide one partner with an agreed portion of profits in priority to the others) or whether the recipient is merely an employee in receipt of a salary who is described as a 'partner'. HMRC will consider all the facts and the terms of the partnership agreement entered into by the parties. The terms of the agreement are not conclusive (*Stekel v Ellice* [1973] 1 WLR 191). Where salary is an allocation of profit, it is not deductible from the firm's taxable profits. Where it is a true salary, it is deductible and will be assessed under the Income Tax (Earnings and Pensions) Act 2003, with tax being deducted at source under the PAYE procedure

(b) *Interest*

'Interest' payable to a partner will not be a deductible expense if it is payable on a partner's contribution of capital to the firm. Such a payment is regarded as part of the agreed method of allocating profits. However, if a partner makes a loan to the partnership, interest payable on the loan will normally be a deductible expense

(c) *Rent*

Where a partnership pays rent to a partner for the use of assets owned by the partner, the rent will be a deductible expense (unless it is excessive).

17.5.3 Mechanics of assessment—current year basis

Partners are assessed to tax on an individual basis rather than being jointly liable as with all other partnership liabilities (see 3.2).

Each partner must include his share of partnership profits in his tax return and is liable for the tax on that share but not that of any other partner. The partnership is required to submit a set of accounts and a tax return in respect of total partnership profits. Once these are agreed with HMRC, the final profit figure will be apportioned amongst the partners according to the profit-sharing ratio in force during the accounting period in question. The deadline for submission is 31 October for paper returns and 31 January for electronic returns, following the tax year of assessment. Thus, paper tax returns for the year 2011/12 would have been submitted by 31 October 2012 and online returns by 31 January 2013.

17.5.4 Losses of a partnership

When a partnership makes a loss, each partner can choose what type of relief to claim in respect of his share of the loss. Thus, some partners may claim relief under s. 64 ITA 2007 immediately; others may prefer to wait and claim relief under s. 83 ITA 1988.

17.5.5 National insurance

Partners, being self-employed, are liable to make Class 2 and Class 4 National Insurance contributions at a rate lower than the rate applicable to employees (but the benefits are correspondingly lower), and they are entitled to deduct one half of their contributions when calculating their income tax liability.

online resource centre

For further resources and online chapters please visit the Online Resource Centre at www.oxfordtextbooks.co.uk/orc/business13_14/.

18 The corporation tax system

This chapter covers the following topics:

18.1 Introduction

This chapter deals with the corporation tax system, which determines the tax liability of companies. The tax liabilities of those who invest in companies (whether by way of shares or debentures) are considered in **Chapter 20**. The inheritance tax and capital gains tax liabilities of shareholders are considered in **Chapter 22**. The principal statutes which deal with corporation tax are the Corporation Tax Act 2009 (CTA 2009) and the Corporation Tax Act 2010 (CTA 2010).

18.2 Calculation of profits

18.2.1 Profits

Companies pay corporation tax on their profits. 'Profits' means income and chargeable gains (s. 2(2) CTA 2009). The amount of profits on which corporation tax is payable is calculated according to steps set out in s. 4 CTA 2010. The first step is to calculate the amount in respect of which the company is chargeable to corporation tax on income. This is calculated according to various provisions in the Corporation Tax Acts, taking into account any reliefs available. Added to this figure is any amount in respect of chargeable gains (see s. 8 TCGA 1992), again taking into account any reliefs available. The sum of these two amounts produces the 'total profits' of the company (s. 4 CTA 2010). There may also be reliefs available on this figure. Having deducted any such reliefs, corporation tax is chargeable at the relevant rate on this final figure—the company's 'taxable total profits'.

EXAMPLE

Taking the steps above, a company's taxable total profits chargeable to corporation tax are calculated by:

(i) adding:

the amount chargeable to corporation tax on income after any applicable reliefs

plus

any amount in respect of chargeable gains after any applicable reliefs

which provides the 'total profits' of the company, then

(ii) deducting:

any amounts which can be relieved against the total profits

to find the final taxable total profits.

Note that the reliefs available against income or chargeable gains in (i) above will be reliefs that specifically reduce either the *income* or *chargeable gains* respectively, *before* calculation of the total profits. An example of a relief available *against* total profits (see (ii) above) is provided for in s. 189 CTA 2010, which allows a company to deduct certain qualifying charitable donations from total profits.

18.2.2 Income

The principal income on which most companies will be charged corporation tax will be trade profits (s. 35 CTA 2009). These must be calculated in accordance with generally accepted accounting practice, subject to any regulatory adjustments for corporation tax purposes (s. 46 CTA 2009). Part 3 of CTA 2009 contains specific rules applying to the calculation of trade profits, defining receipts and expenses, and allowing or restricting specific deductions to be made. It should be noted that, to be deductible for tax purposes:
—expenses must be incurred wholly and exclusively for the purposes of the trade; and
—losses must be connected with or arise out of the trade.

Companies may also be charged corporation tax on other forms of income, such as income from property, loan relationships, or various types of derivative contracts. CTA 2009 contains detailed rules on the calculation of profits in relation to these other forms of income.

Note that, unlike individuals, companies are not entitled to any personal allowance in calculating income.

18.2.3 Chargeable gains

Chargeable gains realised by companies are calculated according to general capital gains tax principles as set out in TCGA 1992 (see **Chapter 22**). However, there are certain key points to note:

(a) Companies are not entitled to the annual exemption.

(b) Most reliefs available to individuals are not available to companies, although companies can claim roll-over relief on the replacement of business assets.

(c) Companies do, however, receive an indexation allowance, which is *not* available to individuals and partnerships. (The removal of the allowance for these parties coincided with the reduction, introduced in the tax year 2008/09, of the capital gains tax rate for individuals and partnerships to 18%.)

18.2.3.1 Indexation allowance

When capital gains tax was originally introduced, no allowance was given for inflation. The result was that, in times of raging inflation, tax would be charged on 'gains' arising as a result of inflation, rather than as a result of a real increase in the asset's value. This unfairness was addressed by the introduction of an 'indexation allowance' which effectively removes inflationary gains from the charge to tax. The allowance is calculated by multiplying the initial and subsequent allowable expenditure by a decimal fraction produced by the following formula:

$$\frac{RD - RI}{RI}$$

where RD is the retail prices index for the month of disposal and RI is the retail prices index for the month in which the expenditure was incurred. (HMRC publishes tables containing the relevant retail price indices.) The resulting figure can then be deducted from the consideration for the disposal, together with any allowable expenditure, to reduce further the actual gain subject to tax.

For all disposals no capital gains tax is levied on gains arising in respect of periods of ownership prior to 31 March 1982. Effectively, companies are treated as having disposed of assets on 31 March 1982 and then immediately re-acquired them at their market value at that date.

18.2.3.2 Gains on appreciating assets and 'double taxation'

Retaining appreciating assets in a company can lead to an element of double taxation since, on a sale of the asset, the company pays tax (subject to any relief for replacement assets). The company's gain after tax may be reflected in an increase in the overall value of the company's assets because of the receipt of money from the sale of the asset. This may then cause the value of the shares in the company to increase, which could in turn result in a greater gain being realised (subject to exemptions and reliefs) on a disposal of shares by a shareholder.

18.2.4 Capital allowances

Companies are entitled to claim capital allowances at the same rates as individuals (see **Chapter 21**). Capital allowances of companies are treated as trading expenses of the accounting period in respect of which they are claimed and balancing charges are treated as trading receipts of that period. They should therefore be considered when calculating income for corporation tax purposes (see **18.2.2**).

18.3 Assessment

18.3.1 Basis of assessment

Corporation tax is calculated by reference to profits (see **18.2.1**) made in each accounting period of the company (s. 8 CTA 2009). An accounting period is normally 12 months ending with the company's accounting date—the date to which its accounts are made up. If the accounts are made up for a period of less than 12 months, then the accounting period is also less than 12 months; if for a longer period, special rules apply and the profits are divided on a time basis between two or more accounting periods, none of which may individually be longer than 12 months.

18.3.2 Basis of payment

Corporation tax is currently payable nine months after the end of the accounting period so that the date chosen does not affect the length of time between the end of the period and the date of payment. However, large companies—those with annual profits of not less than £1.5 million—are obliged to account for corporation tax on an instalment basis. Such instalments are payable on the 7th and 10th months during the accounting period being assessed, and on the 13th and 16th months thereafter.

EXAMPLE

Wolfe Industrials plc has an accounting reference date of 31 December. In relation to its accounting year ending on 31 December 2013 its corporation tax payments will be payable in July and October 2013 and January and April 2014.

Companies must comply with a 'pay and file' system. This requires companies to estimate their profits and assess their own tax liability, then submit a return together with accounts to substantiate it. Companies have up to 12 months from the end of each of their accounting periods to submit this return but must always satisfy their tax liabilities on the dates set out above. Where under- or over-payments of tax are made, interest (at rates set by statutory instrument) will be payable.

18.3.3 Rates of tax

18.3.3.1 Rates for financial year 2013/14

The rates of corporation tax for the year 2013/14 as determined by companies' profits are set out in the table below. They are announced by the Chancellor of the Exchequer in the annual Budget and legislated annually in the Finance Act. Although companies pay tax on the profits of their own accounting periods, the rates of tax are fixed for financial years, periods starting on 1 April and ending on the following 31 March. Therefore, the financial year 2014 (often shortened to 'FY14') runs from 1 April 2013 to 31 March 2014.

Rate	Company profits (£)
Small profits rate: 20%	0–300,000
Marginal relief applies	300,001–1,500,000
Main rate: 23%	1,500,001 or more

In the March 2013 Budget, it was announced that the main rate will be cut to 21% for the financial year beginning 1 April 2014, and then to 20% for the financial year beginning 1 April 2015. The latter reduction will create a unified 20% rate for all profits, simplifying the corporation tax system. The following paragraphs describe the way in which the current rates operate.

18.3.3.2 Main rate

For the financial year 2014, for companies with profits in excess of £1,500,000, the main rate is 23%. This is applied to the entire amount of the profits. A company with profits of £2,000,000 will therefore, before any reliefs are applied, be liable to pay corporation tax of £460,000.

Unless the company happens to make up its accounts to 31 March the profits are apportioned (on a time basis) between two financial years if different rates apply.

EXAMPLE

A company makes up its accounts to 31 December. Its profits for the accounting period ending on 31 December 2013 are £1,600,000—the rate of corporation tax for the financial year 2013 (1 April 2012–31 March 2013) was 24% and for the financial year 2014 (1 April 2013–31 March 2014) the rate is 23%. Corporation tax for the accounting period is therefore:

$$\frac{90}{365} \times 1{,}600{,}000 \times 24\% = £94{,}684$$

plus

$$\frac{275}{365} \times 1{,}600{,}000 \times 23\% = \underline{£277{,}260}$$

$$\underline{£371{,}944}$$

18.3.3.3 Small profits rate

Where a company's taxable profits are between £0 and £300,000, the rate of corporation tax for the financial year 2014 is 20%. This small profits rate is made under the provision of s. 18 CTA 2010. As with the main rate, the rate is applied to the total amount of profits within the band. A company with profits of £225,000 would therefore be liable, before any reliefs were applied, for corporation tax of £45,000.

18.3.3.4 Marginal relief

For those companies with taxable profits between £300.000 and £1,500,000, marginal relief is available under s. 19 CTA 2010. The effect of this is to ease the transition between the small profits and main rates.

The law provides that if taxable profits *including dividends* received fall within the band in which marginal relief applies, they should first be taxed at the main rate of 23%. The resulting liability is then reduced by marginal relief, as seen in the table below. (Should profits including dividends be £300,000 or less, or more than £1,500,000, then marginal relief is irrelevant and the normal rates apply.)

Profits including dividends (£)	Rate of tax
0–300,000	Small profits rate: 20%
300,001–1,500,000	Main rate: 23% *then* reduced by marginal relief
More than 1,500,000	Main rate: 23%

18.3.3.5 Calculation of marginal relief

Statutory formula

To establish the amount of marginal relief by which tax liability is to be reduced, the following statutory formula must be applied:

(M – P) × (I/P) × Statutory Fraction

Where:

M = Higher relevant maximum amount

P = Total profits including non-group dividends

I = Profits excluding non-group dividends

Statutory Fraction = 3/400 (these fractions are set each year by the Finance Act).

The figure resulting from application of the statutory formula should then be deducted from the figure resulting from the application of the main rate to the company's profits, to provide the amount of corporation tax payable.

Marginal tax rates

There is an alternative means of calculating the amount of corporation tax payable where marginal relief is given. It is possible, from the application of the statutory formula, to calculate an effective tax rate to be applied to the profits which fall within the marginal relief band. For the tax year commencing 1 April 2013, this rate is 23.75%, known as the marginal tax rate.

The following example shows application of both the formula and the marginal tax rate to a company's profits which fall within the marginal relief band. Note that the company in question has not received any profits by way of non-group dividends.

EXAMPLE

Clarke Knitwear Limited has total taxable profits of £600,000 for the accounting year.

£600,000 × 23% = £138,000

Marginal relief = (£1,500,000 – £600,000) × (600,000/600,000) × 3/400

= £6,750

Deducting the marginal relief from tax liability at the full rate (i.e., (£600,000 × 23% = £138,000) *less* (£6,750)) gives a figure of £131,250.

Applying the upper marginal rate:

£0–300,000 × 20% = £60,000

£300,000–600,000 × 23.75% = £71,250

Total tax = £131,250

Note how the application of the marginal rate produces the same result as application of the statutory formula.

18.3.3.6 Calculation of marginal relief where profits include dividends

Where a company's profits include dividends from another company the situation is more complex. These dividends are not actually taxable in the hands of the recipient company but do have an impact on taxable profits because they must be included in the company's profits total to determine the extent to which a company may benefit from marginal relief. This is why the statutory formula shown above makes a distinction between profits including and not including non-group dividends. The basic effect of the statutory formula is that the higher the proportion of total profits which is made up of dividends, the less marginal relief there is available for the actual profits taxed.

For the purposes of the formula, dividends do not include dividends paid from another company in the same group as the recipient. It is beyond the scope of this book to examine what constitutes a 'group', suffice it to say that a common example of a payment within a group would be from a wholly-owned subsidiary to its parent. The following example shows the effect which dividends can have on the application of marginal relief.

EXAMPLE

In the financial year 2014, Fallon Limited has trading profits of £300,000 and gross dividend receipts (non-group) of £200,000. Although such dividends will not be taxed in the hands of Fallon Limited, when they are added to the trading profit figure the total amount is £500,000 which means that the trading profit will be subject to the main rate of 23% then reduced by marginal relief.

Applying the statutory formula, the corporation tax liability will be £64,500. This is because tax at 23% on the trading profits of £300,000 is £69,000 and marginal relief reduces this by £4,500 to £64,500. The amount of marginal relief is calculated as follows:

	£
(1,500,000 – 500,000) × 300,000/500,000	= 600,000
600,000 × 3/400	= 4,500

It will be noted that, had the company only had its trading profits of £300,000 in that year, then the small profits rate would have been payable: 20% of £300,000 = £60,000. It can therefore be seen that dividends, although not actually taxable, have a considerable impact on the company's tax liability.

18.4 Loss relief

18.4.1 Introduction

Trading losses of companies are relieved in a number of ways; the scheme of the legislation is very similar to the one which applies for income tax (see **Chapter 17**).

18.4.2 Relief for trade losses against total profits

A company may set off a loss made during an accounting period against any profits of the same accounting period (s. 37 CTA 2010). The claim for relief must be made within two years of the end of the accounting period in which the loss was made. As corporation tax 'profits' include both income and chargeable gains, a company may set an income loss (from a trade) against a chargeable gain. If the loss is not entirely relieved by setting it off against profits of the same accounting period, the company may also make a claim for the unrelieved losses to be set against profits (including chargeable gains) of previous accounting periods so far as they fall wholly or partly within the 12 month period ending immediately before the loss-making period began. A loss cannot be carried back under this provision to a period when the company was not carrying on the business and there are no corporation tax provisions corresponding with s. 72 ITA 2007 (income tax loss relief for the early years of a new trade—see **17.4.4**).

18.4.3 Carry forward

Under s. 45 CTA 2010, a company can carry forward a trading loss and use it to reduce profits derived from the same trade in future accounting periods. This relief applies to trading profits only; it does not apply to chargeable gains. (However, note that capital losses may be carried forward and offset against future capital gains (see **18.4.5**).) The relief given will be for that part of the trading loss for which no relief has been claimed under s. 37 (see **18.4.2**) or surrendered as group relief (see **18.4.6**). No claim needs to be made for trading losses to be carried forward; it will happen automatically provided the company's tax return is completed appropriately.

EXAMPLE

To illustrate the application of ss. 37 and 45 CTA 2010, the company has an accounting period corresponding with calendar years and its profits and losses are as follows:

	Trade I	Trade II	Chargeable Gains
	£	£	£
2008	75,000	25,000	Nil
2009	100,000	50,000	Nil
2010	100,000	50,000	20,000
2011	(300,000) loss	50,000	30,000
2012	100,000	50,000	10,000
2013	200,000	50,000	Nil

The £300,000 loss made in Trade I in 2011 can be used to relieve fully the Trade II profits and chargeable gains for that year by making a claim under s. 37 CTA 2010. This leaves losses of £220,000. These can be carried back against the total profits (income and chargeable gains) for 2010 of £170,000, again by making a claim under s. 37 CTA 2010). This leaves losses of £50,000.

These will be carried forward against the profits for Trade I in 2012 under s. 45 CTA 2010. Note that these may not be applied against the profits for Trade II or the chargeable gains.

18.4.4 Tactical considerations

In deciding which method of relief to use, the company will wish to ensure, so far as possible, that the maximum tax saving is achieved (e.g., by setting the loss against those profits which are subject to tax at 23% rather than any lower rate). However, the cash flow problem of having to meet a tax bill at a time when the cash reserves may be low often means it is preferable not to carry forward the relief but to make a claim under s. 37 so that they can be used as soon as possible.

The possibility of carrying forward losses is lost in certain cases where there are substantial changes in both the ownership of the company and in the nature of its trade. This is an anti-avoidance provision designed to prevent the purchase of a company simply to take advantage of its tax losses.

18.4.5 Capital losses

If a company makes a capital loss (calculated in the same way as a chargeable gain), it may be set off against chargeable gains of the same accounting period and, if unrelieved, may be carried forward and set off against chargeable gains of later accounting periods (s. 8 TCGA 1992). Although trading losses may be set off against chargeable gains under s. 37 CTA 2010, there are no provisions allowing capital losses to be set off against income profits. Indexation allowances (see **18.2.3.1**) may operate to reduce losses. Where this occurs, note that the indexation allowance can only be used to the extent that it extinguishes any gain. It cannot create or increase losses.

EXAMPLE

If A disposes of an asset for £60,000 and the base cost for that asset is £45,000, A is left with a gain of £15,000. If the base cost also attracted an indexation allowance of £20,000, this could be used to wipe out the gain, but could not create a loss of £5,000.

18.4.6 Group relief

Section 130 CTA 2010 makes provision for group relief. In outline, where a company is a member of a group it may surrender losses and other amounts defined in s. 99 CTA 2010 (for example, excess capital allowances or qualifying charitable donations) to another company in the same group. The latter then deducts the loss from its total profits as if it were its own loss (s. 137 CTA 2010). Companies are in the same group, if one is the 75% subsidiary of the other or both are 75% subsidiaries of a third company (s. 152 CTA 2010).

18.5 Close companies

18.5.1 Definition

A close company is a company controlled by five or fewer participators or any number of participators who are also directors (s. 439 CTA 2010). 'Participators' are shareholders, loan creditors, and certain others entitled to participate in the distributed income of the company. 'Control' includes, inter alia, ownership of a majority of the share capital or a majority of the votes or a right to a majority of the dividends. In assessing control, the rights of 'associates' must be added to the rights of a participator—associates include, among others, the participator's spouse, parents, remoter forebears, children, remoter issue, brothers, and sisters. The above definition is only a very brief summary but it is sufficient to show that nearly all private companies are close companies (for example, if a company has nine or fewer shareholders, it must be under the control of some five of them even if none of them is related to each other—it will therefore be a close company unless it falls into one of the small number of cases excluded from the definition).

18.5.2 Taxation considerations

Close companies are subject to certain special tax rules. These are designed to prevent the use of the company as a vehicle for tax avoidance.

If a loan is made to a participator or his associate then, under s. 455 CTA 2010, the company must pay a levy equal to 25% of the loan within nine months of the end of the accounting period in which the loan was made. This currently means that for every £4 lent an additional £1 must be paid to the Revenue. The levy will be repaid to the company whenever the loan is repaid, waived, or written off.

If the borrower pays back the debt in full, no taxation issues arise for the borrower (except, perhaps, for the fact that any interest which has been forgone or which has been paid at less than the official rate, may result in an income tax liability for the debtor based on that sum). However, if the loan is written off or waived by the company, the borrower benefits from a 'windfall'. As such, income tax will be payable. If the borrower is a basic rate taxpayer, no extra tax will be payable. However, if the borrower is a higher rate taxpayer, the amount written off will be grossed up at the 10% dividends rate of income tax and the resulting sum taxed at 32.5% (or 42.5%, if liable at the additional rate of income tax).

One very important exception is that the above rules do not apply if the amount of the loan does not exceed £15,000 and the borrower owns less than a 5% shareholding in the company.

If a close company provides living accommodation or other 'benefits in kind' for a participator or his associates who are neither directors nor higher paid employees of the company (see **19.3.3(f)**), then the company will be treated as making a distribution (see **Chapter 20**).

If the close company is a 'close investment holding company', the small companies rate of corporation tax will not be available. The company will instead pay corporation tax on its profits, whatever the amount, at the full rate. To fall within this category of close companies, the company must be neither a trading company nor a member of a trading group. Companies which deal in land, shares, or securities and companies carrying on property investment on a commercial basis are all treated as trading companies and so outside the scope of this anti-avoidance provision.

Companies are not normally liable to inheritance tax (IHT) if they make gifts. However, if a close company makes a gift (or other transfer of value), IHT will be charged as if each shareholder in the company (except those with very small interests) had made a transfer of value proportionate to their shareholding (s. 94 IHTA 1984). The transferor company is primarily liable for any IHT payable but if it does not pay within the appropriate time frame, the shareholders can become liable personally (s. 202 IHTA 1984).

online resource centre

For further resources and online chapters please visit the Online Resource Centre at www.oxfordtextbooks.co.uk/orc/business13_14/.

19

Taxation of directors' fees and employees' salaries

This chapter covers the following topics:

19.1 Introduction
19.2 The employer's perspective
19.3 The employee's perspective
19.4 The proprietors of a business
19.5 IR35 companies.

19.1 Introduction

One of the largest ongoing expenses of any business is likely to be wage costs. In addition, it is the way in which most people receive a regular income. This chapter considers the taxation treatment of salaries, from the perspectives of both employer and employee. Remember that any type of business can act as an employer. Also, note that employees can be rewarded in ways other than pure salary, such as health insurance or company cars. In most instances, these rewards will result in a tax liability for the employee.

19.2 The employer's perspective

19.2.1 Deductibility of employee remuneration

An employer will wish to ensure that any remuneration or reward paid to its employees will entitle it to claim a pre-tax deduction and reduce its taxable profits. As seen in **Chapter 17**, to be deductible, any expense must satisfy two conditions, namely that the payments must be:

(a) of an income nature as opposed to a capital outlay; and
(b) incurred wholly and exclusively for the purpose of the trade or profession.

Applying this rule, payments that are deductible include the payment of salaries, wages, pension contributions, and even lump sum payments in compensation for loss of the employee's office.

The following specific aspects of this general proposition should be noted.

(a) '*Wholly*'

The word 'wholly' relates to quantum, so that excessive payments cannot be deducted. In *Copeman v William J. Flood and Sons Ltd* [1941] 1 KB 202, it was decided that where a payment is held to be excessive, only such proportion of the payment as is reasonable in the light of the employee's work can be deducted.

With regard to pensions, the pension paid to an ex-employee is deductible even if it is paid voluntarily by the employer. In practice most employers who provide pensions do so by setting up a fund managed by an insurance company. Contributions paid into the fund by the employer are deductible as business expenses provided the scheme is a retirement benefit scheme as defined by s. 590 ICTA 1988.

(b) *Compensation for loss of office*

Lump sum payments for loss of office are deductible if they satisfy the conditions set out above, even though they may be one-off payments. In *Mitchell v B. W. Noble Ltd* [1927] KB 719, compensation payments made to directors who were liable to dismissal because of their misconduct but who resigned to avoid bad publicity were held to be deductible on the basis that their retirement was in the interests of the business. Conversely, payments made to former employees to persuade them to enter into restrictive covenants have been held not to be deductible, since the payments were intended to buy off potential competitors and so amounted to a capital payment (*Associated Portland Cement v Kerr* (1945) 27 TC 108 (CA)). This position has now been changed statutorily, such that the payment will be both taxable as income in the hands of the recipient and an income deductible expense for the company (see **19.3.5**). If the employee is redundant and receives a redundancy payment, such payments are deductible and are treated as having been paid on the last day on which the business was carried on if made after the discontinuance of the trade, profession, or vocation.

(c) *The provision of benefits*

Many employers provide their employees with benefits over and above their salary, such as company cars, free meals, and so on. The cost of providing such benefits will be deductible if the payments are made wholly and exclusively for the purposes of the trade. Thus, if cars are provided for salesmen, the outlay will be deductible, but if they are for private use they will only be deductible if they can be regarded as reasonable remuneration.

19.2.2 Social security contributions

Although it is beyond the scope of this book to consider the social security legislation in detail, it should be noted that the employer is obliged to make National Insurance contributions ('NICs') in respect of each employee who has wages above a weekly threshold (as well as deducting the NICs of the employee before paying over the net wages). Both employee and employer NICs rates (referred to respectively as 'primary' and 'secondary') are set for each tax year, and vary according to earnings thresholds and employee categories. The employer secondary NICs effectively means that there is an additional cost to the employer over and above the salary it pays. The employer's contributions are deductible in computing the tax liability of the employer.

19.3 The employee's perspective

19.3.1 Income Tax (Earnings and Pensions) Act 2003

The system for taxation of employees' income is contained in the Income Tax (Earnings and Pensions) Act (ITEPA) 2003. In addition to setting out the basis of the tax charge, it contains provisions which provide for the mechanism by which income tax is deducted at source from an employee's wages and accounted for by his employer to HMRC under the PAYE (Pay As You Earn) scheme—see Pt 11 ITEPA. (Contrast this with 'self-employed' income, where recipients must account for tax themselves, normally some time after receipt—see **17.3** for more details).

Section 6 ITEPA imposes a charge to tax on 'employment income', which is a charge to tax on, inter alia, 'general earnings'. Section 7 ITEPA defines both these terms by reference to s. 62, which states that 'earnings' mean, in relation to an employment:

(a) any salary, wages, or fee;

(b) any gratuity or incidental benefit of any kind obtained by the employee if it is money or money's worth;

(c) anything which constitutes an emolument of the employment.

Employment income is taxed in the tax year in which it is received, irrespective of whether or not it is actually earned in that year (see Pt 2, Chapter 4, Pt 1 ITEPA).

The term 'employment' is clearly important and is defined in s. 4 ITEPA to include a contract of service. Section 5 operates to include 'offices' and 'office-holders' within employment. Neither of these definitions is absolute, so it is worthwhile considering case law for guidance in these areas.

(a) *Office*

Rowlatt J in *Great Western Railway Co v Bater* [1920] 3 KB 266, said that 'office' meant 'a subsisting, permanent, substantive position which had an existence independent of the person who filled it, which went on and was filled in succession by successive holders', although Lord Wilberforce and Lord Lowry, in *Edwards v Clinch* [1981] 3 All ER 543, felt the definition should be refined. Lord Wilberforce accepted that 'a rigid requirement of permanence is no longer appropriate . . . and continuity need not be regarded as an absolute qualification. But still, if any meaning is to be given to "office" in this legislation . . . the word must involve a degree of continuance (not necessarily continuity) and of independent existence: it must connote a post to which a person can be appointed, which he can vacate and to which a successor can be appointed.'

Over the years office holders have been held to include directors of UK companies, NHS consultants, bishops, judges, and personal representatives. (Remember that a director may hold the office of director and may simultaneously be an employee, by performing an executive function. (See **19.4** for further discussion of the taxation of directors' salaries.))

(b) *Employment*

Pennycuick V-C said in *Fall v Hitchen* [1973] 1 All ER 368, that 'unless some special limitation is to be put upon the word "employment" in any given context, the expression "contract of service" appears to be coterminous with the expression "employment"'. The case involved a ballet dancer who entered into a contract having the attributes of a contract of service, in that he was paid weekly regardless of whether a performance was given or a rehearsal attended; the 'employer' paid national insurance contributions on the dancer's behalf as if he were an employee and the dancer worked only for the employer. This contract was therefore assessable, even though it had been entered into in the normal course of carrying on his profession of dancer. Conversely, if it can be shown that the taxpayer's method of earning a livelihood does not consist of obtaining a post and remaining in it (as was the case in *Fall v Hitchen*), but consists of engagements and moving from one engagement to another, he is assessed under ITTOIA (see **Chapter 17**) and not ITEPA, provided the engagements are entered into as part of his profession (*Davies v Braithwaite* [1931] 2 KB 628).

19.3.2 Taxable receipts by employees

A director or other employee who receives salary, wages, or a bonus from his employer is obviously assessable under ITEPA. However, rewards for employees, and particularly directors, tend to comprise more than just salary. Perhaps the most common example is that of the company car, but others can have considerable worth, such as loans on favourable terms and subsidised or free living accommodation. Such 'perks' will amount to benefits of money or money's worth and, therefore, will be taxable along with other earnings.

ITEPA contains the 'Benefits Code' in Chapter 2, Pt 3, which deals with such benefits and will now be considered.

19.3.3 The Benefits Code

(a) Benefits generally

Benefits from employment generally fall into two categories: either they amount to cash or its equivalent or they amount to the use of something at the employer's expense. An example of the former might be the payment of premiums on private health insurance; an example of the latter would be the use of a company car.

Under s. 204 ITEPA, the general rule is that the cost to the employer of providing the benefit will be treated as earnings by the employee. However, a number of specified benefits are subject to their own rules.

(b) Living accommodation

Chapter 5 of Pt 3 ITEPA covers this benefit and provides rules on how much an employee is deemed to receive in monetary terms. An employee who occupies premises by reason of his employment is taxed on the greater of either the rent paid by his employer or the deemed 'annual value' of the accommodation less the rent actually paid by the employee. 'Annual value' means the market rent that could be obtained for the premises on the assumption that the landlord will bear the costs of repair and insurance.

EXAMPLE

Scenario one

Employer buys a property for £60,000 to provide accommodation for Employee. Employee pays an annual rent of £4,000 to Employer. The deemed market rent of the property is £10,000 per annum. Employee, therefore, receives a taxable benefit of £6,000—the difference between the deemed market rent and the actual rent paid by the employee.

Scenario two

Employer rents a property for £8,000 per annum to provide accommodation for Employee. Employee pays an annual rent of £4,000 to Employer. The deemed market rent of the property is £6,000 per annum. Employee, therefore, receives a taxable benefit of £4,000—the difference between the actual rent paid by Employer (as it is higher than the deemed rent) and the actual rent paid by Employee.

Where it costs an employer more than £75,000 to provide accommodation for an employee, an employee's liability is calculated on a slightly different basis. In this instance, an employee will be treated as receiving a percentage (based on an official rate of interest in line with mortgage rates) of the amount in excess of £75,000 which the employer has spent on providing the accommodation (so-called 'additional yearly rent'), as well as taking into account any deemed receipt which the employee would normally be taxed upon under the rule above.

EXAMPLE

Employer buys a property for £100,000 to provide accommodation for Employee. Assume the deemed percentage is 5%. Therefore, Employee is treated as receiving additional yearly rent of 5% of £25,000 (the amount over £75,000 paid by Employer for the property) = £1,250.

The deemed market rent of the property is £10,000 per annum and Employee pays an annual rent of £6,000 to Employer.

Employee's total taxable liability for the property is, therefore:
(£1,250 + £10,000) – £6,000 = £5,250.

(c) Expenses

Any allowance for expenses payable to an employee will be a taxable benefit, subject to whatever percentage of that allowance is spent on expenses incurred wholly, exclusively, and necessarily in the performance of the duties of employment, in which case, such expenses are deductible pursuant to s. 336 ITEPA. For example, if a director has an expense allowance of £1,000 per month and regularly incurs deductible expenses of £800 per month, only the difference will be taxable.

The test for deductibility is stringent, particularly as expenditure has to be shown as necessarily incurred. It is always open to the Revenue to argue that such necessity did not exist.

In many instances, an employee will, instead, incur the expense first and be reimbursed by his employer. This does not normally produce a taxable receipt for the employee, so long as the expense fulfils the test for deductibility. As a sizeable proportion of an employee's expenses claims tends to refer to travelling costs, it is worth noting two specific aspects of the system:

(i) the test for deductibility of travel expenses is less demanding, the rule being that these expenses must be necessarily incurred in the performance of an employee's duties (s. 337 ITEPA);

(ii) in relation to mileage allowance, s. 229 ITEPA exempts from taxation any allowance of 40 pence per mile up to the first 10,000 miles and 25 pence thereafter.

(d) Motor vehicles

As with living accommodation, an employee who is provided with a company car is deemed to receive an annual sum to represent the cash equivalent of the vehicle. This sum can be between 0% and 35% of the list price of the vehicle provided, depending on its carbon dioxide emissions (see Chapter 6, Pt 3 ITEPA for full details).

(e) Beneficial loan arrangements

Loans from an employer can be attractive if the rate of interest is lower than that in the marketplace. As such, Chapter 7, Pt 3 ITEPA attributes to an employee the value of this difference as earnings. This is done by comparing the actual interest payable by the employee with an official rate of interest, which itself reflects the market rates in force (s. 175(3) ITEPA).

EXAMPLE

Martha is lent £20,000 by her employer. The rate of interest she pays on this to her employer is 2% per annum. As such, she pays £400 interest per annum. Assume that, according to the Revenue's official rates, interest upon such a loan is expected to be 6%, that is, £1,200 per annum. Martha will, as a consequence, be deemed to receive a taxable benefit worth £800.

There are a number of exceptions to this rule, but the one of general application is that, if the aggregate amount owing to the employer by the employee does not exceed £5,000, ITEPA will not bite (s. 180 ITEPA).

Should the whole or part of a loan be written off or released by the employer, the amount released or written off will be treated as earnings (s. 188 ITEPA).

(f) Lower paid employees

Section 216 ITEPA recognises a category of lower paid employees (that is, employees earning less than £8,500 per annum) who receive a more lenient treatment of benefits. For example, expense allowances, company cars, and beneficial loans provided to lower paid employees will not be subject to income tax.

To avoid abuse of this system, that is, by paying an employee an artificially low salary and then supplementing this with substantial benefits, the cash equivalent of all benefits received must be included in the employee's earnings total for the purpose of the £8,500 threshold (s. 218 ITEPA).

EXAMPLE

George's remuneration package is made up as follows:

Salary of £6,500 per annum
Company car with a cash equivalent of £1,750 per annum
Expenses allowance of £1,200 per annum.

George's total earnings for the purposes of s. 218 ITEPA are £9,450. As such, George is not a lower paid employee.

Finally, as a rule of thumb, a director will never qualify as a lower paid employee, unless he is a full-time working director with no more than a 5% shareholding in the company and earning less than the specified amount.

19.3.4 Terminal payments

(a) General principles

The mere fact that the payment is made on the termination of the contract (or the alteration of its terms) does not preclude its taxation under ITEPA, if it is 'something in the nature of a reward for services, past, present or future' (per Upjohn J in *Hochstrasser v Mayes* [1959] Ch 22). As a result of this, sums paid at the end of an employment in accordance with the terms of the employment contract will be taxable since they will represent deferred or advance remuneration (*Dale v De Soissons* [1950] 2 All ER 460). Thus, if an employee is to be paid £10,000 a year for ten years but under the contract is to receive a lump sum of £50,000 on either the commencement or termination of the term, the sum is fully taxable under ITEPA (see *Williams v Simmonds* [1981] STC 715). However, it is more common for an employee's contract to be terminated and for the employee to be allowed to work out his notice or to be denied this right and paid a lump sum to reflect the money that he would have earned had he been allowed to do so, i.e., a payment in lieu of notice. It is at this point that some important distinctions must be made.

If an employee is allowed to work his notice period or is kept on for the period of his notice, but not allowed to work (so-called 'gardening leave'), the payments made to the employee will be taxable in the usual way. This should be contrasted with the situation where the employee is dismissed without notice and is paid in lieu of notice. Such a payment constitutes damages for breach of contract by the employer, and, as such, will not be treated as taxable as an emolument. Instead it will be taxable under s. 401 ITEPA (see (b) below).

Some employment contracts specifically provide the option for an employer to make a payment in lieu rather than give notice. This is in an attempt to avoid the deeming of a breach of contract, thus preserving many of the terms of the contract, specifically any restrictive covenants. Any payment made under such a provision is taxable as an emolument, as it arises from the operation of the contract.

As such, the exact nature of any lump sum termination payment made to an employee needs careful consideration to determine its status for tax purposes.

(b) Payments under s. 401 ITEPA

A lump sum payment made to an employee on early termination of the contract by the employer which is not assessable under the general principles may be taxable under s. 401 ITEPA. This taxes a payment on the termination of employment that is not otherwise chargeable to tax (under the general principles). However, the great advantage to the taxpayer of a payment falling within s. 401 is that only if the sum received exceeds £30,000 will any tax be payable and, in such case, only the amount in excess of £30,000 (s. 403 ITEPA).

A common example of a s. 401 payment is a payment in lieu of notice which amounts to damages for breach of contract (see (a) above). This can lead to the unusual situation that an employee who is paid £25,000 in lieu of notice pursuant to a contractual provision will pay tax on this amount, whereas an employee who is paid the same sum, but which amounts to damages for breach, will pay none.

Another example of payments falling within the ambit of s. 401 are ex gratia payments or 'golden handshakes'.

A terminal payment paid to a director near retirement age needs careful consideration, as such a payment may instead be treated by the Revenue as a payment out of an unapproved pension scheme, in which case it will not attract the £30,000 exemption and will be taxed in full under s. 394 ITEPA.

Statutory redundancy payments and, since *Mairs v Haughey* [1993] 3 All ER 801, non-statutory redundancy payments are only taxable under s. 401. However, only genuine redundancy payments are caught. So an attempt to class a payment of less than £30,000 to a director as a redundancy payment to take advantage of the exemption will be closely scrutinised by HMRC. (See Statement of Practice SP 1/94.)

19.3.5 Restrictive covenant payments

If an employee receives a payment in consideration of entering into a restrictive covenant, this is regarded as being a capital outlay by the employer. As such, it should be a capital receipt in the hands of the employee and so not taxable as part of the employee's income. However, s. 225 ITEPA levies income tax on such payments. They are fully taxed in the recipient's hands and the paying employer can deduct them when calculating income profits.

19.3.6 Social security contributions

In the same way that employers must make National Insurance contributions in respect of employee's salaries, employees are also liable to make such contributions. The contributions deducted by the employer from the employee's salary (see **19.2.2**) are not deductible when calculating the employee's tax liability. Employees' contributions are greater than those levied on the self-employed but, in compensation, the benefits available to employees are greater than those available to the self-employed. (The details of the benefits are beyond the scope of this book.)

19.4 The proprietors of a business

Some important distinctions need always to be borne in mind when considering the proprietors of a business. First, sole traders cannot earn a salary from their businesses. The profits they make are taxed as a receipt under the Income Tax (Trading and Other Income) Act 2005 (see **Chapter 17**). The same applies to partners who are 'true' partners in a partnership. If any such partners pay themselves a salary (in addition to taking any profit share), their total receipts from the business will be taxed in the same way as a sole trader. (See *MacKinlay v Arthur Young McClelland Moores & Co* [1990] 1 All ER 45 for judicial discussion of this point.) However, 'salaried partners', that is, partners who have no stake in the business in question, are not entitled to any profit share and are remunerated solely by salary (and for whom the title 'partner' is, therefore, somewhat of a misnomer) will be taxed as employees.

The position of a company and its directors is different. As the company is a legal personality separate from its owners and managers, directors who work full-time in the company are treated as its employees and taxed on the salaries they receive. As such, a company pays tax on its profits and directors pay tax on their salaries. With a partnership, there is only the single liability of the partner to tax.

The significance, therefore, of this distinction becomes clear in the context of deductibility. Salaries payable by a company to its directors (as employees) will be deductible from the company's overall taxable profits. 'Salaries' payable to true partners will not be deductible. This does provide the opportunity to manipulate a company's profits by paying directors substantial sums, such that the company incurs little or no liability to corporation tax (although note the discussion at **19.2.1** about excessive salary payments). In many closely held private companies this can be a common method of extraction of profit from the business, although it should be borne in mind that increased salaries will also result in increased National Insurance payments from both the company and its directors (see **19.2.2** and **19.3.6**). By contrast, in a listed public limited company, such manipulation of profit will be prevented by corporate governance rules and will usually be of limited impact due to the substantial profits earned by such companies.

19.5 IR35 companies

Because of the financial and practical burden of the PAYE scheme and National Insurance, employers began to favour an alternative method of rewarding certain staff. Instead of being taken on as employees, the persons in question would create a single shareholder/director company and the 'employer' would then contract with that company for it to provide the services of the shareholder/director (effectively the 'employee'). Payments made to the company by the 'employer' would not be treated as an emolument of the 'employee', but a receipt of the company, thus escaping the PAYE/National Insurance burden on the 'employer'. However, those payments would still amount to a deductible business expense for the paying 'employer'. The 'employee', as a shareholder of the company, could then extract the profits from the company by way of dividend, again avoiding any PAYE/National Insurance obligation, and the corporation tax liability incurred by the company may have been less than the income tax liability on any salary paid direct. (See **Chapter 18** for an explanation of the rates of corporation tax.)

In 1999, Revenue Budget Press Release IR35 was published, explaining that this manipulation of the rules would be prevented in the future. The current legislation is found in ss. 48–61 ITEPA 2003. However, the reference to 'IR35' has remained.

The basic effect of the rules is that in cases where there is, in effect, an employer/employee relationship, payments made into the intermediate company will be treated as deemed employment income of the proprietor of the company and, therefore, subject to PAYE and National Insurance liability in the usual way. This will be the case even if the company pays out no monies to the proprietor or if it pays them out in the form of dividends (in which case there will be set off between the liability incurred on the deemed payment and the liability on the dividend payment). Should the reader want further details of this very complex area, a recommended starting point is the special website set up by the Inland Revenue—www.hmrc.gov.uk/ir35.

online resource centre

For further resources and online chapters please visit the Online Resource Centre at www.oxfordtextbooks.co.uk/orc/business13_14/.

20

Taxation of distributions and debenture interest

This chapter covers the following topics:

20.1 Introduction

Those involved with companies can receive a return from their investment in a variety of ways. Therefore, awareness and understanding of the different tax consequences is important.

This chapter deals with the taxation of distributions by way of dividend and of debenture interest. The common factor is that both dividends and debenture interest are income returns on investments made in companies and, therefore, subject to income tax.

EXAMPLE

Titus is a director of a private limited company. He is also a shareholder of the company and holds debentures issued by the company in respect of a loan he has made to the company. Three possible income tax events could arise in this situation, namely:

(a) Titus is paid a salary or fee as a director (covered in **Chapter 19**).

(b) Titus is paid a dividend in respect of his shareholding.

(c) Titus is entitled to annual interest in respect of the debentures he holds.

20.2 Taxation of distributions by way of dividend

20.2.1 Definition of distribution

A shareholder is liable to income tax on any 'distribution' which he receives in respect of shares. The definition of distribution is complicated but the following types of receipt are the most important:

(a) any dividend paid by the company including a capital dividend;

(b) any other distribution out of assets of the company in respect of shares;

(c) any interest on securities (e.g., debentures) where the interest varies with the profits of the company;

(d) in some circumstances, the issue of bonus shares following a reduction of share capital or the repayment of share capital after a bonus issue.

It should be noted that an issue of bonus shares (that is, shares treated as paid up out of the profits of the company) is not a distribution for tax purposes unless share capital has previously been reduced. However, if the shareholders are given a choice between receiving a cash dividend (which is, of course, a distribution) or bonus shares, those who choose to take the bonus shares are taxed on the amount of cash dividend forgone in almost the same way as if it were a distribution.

20.2.2 Tax consequences for the company of the payment of a dividend

The payment of a dividend or other distribution is neither an expense of a company's business nor a charge on its income. The amount of any dividend paid does not, therefore, reduce a company's liability to corporation tax.

20.2.3 Taxation of a recipient of a dividend

20.2.3.1 Corporate recipient

Where a UK company receives a dividend or other distribution from another, the general rule is that these sums are not subject to corporation tax in the hands of the recipient. (However, as was explained at **18.3.3.6**, dividends received may determine the rate at which a company's taxable profits are taxed.)

20.2.3.2 Individual recipient

An individual shareholder who receives a dividend from a company is treated for tax purposes as receiving a sum equivalent to the actual dividend plus a tax credit. The latter is equivalent to 10% of the dividend as grossed up by a tax credit fraction. The current fraction is 10/90.

EXAMPLE

Shareholder receives a dividend of £500. For tax purposes, he is treated as receiving:

The actual dividend	£500
Plus	
10% of £500 grossed up (i.e., £500 plus (10/90 × £500))	£55.56
Total	£555.56

The shareholder is liable to pay tax on this grossed-up amount. For the tax year 2013/14, the basic tax rate for individuals on dividends is 10% and the higher rate is 32.5%. There is also an additional rate of 37.5% for those whose taxable income exceeds £150,000.

Dividend income is treated as the top slice of the shareholder's income. Where dividend income falls entirely within the basic rate band of taxable income, the tax credit will satisfy the entire liability to tax. If dividend income falls entirely within the higher rate band of income, an amount of 32.5% of the grossed-up dividend will be due from the shareholder minus any tax credit. Where the income cuts across the basic and higher rate bands, the dividend must be apportioned between them and the tax credit deducted from the resulting sum. The balance will be the amount of tax outstanding. (The same is true when the dividend cuts across the higher rate and additional rate bands.) Should a shareholder not be liable to tax, there is no ability to claim a repayment of the tax credit.

EXAMPLE

In all the examples which follow, the relevant income tax bands are those for the tax year 2013/14.

Example one

A has taxable income of £15,000 and receives a gross dividend of £555.56 (i.e., £500 cash plus tax credit of £55.56). The total dividend falls within the basic rate income tax band. Tax is therefore:

£555.56 × 10% = £55.56

The tax liability is fully satisfied by the tax credit.

Example two

B has taxable income of £38,000 and receives a gross dividend of £1,666.67 (i.e., £1,500 cash plus tax credit of £166.67). The total dividend falls within the higher rate income tax band. Tax is therefore:

£1,666.67 × 32.5% = £541.67

The tax liability is satisfied to the extent of the tax credit, i.e. £166.67. The shareholder is required to pay the remaining tax due of £375.

Example three

C has taxable income of £30,000 and receives a gross dividend of £7,777.78 (i.e., £7,000 cash plus tax credit of £777.78). The dividend falls within both the basic and higher rate income tax bands. Tax is payable as follows:

£2,010 × 10% = £201

£5767.78 × 32.5% = £1874.53

Total tax payable = £2,075.53

The tax liability is satisfied as to the extent of the tax credit, i.e., £777.78. The shareholder is required to pay the remaining tax due of £1,297.75.

20.3 Debenture interest

20.3.1 Introduction

The tax treatment of interest on debentures will be looked at for two reasons:

(a) it can be contrasted with the tax treatment of dividends;

(b) an investment made into a company by way of debt (loan) funding has consequences for both the investor and the company.

20.3.2 Tax consequences for the paying company

When a company issues debentures or another type of debt instrument in respect of debt funding it receives, the holder of such debenture is likely to receive interest as part of this arrangement. The payment of interest by a company will usually result in a tax saving to the company because the interest will be a business expense deductible in computing profits. This is because interest payments made by companies usually fall within the 'loan relationships' rules, as set out in Pt 5 of the Corporation Tax Act 2009. It is beyond the scope of this book to look at these rules in detail as they are complex and cover many situations other than debenture interest. However, a brief summary follows.

20.3.2.1 Definition of loan relationships

A company has a loan relationship where it stands in the position of a creditor or debtor as regards any money debt and that debt arises from a transaction for the lending of money. As such, borrowing in the form of debentures comes within the definition.

20.3.2.2 Taxation of loan relationships

Very simply, the taxation of loan relationships works on the basis of a system of credits and debits; money received from a loan relationship is a credit and money paid out is a debit. As such, interest paid on borrowings is a debit, whilst interest received on lending would be a credit. Also, charges and expenses incurred in setting up the loan relationship (in this instance, legal or administrative) can also be treated as debits.

The way in which credits and debits are taxed is determined by whether or not they are 'trading' or 'non-trading'. In very general terms, if a company raises money by borrowing which is for the purposes of its trade, then any interest thereon will be deductible from trading receipts in calculating its taxable profits (s. 297 CTA 2009). However, where the borrowing does not support trade carried on by the company, interest thereon is treated as a 'non-trading debit'. Such a sum must first be deducted from any 'non-trading credits' (i.e., profits which a company has made from lending money where this is not the trade of the company). If such credits exceed debits, the resulting sum (a 'non-trading profit') is charged to corporation tax (s. 299 CTA 2009). However, where the situation is in reverse (a 'non-trading deficit'), the company may, very simply, use that deficit and set it off against any profits of the same accounting period or carry it back against any profits of earlier accounting periods (s. 300 CTA 2009).

In summary, therefore, interest paid out by a company to debenture holders could be treated in a variety of ways. However, the general effect will usually be that the amounts in question will be tax-deductible for the purposes of corporation tax.

20.3.3 Deduction of tax

In a number of situations, the payer of a taxable sum is required to deduct tax at source and make the payment net. For these purposes any company paying 'yearly' interest to individuals is subject to such an obligation and must deduct basic rate income tax of 20% (s. 874 ITA 2007). Yearly interest arises where the relevant loan is expected to last for more than one year.

When the company deducts tax it must account to HMRC for the sum deducted. For example, a company borrows £1,000 at 10% interest from an individual. Each year (assuming tax rates remain the same) it will pay £80 interest to the lender and £20 to the Revenue.

20.3.4 Taxation of the recipient

The gross amount of interest received by a debenture-holder is taxable. As we have just seen, the company usually deducts the 20% tax from the payment so that the amount received is a net amount. To calculate the amount of tax payable it is, therefore, first necessary to calculate the gross amount of interest. This is done by multiplying the net amount actually received by 100/80 (e.g., £80 × 100/80 = £100). If the tax rate changes so will the fraction—the '80' represents 100 minus the rate of tax. Of course, if no deduction of tax has been made at source, this calculation is unnecessary.

The gross amount of interest is investment income in the hands of the recipient and is liable to higher rate tax if the recipient's income is large enough.

EXAMPLE

P has taxable income of £30,000 in the tax year 2013/14. He therefore has £2,010 of the basic rate band still unused. He received £10,000 gross interest on a loan to a company.

(a) P's net receipt was £8,000 plus credit for £2,000 tax deducted at source by the paying company.

(b) Tax to pay (on gross sum):

£0 to 2,010 × 20%	= £402
£2,011 to 10,000 × 40%	= £3,196
	= £3,598

(c) Tax deducted satisfies £2,000 of the above liability—balance to pay of £1,598.

---

online resource centre

For further resources and online chapters please visit the Online Resource Centre at www.oxfordtextbooks.co.uk/orc/business13_14/.

21 Capital allowances

This chapter covers the following topics:

21.1 Introduction

21.1.1 General

Most businesses will need to acquire fixed assets for use in the business. Nearly all will depreciate in value over time due to wear and tear arising from their use in the business. This depreciation may not be deducted from the business's trading profits. However, certain limited types of fixed asset entitle a business to claim relief in the form of a capital allowance, which can be deducted when calculating taxable profits. The purpose of this allowance is to give tax relief for the depreciation in value of specific assets bought and owned for business use, by allowing the owner to write off their cost against the taxable income of the business. The amount which can be written off is calculated according to a fixed formula.

Relief is only available if the capital expenditure has been incurred in respect of the items of expenditure prescribed by the governing statute, the Capital Allowances Act 2001. Under this Act, the principal allowances relate to expenditure incurred on plant and machinery (although expenditure on some other items is deductible under the terms of the Act).

The allowances can be claimed by companies, partnerships, sole traders, and self-employed persons.

Capital allowances are treated as trading expenses incurred in the accounting period in which they are claimed. They are, therefore, deductible from income receipts from the same period.

21.2 The capital allowances system

21.2.1 Plant and machinery

The Capital Allowances Act 2001 does not define either 'plant' or 'machinery' and therefore whether the capital expenditure will attract the allowances will depend on the facts in each case. This means that a precise definition cannot be given. However, HMRC does provide guidance on the items on which capital allowances may be claimed. The principal items will be equipment owned and used in the business: tools; machinery; office equipment; computers; vehicles; plant; and factory equipment. Capital allowances *may not* be claimed on items that a business buys and sells as part of its trade. These are normally treated as purchases and sales of stock or goods, and taken into account in calculating trading profits.

In most cases, capital allowances cannot be claimed in respect of the purchase or investment in land, buildings, and property. (Until April 2011, allowances could be claimed in respect of industrial buildings but these are no longer available.) The Act also provides that allowances may be available in respect of:

(a) agricultural forestry buildings;
(b) scientific research;
(c) patents and 'know-how';

(d) mines, oil wells, mineral rights, cemeteries, crematoria, and dredging;
(e) hotels; and
(f) certain research and development activities and facilities.

21.2.2 The allowances

21.2.2.1 Writing down allowance

If the expenditure is incurred on an item of 'plant or machinery', it will qualify for a 'writing down allowance' of up to 18% of the 'qualifying expenditure' in the first and subsequent years. Allowances are then effectively set against profits in the same way as a deductible trading expense, to reduce the tax liability of the business.

The 18% rate was introduced with effect from 1 April 2012 for companies paying corporation tax and 6 April 2012 for businesses subject to income tax. Prior to April 2008, the relevant rate was 25%, and between April 2008 and April 2012 it was 20%. Where a business's chargeable period spans relevant dates when the rates change, then a hybrid rate will operate, effectively calculating allowances by apportioning the chargeable period either side of those dates at the rate in effect for each portion.

The term 'qualifying expenditure' means the original cost of the asset less any allowances already given. The allowance may be claimed in whole or in part by sole traders or partners.

EXAMPLE

Machinery was purchased for £50,000 on 1 April 2010 and the full writing down allowance of 20%* claimed. This provided an allowance of £10,000 in the first year of ownership. In the three subsequent years, the allowance available is:

	Written down value		Allowance
Year 2	£50,000–£10,000 (1st Year WDA)	= £40,000	£8,000*
Year 3	£50,000–£18,000 (£10,000 + £8,000)	= £32,000	£5,760**
Year 4	£50,000–£24,400 (£10,000 + £8,000 + £5,760)	= £23,760	£4,276**

* 20% rate in force April 2008–April 2012
** 18% rate in force April 2012 onwards

The example set out above shows that the allowance is of the relevant percentage of the *unrelieved expenditure* (that is to say, the purchase price less the allowances already taken). Thus, the annual allowance is a percentage of an ever-reducing balance so that it can take many years for the entire expenditure to be set against profits, subject to any balancing charge (see **21.2.2.2**) becoming payable.

21.2.2.2 Balancing charge or allowance

When the asset is sold at a price which differs from the written down value, there will be:
a *balancing charge* if the asset is sold for *more* than the written down value; or
a *balancing allowance* if the asset is sold for *less* than the written down value.

EXAMPLES

In the example above (21.2.2.1) the written down value after the fourth year was £19,484 (£23,760 – £4,276). Compare the following examples:

Written down value	Sale price	Balancing charge
£19,484	£22,000	£2,516

Written down value	Sale price	Balancing allowance
£19,484	£18,000	£1,484

A balancing charge is added to profits for the purpose of calculating tax, whereas a balancing allowance provides further relief, being deductible from profits. The effect of both is to ensure that, taking all the years together, the total relief given is equal to the amount of the actual depreciation.

Note that a balancing charge can never be more than the total amount of allowance given—any actual profit made on the sale of the asset being liable to capital gains tax, if taxable at all.

21.2.3 'Pooling'

21.2.3.1 General

So far, we have looked at the rules as they apply to the acquisition and subsequent disposal of a single item of plant or machinery. If several items of plant and machinery are owned by the business (as is more likely to be the case) the allowances are given by reference to a 'pool' of expenditure. This will mean that all of the assets in the pool are treated as if they were one asset. The amount of the writing down allowance on the 'pool' of expenditure will be up to 18% of the total of expenditure on machinery and plant less all allowances so far claimed. Where one item included in the pool is disposed of, the sale price of that item is deducted from the written down value of the pool (this deduction being known as a 'balancing adjustment'), so that smaller allowances will be available in later years. A 'balancing charge' will only apply where pooled items are sold for more than the written down value of the whole pool.

Given changes in writing down allowance rates made in 2008 and 2012, special rules, including a hybrid rate (see **21.2.2.1** above), apply to calculate the overall allowances available to businesses that have pools of assets and whose chargeable periods span the relevant date on which the rate changed.

21.2.4 Using the allowances

Writing down allowances are available both in the accounting period in which the asset was purchased and in all subsequent accounting periods during which the asset is owned.

While the system does not lend itself to simplification (especially from the corporation tax perspective), the basic use of a writing down allowance for a company, partnership, or sole trader is that of a deductible trading expense. If such allowances exceed income receipts, the loss incurred attracts loss relief in the usual way.

21.2.5 Special allowances and rules

21.2.5.1 Annual Investment Allowance for small and medium-sized businesses

Small and medium-sized businesses (which account for around 99% of businesses in the UK) are entitled to a 100% Annual Investment Allowance (AIA) on purchases of most plant and machinery up to £25,000 in any one year as from 1 April 2012. This allowance, like other capital allowances, is treated as a trading expense and can thus be set off against income receipts when calculating tax. Where a qualifying business spends more than £25,000 in any one year on plant and machinery, the balance above £25,000 will qualify for standard capital allowances and enter any existing pool of assets. The AIA is designed to encourage investment by providing increased cash-flow benefits. Between April 2008 and 2010, the AIA was £50,000, and between April 2010 and 2012 it was £100,000. Any business with chargeable periods which span the dates when AIA limits changed will have its allowance apportioned accordingly.

EXAMPLE

Machinery was purchased for £60,000 on 1 April 2012. The first £25,000 will qualify for the AIA, whilst the remaining £35,000 will qualify for standard capital allowances. Therefore, the written down value for Year 2 will be: £60,000 – (£25,000 (AIA) + £6,300 (18% of £35,000)) = £28,700

21.2.5.2 Long-life assets

Long-life assets are those with a useful economic life of more than 25 years. Plant and machinery which falls within this category attracts a writing down allowance of 8%. In addition, certain integral features of premises may also attract this allowance.

These provisions only affect large concerns. As such, any business which spends less than £100,000 a year on long-life assets is excluded and will still be able to claim the full 18% capital allowance. Certain categories of assets are also excluded, the most relevant being motor cars.

Because these rules result in allowances being claimed at a slower rate than normal, businesses could be tempted to sell off assets prematurely at less than their written down value so as to bring an immediate balancing allowance into effect. The legislation contains provisions to defeat such activity by deeming the sale to have been at the relevant written down value.

21.2.5.3 Short-life assets

A short-life asset is one that the owner expects to keep for no more than eight years after the end of the accounting period in which it was bought, or to have worn out or broken within such period. A business must elect to treat an asset in this way and inform HMRC of this decision. Having done so, the business may treat this and similar assets as a separate 'pool' of assets (see **21.2.3**) to which it can then apply the 18% capital allowance rate for a maximum of five accounting periods. This election and separation of assets is designed to enable businesses to obtain allowances for the actual net cost of the assets during their lifespan in the business if they are scrapped or sold before the end of the eight year period.

If the business sells the asset during this period, then a balancing charge or allowance will apply (see **21.2.2.2**). Should it still own the asset at the end of this period, it must transfer its residual value back into its main 'pool' (see **21.2.3**) where it will be treated in the standard way.

The type of assets which qualify as short-life assets are also likely to qualify for the AIA (see **21.2.5.1**). Therefore, the short-life assets rules will principally benefit those businesses investing amounts in plant and machinery in excess of the AIA limit for the year of purchase, given that the latter provides a 100% allowance.

21.2.5.4 Leased assets

There are special rules on the availability of capital allowances to the lessor when plant and machinery is bought in order to be leased. There are also special rules for the lessees of equipment. It is important to distinguish between arrangements which are 'pure' leasing contracts, where the title in the assets leased always remains with the lessor, and those which constitute lease-purchase (and hire-purchase) arrangements where the lessee (or hirer) becomes the ultimate owner of the assets, normally upon payment of a final capital sum. In the former case, the lessor will be able to claim writing down allowances; in the latter it will be the lessee. Because of the amount of assets either leased or subject to lease-purchase in the UK, these rules should not be overlooked. The detail of these rules is beyond the scope of this book.

21.2.5.5 Motor cars

Cars that are used only for business purposes and have been bought since April 2009 qualify for writing down allowances of either 10%, 20%, or up to 100%, depending on carbon emission levels. Cars provided to employees that are also used for private purposes are treated as being used only for business purposes. Individuals or partners in a partnership, however, who use cars partly for private purposes are required to reduce their claims by the proportion of private use made of the car.

Cars bought before April 2009 qualified for an allowance at the rate in force at the time, varied according to the original cost and the extent of non-business use.

online resource centre

For further resources and online chapters please visit the Online Resource Centre at www.oxfordtextbooks.co.uk/orc/business13_14/.

22

Capital gains tax and inheritance tax on business assets

This chapter covers the following topics:

22.1 Introduction

One of the principal motivations for people going into business is to earn a living from the income they derive from the enterprise. For many people an equally important motivation is to create a capital asset which they can either sell or give away (whether during their lifetime or on death). The tax charges which can arise on these events are therefore of importance to business people. In this chapter we will examine the capital gains tax and inheritance tax regimes which apply to individuals in relation to businesses and business assets. Companies are also liable to pay tax on capital gains and there is explanation of this in **Chapter 18**.

22.2 Capital gains tax

22.2.1 General

In the same way that people can generate money through income transactions, it is also possible to generate money through the disposal of a capital asset, for example, the sale of land or shares. The capital gains tax regime exists to bring the proceeds of such disposals into the taxation net.

Under the provisions contained in the Taxation of Chargeable Gains Act (TCGA) 1992, capital gains tax is payable when a taxable person makes a disposal of chargeable assets giving rise to a chargeable gain unless an exemption or relief applies. Capital gains tax is charged by reference to gains made during a tax year (as with income tax). What follows in this section is an explanation of the various rules which need to be considered to establish a taxpayer's capital gains tax liability on any given disposal.

22.2.2 The requirements for a charge to capital gains tax

For the charge to tax to arise, a *taxable person* must make a *disposal of a chargeable asset*.

A 'taxable person' for CGT purposes is anyone who is resident or ordinarily resident in the UK (including the personal representatives of a deceased person).

A 'disposal' is not exhaustively defined in the Act but includes a sale, gift, or part disposal.

A definition of 'assets' for capital gains tax purposes is contained in s. 21(1) TCGA 1992, which widely defines it as including 'all forms of property . . . '.

Only 'chargeable' assets can give rise to a liability to the tax but virtually all 'assets' are chargeable assets subject to a few exceptions (such as motor cars and pounds sterling).

22.2.3 The basic calculation

For the tax to become payable, the disposal of chargeable assets has to give rise to a gain, which will occur if the 'consideration for disposal' exceeds the 'allowable expenditure' permitted by the Act. The 'consideration for disposal' equates to the sale price of the asset. 'Allowable expenditure' consists of:

(a) the initial expenditure (that is, the original purchase price or market value if the asset was acquired by way of gift) plus incidental costs incurred in acquiring the asset;

(b) subsequent expenditure (such as money spent on enhancing the value of the asset); and

(c) incidental costs of disposal.

EXAMPLE

Natalie bought a 15% shareholding in Transit Commercial Vehicle Hire Limited five years ago for £75,000. Legal fees incurred in negotiating the purchase amounted to £3,000.

Natalie has recently sold her entire shareholding for £135,000. Legal fees incurred in negotiating the sale amounted to £5,000.

At its simplest, therefore, Natalie's capital gain is:

Consideration for disposal	£135,000
Less allowable expenditure, being:	
Initial expenditure:	
Purchase price	£75,000
Legal fees	£3,000
Deduct subsequent expenditure:	
N/a	
Deduct incidental costs of disposal:	
Legal fees	£5,000
Capital Gain	£52,000

(Note: the calculation of tax on this gain is shown in the example at **22.2.6**.)

22.2.4 Annual exemption

Aside from the deductions mentioned already, every individual has an annual exemption from capital gains tax. For the current tax year, the first £10,900 of capital gains made in that tax year is exempt from liability to tax (s. 3 TCGA 1992).

22.2.5 Rate of tax

For individuals, whatever chargeable gain is to be taxed is treated as if it were the top slice of a taxpayer's taxable income, that is, it must be added onto the taxpayer's taxable income to determine how much of the gain falls within the basic rate band for income tax and how much falls beyond it. Any gain which falls wholly into the basic rate band is taxed at 18% and any gain which falls above the basic rate band is taxed at 28%. Gains which straddle these rate bands must be apportioned accordingly and a percentage taxed at 18% and the remainder at 28%.

For the current tax year the relevant income tax bands are:

£0 – 32,010	= Basic Rate (i.e., 18% CGT)
£32,010 upwards	= Higher Rate (i.e., 28% CGT)

EXAMPLE

(a) Taxpayer A has no taxable income for the tax year in question and a chargeable gain of £25,000: the whole gain falls within the basic rate band and will be taxed at 18%.

(b) Taxpayer B has taxable income for the tax year in question of £55,000 and a chargeable gain of £25,000: the whole gain falls within the higher rate band and will be taxed at 28%.

(c) Taxpayer C has taxable income for the tax year in question of £30,000 and a chargeable gain of £25,000: £2,010 of the gain falls within the basic rate band and will be taxed at 18% and the remaining £22,990 will be taxed at 28%.

22.2.6 The CGT calculation

The following is an example of a simple CGT calculation, continuing the example given at 22.2.3.

EXAMPLE

Natalie bought a 15% shareholding in Transit Commercial Vehicle Hire Limited five years ago for £75,000. Legal fees incurred in negotiating the purchase amounted to £3,000. Natalie has recently sold her entire shareholding for £135,000. Legal fees incurred in negotiating the sale amounted to £5,000. Natalie's taxable income for the tax year in question was £90,000 and so she is a higher rate tax payer.

Capital Gain	£52,000
Deduct annual exemption	£52,000 − £10,900 = £41,100
Final CGT liability	£41,100 × 28% = £11,508

22.2.7 Disposals other than at arm's length

Where a disposal is other than at arm's length, i.e., where there is a gift element to the disposal, the market value of the asset at the time of disposal is treated as the consideration received. Any transfer between connected persons is always deemed to be otherwise than at arm's length, resulting in this rule applying. Connected persons are defined by s. 286 TCGA 1992. The basic categories are:

(a) a spouse, direct relatives, and relatives of the spouse of the disponer;

(b) companies under common control;

(c) partners in a business and spouses of partners;

(d) trustees and settlors (and any persons connected with the settlor).

This rule is of particular relevance to sales at an undervalue. Such a sale can be an arm's length, commercial transaction, in which case the actual price paid will be the relevant consideration for CGT purposes. However, any such undervalue transaction between connected persons will result in the market value of the asset being substituted.

EXAMPLE

Jo is selling a plot of land to Sheila. The land is worth £120 000, but Jo needs to raise money quickly and Sheila is currently the only interested party. As such, Jo sells the land for £100,000.

If Jo and Sheila are not connected persons, Jo will be treated as receiving £100,000 for CGT purposes.

If Jo and Sheila are connected persons, Jo will be treated as receiving £120,000 for CGT purposes.

22.2.8 Part disposals

Special rules apply in relation to the allowable deductions if there was a partial disposal of the asset. The effect of these rules is to permit the taxpayer to deduct only a proportion of the 'allowable expenditure'. This proportion is equal to the proportion which the part of the asset disposed of bears to the whole asset.

EXAMPLE

X sells part of a piece of land for £50,000. Total allowable expenditure on the whole plot of land amounts to £30,000. If the remaining land is worth £100,000, X can use a percentage of the allowable expenditure calculated as follows:

£50,000 ÷ (£50,000 + £100,000) = 0.33

0.33 × £30,000 = £10,000 allowable expenditure available.

22.2.9 Creation of losses by allowable expenditure

It may be that the 'allowable expenditure' in respect of a particular asset exceeds the sale price or market value. In those circumstances, the loss arising can be set off against other gains made during the current tax year. The gains in the current year must be reduced to nil. Only the balance of the loss once all other gains have been completely wiped out can be carried forward. Such losses can be carried forward indefinitely until gains arise in future years (although a carried forward loss must be set off against future gains as they arise). In contrast to the position for the year in which the loss initially arises, carried forward losses need only be set against the gains of future years to the extent necessary to bring that year's gains down to the amount of the then current annual exemption (see **22.2.4**).

EXAMPLE

Alan disposed of an asset in 2010/11 for £60,000. The allowable expenditure for that asset was £85,000. Alan was therefore left with a loss of £25,000. In the same tax year, Alan also realised a capital gain of £10,000. As such, this gain would be wiped out by the loss, leaving a balance of £15,000 of the loss to carry forward.

In 2011/12, Alan disposed of another asset, this time for £50,000. The allowable expenditure for that asset was £30,000. Alan therefore made a gain of £20,000.

Alan could then set off sufficient of the carried forward loss against the £20,000 gain to result in a net gain equal to the annual exemption for that tax year. The result would be that Alan would pay no CGT in that tax year (assuming no other disposals take place in 2011/12).

Whatever unused CGT loss remains can be carried forward indefinitely to be set off against future gains as they arise.

22.2.10 Exemptions for specific assets

The TCGA 1992 contains a variety of exemptions for specific assets, the details of most of which are beyond the scope of this book. They include exemption for:

(a) the taxpayer's only or main residence (s. 222 TCGA 1992);

(b) tangible movable chattels having a predictable useful life not exceeding 50 years, e.g., cars and items of plant and machinery (wasting assets) (s. 45 TCGA 1992); and

(c) non-wasting chattels where the consideration for disposal does not exceed £6,000, e.g., paintings and antiques (s. 262 TCGA 1992).

In the case of wasting assets, the effect is normally that the taxpayer cannot claim any allowable loss, as most such assets rarely appreciate in value. In the case of non-wasting chattels, the rule operates as a *de minimis* threshold—HMRC is simply not concerned with the small gains which may ensue from such disposals.

22.2.11 Deferment of tax

It is possible, in certain circumstances, to postpone or defer the payment of tax, as follows:

(a) If the disposal is by way of a gift, or there is a sale at an undervalue, the donor and donee can elect to 'hold over' any gain arising. This will result in the donee being treated as acquiring the asset at the donor's acquisition value. The basic effect of this arrangement is that, when the donee makes a chargeable disposal of the asset in the future, any CGT liability will be based both upon any gain made whilst the asset was in the donee's possession and the gain which was held over (see **22.2.12**).

(b) In certain circumstances, where the owner of certain types of assets sells them (even at full value), he can elect to 'roll over' the gain arising into replacement assets. The effect will be to reduce the acquisition cost of the new assets by the amount of the 'rolled over' gain. Any subsequent disposal of the replacement asset will bring both the rolled-over gain and any actual gain on that asset into the charge to CGT (see **22.2.13**).

(c) Gains realised on the disposal of any asset may be deferred into an investment in shares in a private limited company (see **22.2.14**).

Each of these will now be looked at in more detail.

22.2.12 Hold-over relief

Hold-over relief is available in circumstances including:

(a) transfers between spouses (s. 58 TCGA 1992);

(b) gifts or sales at undervalue of business assets (s. 165 TCGA 1992), in which case a joint election can be made by the transferor and transferee and any gain arising will be held over (for these purposes, business assets are those used for the purposes of a trade, profession, or vocation carried on by the transferor or his personal company and also include shares in an unquoted company or in the transferor's personal company; 'personal company' means that the donor holds at least 5% of the voting rights).

It should be noted that a claim for hold-over relief will mean that the whole gain in question must be held over and cannot be reduced by the donor's annual exemption.

EXAMPLE

A gifts an asset to C when the asset is worth £20,000. A's base cost for the asset is £8,000. Ignoring any other allowable expenditure, the gain on the disposal is £12,000. If A and C elect to hold over the gain, C takes over the asset with a base cost of £8,000.

If C disposes of the asset five years later when it is worth £30,000, ignoring any other allowable expenditure, C's taxable gain is £22,000.

A sale at an undervalue produces different results in that the whole of the actual chargeable gain cannot be held over and is, instead, reduced by the amount actually received by the seller in excess of the base cost of the asset sold.

EXAMPLE

S bought an asset for £10,000. S sells this asset to T for £20,000 when it is worth £25,000. S is deemed to receive £25,000, and so, the whole chargeable gain is £15,000.

If S and T elect to hold over, the chargeable gain must be reduced by the amount received by S in excess of the base cost, i.e., £15,000 is reduced by £10,000, which leaves £5,000, the amount of gain which can be held over. Thus, T will take the asset with a base cost of £20,000 (the market value of £25,000 less the £5,000 held over gain). S will be taxed on £10,000 worth of the gain.

22.2.13 Roll-over relief

There are two main types of roll-over relief:

(a) roll over on the replacement of certain business assets, pursuant to s. 152 TCGA 1992; and

(b) roll over of any gain from the disposal of any asset into a qualifying investment in shares.

Details of (b) are given at **22.2.14**. Type (a) is explained here.

The conditions to be fulfilled to benefit from replacement asset roll-over relief are:

(a) The original and the replacement asset must both fall within limited categories. The most common are land, buildings, and plant and machinery. Both the original and the replacement asset must be used as business assets throughout their periods of ownership.

(b) The purchase of the replacement asset must take place within the 12-month period before, or the 3-year period after, the disposal of the original asset.

(c) To roll over the whole gain realised on the original asset, the full proceeds of sale must be used to purchase the replacement. If a lesser sum is used, an amount equivalent to that by which the sale proceeds of the original asset exceed the cost of the replacement asset will become chargeable to tax immediately. This may result in the whole gain becoming chargeable, even though the relief is theoretically available.

Note that this relief is available both to individuals and companies disposing of business assets.

EXAMPLE

Ovid Limited is considering selling its trading premises and buying new ones. The proceeds from the sale are likely to be £155,000. It is considering three potential sites; one at £175,000 (Premises A); one at £145,000 (Premises B); and one at £130,000 (Premises C).

Assuming the gain on any sale of the original premises would be £20,000, the following would result:

Premises A—Total gain rolled over, as whole of proceeds of sale used; base cost of new premises for future CGT calculations = £155,000 (£175,000 − £20,000).

Premises B—Percentage of gain rolled over (£10,000); base cost of new premises for future CGT calculations = £135,000 (£145,000 − £10,000). Tax payable on £10,000 of gain.

Premises C—No amount of gain rolled over—difference in value between original and replacement asset is greater than amount of gain; base cost of new premises for future CGT calculations = £130,000.

22.2.14 EIS deferral of chargeable gains

As well as being a method of filling the public coffers, the taxation system can also be used to 'engineer' certain types of behaviour. One beneficial activity for business is to encourage high net worth individuals to invest in growing private companies, by affording such investment preferable tax treatment.

The Enterprise Investment Scheme (EIS) attempts to achieve this by offering three tax incentives:

(1) Income tax relief equal to 30% of any investment (subject to an investment limit of £1,000,000).

(2) CGT exemption for any gains on the investment (if held for more than three years).

(3) The deferral of an existing CGT liability by the investment of the proceeds of disposal, which would otherwise attract CGT.

It is beyond the scope of this chapter to examine the intricacies of the scheme as it applies to income tax. Furthermore, the CGT *exemption* is linked to the eligibility to income tax relief, so discussion will be limited to its impact as a capital gains tax *deferral* mechanism, that is, the third category of incentive mentioned above.

Any gain realised upon the disposal of *any* asset by an individual can benefit from the relief. However, to qualify, the investment can only take a specified form, that is, it must be:

(a) an allotment of fully-paid ordinary shares, with no rights of redemption or preference in whatever form for three years;

(b) in a company whose shares are unquoted;

(c) in a company which only carries on regular trading activities, e.g., is not an investment, property development, farming, or forestry company or the like, mainly in the UK;

(d) which does not have a gross assets value of more than £15 million before the investment (such value to include the value of assets owned by subsidiaries);

(e) which has fewer than 250 full-time employees at the time the investment is received; and

(f) which is not controlled by another company and which does not have any subsidiaries other than ones which also fulfil the requirements in (b) to (d).

In addition, the investment must take place no more than 12 months before or 3 years after the original disposal.

Because this is a scheme to encourage start-up/development capital for companies, any attempt to use the system solely to achieve a tax benefit or failure to use the funds realised in the trading activities of the company will result in the relief being withdrawn, resulting in an immediate liability to tax on the gain deferred. Also, for the same reason, it is not possible to sell shares in a company and then re-invest in that same company.

The investor will not be liable for tax on the deferred gain until such time as the shares are sold; there is no required minimum period of ownership.

It is not necessary to invest all of the proceeds of the original disposal to claim the deferral, an investment of an amount equivalent to the gain will be sufficient to defer the full value of it. Once the shares are sold any increase in their actual value will be subject to capital gains tax (unless the CGT exemption mentioned at the outset also applies).

EXAMPLE

Sumiya disposes of an asset in January 2005 and realises a gain ('the original gain') of £40,000. In June 2006 she invests in EIS-qualifying shares worth £85,000. These shares are sold in May 2010, realising a gain of £35,000. Issues to note are:

(a) The deferral takes place within three years of the original gain, so is within the time limits.

(b) The amount of the EIS investment exceeds the original gain, so the full amount of this gain is deferred.

(c) The sale in 2010 results in the original gain being taxed.

(d) The sale in 2010 also results in the gain of £35,000 being taxed (unless the further CGT exemption is also available under the EIS scheme).

22.2.15 Relief on disposal of a business (entrepreneurs' relief)

22.2.15.1 Introduction

This relief came into effect from 6 April 2008 and is aimed at providing relief from capital gains tax to qualifying individuals who dispose of all or part of a trading business, assets used in such a business, or shares in a trading company. Unlike the other reliefs considered so far, this relief actually reduces the taxpayer's CGT liability, rather than simply deferring it.

22.2.15.2 Availability of relief

The relief is available in respect of gains made on the disposal of:

(a) all or part of a business carried on by an individual, alone or in partnership (including professions and vocations but not property letting businesses, save for furnished holiday lettings); or

(b) assets following the cessation of a business, which assets were formerly used in that business and are disposed of within three years of cessation; or

(c) shares in a trading company (or a holding company of a trading group) where the individual disposing of the shares has been an officer or employee of that company (or a company in the same group) and owns 5% or more of its ordinary share capital which enables the exercise of at least 5% of the voting rights in that company.

An individual will be able to make claims for relief on more than one occasion. The lifetime limit on qualifying gains made after 6 April 2011 stands at £10 million.

22.2.15.3 Effect of relief

The effect of the relief is to tax qualifying gains at 10%. The qualifying gains are the aggregate of gains and losses relating to relevant assets.

EXAMPLE

Kumar realises a capital gain of £100,000.

Kumar is a higher rate taxpayer for income tax purposes, so, in normal circumstances, he would pay CGT at a rate of 28% on the gain = £28,000 payable.

If entrepreneur's relief applies to this gain, the effective rate of CGT is reduced to 10% = £10,000 payable.

It may be that a taxpayer realises more than one capital gain in a particular tax year, only one of which attracts entrepreneur's relief. In those circumstances different rates of tax must be applied to the different gains. Further, the gain which attracts entrepreneur's relief must first be aggregated with any income in the tax year, which may push other gains out of the basic rate band (although such other gains could benefit from the application of the annual exemption). However, this will only be a material consideration where a taxpayer has a small amount of taxable income or where the gain which attracts entrepreneur's relief is small. (See **22.2.5** for an explanation of the interaction between the income tax bands and the rate of CGT.)

EXAMPLE

Vincent has taxable income of £10,000.

He has also realised in the same tax year:

(i) a gain of £20,000 which attracts entrepreneur's relief ('Gain A'); and

(ii) a gain of £30,000 ('Gain B'), which does not.

Gain A will attract CGT at a rate of 10%.

Gain B will form the highest slice of Vincent's taxable receipts (i.e., after Gain A has been aggregated with his taxable income). A large percentage of Gain B will, therefore, fall entirely outside the basic rate band and attract CGT at a rate of 28%.

(i) £10,000 + £20,000 (Gain A) = £30,000

(ii) Balance of basic rate band = £2,010

Ignoring the Annual Exemption
Gain B taxed as follows:

£2,010 x 18%	= £361.80
£27,990 x 28%	= £7,837.20

If, alternatively, Vincent's taxable income had been in excess of the basic rate band or the gain attracting entrepreneur's relief had been, for example, £25,000, then all of Gain B would have attracted CGT at 28% (£10,000 + £25,000 exceeds the basic rate threshold).

22.2.15.4 'Associated disposal' of business assets

Where an individual qualifies for entrepreneurs' relief on a disposal of shares or securities, relief is also available for any 'associated disposal' of an asset which was used in the company's (or group's) business. For example, if a company director who owns the premises from which the company carries on its business sells the premises at the same time as he sells his shares in the company, the sale of the premises may count as an 'associated disposal' and qualify for entrepreneurs' relief. The relief on an associated disposal is restricted where the asset in question was not wholly in business use throughout the period it was owned.

A similar rule allows relief on an 'associated disposal' by a member of a partnership who is entitled to relief on disposal of his interest in the assets of the partnership. Again, relief is restricted where the asset in question was not wholly in business use throughout the period of ownership.

22.2.16 Death of taxpayer

No capital gains tax is payable when a person dies. The personal representatives of the deceased under the will or intestacy are deemed to acquire the deceased's assets at market value at the time of death. As such, there is neither a gain nor loss. Moreover, all legatees of the estate are deemed to acquire any assets at the base cost of the personal representatives. However, should an asset appreciate in value whilst in the hands of the personal representatives and be disposed of by them to third parties (as opposed to being distributed to legatees), this will result in a gain in the hands of the personal representatives.

22.3 CGT in the business context

Liability to capital gains tax can arise in a variety of situations. The purpose of the following sections 22.4 to 22.7 is to look at the common business scenarios where such liability is likely to arise and to consider the applicability of reliefs and exemptions in such situations.

22.4 Disposals of partnership property

22.4.1 General

When a firm disposes of one of its assets, normal CGT principles apply in determining what gain, if any, the firm has made. There are difficulties involved in applying the normal CGT principles to a partnership context. The premise on which HMRC operates is for each partner to be treated as owning a fractional share of each of the chargeable assets of the partnership (including goodwill) and not, for this purpose, as owning an interest in the business as a whole. When the firm disposes of an asset to an outsider, each partner is treated as making a disposal of his fractional share in the asset.

What follows is concerned with the disposal by a firm of its assets. CGT issues can also arise when partners leave and join partnerships. These are discussed in **Chapter 23**.

22.4.2 Assessment

The assessment and collection of CGT is treated differently from the assessment and collection of income tax. The precedent partner delivers a return to HMRC giving full details of disposals. The assessment is made on the individual partners. Each partner's share in the gain is calculated in accordance with his share in the asset disposed of.

In order to calculate the CGT liability of the individual partners in relation to the disposal of assets it is, therefore, necessary to know the proportions in which assets are owned. This is often referred to as the partners' 'asset surplus ratio'.

22.4.3 Asset surplus ratio

The partnership deed may specify the proportions in which asset surpluses are to be shared. If it does, it is conclusive. If there is no express provision in the partnership deed, the asset surplus sharing ratio is deemed to be the ratio in which profits are shared. It is common for a partnership deed to provide an asset surplus sharing ratio which is different from the profit sharing ratio. For example, the agreement may provide for an individual partner's right to share in an asset surplus to be greater than his right to share in income profits, to reflect the fact that he has made a substantial capital contribution to the firm while contributing comparatively little to earning income profits.

When an asset is acquired by a partnership, each partner's share in the acquisition value is determined by his share in the asset surplus *at that time*. Similarly, in a disposal, each partner's share in the proceeds of disposal is determined by his share in the asset surpluses *at that time*.

EXAMPLE

A and B are in partnership. They share profits equally and have made no special agreement as to sharing asset surpluses. They acquire an asset for £20,000. The acquisition value for each partner is:

A	½	£10,000
B	½	£10,000

They sell the assets for £36,000. The share in the proceeds of the disposal of each partner is:

A	½	£18,000
B	½	£18,000

The chargeable gain of each partner is:

A	£18,000 – £10,000 = £8,000
B	£18,000 – £10,000 = £8,000

Each partner is personally liable for his own chargeable gain and will be assessed for tax at the rates appropriate to his level of income.

22.4.4 Reliefs

If there is a gain realised on the disposal, the exemptions and reliefs already referred to may be available. To the extent that there is a gift element in a disposal, hold-over relief is available to postpone the payment of tax.

A disposal of partnership property in circumstances where the partners intend to re-invest the sale proceeds can attract roll-over relief (under ss. 152–160 TCGA 1992).

22.5 Disposals of shares

22.5.1 Disposals by individuals

A capital profit on the sale of shares by an individual will in most cases attract a liability to capital gains tax and the general principles and reliefs already referred to will apply, with the exception of roll-over (replacement asset) relief under s. 152 TCGA. However, there is a notable exception to this rule when the purchaser of the shares is the company in which the shares were issued. This is dealt with at **22.7**.

22.5.2 Disposals by companies

A disposal by a company of shares it owns in another company will be subject to capital gains. However, the following should be noted:

(a) Companies can claim indexation allowance for the full period of ownership (see **Chapter 18**).

(b) Any capital gain realised by a company will form part of its profits for corporation tax purposes (see **Chapter 18**).

(c) Should the disposal be of a 'substantial shareholding', no charge to tax will arise. A company will be treated as disposing of a substantial shareholding if such shareholding comprises at least 10% of the ordinary share capital and both the selling company and the company in which it owns shares are trading companies and have been for a two-year period prior to disposal. In addition, the shareholding in question must have been owned for a period of at least 12 months in the two-year period prior to the sale.

22.6 Disposals of business assets owned by those involved in the business

22.6.1 Reliefs

It is not uncommon for shareholders/directors or partners to own assets which are used by their respective companies or partnerships. The disposal of such assets may result in a CGT liability for the person concerned.

However, many of the reliefs mentioned above will be available: roll-over (replacement asset) relief; hold-over relief; and entrepreneurs' relief.

22.6.2 Wasting assets

Should the asset have a predictable, useful life of less than 50 years, it will be CGT-exempt in any event. Many such assets do not appreciate in value and are more likely to be sold at a loss, however, so this exemption will then work against the taxpayer, as no allowable loss will be created.

22.7 The purchase by a company of its own shares

22.7.1 The basic position

Where a company redeems or buys its own shares, tax will usually become payable. The amount received from the company is in most cases treated as a dividend (and so is subject to income tax in the hands of the recipient) to the extent that it exceeds the original investment in the company. (See **20.2.3** for further discussion of the income tax treatment of dividends.) The return of the original cost of the shares is a capital sum.

EXAMPLE

Purchase Ltd buys back shares from A for £9,000. A originally subscribed for his shares at a nominal value of £1,000. Purchase Ltd is treated as making a dividend of £8,000. A receives the return of his investment of £1,000 at the same price as he paid for it, so there are no capital gains tax consequences (ignoring any items of actual allowable expenditure, etc.). A also receives a dividend of £8,000 which has borne basic rate income tax at source. The consequences of this are as follows:

(a) if the dividend falls to be taxed entirely at basic rate income tax, A need pay no further tax;

(b) if some or all of the dividend falls to be taxed at higher rate income tax, A must account for the balance of the tax due;

(c) if some of the dividend is exempted from tax by falling within A's personal allowance, A will be unable to claim back any of the tax already deducted;

(d) if A has tax-exempt status, for example, as a charity or pension fund, again, as in (c), A will be unable to claim back any tax.

Payments to buy back members' shares are not deductible in calculating the company's profits for corporation tax purposes.

22.7.2 The capital gains tax alternative

Section 1033 Corporation Tax Act 2010 contains provisions excluding such a payment from the definition of a distribution in certain circumstances. Where the payment is so excluded, the redemption or repayment is treated wholly as a disposal for CGT purposes as if it were a sale and capital gains tax will be payable on any increase in the value of the shares during the period of ownership.

This may or may not have beneficial consequences for the relevant shareholder. We will examine this issue after we have considered the effect of s. 1033.

A redemption, repayment, or purchase by the company is excluded from the definition of a distribution if the company is a trading company and the transaction is made 'wholly or mainly for the purposes of benefiting a trade carried on by the company'. Presumably, the transaction will be made for such a purpose if the object of it was to enable a shareholder of the company who disagreed with the policy of the directors to retire from the business if the company had more capital than it required. A transaction designed to enable the proprietors to take an income tax-free profit would not be covered, and this is reinforced by the further requirement that the main purpose or one of the main purposes of the scheme must not be 'to enable the owner of the shares to participate in the profits of the company without receiving a dividend or the avoidance of tax'. A redemption, repayment, or purchase is also excluded from the definition of a distribution if the proceeds are intended to be used (and are used within two years) for the payment of inheritance tax (IHT). The IHT must have arisen on a death and the shareholder must show that undue hardship would have arisen if the shares had not been purchased by the company.

In addition to the basic requirements of s. 1033, income tax is only avoided if the following conditions are satisfied:

(a) the owner of the shares is resident and ordinarily resident in the UK at the time of the purchase;

(b) he has owned the shares for five years;

(c) the sale is of a substantial part of his shareholding taking into account any holding of his associates (which term includes close relatives, partners, and trustees of certain settlements); and

(d) certain special conditions apply only in the case of groups of companies.

The object of these rules is to ensure that tax avoidance or tax advantages cannot be obtained by a purchase of its own shares by a company, but that 'genuine' transactions should give rise to CGT liability only. It is possible to apply for advance clearance when a scheme to buy back shares is proposed which, if granted, will ensure that putting the proposal into effect will not give rise to an income tax charge.

EXAMPLE

Suppose in the above example the receipt by A fell within s. 1033. A would receive a capital sum of £9,000, from which the base cost of his shares could be deducted, resulting in a capital gain of £8,000.

A taxpayer will wish a buyback to fall within s. 1033 if the application of CGT results in a lower tax charge than if income tax were payable. For example, the taxpayer may have incurred capital losses which could be set off against the gain; or a capital gain may be a lesser amount than an income gain; or the shareholder might be in a position to claim entrepreneurs' relief. Also, whilst most taxpayers will normally have other income sufficient to use up their personal allowance, if no other chargeable gains have been incurred in the tax year in question, the full CGT annual exemption will be available.

EXAMPLE

Five years ago Rehana was allotted 10,000 shares at par in Surface Solutions Limited. The nominal value of each share was £5. Surface Solutions is to buy back 2,000 of Rehana's shares at £15 per share for a total consideration of £30,000. Rehana has taxable income of £43,000.

Income tax position

Capital sum returned	£10,000
Net income received	£20,000
(plus tax credit of £2,222)	______
Gross income received	£22,222

Rehana is a higher rate taxpayer, therefore gross income receipt taxed at 32.5%, less the tax credit, gives an income tax liability of £5,000.

Section 1033 alternative

Capital sum received	£30,000
Less:	
Base cost	£10,000
Chargeable gain	£20,000
Less:	
Annual exemption	£10,900

This would leave Rehana liable to pay CGT at 28% on £9,100, giving a CGT liability of £2,548.

22.8 Inheritance tax

22.8.1 General

Inheritance tax (IHT) is payable under the provisions of the Inheritance Tax Act (IHTA) 1984 where there is a *chargeable transfer*. The chargeable transfer is defined as 'any *transfer of value* which is made to an individual but is not . . . an exempt transfer'. A transfer of value is defined as 'a *disposition* made by a person . . . as a result of which the value of his estate immediately after the transfer is less than it would be but for the disposition . . . '. Inheritance tax is payable on the *value transferred* which is the amount by which the value of the transferor's estate is reduced as a result of the disposition.

Transfers of value can be made either *inter vivos* as a result of gifts or sales with a gift element or on death. In this section, we only give an outline of the principal aspects of the tax.

The reader is referred to one of the standard tax textbooks for full details of all of the aspects of the tax.

As *inter vivos* gifts and sales at an undervalue can also attract CGT (see **22.2.2**), it is important to consider both capital taxes in such a context. This will be unnecessary on the death of a taxpayer, as only inheritance tax will be payable.

22.8.2 Types of transfer

There are three types of transfer which can give rise to inheritance tax (subject to the availability of any exemptions or reliefs). These are:

(a) a transfer on death which will attract tax at the full rate of 40%;

(b) a potentially exempt transfer (PET) which is an *inter vivos* transfer of value made by an individual as a result of which property becomes part of the estate of another individual or is transferred to certain types of trust. (As such, transfers to companies do not qualify as potentially exempt.) A PET will become fully exempt if the transferor lives for seven years after the transfer. Death within those seven years will result in the transfer becoming chargeable at the rates of tax in force at the date of death. Most likely examples are gifts of cash, real property, or shares; and

(c) a chargeable transfer made before death which is immediately taxable but at only half the rates which apply on death; that is, 20%. The death of the transferor within seven years will lead to the transferee becoming liable to tax at the full rates in force at the date of death. There are very few instances of such chargeable transfers, the most likely being the transfer of property into a discretionary trust.

22.8.3 Cumulation

There are only the above two rates of inheritance tax. There is a nil rate band for the current tax year of £325,000 and any excess is taxed at the rate of 20% or 40%, depending on the type of transfer—see **22.8.2** above. However, no transfer can be looked at in isolation. Whether or not the nil-rate band has been used up in relation to a particular chargeable transfer will depend on the total value of all previous chargeable transfers which the transferor has made within the immediately preceding seven years (this includes lifetime chargeable transfers and PETs which become chargeable because of death). This process of cumulation will mean that the tax on the present transfer will be calculated as if it were the top slice of a single transfer equal in value to all of the transfers (including the one in question) made during the last seven years.

In a great many instances, the issue of cumulation will not arise and only the total value of the taxpayer's estate will be subject to the nil-rate band. However, this will not be so where any transfers have been made out of the taxpayer's estate prior to death.

EXAMPLE

Example one

Keith dies in June 2010 and the value of his estate at the time of his death is £375,000. If he has made no transfers out of his estate at any relevant time the amount of £50,000 in excess of the nil-rate band will be taxed at 40%.

However, should Keith have made the following transfers, cumulation would have to be considered:

March 1999—PET of £50,000
June 2003—PET of £70,000
February 2006—PET of £100,000

The PET in 1999 is more than seven years before Keith's death, so falls out of the picture. However, the other two PETs are both within seven years of his death, becoming chargeable to tax as a result. The cumulative total of the PETs is £170,000. As this total does not exceed the nil-rate band, no tax is payable on them. However, as Keith's death estate must be cumulated with the PETs, this means that only £155,000 of the nil-rate band will be available to set against his death estate. As such, £220,000 of his death estate will be taxed.

Example two

In real terms, the giving away of PETs is quite likely to reduce the value of the death estate. Therefore, the above rule may not be quite so harsh.

Assume that if Miranda had made no transfers during her lifetime, her estate would have been worth £700,000. On her death in May 2010, £375,000 of her estate would have been chargeable to tax.

If, instead, she had made the following transfers:

January 2004—PET of £50,000
August 2005—PET of £200,000

the value of her estate at death could be assumed to be reduced to £450,000.

Therefore, whilst the two PETs become chargeable, thus using up some of Miranda's nil-rate band, her death estate is correspondingly reduced. (Moreover, PETs attract an annual exemption, which may mean a small amount of the estate is free from IHT totally—see **22.8.5**.)

Example three

Lifetime chargeable transfers (LCT) complicate matters. As they are taxable at the time they are made, they must be cumulated with any other chargeable transfers in the previous seven years and then have the nil-rate band applied to them.

Raj, who is still living, has so far made the following transfers:

March 2009—PET of £150,000
June 2011—LCT of £183,000
February 2012—PET of £100,000

His current IHT position is that neither of the PETs attracts any tax. The LCT should be cumulated with any chargeable transfers in the previous seven years (there are none) and have the nil-rate band applied to it. Any excess over the nil-rate band should be taxed at 20%. At this stage, therefore, the LCT bears no tax.

If Raj dies in January 2015, all his lifetime transfers must be re-examined. The effect will be as follows:

(a) The March 2009 PET becomes chargeable and becomes subject to the nil-rate band. Accordingly it will bear no tax.
(b) The LCT must now be cumulated with the March 2009 PET, which means that the revised cumulative total becomes £333,000 and therefore £8,000 worth of the LCT is now subject to tax at 40%.
(c) The February 2012 PET becomes chargeable and must be cumulated with all chargeable transfers in the previous seven years. The cumulative total at this stage is now £433,000 and all this PET is taxed at 40% as the whole of the nil-rate band has been used up.
(d) Raj's death estate must be cumulated with all chargeable transfers in the previous seven years, that is, all the previous three (now) chargeable transfers. As a consequence, the whole of the death estate will also be taxed at 40%.

What should be noted from this example is that it is incorrect to think of a taxpayer only having one cumulative total. Depending on the taxpayer's circumstances, a number of cumulative totals may have to be considered and re-considered as part of the taxpayer's changing IHT profile.

The full rate of 40% only applies where the transfer is made on death or within three years of death. If the transfer is a potentially exempt transfer or a chargeable transfer which occurs within four to seven years of the death of a taxpayer, a sliding scale applies to determine the value of the transfer which will be subject to tax at the full rates in force at the time of death. This relief operates on the basis of a reduction in the amount of tax which would normally be payable at the full rate as follows:

(a) transfers six to seven years before death—20% of the tax payable;
(b) transfers five to six years before death—40% of the tax payable;

(c) transfers four to five years before death—60% of the tax payable;

(d) transfers three to four years before death—80% of the tax payable.

EXAMPLE

Talbot made a PET of £400,000 five-and-a-half years before he died. He made no other transfers during his lifetime. On his death, the nil-rate band would be applied to the PET and the balance of £75,000 would have to be taxed at 40%. The full tax charge is therefore £30,000. However, only 40% of this is payable as the PET occurred between five and six years before death. The actual liability will be £12,000.

22.8.4 Value transferred

The value of the property transferred plays an important part in the calculation of the liability to inheritance tax. For the purposes of inheritance tax, the value of particular items which have been given away will be the price which the property might reasonably be expected to fetch if it was to be sold in the open market at the time of the gift. Quoted stocks and shares can usually be valued by reference to the price at which they were being traded on the relevant day. The value of unquoted shares (normally those in private companies) will be determined by the normal market value rule but it is sometimes extremely difficult to value such shares accurately. The facts that have to be taken into account include the company's profitability, its dividend record, the level of retained earnings, and the value of the assets which the company owns. Should the shares be sold subject to pre-emption rights, the market value will be determined on the assumption that the pre-emption rights did not apply to the hypothetical sale. However, those rights will be assumed to apply to the hypothetical purchaser (which will mean that the value so determined would be the one which a purchaser was likely to pay in the full knowledge that the pre-emption rights will apply to their shares in the future).

Although not exclusively applicable to shares, a further rule of particular relevance when valuing shareholdings is the rule relating to 'related property'. This rule recognises the fact that some assets can be more valuable when combined with other assets of the same type than when they are owned individually. Shares which form part of a majority holding in a company will, for example, be more valuable than shares which form part of a minority shareholding. The IHTA 1984 defines a variety of items of property as being related property. This can include any item of property owned by the transferor's spouse at the time of the transfer. If the transfer is made of related property, the property actually transferred and the property to which it is related are valued as a single asset and tax is then calculated on the proportion of the total value which is transferred.

(This textbook does not cover any of the other detailed rules on the calculation of tax, such as the rules relating to gifts with a reservation or changes in values of gifts within seven years of death.)

22.8.5 Exemptions

At the start of this section, we stated that a chargeable transfer was any transfer of value which is not an *exempt* transfer. An exempt transfer will not attract tax and it will not be included in the transferor's cumulative total. The exemptions which can be claimed include the spouse exemption which is available both during lifetime and on death (thus, all gifts irrespective of value, between spouses are exempt from inheritance tax provided the recipient spouse is domiciled in the UK). An annual exemption of £3,000 per year is available on transfers made before death. If the annual exemption for any year is not used either wholly or partially, the unused part can be carried over for one year but no longer. In addition, small gifts to individuals up to £250 per recipient are exempt.

EXAMPLE

Consider again Keith's estate in the example at **22.8.3**. Applying the annual exemption to each PET which becomes chargeable to tax, it will be seen that £6,000 can be deducted from each one, being the annual exemption for the year in question together with the unused exemption from the previous year.

June 2003—PET of £70,000 – £6,000 = £64,000

February 2006—PET of £100,000 – £6,000 = £94 000

As such, the cumulative total of the chargeable PETs at the time of Keith's death is reduced to £158,000, freeing up an extra £12,000 of the nil-rate band to apply against his death estate.

22.8.6 Business property relief

22.8.6.1 General

In addition to the exemptions, the IHTA 1984 also makes various reliefs available which include quick succession relief, agricultural property relief, and business property relief. The effect of a relief being available is to reduce the value of the relevant property with a resultant reduction in the amount of inheritance tax payable.

In this section we will look only at business property relief, which is available provided the property was 'relevant business property'. This term is defined as:

(a) property consisting of a business or an interest in a business (and so it includes the interest of a sole proprietor or a partner in a business);

(b) shareholdings in unquoted companies or companies quoted on the Alternative Investment Market;

(c) shareholdings in quoted companies which alone or with other shares owned by the transferor or with related property gave the transferor control immediately before the transfer (control means being able to exercise more than 50% of the votes in general meeting—temporary control will suffice);

(d) land or buildings, or machinery or plant used immediately before the transfer wholly or mainly for the purposes of a company controlled by the transferor or of a partnership of which he was a member;

(e) land or buildings, machinery or plant used immediately before the transfer for the purposes of a business carried on by the transferor and which was settled property in which the transferor had an interest in possession.

The relief on such a property is a reduction in the value transferred of 100% (in the case of property falling within (a)–(b) above) or 50% (in the case of property within (c)–(e) above).

22.8.6.2 'Business'

For the purposes of this relief, 'business' includes a profession or a vocation but does not include a business carried on otherwise than for gain. Agriculture is a type of business and so business property relief may be available to the extent that agricultural relief is not. If the business consists of dealing in securities, stocks, shares, land or buildings, or of holding investments, the relief is not available. However, business property relief will be available where the business is the active management of land.

The reduction in value is given on the net value of the business property (that is to say, after the liabilities have been deducted).

Even if the property falls within the categories set out above, relief will not be available unless the transferor has owned the property throughout the two years before the transfer. If property replaces other relevant business property (other than in the case of minority shareholdings), relief is available provided the aggregate period of the ownership of the original and replacement property exceeds two years in the five years before the time of transfer. If the transferee of relevant business property himself makes a transfer of the same property before he has owned the property for two years, this will not prevent the relief being claimed provided the relief was available on the original transfer and one of the transfers was a transfer on death. If property is received on the death of a spouse, the surviving spouse can aggregate the deceased spouse's period of ownership with his own in order to satisfy the two-year period of ownership requirement.

22.8.6.3 Period of ownership

If a business (or other relevant business property) has been owned for two years (or more), business property relief at the appropriate percentage is available on the full value at the time of transfer. There is no obligation to show that particular assets of business have been owned for two years. Having said that, the value of an asset will be excluded from relief if it has not been used wholly or mainly for the purpose of the business throughout the two years preceding the transfer or throughout the period since it was acquired, if later.

22.8.6.4 Anti-avoidance

As a way of preventing taxpayers placing private assets in a business and then trying to obtain business property relief on them, s. 112 IHTA 1984 provides that relief is not available on 'excepted assets'. These are assets which are neither:

(a) used wholly or mainly for the purposes of the business concerned throughout the whole of the previous two years; nor

(b) required at the time of the transfer for future use.

These are alternative requirements. An asset which fulfils either one of the requirements will not be an excepted asset. However, (b) is not available where relief is claimed on an asset used by a company controlled by the transferor or by a partnership of which he is a member.

22.8.6.5 Potentially exempt transfers

Where a transfer is made before death (whether it is chargeable or potentially exempt) and the transferor dies within seven years, the relief is available only if the property originally given or qualifying property representing it has remained as relevant business property in the ownership of the transferee from the date of the transfer to the date of the death of the transferor. If the transferee dies before the transferor within the seven-year period, relief is only available on the death of the transferee if the same condition is satisfied. The property must remain relevant business property in the hands of the transferee. If only a proportion of the property originally given or qualifying property representing it remains in the ownership of the transferee at the date of death, relief is available on the proportion of the property owned at that date. It is sufficient if 'property representing' the original property is in the hands of the donee at the relevant date. It should, however, be noted that:

(a) the whole of the consideration must have been applied on acquiring the replacement property;

(b) replacement property must be acquired within three years after the disposal of the original property; and

(c) the provision applies only to the first replacement and not to subsequent ones.

It is not our intention to deal with the complex rules for determining who is liable to account for inheritance tax to the Inland Revenue on death, nor to consider the rules on the burden or incidence of inheritance tax.

22.8.7 Payment of IHT

Tax on a chargeable transfer made before death must be paid six months after the end of the month in which the transfer is made or, if the transfer is made after 5 April and before 1 October, at the end of April in the next year. Tax in relation to a death is payable six months after the end of the month in which the death occurred. If tax is paid late, interest will be charged.

Inheritance tax on certain types of property can be paid by 10 annual instalments. The instalment option is available in respect of:

(a) land of any description;

(b) shares or securities in a company giving the transferor control of the company immediately before death;

(c) unquoted shares or securities which do not give the transferor control (provided paying the tax in one lump sum will not cause any hardship);

(d) unquoted shares or securities not giving the transferor control in the company, provided at least 20% of the tax paid by the person paying the tax on the shares is either tax on those shares or on those shares and other instalment options;

(e) unquoted shares which did not give the transferor control and the value of which exceeds £20,000, provided they are at least 10% of all the shares of the company or are ordinary shares and at least 10% of the ordinary shares in the company; and

(f) business or interest in a business including a profession or vocation.

Shares quoted on the Alternative Investment Market are still 'unquoted' for these purposes. Control means voting control on all questions affecting the company. The relief is available whether the transfer is on death or *inter vivos* but, in the latter case, the relief is only available if the *transferee* pays the inheritance tax. The instalment option must be claimed by a written notice to the Revenue and the outstanding instalments must be paid off if the assets are sold within the 10-year period.

If the instalment option is available, the first instalment is generally due six months after the end of the month in which the gift has been made. No interest is charged on the tax provided the instalments are paid on time. Although the instalment option does not reduce the amount of tax, the relief is nonetheless beneficial.

The primary liability for IHT on lifetime chargeable transfers falls on the transferor. However, it is also possible for the transferee(s) to meet this liability. If the tax is paid by the transferor, the loss to the transferor will be the value of the gift plus any inheritance tax on it. This will mean that the inheritance tax calculation will be based on the gross loss to the donor. In those circumstances, it will be necessary to 'gross-up' the net gift before the calculation of the tax can be made. If the transferee(s) pay the IHT, no such considerations come into play. This will result in a smaller IHT bill.

The IHT liability arising on death will be met primarily by the personal representatives of the deceased out of the death estate. The liability of the personal representatives is limited to the amount they receive in their capacity as personal representatives.

22.8.8 Partnerships

The IHT legislation contains few provisions dealing specifically with partnerships. According to the general principle of IHT, any transfer of a partnership asset, or of an interest in a partnership, will be a transfer of value by the individual partners if the transfer is by way of gift or there is an element of gift in the disposition.

The transfer will be exempt if it is made between spouses. It will also be exempt if it was not intended to, and was not made in a transaction intended to, confer any gratuitous benefit and either it was an arm's length transaction between unconnected persons or was such as might be expected to be made between unconnected persons.

As a result of this provision, many *inter vivos* transfers which might appear to be transfers of value will escape inheritance tax. For example, when a new partner is admitted and is given a share in the assets without making a payment, there would be a transfer of value were it not for this provision. This is considered in **Chapter 23**.

On death, a deceased partner's interest in the partnership will be part of his estate. The position is considered more fully in **Chapter 23** but business property relief (see **22.8.6**) will normally be available.

22.8.9 Shareholdings

The gift of shares may give rise to inheritance tax (and capital gains tax) since inheritance tax is chargeable on the 'loss to the donor's estate'. This normally means the market value of the asset given away, but in some cases the loss is considerably more than market value. For example, if a controlling shareholder gives away enough shares to lose control of the company, the loss to his estate will be very much more than the value of the shares given away.

The most important (but not only) 'reliefs' which will be relevant when shares in a company are given away are 'business property relief' and the instalment option (considered in **22.8.7**).

These reliefs exist because the Government recognises that too high a tax burden on the disposal of shares in a company could lead to the break-up of a company as being the only way of raising funds to pay the tax. It should not be forgotten that the general exemptions (such as the spouse exemption and the annual exemption) will be available in respect of business property, as well as the business property relief.

Anybody in business should consider the possible impact of tax on his family from a relatively young age. It should be clear from the rules described in this chapter that there is a very considerable fiscal advantage in disposing of assets *inter vivos* so as to take account of the fact that the IHT lifetime rates are lower than the death rates, and tax can be avoided altogether if the donor survives seven years after a potentially exempt transfer has been made. Since transfers of value are only cumulated for seven years after they are made (i.e., transfers made more than seven years ago are ignored in calculating the amount of tax), there is an advantage to be gained from making gifts of shares over a considerable period of time rather than all at once. The burden of IHT can also be reduced in the long run by making use of the spouse exemption to ensure that both husband and wife leave enough to take maximum advantage of the nil-rate band that they each have.

online resource centre

For further resources and online chapters please visit the Online Resource Centre at www.oxfordtextbooks.co.uk/orc/business13_14/.

23

Tax consequences of leaving and joining a partnership

This chapter covers the following topics:

23.1 Introduction

In **Chapter 5** we saw that it was possible for an individual to cease to be a partner on the happening of one of the following events:

(a) the dissolution of the partnership;

(b) retirement or death; or

(c) expulsion from the partnership.

Having considered the legal consequences of the occurrence of these events in **Chapter 5**, we will concentrate in this chapter on the tax consequences (particularly the circumstances in which tax charges can arise). We will only consider the tax exemptions and reliefs where they are of special relevance.

We will also consider the position of a new partner joining the firm, whether or not as a replacement for a deceased, retired, or expelled partner.

In this chapter we will not repeat the legal consequences so the reader is recommended to review **Chapter 5** for this information.

Reference is made throughout this chapter to both capital gains tax and inheritance tax. It is recommended, therefore, that **Chapter 22** has been read beforehand.

23.2 Tax consequences of the dissolution of a partnership

23.2.1 Introduction

If a partnership is dissolved by one of the methods explained in **Chapter 5**, the partnership relationship ceases and the assets of the business may be realised. From this will flow various tax consequences.

23.2.2 Income tax

If there is a permanent cessation (on a closure of the business) the relevant closing year rules will be applied (see **17.3.2.3**).

If the partnership has been claiming capital allowances on, for example, the plant and machinery used in the business, balancing charges may be levied if the assets are disposed of for more than their written down value on cessation. Balancing allowances may be claimed if the market value of the assets is less than their written down value.

Finally, if the partnership has made losses, loss relief under s. 89 ITA 2007 in respect of the final tax year of the trade may be claimed. Terminal loss relief will permit the partners to carry back losses made in the final 12 months of the trade against the profits of the same trade during the immediately preceding three tax years or set them off against other income in the year of cessation (see **17.4**).

23.2.3 Capital gains tax

If the partnership property is sold to outsiders following dissolution any gains realised by each partner on the disposal of his fractional share of the assets will be taxable in accordance with general principles. The general principles will also apply when a partner disposes of assets he owns personally but which have been used by the partnership.

23.2.4 Inheritance tax

If the assets of the partnership are disposed of at full market value on dissolution, there will be no reduction in the value of the transferor's estate and, therefore, no transfer of value. If there is no transfer of value there cannot be any IHT liability.

23.3 Tax consequences of the retirement of a partner

23.3.1 Introduction

As we explained in **Chapter 5**, while 'retirement' implies a person retiring from full-time work having reached normal retirement age, in the partnership context 'retirement' simply means leaving the partnership voluntarily so that the age of the 'retiring' partner is irrelevant. In this section we have examined the tax charges which can arise when there is such a change in the partnership.

23.3.2 Income tax

When any partner retires, the closing year rules will apply in order to calculate that partner's final income tax liability on partnership earnings (see **17.3.2.3**).

23.3.3 Capital gains tax

23.3.3.1 Disposals amongst partners

Where one partner retires from the business he will normally relinquish his interest in the partnership assets in consideration of a capital sum and/or the provision of an income. The retiring partner's present interest in the business is shown on his capital account. He will be treated as making a disposal of that interest to the continuing partners. The continuing partners will acquire his interest and will thereafter have a greater interest in the business.

Originally, the lack of a comprehensive body of legislation dealing with the taxation of capital gains realised by partners led to HMRC introducing Statement of Practice D/12, which sets out their view of the way in which general capital gains tax principles apply in a partnership context. The underlying principle on which the Statement of Practice D/12 is based is that each partner is to be treated as owning a fractional share of each of the chargeable assets of the partnership (including goodwill).

EXAMPLE

A, B, C, and D share profits (and asset surplus) equally. The assets of the firm were acquired for £60,000. A is retiring and once he has retired, all the profits will be divided equally between B, C, and D. The asset-sharing ratio will change as follows:

	Before	*After*
	£	£
A	15,000 (1/4)	(—)
B	15,000 (1/4)	20,000 (1/3)
C	15,000 (1/4)	20,000 (1/3)
D	15,000 (1/4)	20,000 (1/3)

A has disposed of his quarter interest to the continuing partners and is left with nothing. Each of the continuing partners receives one-third of A's quarter share (i.e., one-twelfth share in the partnership property). They will, naturally, each pay A for such share.

It can be clearly seen from the above example that the retiring partner has made a disposal to the continuing partners. The question then arises of whether or not the disposal has realised a gain (or a loss). Where the assets have not been revalued in the accounts and the retiring partner receives an amount equivalent to the balance on his capital account, he is simply receiving the return of his original capital contribution. There will be no gain and no loss (D/12, para. 4). For example, in the above illustration, if A was paid £15,000 he would realise neither a gain nor a loss.

However, there will be a gain on disposal where assets have been revalued in the accounts (D/12 para. 5). Where assets have increased in value since the date of acquisition the partners may wish to record this increase in the accounts: the process is referred to as a 'revaluation'. The values of the various assets are increased in the accounts and the balances on the partners' capital accounts are increased by a corresponding amount in order to reflect the increase in the worth of the business. A revaluation of itself gives rise to no charge to CGT since there has been no disposal. However, if after a revaluation there is a change in the asset surplus sharing ratio, for example on retirement, the disponer partner will receive more than his original capital contribution and (subject to reliefs) there will be a charge to capital gains tax.

EXAMPLE

The facts are as in the previous example but the partnership decides that prior to A's retirement the assets should be revalued from £60,000 to £90,000. A's share will be worth £22,500. Therefore A will be treated as disposing of assets for £22,500 which were acquired for £15,000, and will have a capital gain of £7,500.

	Before	*On revaluation*	*After*
	£	£	£
A	15,000(1/4)	22,500(1/4)	–
B	15,000(1/4)	22,500(1/4)	30,000(1/3)
C	15,000(1/4)	22,500(1/4)	30,000(1/3)
D	15,000(1/4)	22,500(1/4)	30,000(1/3)
	60,000	90,000	90,000

B, C, and D will each be treated as acquiring £7,500 worth of A's share in the assets and therefore their respective base costs will increase from £22,500 to £30,000. They are, therefore, holding assets which have increased in value to them from £15,000 to £30,000. When they realise the assets, there will be a CGT liability.

The members of the partnership, in order to minimise the burden of finding large capital sums, may agree not to revalue assets as and when partners retire. It could be argued that this is a gift by each retiring partner of his share in the increased value of the asset. In the case of a gift (or sale at an undervalue), HMRC can treat the disposal as made for market value unless it was a bargain made at arm's length. In the case of connected persons, transfers are always treated as otherwise than by way of bargains made at arm's length. Partners are normally connected but will not be when transferring property to each other provided the disposal *was pursuant to a bona fide commercial arrangement.* Thus, provided there is some bona fide commercial reason for not revaluing, HMRC will not seek to substitute market value.

Even where the partners are connected other than by partnership (for example, father and son) HMRC has stated that it will only seek to substitute market value where the transaction would not have been entered into by persons who were not at arm's length.

23.3.3.2 Entitlement to reliefs

If a charge to tax arises on the disposal by a partner of his interest in partnership property, the disponer will be entitled to claim the benefit of the CGT exemptions and reliefs in the normal way.

Details of relevant reliefs are given in **Chapter 22**.

23.3.3.3 Disposal of assets owned by partners personally

Where a partner disposes of an asset which he owns personally but which is used by the partnership, the Statements of Practice are not relevant. On such disposals the normal CGT principles are applied to ascertain whether a gain or loss has arisen. Similarly, the disposing partner will be able to claim any relevant exemptions or reliefs.

23.3.4 Inheritance tax

Normal principles of IHT apply in the partnership context. Thus, where a partner sells an interest in the partnership for full consideration there is no transfer of value and therefore no charge to IHT arises. If a partner sells an interest for less than full consideration or transfers it for no consideration at all, prima facie a charge to IHT will arise. However, s. 10 IHTA 1984 provides that a disposition is *not* a transfer of value if it was not intended to confer gratuitous benefit and was either made at arm's length between unconnected persons or, if between connected persons, was such as might be expected to be made between unconnected persons. Partners are not connected persons in respect of transfers between partners of partnership assets pursuant to bona fide commercial arrangements. Thus, many transfers which might appear to be chargeable may escape IHT on the ground that there was no intention to confer a gratuitous benefit.

23.4 Tax consequences of death of a partner

23.4.1 Introduction

As we saw in **Chapter 5**, under the Partnership Act death causes the automatic dissolution of a partnership, although it is common to provide in partnership agreements that this will not happen. In this section, we look at the tax consequences of the death of a partner.

23.4.2 Income tax

The deceased partner's income earned during the relevant tax year will be subject to the closing year rules.

23.4.3 Capital gains tax

The deceased partner's interest in the partnership assets is *acquired* by his personal representatives at market value on the date of death. Since a disposal is a prerequisite for liability to CGT, this means that no CGT is payable on death and that unrealised gains arising during the deceased's lifetime escape the charge to tax.

23.4.4 Inheritance tax

23.4.4.1 General

The estate of a deceased partner will include his interest in the partnership assets. Under s. 4(1) IHTA 1984, the partner is deemed to make a transfer of value on his death and the value transferred is the value of the assets in his estate immediately before his death. Accordingly, subject to exemptions, reliefs, and the deceased partner's cumulative total at the date of death, IHT will be payable in respect of the market value of his share in the partnership.

Changes in the value of assets resulting from death are taken into account for IHT purposes. If all or part of the value of the goodwill of the business was personal to the deceased partner the value of the goodwill, and therefore of the business, will fall as a result of the death. The reduced value of the deceased partner's share in the business will then be included in his estate for IHT purposes.

23.4.4.2 Business property relief

Where an IHT liability does arise on death it may be reduced by virtue of the relief for business property given by ss. 103–114 IHTA 1984. An interest in the partnership is relevant business property qualifying for business property relief at 100%. For land, buildings, plant or machinery owned by a partner personally but used wholly or mainly for the purpose of the partnership of which he is a member, a reduction of only 50% is available. (See **22.8.6** for a full discussion of this relief.).

However, there is no entitlement to claim the relief if the assets are the subject of a binding contract for sale at the time of death. A clause in the partnership agreement to the effect that the surviving partners are *obliged* to buy and the personal representatives of the deceased partner are *obliged* to sell the deceased partner's share may have been included in the agreement for sound commercial reasons but it will result in the loss of business property relief. This is because HMRC regards such clauses as amounting to binding contracts (see Statement of Practice 12/80 dated 13 October 1980). If there is no *obligation* to buy and sell, the relief is available and so this difficulty can be avoided by the use of an option arrangement or an automatic accruer clause.

23.4.4.3 Instalment option

IHT attributable to an interest in partnership property can be paid in 10 yearly instalments under ss. 227 and 228 IHTA 1984. The first instalment is due six months after the end of the month of death and no interest is due unless an instalment is late. If the interest in partnership property is sold, all outstanding IHT must be paid off. Where the continuing partners purchase the interest of a deceased partner the instalment option will not thereafter be available to the deceased partner's estate.

23.5 Tax consequences of expulsion from a partnership

In **Chapter 5** we saw that s. 25 of the Partnership Act 1890 provides that the majority of the partners can expel any partner unless a power to do so has been conferred by express agreement between the partners. If the partnership agreement does contain such a power and it is exercised, the tax consequences of expulsion are the same as for retirement.

23.6 Tax consequences of admission of a new partner

23.6.1 Introduction

Although this chapter is primarily concerned with leaving a partnership, the admission of new partners is a topic so closely connected that it seems appropriate to deal with it here.

23.6.2 Income tax

Because partners are treated as notional sole traders for tax purposes, when a partnership starts up, all partners will be equally subject to the opening year rules (see **17.3.2.2**). Accordingly, when a new partner is admitted to an existing partnership, that partner will be treated as if starting up a trade and will initially be subject to the opening year rules, while the original partners will continue to be taxed on the normal current year basis.

EXAMPLE

Y and T are in partnership sharing profits equally. The accounting year end for the business is 30 June. On 1 January 2012, W is admitted to the partnership and will share profits equally with Y and T. W joins, therefore, in the tax year 2011/12.

The tax liability of Y and T for the tax year 2011/12 will be based on profits to the year end 30 June 2011. W's tax liability for his year of joining (2011/12) will, according to the opening year rules, be based upon his profit entitlement from 1 January 2012 to 5 April 2012.

The tax liability of Y and T for the 2012/13 tax year will be based on the share of profits earned during the accounting year ending on 30 June 2012; one-half of profits each up to the date of W's joining and one-third each thereafter.

The tax liability of W for the 2012/13 tax year will be based on W's share of profits for his first 12 months of notional trading, i.e., from 1 January 2012 to 31 December 2012. (This is because the relevant year end in this tax year is not more than 12 months from the date of W's joining.)

For the tax year 2013/14 all three partners will be assessed on a current year basis on profits up to the year end 30 June 2013, i.e., from 1 July 2012 to 30 June 2013.

It will be noted that W's tax liability is based upon a certain amount of double taxation; the profits from 1 January 2012 to 5 April 2012 are taxed twice along with profits from 1 July 2012 to 31 December 2012. C may be able to claim overlap relief in respect of this.

If the new partner has to borrow money to raise the funds to buy into the partnership, the borrower will be able to deduct the interest as a charge on his income. The same relief is available if the borrower uses the funds to contribute additional capital to the partnership or to make a loan to the partnership, if it is used exclusively for the partnership's business purposes.

23.6.3 Capital gains tax

A newly admitted partner will acquire an interest in the partnership assets either by purchase or by gift. Thus, for example, if the old partners give the incoming partner a one-third share in profits and asset surpluses, he will acquire one-third of the value of the partnership assets at that date. That value will be his acquisition value/base cost in respect of any future disposal which attracts CGT.

EXAMPLE

A and B, who share profits and assets equally, decide to admit C and to share profits and assets equally thereafter. The partnership assets are shown in the accounts as worth £120,000 at the date of C's admission.

	Before	*After*
	£	£
A	60,000(1/2)	40,000(1/3)
B	60,000(1/2)	40,000(1/3)
C	—	40,000(1/3)

C's acquisition value is, therefore, £40,000.

23.6.4 Inheritance tax

Inheritance tax is unlikely to be an immediate problem for a newly admitted partner. However, he might be the recipient of a potentially exempt transfer of value. If so, it is possible that the transfer will become chargeable if one or more of the transferor partners dies within seven years.

online resource centre

For further resources and online chapters please visit the Online Resource Centre at www.oxfordtextbooks.co.uk/orc/business13_14/.

24 Value Added Tax

This chapter covers the following topics:

24.1 Introduction

Value Added Tax (VAT) is charged on supplies of goods and services made in the UK. Where a person makes taxable supplies in excess of a set limit in any one-year period, he must register with HM Revenue and Customs (HMRC). He must then account to HMRC for VAT on all taxable supplies made. The total amount payable may be reduced by the amount of VAT which he has paid on certain taxable supplies made *to him*.

The liability to pay VAT to HMRC rests on suppliers of goods and services. However, the cost of the tax is actually borne by suppliers' customers (unless they can recover VAT) who are charged VAT on the goods and services they purchase.

VAT is charged in the UK under the Value Added Tax Act (VATA) 1994. The obligation to charge VAT arose when the UK became a member of the European Economic Community in 1973. VAT is the common tax on business turnover within the European Union and should be applied in the same manner in each Member State.

24.2 Registration

24.2.1 Turnover limits for registration

Under Sch. 1 VATA 1994, a person becomes liable to register for VAT with HMRC if:

(a) at the end of any month, the value of taxable supplies made during the past year exceeds £79,000; or

(b) at any time, there are reasonable grounds to believe that the value of taxable supplies to be made in the next 30 days alone will exceed £79,000.

If, at the end of any month, a person's taxable turnover in the past 12 months or less exceeds £79,000 but HMRC is satisfied that it will not exceed £77,000 in the next 12 months, that person will not have to be registered.

Where a person makes taxable supplies which do not exceed the relevant turnover limits, he may apply to be registered for VAT on a voluntary basis. The relevant turnover limits for registration are those in force from 1 April 2013 and may be altered in the future.

24.2.2 'Person' for VAT purposes

VATA 1994 requires registration by a 'person'. The latter includes an individual, a body corporate, or a partnership (notwithstanding that the latter has no separate legal personality). A person is only entitled to one VAT registration (irrespective of the number of businesses run) and is therefore liable for VAT on taxable supplies made by *all* of their businesses. There are exceptions to this rule, one being that a company which is organised into several divisions may seek registration for each division.

24.2.3 Registration documentation

A person applying for VAT registration must complete an application form, VAT 1. A partnership must also submit details of all the partners on a Form VAT 2. Most registrations can be completed using the HMRC online VAT registration system.

24.2.4 Effect of registration

Once registered, a person is liable to account for VAT to HMRC on all taxable supplies of goods and services made in the UK.

24.2.5 De-registration

A person may apply to be de-registered for VAT if he ceases to make taxable supplies or if he can satisfy HMRC that taxable supplies for the next 12 months will not exceed £77,000. This turnover limit for de-registration is that in force from 1 April 2013 and may be altered in the future.

24.3 Taxable supplies and the charge to VAT

24.3.1 Taxable supplies

VAT is charged on taxable supplies of goods and services made in the UK. A taxable supply is one which is made in the course of furtherance of business and is not classified as exempt from VAT under Sch. 9 VATA 1994. (Examples of exempt supplies include most sales of land and buildings, insurance, doctors' services, and certain types of education services.)

24.3.2 Rates of VAT on taxable supplies

A taxable supply will be charged at one of three rates: standard, reduced, or zero. The standard rate of VAT (which has been in place since 4 January 2011) is 20%. The reduced rate is 5% and applies to a limited range of goods and services, such as energy supplies. Its application may vary according to circumstances or who a customer is, so is subject to specific rules. Zero-rated supplies do not actually give rise to a VAT charge, They may, however, allow a person to recover input tax paid on supplies *received by the supplier* (see **24.4.4**).

Zero-rated supplies are set out in Sch. 8 VATA 1994 and include:

(a) food (except restaurant);

(b) children's clothing and shoes;

(c) books and newspapers; and

(d) sales of new houses.

24.4 Accounting for VAT

24.4.1 Charging VAT to customers

A person should start charging VAT to his customers and keep relevant records as soon as he realises that he is liable to register for VAT with HMRC.

24.4.2 Invoice to customers

Once registered, a person will be given a VAT registration number. This must be included on tax invoices sent to customers for supplies of goods or services. The tax invoice should also include the date of supply, type of supply, total amount payable, and the amount of VAT chargeable at the relevant rate. This VAT, charged to customers, will meet the liability to HMRC.

24.4.3 VAT Return

A registered person is required to make a VAT Return every three months (although monthly or annual Returns may be agreed with HMRC). The Return determines a person's VAT liability to HMRC and thus a system of *self-assessment* operates. The Return must be completed and the relevant tax paid within a month from the end of the three-month period to which it relates.

From April 2012, all businesses (save for a very small number of exempt businesses) have been required to complete their VAT Returns online and make electronic payments of VAT.

There is an option, for businesses with an estimated VAT taxable turnover of up to £1,350,000, to join an annual accounting scheme. This allows a business to submit a single VAT Return each year. The business makes either three (quarterly) or nine (monthly) advance payments to HMRC of the VAT it expects to owe at the end of the year. The business's VAT Return is then sent in at the year-end, together with any outstanding VAT payable. If the business has overpaid VAT, it will be returned by HMRC. The scheme is intended to assist businesses in managing cashflow by making regular payments.

24.4.4 Amount of VAT payable

24.4.4.1 Standard method of calculating net tax due

The amount of VAT payable by a taxable person will effectively be the standard rate of 20% as charged on all supplies of goods and services made in the relevant three-month period. This is often referred to as *output tax*, i.e., the amount of VAT charged to customers on supplies *made* by a taxable person.

Output tax may be reduced by *input* tax. This is VAT which the taxable person has paid on supplies *made to* him. However the amount of input tax which can be set off against output tax is limited to the input tax attributable to taxable supplies made by that person. Put another way, you can only set off input tax relating to supplies which are used in some way in making taxable supplies to others.

If a person makes zero-rated supplies, there is no output tax charge. From a customer's perspective, it is as if it is an exempt supply. However, the taxable person is entitled to recover any input tax attributable to zero-rated supplies made by him. This is the benefit derived from zero-rated supplies, compared with exempt supplies.

Note that it is possible, particularly where a person makes predominantly zero-rated supplies, for recoverable input tax to be in excess of output tax. In such cases, HMRC will repay any excess.

The ability to recover input tax and the effect of zero-rated supplies is illustrated in the following examples. Note the following:

(a) each example relates to a single three-month VAT period;

(b) the input tax has been assumed to be wholly attributable to the taxable supplies made; and

(c) the supplies received and made figures are shown *exclusive* of any VAT, the latter being shown in a separate column.

EXAMPLE 1

Cost of supplies received	*VAT on supplies received (input tax)*	*Standard rate supplies made*	*VAT on supplies (output tax)*	*Net VAT payable*
1,000	200	1,600	320	120

EXAMPLE 2

Cost of supplies received	*VAT on supplies received (input tax)*	*Zero-rate supplies made*	*VAT on supplies (output tax)*	*Net VAT recovered*
1,000	200	1,600	0	200

24.4.4.2 Optional flat rate scheme

HM Revenue and Customs operates a scheme which enables businesses to calculate their net VAT due simply by applying a flat rate percentage to their tax-inclusive turnover (the total turnover generated, including all reduced, zero-rate, and exempt income). The flat rate percentage will depend upon the trade sector into which a business falls for the purposes of the scheme. For example, the following flat rates currently apply in these sectors: legal services—14.5%; food retailing—4%; and general building services—9.5%. The scheme is limited to businesses with a VAT-exclusive annual taxable turnover of up to £150,000.

The aim of the scheme is to ease the administrative burden on small businesses. Those who opt to use the scheme, in most cases, can work out the net VAT due by simply recording their tax-inclusive turnover and applying the appropriate flat rate percentage for their trade sector. Businesses will still need to issue tax invoices to their VAT registered customers, but will not have to record all the details of the invoices issued or purchase invoices received to calculate their VAT. However, businesses in the scheme may not generally set off input VAT on purchases against VAT on supplies made (see **24.4.4.1**). This is because the flat rate percentages contain an allowance for VAT on purchases. Businesses may be part of both the flat rate and annual Return (see **24.4.3**) schemes.

24.4.5 Calculation of tax on VAT-inclusive figure: the VAT fraction

Calculation of standard rate VAT payable on *VAT-exclusive* figures (as used in the above examples) is comparatively easy. It merely requires calculation of 20% of the VAT-exclusive figure.

A figure which combines both the price of the supply *and* the VAT payable on the supply is said to be *VAT-inclusive*. To calculate the VAT element of a VAT-inclusive figure, you multiply the figure by the fraction which provides the equivalent of 20% on the VAT-exclusive price. That fraction is 1/6 and is known as the *VAT fraction*. It will obviously change with the standard rate of VAT.

EXAMPLE

The VAT-inclusive price of goods supplied is £2,856.
1/6 of £2,856 = £476. This latter figure is the amount of VAT payable.
Therefore, the VAT-exclusive price of the goods is £2,856 – £476 = £2,380.
(NB 20% of £2,380 = £476.)

---

online resource centre For further resources and online chapters please visit the Online Resource Centre at www.oxfordtextbooks.co.uk/orc/business13_14/.

Insolvency

25

Personal bankruptcy

This chapter covers the following topics:

25.1 Introduction

The risk of personal bankruptcy is a spectre which haunts many partners and sole traders. If a partner or sole trader finds that he is unable to pay his debts as they fall due, he may be made personally bankrupt. Thus, the partner or sole trader may be made bankrupt if his liabilities exceed his assets; he faces the same risk if he has insufficient liquid assets to pay his current liabilities even if the value of his total assets exceeds the value of his total liabilities.

It is to avoid this risk that many entrepreneurs choose to trade through a limited company. However, it should not be forgotten that the directors and members of a company may face personal bankruptcy where, for example, they have personally guaranteed a loan to the company.

The members or partners may, of course, also find themselves facing bankruptcy as a result of a financial collapse entirely unconnected with the business of their own company or partnership.

The result, for someone who finds himself unable to meet all his debts in full, is that he may:

(a) be adjudicated bankrupt; or

(b) have his estate administered by a qualified insolvency practitioner under a voluntary arrangement (see **25.9** below).

The law of bankruptcy is now mostly contained in the Insolvency Act (IA) 1986 together with delegated legislation made under its provisions. The Enterprise Act (EA) 2002 amended the 1986 Act in a number of ways. These changes came into force for the financial year 2004 and:

(a) shortened the period for automatic discharge of most bankrupts;

(b) introduced a new Bankruptcy Restriction Order regime;

(c) imposed a time limit within which a trustee in bankruptcy must deal with a family home; and

(d) introduced a fast track individual voluntary arrangement scheme.

The overall intention behind these changes was to promote a more entreprenurial culture within the UK whilst ensuring that the public remains protected from anyone who is irresponsible or reckless in carrying on their business.

25.2 The bankruptcy procedure

25.2.1 Introduction

Bankruptcy proceedings are commenced by the presentation of a petition for a bankruptcy order. The petitioners (who, broadly speaking, simply have to prove that the debtor is unable to pay his debts) are:

(a) a creditor (or creditors jointly) whether secured or unsecured; or

(b) the debtor personally; or

(c) a supervisor of, or a person bound by, a voluntary scheme; or

(d) the Director of Public Prosecutions.

25.2.2 Procedure on a creditor's petition

25.2.2.1 Prerequisites for presentation of a creditor's petition

The court will only entertain a petition presented by a creditor or creditors if certain conditions are satisfied:

(a) The debtor must normally be domiciled or personally present in England and Wales when the petition is presented.

(b) The debt (or debts) which are the basis of the petition must be for a liquidated sum.

(c) The debt (or debts) must amount to at least £750. (This sum can be changed from time to time by statutory instrument.)

(d) The debt must be unsecured. A secured creditor can present a petition but only if he relinquishes his security or petitions only for the unsecured part of the debt.

25.2.2.2 Grounds for presenting a creditor's petition

The petitioning creditor must allege that the debtor appears either:

(a) to be unable to pay; or

(b) to have no reasonable prospect of paying

the debt or debts specified in the petition and that there are no outstanding applications to have a 'statutory demand' set aside. (A 'statutory demand' is a demand in a form which complies with the Insolvency Rules 1986, r. 6.1.) The functions of the demand are described below.

25.2.2.3 Proving inability to pay debt

Before the court will make the order, the debtor's inability to pay his debt or debts may be proved in one of two ways:

(a) by showing that a 'statutory demand' served on the debtor requiring him to pay, secure, or compound for the debt to the satisfaction of the petitioning creditor has not been complied with within three weeks;

(b) by showing that execution or other process issued in respect of the debt as a judgment or order of any court has been returned unsatisfied in whole or in part.

25.2.2.4 Grounds on which court may dismiss petition

Once a petition has been presented by a creditor the court may dismiss the petition if it is shown that the debtor can pay all his debts, including contingent and prospective debts; if the creditor has unreasonably refused any offer made by the debtor in response to a 'statutory demand'; or if it is appropriate to dismiss the petition for any reason, including a breach of the rules.

The court *must* dismiss a petition if a 'statutory demand' has been complied with.

25.2.3 Procedure on a debtor's own petition

The debtor himself may present a petition provided he has a connection with England and Wales. Accordingly the debtor must be able to show that he satisfies the requirements set out in **25.2.2.1(a)** above.

The only ground on which the petition can be based is that the debtor is unable to pay his debts. When presenting the petition, the debtor must lodge a 'statement of affairs' giving full details of his assets, liabilities, and creditors. Once presented, the petition can only be withdrawn with leave of the court.

In most cases the court will order an insolvency practitioner to inquire into the debtor's affairs and report on whether the debtor is willing to make a proposal for a composition with his creditors and/or whether the creditors should be summoned to a meeting at which they will consider such a proposal. Having considered the report of the insolvency practitioner the court can, if it considers it appropriate, make a bankruptcy order. Otherwise the voluntary composition will be pursued or the court can issue a certificate of summary administration.

25.2.4 Presentation of a petition by a supervisor of, or a person bound by, a voluntary arrangement

The supervisor of, or a person bound by, a voluntary arrangement (the details of which are considered below in **25.9**) may base a petition on the following grounds:

(a) that the debtor has failed to comply with his obligations under the scheme (or failed to comply with the supervisor's reasonable requests in connection with the scheme);

(b) that the debtor has provided false or misleading information in connection with entry into the scheme.

25.2.5 Presentation of a petition by the Director of Public Prosecutions

The DPP has power (under the Powers of Criminal Courts Act 1973) to apply to have a person made criminally bankrupt if the person has been convicted of an offence where loss in excess of a specified value has occurred.

25.2.6 Consequences of presenting a petition

25.2.6.1 Restrictions on dispositions

A debtor who is the subject of a bankruptcy petition may be tempted to dispose of property before he is adjudicated bankrupt. The IA 1986 makes void any disposition of property or payment of money made after the presentation of a petition if the debtor is subsequently adjudicated bankrupt unless the court approves the transaction either before or after it takes place.

25.2.6.2 Restrictions on proceedings

The court has power to stay any action, execution, or legal process against the debtor or his assets while bankruptcy proceedings are pending.

25.2.7 Making the bankruptcy order

Once the petition has been presented, the court may exercise its discretion to make a bankruptcy order (or, in the case of a petition presented by the debtor personally, to make an interim order so that a voluntary composition with the creditors can be arranged).

25.2.8 Procedure following the making of the bankruptcy order

25.2.8.1 The official receiver becomes receiver and manager of the estate

Unless a trustee in bankruptcy is appointed at the time the bankruptcy order is made, the official receiver (who is an official of the court) will become the receiver and manager of the bankrupt's estate on the making of the order, pending the appointment of a trustee in bankruptcy.

25.2.8.2 Statement of affairs by the bankrupt

The bankrupt must, unless the official receiver dispenses with the requirement, prepare a statement of his affairs within 21 days (although this time limit may be extended by the official receiver). Failure to do so is contempt of court.

When the debtor presents his own petition he must prepare a statement of affairs which is lodged with the petition.

25.2.8.3 Public examination of the bankrupt

At any time after the order is made and before the bankrupt is discharged, the official receiver can apply for an order that the bankrupt be required to attend a public examination of his affairs.

25.2.8.4 Appointment of a committee of creditors

Following the making of the bankruptcy order, a committee of creditors can be appointed by the creditors (unless the official receiver has been appointed as trustee in bankruptcy, in which case the Secretary of State performs the function of the committee).

25.3 The trustee in bankruptcy

25.3.1 Introduction

The IA 1986 provides that the administration of a bankrupt estate should be carried out by a trustee in bankruptcy.

25.3.2 Appointment

The procedure for appointing a trustee in bankruptcy and the date on which his appointment takes effect differ depending on who makes the appointment.

25.3.2.1 Appointment by creditors

If the official receiver is acting as receiver and manager of the bankrupt's estate, he has 12 weeks from the making of the order to decide whether to call a meeting of the creditors for the purpose of appointing a trustee. If he decides to call such a meeting he must notify the creditors within the 12-week period. He *must* call such a meeting if one-quarter (by value) of the creditors demand it and if he decides not to call a meeting, one-quarter (by value) of the creditors can override his decision. Provided the creditors do not object to no meeting being called, on notifying the court that no meeting will be held, the official receiver automatically becomes the trustee.

25.3.2.2 Appointment by the court

If the order is based on the debtor's own petition, the insolvency practitioner who is appointed to report on the debtor's affairs can be appointed as the trustee.

25.3.2.3 Appointment by the Secretary of State

The Secretary of State has power to appoint the trustee if the creditors fail to make an appointment at their meeting.

25.3.3 Functions of the trustee

The function of the trustee is to get in, realise, and distribute the bankrupt's estate in accordance with the provisions of the Act.

25.3.4 Powers of the trustee

The Act gives the trustee wide powers which he may exercise in the course of administering the bankrupt's affairs. He may:

(a) sell any part of the property for the time being comprised in the bankrupt's estate, including the goodwill and book debts of any business;

(b) give receipts for any money received by him;

(c) prove, rank, claim, and draw a dividend in respect of such debts *due* to the bankrupt as are comprised in the bankrupt's estate;

(d) exercise in relation to any property comprised in the bankrupt's estate any powers which the Act vests in him as trustee;

(e) exercise all the powers of a receiver appointed by the High Court to enable him to collect or retain the bankrupt's estate;

(f) exercise all the powers the bankrupt could exercise to transfer shares, stock, or other property;

(g) exercise extensive powers to require delivery, production, or inspection of books, documents, and records;

(h) apply to the court for orders directing the bankrupt to do any act in connection with the administration of the estate;

(i) hold property, make contracts, sue and be sued, employ agents, execute documents, and do any act which may be necessary or expedient for the exercise of his powers;

(j) disclaim onerous property (e.g., unprofitable contracts).

There are certain further powers which are only exercisable with the consent of the committee of creditors (if there is one) or of the court. These include:

(a) power to carry on the bankrupt's business with a view to a beneficial winding up;

(b) power to mortgage or pledge assets with a view to raising money for the estate;

(c) power to make any compromise or arrangement as may be expedient with the creditors of the estate;

(d) power to require the bankrupt to do any acts in the management or carrying on of the bankrupt's business.

25.3.5 Retirement, removal, and release

25.3.5.1 Resignation

A trustee in bankruptcy may resign only if the resignation is accepted either by a creditors' meeting or by the court. Resignation must arise out of ill-health, retirement from practice, conflict of interest, or other sufficient causes.

25.3.5.2 Removal

The appointees of creditors can be removed either by the court or by the creditors themselves at a general meeting summoned specially for the purpose.

25.4 Effect of the bankruptcy order on the bankrupt personally

If the court exercises its discretion to make a bankruptcy order against the debtor, he will become an undischarged bankrupt and will be deprived of the ownership of his property.

An undischarged bankrupt suffers certain disabilities; for example, he cannot practise as a solicitor or barrister nor act as a director, nor be involved in the management of a company. Furthermore, an undischarged bankrupt faces criminal liability if he commits one of the offences specified in the 1986 Act. These include making gifts of property, concealing property, and obtaining credit without disclosing the bankruptcy.

25.5 Assets in the bankrupt's estate

25.5.1 Introduction

The trustee in bankruptcy is under an obligation to collect the bankrupt's assets and distribute them among the bankrupt's creditors. In this section, we consider which assets can be claimed by the trustee towards payment of the bankrupt's debts.

25.5.2 Avoidance of dispositions made after the presentation of the petition

Any disposition made by the bankrupt in the period between presentation of the petition and the date the estate of the bankrupt vests in the trustee in bankruptcy is void, unless the court gave prior consent to (or subsequently ratifies) the disposition.

25.5.3 Vesting the assets in the trustee

Once the bankruptcy order is made, the undischarged bankrupt is deprived of the ownership of his property.

25.5.4 Bankrupt's family home

The trustee must deal with the bankrupt's interest in the property within three years, failing which it will revert back to the bankrupt unless the trustee:

(a) realises the interest;

(b) applies for an order of sale or possession in respect of the premises in which the interest subsists;

(c) applies for a charging order over the premises in respect of the value of the interest; or

(d) enters into an agreement with the bankrupt regarding the interest.

The three-year period may be extended by application to the court.

25.5.5 Property not available to the trustee

If the bankrupt enjoyed a purely personal right, such as the benefit of the Rent Act statutory tenancy, this is not available to the trustee. The following items are also not available for distribution:

(a) property held by the bankrupt in trust for any other person;

(b) the tools of his trade, as well as such wearing apparel and bedding as is necessary to satisfy the basic needs of the bankrupt and his family;

(c) the personal earnings of the bankrupt to the extent that those earnings are not in excess of what is required to satisfy the reasonable domestic needs of the bankrupt and his family.

25.5.6 Extension of trustee's title to bankrupt's property

The Act gives the trustee power to claim assets which are no longer in the possession or ownership of the bankrupt in the circumstances set out below.

25.5.6.1 Transactions defrauding creditors (ss. 423 to 425)

Grounds

Section 423 IA 1986 can be used to give relief in respect of transactions defrauding creditors. To be within the scope of s. 423 a transaction must be:

(a) a transaction at an undervalue entered into between one person and another; and

(b) be accompanied by the requisite intent, namely that it is done for the purpose of putting assets beyond the reach of a person who is making, or may at some time make, a claim against the relevant person, or of otherwise prejudicing the interests of such a person in relation to the claim which he is making or may make.

Time limit

The transaction that is the subject of an action under s. 423 can have taken place at any time; there is no time limit.

25.5.6.2 Undervalue transactions

If a person who is subsequently made bankrupt has transferred property to, for example, a member of his family or to trustees to hold for the benefit of his family the transaction may be voidable under s. 339 IA 1986.

Grounds on which transaction voidable

If the transaction is at an undervalue and is with a person who is not an associate of the transferor, it is voidable at the instance of the trustee in bankruptcy if the transaction took place within the five years ending with the day on which the bankruptcy petition which ultimately led to the individual being adjudged bankrupt was presented (unless the debtor was solvent at the time of, and despite entering into the transaction). However, if the individual entered into the transaction at an undervalue within two years of the presentation of the relevant bankruptcy petition, the transaction is voidable irrespective of whether the debtor was insolvent at the time of, or as a result of, the transaction.

Transfer to associate

In circumstances where the transferee is an 'associate' of the transferor, transactions entered into during the period of two to five years preceding the presentation of the petition are presumed, unless it can be *proved* to the contrary, to have taken place at a time when the transferor was insolvent. 'Associate' is defined as the bankrupt's spouse or former or reputed spouse, and, in relation to any of them or the bankrupt, a brother, sister, uncle, aunt, nephew, niece, lineal ancestor, or lineal descendant (including relatives of the half-blood, stepchildren, adopted, and illegitimate children). A company controlled by the bankrupt or any associate(s), as defined, is an associate.

25.5.6.3 Voidable preferences

A debtor who is in financial difficulties may not only make an undervalue transaction (as described in **25.5.6.2** above) but he may also be tempted to give a 'voidable preference' (s. 340 IA 1986).

Grounds

A 'voidable preference' consists of the debtor doing or suffering anything to be done at a time when he is insolvent which 'has the effect of putting [the person who benefits from the preference] into a position which, in the event of the [debtor's] bankruptcy, will be better than the position he would have been in if that thing had not been done'. Thus, a debtor discharging one of his unsecured, ordinary creditor's debts in full at a time when his assets are insufficient to discharge *all* his debts in full may have given a voidable preference.

If the trustee in bankruptcy considers that a voidable preference has been made, he may apply to the court to remedy the preference. However, an order can only be made where it can be proved that the debtor was 'influenced in deciding to give it by a desire' to improve the position of the creditor. Under these provisions the intention to prefer the particular creditor need not be the *dominant* intention.

Preference given to 'associate'

In cases where the preference is given by an individual to his 'associate' (see **25.5.6.2** above), there is a *presumption* that the debtor was influenced by the desire which would make the preference voidable, unless the contrary is proved.

Time limits

A preference is voidable if it takes place within the two years ending with the presentation of the bankruptcy petition, if the person preferred is an associate, but in other cases the preference is only actionable if it took place in the six months preceding the presentation of the petition.

25.5.6.4 Family homes

The Insolvency Act contains provisions designed to protect the family home of the bankrupt for the benefit of his family (see also **25.5.4**).

If the family home is owned in the sole name of the bankrupt the 1986 Act charges the right of occupation of the spouse of the bankrupt on the interest of the trustee in bankruptcy in the matrimonial home. If an application is made to realise the bankrupt's interest in the house the court will consider certain factors when deciding whether to grant an application for sale of the house. These factors include the creditors' interests, the needs and resources of the spouse, the needs of the children, whether the spouse's conduct contributed to the bankruptcy, and all other relevant circumstances. (If the matrimonial home is owned in joint names by the bankrupt and his spouse, the discretionary factors listed above will be taken into account when the trustee applies under s. 30 of the Law of Property Act 1925 to realise the bankrupt's interest.) If the application is made after one year has elapsed since the bankrupt's property vested in the trustee in bankruptcy, the interests of the creditors will be paramount.

If the bankrupt's minor children lived in the home at the time of presenting the petition and when the bankruptcy order was made, the bankrupt cannot be evicted without a court order. The court will consider the creditors' interests, the bankrupt's financial resources, the needs of the children, and all the circumstances when deciding whether to make the eviction order. If the application is made after one year has elapsed since the bankrupt's estate vested in his trustee, the interests of the creditors will outweigh all other considerations, unless the circumstances are exceptional.

25.6 Distribution of the bankrupt's assets

25.6.1 Distribution procedure

Having realised as much of the bankrupt's assets as possible without needlessly protracting the administration of the estate, the trustee must notify the creditors that he intends to declare a final dividend (or that no dividend will be declared). The notice must also state a final date for the proving of claims (although the court has power, on application by any person, to postpone this date). Subject to any postponement, any creditor who fails to prove by the final date may be ignored in the final dividend.

25.6.2 Order of priority for payment of debts

The distribution of the bankrupt's assets must be made strictly in accordance with the statutory order for payment of debts which is as follows:

(a) secured creditors, who take the mortgaged or charged property in priority to all other claims. However, if the security is insufficient to meet the debt, as far as the excess is concerned, the secured creditor claims as an ordinary creditor;

(b) the administration costs of the bankruptcy paid to the official receiver, the trustee in bankruptcy, and others, including professional advisers who have given assistance;

(c) certain sums paid to masters by their apprentices;

(d) the preferential debts which are the same as those relevant on a company liquidation (see **26.8.4**). These debts are calculated by reference to the 'relevant date', which, generally, is the date the bankruptcy order is made (unless an interim receiver is appointed following the presentation of the petition, in which case the date is that on which the receiver is first appointed), and include:

(i) employees' arrears of wages or salary (including time or piece work and commission) for four months prior to the relevant date subject to an overall financial limit prescribed by delegated legislation (currently £800). These sums include sick pay, protective awards, and payments for time off work, such as on trade union work;

(ii) accrued holiday remuneration;

(e) the ordinary unsecured creditors;

(f) statutory interest which will be paid if a surplus remains after all previous claims have been paid. This interest is paid from the date of the order to the date of payment and the rate is the greater of the rate provided for in s. 17 of the Judgments Act 1838 and the rate the bankrupt would have had to pay on the debt if he had not been made bankrupt;

(g) the postponed creditors such as the spouse of the bankrupt who has a provable debt as a result of a loan to the bankrupt spouse;

(h) the bankrupt receives any surplus.

Each class of creditor must be paid in full before the next class receives anything. If the assets are insufficient to meet the debts owed to the creditors of the class, they are paid rateably according to value.

25.7 Duration of the bankruptcy and discharge of the bankrupt

25.7.1 Discharge of the bankrupt

The majority of those made bankrupt are automatically discharged one year after the date of the bankrupt order. The period may even be shorter if:

(a) a bankrupt fully co-operates with the official receiver and/or trustee;

(b) creditors do not raise any matters relating to the bankrupt's conduct and affairs which require further investigation; and

(c) the official receiver files a notice at the court stating that the investigation of the bankrupt's affairs has been concluded or he thinks an investigation is unnecessary.

A bankrupt will not be discharged if there is a court order suspending his discharge. This could be the case where the bankrupt has not co-operated with the official receiver or trustee in bankruptcy.

25.7.2 Effect of discharge

Once the bankrupt has been discharged, he is normally freed from the disqualifications suffered by undischarged bankrupts and from liability to meet his bankruptcy debts.

25.7.3 Bankruptcy Restrictions Order (BRO)

Where a trustee considers that the bankrupt's conduct has been irresponsible or reckless, the court may make a BRO for a period of between 2 and 15 years, depending on the circumstances of the case. The BRO imposes restrictions which will generally take effect following the discharge of the bankrupt. These will include:

(a) it being an offence for the bankrupt to be involved as an officer or in the management or promotion of a company without the leave of the court;

(b) being unable to obtain credit in excess of £500 without first disclosing the BRO;

(c) only being allowed to trade in their own name or that in which they were adjudged bankrupt.

25.8 Fast track voluntary arrangement

The Enterprise Act 2002 introduced a fast track voluntary arrangement scheme (FTVA). An individual can only enter into a FTVA *after* he has been made bankrupt. This differs from an IVA which is intended as an *alternative* to bankruptcy (see **25.9**). Under the scheme, the official receiver is the proposed nominee. An FTVA proposal is agreed with the official receiver and filed with the court, without the need for a creditors' meeting. Instead, the official receiver sends the proposal to creditors by post. The latter either agree to or reject the proposal; there is no facility to modify it. Assuming the proposal is approved, the official receiver supervises the FTVA and notifies the court which annuls the bankruptcy order, removing it from the bankruptcy records. This will usually occur between five to seven weeks after the commencement of the FTVA. Once this has occurred, the individual is no longer subject to any of the restrictions applicable in bankruptcy, and any assets not included in the FTVA will be returned.

25.9 Individual voluntary arrangement

25.9.1 Introduction

While formal bankruptcy may be the appropriate method of dealing with many debtors who find themselves in financial difficulties, there will be certain cases where the debtor involved may be able to come to terms with his creditors without involving the full rigour of the bankruptcy procedure. The Insolvency Act 1986 introduced an alternative method—with the aim of avoiding bankruptcy—by which debtors can come to binding arrangements with their creditors. This allows debtors to propose a composition or scheme of arrangement to creditors. This is known as an individual voluntary arrangement, usually referred to in practice as an 'IVA'. The procedure for this is set out in Pt VIII IA 1986 and is considered further below. There has been increasing use made of the IVA scheme over bankruptcy orders: in 2010 in England and Wales there were 59,173 bankruptcy orders made and 50,693 IVAs; provisional figures for 2012 show 31,756 bankruptcy orders and 46,694 IVAs.

25.9.2 Interim order

25.9.2.1 Application by debtor

If a debtor in financial difficulties wishes to propose a voluntary arrangement to his creditors, he must first apply to the court, even if a petition for his bankruptcy has already been presented, for an interim order to be made. The debtor must have in place an insolvency practitioner who is willing to act in relation to the proposed voluntary arrangement. The latter is known as the 'nominee'.

25.9.2.2 Effect of interim orders

Once the interim order is made, no bankruptcy petition can be presented against the debtor and no other proceedings, execution, or legal process can, without the leave of the court, be commenced or prosecuted against the debtor or his assets. (It should be noted that legislation has been proposed to allow a proposal to be made for a voluntary arrangement *without* first applying for an interim order. Obviously, in such a situation, the debtor would not have the benefit of the interim order.)

25.9.2.3 Period of interim order

The interim order is relatively short-lived since it will cease to have effect at the end of the period of 14 days beginning with the day after the order was made, although the court has power to extend the period.

25.9.3 Procedure following the making of the interim order

25.9.3.1 Debtors to provide statements to nominee

After the order has been made the debtor must provide the nominee with a statement giving details of the proposed voluntary arrangement. He must also give a statement of his affairs, which will give details of his assets and liabilities. Failure to do so may result in the interim order being discharged.

25.9.3.2 Nominee's report to court

The nominee is required to report to the court, stating whether the voluntary arrangement has a reasonable prospect of being approved and implemented. In addition, he is required to state whether a meeting of creditors should be called to consider the proposed voluntary arrangements. Should the nominee fail to deliver the report to the court before the interim order expires, the debtor can apply to the court to have the order renewed or extended and the debtor may also apply to have the nominee replaced.

25.9.3.3 Discharge of interim order

If the nominee decides that a meeting of creditors should not be called and the court agrees, the interim order may be discharged.

25.9.4 Consideration of the debtor's proposals

If the nominee has submitted a report to the court recommending that a creditor's meeting be called to consider the debtor's proposals, subject to any directions made by the court, the nominee gives notice of the meeting (at the date, time, and place specified in his report to the court) to all creditors of whom he is aware.

At the meeting the proposals will be considered and the proposals may be approved as proposed or with any changes thought appropriate.

25.9.5 Effect of accepting the proposal

Once the proposal is approved, all persons who had notice of the meeting and who were entitled to vote at the meeting (irrespective of whether they did so vote) are bound by the composition or scheme as if they were parties to it. Any creditor who would have been entitled to vote at the meeting, had they been given notice of it, will also be bound by the proposal.

Subject to any challenges within the 28-day period referred to in **25.9.6** below, once the proposal has been accepted, any interim order in force ceases to have effect and any bankruptcy petition which was stayed by the interim order is deemed to have been dismissed (subject to a court order to the contrary).

25.9.6 Challenging the decision of the creditors' meeting

25.9.6.1 Parties who may challenge

Once the creditors' meeting has reported its decision to the court, at any time during the 28 days commencing with the day the report is made to the court, that decision may be challenged by:

(a) the debtor;

(b) any person who was entitled to vote at the meeting;

(c) the nominee (or his replacement).

25.9.6.2 Grounds

The grounds of challenge are limited to the following:

(a) that the composition or scheme accepted by the meeting unfairly prejudices the interests of a creditor; and/or

(b) that there was a material irregularity at, or in relation to, the meeting.

25.9.6.3 Effect of challenge

If the court confirms the challenge, the approval of the meeting may be revoked or suspended. Alternatively, the court may order a further meeting to be held to consider any revised proposal or (if the challenge is based on 'material irregularity' in relation to the meeting) order that the meeting be held again to reconsider the proposal.

Having ordered a further meeting to be held, the court can extend or renew the interim order. However, if the court is satisfied that no revised proposal will be submitted by the debtor, the order to hold a further meeting will be revoked and the approval given at the original meeting will be revoked or suspended.

online resource centre

For further resources and online chapters please visit the Online Resource Centre at www.oxfordtextbooks.co.uk/orc/business13_14/.

26

Company insolvency proceedings

This chapter covers the following topics:

26.1 Introduction

All statute references in this and the following chapter are to the Insolvency Act 1986 except where otherwise stated.

In this chapter we shall deal with the procedures available when a company is insolvent or facing financial difficulties. In the final section of this chapter we shall look at the way in which insolvent partnerships can be subject to the same procedures as companies.

The law relating to these matters is principally contained in the Insolvency Act 1986 together with the Insolvency Rules 1986, as amended by the Insolvency Act 2000 and the Enterprise Act 2002.

The insolvency legislation provides four procedures for companies in financial difficulties: administration; voluntary arrangement; receivership; and liquidation. The Insolvency Service's provisional statistics indicate that nearly 21,000 companies were the subject of one of these procedures in 2012, with: 2,532 administrations; 839 voluntary arrangements; 1,222 receiverships; and 16,138 liquidations. Note that, whilst the text refers to 'company' or 'companies', these procedures are also applicable to limited liability partnerships (LLPs). For partnerships which are not LLPs, see **26.10** below.

26.1.1 Administration order

This procedure is directed principally at rescuing companies as going concerns. Following the Enterprise Act 2002, administration may be commenced without a court hearing, although a number of formalities must be observed.

26.1.2 Voluntary arrangement under the Insolvency Act 1986

This procedure enables a variety of schemes to be implemented (with the agreement of the company and its creditors) to either avoid or supplement other types of insolvency procedure.

26.1.3 Receivership

A receiver is appointed by a lender who holds a charge over some or all of the company's assets. The main responsibility of the receiver is to take control of the company so as to pay off the appointing creditor. However, the law recognises that this may have a considerable and permanent effect on the company and its other creditors. Therefore, various statutory powers are granted to the receiver and a number of obligations imposed on him.

Prior to the Enterprise Act 2002, the majority of receiverships were administrative receiverships (see **26.4.3**). However, this procedure is now only available in the case of certain specified transactions.

26.1.4 Liquidation (or winding up)

There are two types of liquidation: liquidation by the court (compulsory winding up) and voluntary liquidation. Provisional government statistics for 2012 show that there were 4,243 compulsory liquidations (see **26.5.2**) and 11,896 creditors' voluntary liquidations (see **26.5.3.2**). There are many procedural and other differences between these types of liquidation but each is designed to achieve the same thing, that is, the collection and distribution of all the company's assets. The effect of liquidation is that the company ceases to exist as a *commercial* entity. When the liquidation is over the company is 'dissolved', that is, it ceases to exist as a *legal* entity.

Liquidation by the court is initiated by petition and, in certain circumstances, the appointment of an administrator may still be sought via a court application. There are other elements of all of the above procedures which may require applications to the court at various stages. The High Court has jurisdiction to deal with any such petition or application where the company is registered in England and Wales. This type of business is assigned to the Chancery Division. In addition, the county court of the district in which the company's registered office is situated has concurrent jurisdiction where the company's paid-up share capital does not exceed £120,000.

26.2 Administration orders

26.2.1 Background to administration procedure

Administration was introduced in the 1980s as an alternative to winding up. The original procedure involved a relevant party petitioning the court for an administration order on the grounds that the order would achieve one or more of a number of statutory purposes as regards a company in financial difficulties. These included: saving some or all of the company as a going concern; obtaining better realisations for creditors than would be achieved on a winding up; and seeking a voluntary arrangement. On the making of the petition, a moratorium would become effective, preventing any further action against the company until the hearing of the petition, unless the court gave leave. If the petition was successful, an administration order would be made and an administrator appointed to take control of the company. The moratorium would continue during the period of the order, allowing the administrator 'breathing space' to attempt to achieve the relevant statutory purpose or purposes for which he had been appointed.

A disadvantage of administration was the cost and complexity of seeking an administration order. The petitioner was required to show that the company was either unable or likely to become unable to pay its debts. This had to be supported by a report from an independent insolvency practitioner setting out their reasons for believing that at least one of the statutory purposes could be achieved. These steps, together with the court hearing, may have precluded some companies from pursuing administration as an option when they faced financial difficulties.

The Enterprise Act 2002 introduced a new procedure to allow companies, their directors and floating charge-holders to appoint an administrator without petitioning the court. This enables parties to pursue administration where historically they might not have done so. (The existing court procedure remains an option.) In addition, the statutory purposes have been replaced with three objectives, with the primary one being to rescue the company as a going concern. The moratorium on creditor action and flexibility given to the administrator, once appointed, has been retained. The overall aim is to maintain all the benefits of the original procedure whilst making access easier and the procedure faster and fairer. The statutory provisions on administration are now contained in Sch. B1 to the Insolvency Act 1986. Any references below to paragraph numbers are references to paragraphs of Sch. B1.

26.2.2 Persons entitled to appoint an administrator

A person may be appointed as an administrator of a company by:

(a) the holder of a floating charge (para. 14);
(b) the company or its directors (para. 22); or
(c) an administration order of the court (para. 10).

Any administrator appointed must be qualified to act as an insolvency practitioner in relation to the company. Once appointed, an administrator is an officer of the court, whether or not appointed by the court.

26.2.3 Objectives of administrator

Paragraph 3(1) requires an administrator to perform his functions with the objective of:

(a) rescuing the company as a going concern; or
(b) achieving a better result for the company's creditors as a whole than would be likely if the company were wound up (without first being in administration); or
(c) realising property in order to make a distribution to one or more secured or preferential creditors.

The three objectives are, in fact, a hierarchy. The first objective is the primary aim of the new administration regime. The administrator is required to perform his functions to achieve that objective unless either it is not reasonably practicable to do so or the objective in (b) would achieve a better result for the company's creditors as a whole. Furthermore, the administrator may perform his functions to achieve the objective in (c) only if he thinks it is not reasonably practicable to achieve either (a) or (b) and he does not unnecessarily harm the interests of creditors of the company as a whole.

Overall, the administrator must perform his functions in the interests of the company's creditors as a whole, subject to performing them as quickly and efficiently as is reasonably practicable.

26.2.4 Appointment of administrator by holder of floating charge

26.2.4.1 Power to appoint

An administrator may be appointed to a company by the holder of a qualifying floating charge over the company's property, as defined in paras 14(2) and (3). The charge in question must be enforceable at the time of the appointment. The holder must first give at least two business days' written notice to the holder of any prior qualifying floating charge or obtain written consent to the appointment from such person. The holder of a floating charge may not appoint an administrator if a provisional liquidator has been appointed or an administrative receiver is in office.

26.2.4.2 Notice of appointment

The appointing charge holder must file with the court a notice of appointment in prescribed form. This must include a statutory declaration by or on behalf of the person who makes the appointment that:

(a) the person is the holder of a qualifying floating charge in respect of the company's property;

(b) each floating charge relied on in making the appointment is (or was) enforceable on the date of the appointment; and

(c) the appointment is in accordance with Sch. B1.

The statutory declaration must be made within a prescribed period.

The notice of appointment must identify the administrator and be accompanied by a statement from the latter:

(a) that he consents to the appointment;

(b) that in his opinion the purpose of administration is reasonably likely to be achieved; and

(c) giving any other information and opinions as may be prescribed.

The administrator may, in making his statement, rely on information supplied by the company's directors (unless he has reason to doubt its accuracy).

26.2.4.3 Time at which appointment takes effect

The appointment of an administrator by a holder of a qualifying floating charge takes effect when the notice provisions set out above have been satisfied.

26.2.5 Appointment of administrator by company or directors

26.2.5.1 Power to appoint

Paragraph 22 gives power to appoint an administrator to a company or its directors to appoint an administrator of that company. This power is restricted if:

(a) the company has been in administration in the past 12 months (para. 23);

(b) the company has been subject to a moratorium in respect of a failed creditors' voluntary arrangement under Sch. A1 in the previous 12 months (para. 24);

(c) there is a pending petition for the winding up of the company (para. 25(a));

(d) an administration application has been made to court and is not yet disposed of (para. 25(b)); or

(e) an administrative receiver is in office (para. 25(c)).

26.2.5.2 Notice of intention to appoint

Directors or companies using the out-of-court route must give at least five business days' notice to any person holding a qualifying floating charge or entitled to appoint an administrative receiver. This notice must identify the proposed administrator and be in the prescribed form. A copy of this notice must also be filed with the court and be accompanied by a statutory declaration that:

(a) the company is or is likely to become unable to pay its debts;

(b) the company is not in liquidation; and

(c) the appointment is not prevented by paras 23 to 25.

The charge-holders to whom notice has been given may either agree to the proposed appointment or appoint an alternative administrator, although a moratorium (as described in **26.2.7.1**) will take effect immediately the notice of intention has been filed at court by the company or directors. (It should be noted that this moratorium can only be lifted with the leave of the court, i.e., as no administrator has yet been appointed, his consent cannot be given.)

If charge-holders do not respond to the notice of intention to appoint, the company's or directors' appointee will take office after the notice period has expired and a notice of appointment is filed at court.

26.2.5.3 Notice of appointment

The administrator takes office when a notice of appointment is filed with the court. An appointment may not be made after a period of 10 business days beginning with the date on which the notice of intention to appoint is filed under para. 27.

The notice of appointment must include a statutory declaration stating that the application meets all the necessary requirements set out in para. 29. It must also identify the administrator and be accompanied by a statement from the latter:

(a) that he consents to the appointment;

(b) that in his opinion the purpose of administration is reasonably likely to be achieved; and

(c) giving any other information and opinions as may be prescribed.

The administrator may, in making his statement, rely on information supplied by the company's directors (unless he has reason to doubt its accuracy).

26.2.6 Appointment of administrator by court

26.2.6.1 Application for administration order

The following may apply to court for an administration order in respect of a company:

(a) the company;

(b) the directors of the company;

(c) one or more creditors of the company;

(d) the justices' chief executive for a magistrates' court (where a fine has been imposed on a company); or

(e) a combination of (a) to (d).

It should be noted that this court route preserves a means of putting a company into administration for creditors without qualifying floating charges (e.g., unsecured creditors).

26.2.6.2 Notice of application

An applicant must, as soon as reasonably practicable after making the application, notify:

(a) any person who has appointed or is or may be entitled to appoint an administrative receiver; or

(b) any person entitled to appoint an administrator by virtue of holding a qualifying floating charge.

26.2.6.3 Effect of application

Where an application has been made but not yet granted or dismissed, or it has been granted but an administration order has not yet taken effect, a moratorium (as described in **26.2.7.1**) takes effect. However, it should be noted that this moratorium can only be lifted with the leave of the court (i.e., as no administrator has yet been appointed, his consent cannot be given).

26.2.6.4 Powers of court

On hearing an administration application the court may:

(a) make an administration order;

(b) dismiss the application;

(c) adjourn the hearing;

(d) make an interim order;

(e) treat the application as a winding-up order; or

(f) make any other order it thinks appropriate.

26.2.6.5 Time at which appointment takes effect

Where the court makes an administration order, the appointment takes effect at the time appointed by the order or, if no time is appointed, at the time the order is made.

26.2.7 Effect of administration

26.2.7.1 Moratorium

Once a company is in administration, creditors may not, without the consent of the administrator or the permission of the court:

(a) take steps to enforce security over the company's property;

(b) repossess goods in the company's possession under a hire-purchase agreement;

(c) commence or continue any legal process against the company or its property; or

(d) exercise a right of forfeiture in respect of premises let by the company.

In addition, no resolution may be passed for the winding up of the company and no winding-up order made.

The object of these rules is to preserve the assets of the company so that an administrator has a better chance of rescuing the company as a going concern.

26.2.7.2 Effect on winding up

In addition to the effect of the moratorium (see **26.2.7.1**), a petition for the winding up of a company will be dismissed on the making of an administration order. While a company is in administration following an appointment by the holder of a qualifying floating charge, a winding-up petition will be suspended (para. 40).

26.2.7.3 Effect on receivership

Administration and administrative receivership are mutually exclusive. As we have seen, notice of an administration application or intended appointment must be given to any person who is entitled to appoint an administrative receiver. An administrator cannot be appointed by a qualifying floating charge-holder, the company, or its directors if an administrative receiver is in place. As regards an administration application, the court will dismiss the application if there is an administrative receiver of the company unless either the creditor who appointed the administrative receiver consents or it is shown that his security would be liable to be set aside under ss. 238, 239, or 245 (see **Chapter 27**) (para. 39).

When an administration order takes effect in respect of a company where an administrative receiver is in office (e.g., the creditor who appointed the administrative receiver has consented to the order), that administrative receiver is required to vacate office. During the course of administration, the administrator may require any receiver of any part of the company's property to vacate office.

26.2.8 The administration process

26.2.8.1 Announcement of appointment

The administrator must send notice of his appointment to the company and publish a notice of his appointment in the prescribed manner as soon as reasonably practicable. Notice must also be sent to the Registrar of Companies within seven days of appointment (para. 46(1)) and to the company's creditors.

26.2.8.2 Statement of affairs

The administrator must require a statement of affairs to be prepared (para. 47(1)). This will usually be required from the directors of the company but the legislation allows the administrator to require the others involved in the company's business to provide or contribute to the statement. The statement must be provided within 11 days of the date on which notice of the requirement is received.

26.2.8.3 Powers of administrator

The appointed administrator will run the company and its business with a view to achieving the purpose of administration. The administrator is given power to do anything necessary or expedient for the management of the affairs, business, and property of the company (para. 59). His specific powers are those set out in Sch. B1 IA 1986. These include: power to sell assets; borrow money; insure; bring and defend proceedings; and appoint agents. The administrator also has powers to dispose of charged property as if it were not subject to the charge (paras 70 and 71) and to dispose of hire-purchase goods as if the rights of the owner were vested in the company (para. 72).

In cases of difficulty, the administrator may apply to the court for directions. The management powers of the administrator override those of the company and its directors; they may not exercise any management powers without the consent of the administrator.

26.2.8.4 Proposals

The administrator is required to prepare proposals for achieving the purpose of administration. These must be sent to the Registrar of Companies, all creditors (so far as he is aware of their claims and addresses), and all members (so far as he is aware of their addresses). The proposals must be sent as soon as reasonably practicable but in any event within eight weeks from the commencement of administration.

26.2.8.5 Creditors' meeting

The administrator must hold an initial creditors' meeting within 10 weeks of the commencement of administration. There are exceptions to this requirement (para. 52). No meeting is required where the administrator believes that:

(a) there are no funds available from the insolvent estate for unsecured creditors, outside those flowing from the abolition of Crown preference (see **26.8.4**);

(b) neither the company rescue nor the better result for creditors objective apply (see **26.2.3**); or

(c) that the company has sufficient property to pay each creditor in full.

The creditors may either approve the proposals without modification or approve them with modification to which the administrator consents.

Should the administrator need to make substantial modifications to the approved proposals at any time, he is required to call another creditors' meeting for this purpose.

26.2.8.6 Distributions

An administrator may make distributions to secured creditors and preferential creditors without court permission, and distributions to unsecured creditors with court permission. The administrator may also make payments if he thinks that the payment is likely to assist in achieving the purpose of the administration.

26.2.8.7 Fulfilling the purpose of administration

The question arises as to the practical outcomes of administration. The Insolvency Service (part of the Department for Business, Innovation and Skills) has stated that 'for administration to be successful it needs to have clear exit routes tied to its purpose'. It is for this reason that the legislation provides that:

(a) The administrator's proposal may include a proposal for a company voluntary arrangement (CVA) under the Insolvency Act 1986 or a proposal for an arrangement under Pt 26 of the Companies Act 2006. A company rescue is most likely to involve one of these procedures.

(b) If the company cannot be rescued, then the administrator will aim to achieve a better realisation of the company's assets than would be achieved on an immediate liquidation.

(c) Where there are no funds available for the unsecured creditors, the administrator will realise the company's assets and make payments to preferential creditors and fixed and floating charge-holders and will arrange for the dissolution of the company simply by sending a notice to the Registrar of Companies.

(d) If there are funds available for the unsecured creditors, the company will be put into voluntary liquidation, again simply by sending a notice to the Registrar of Companies.

Where the administrator thinks the purpose of administration cannot be achieved, the administrator is required to apply to court.

26.2.8.8 Ending administration

The appointment of an administrator will automatically end 12 months after the date it commenced. However, this may be extended for up to six months with the consent of the creditors or for a specified period by court order.

26.3 Voluntary arrangements

26.3.1 Proposals and nominee's report

The Insolvency Act 1986 seeks to promote agreement between a company in difficulties and its creditors. The directors or (where the company is being wound up) the liquidator or (where a company is in administration) the administrator may make proposals for a voluntary arrangement to the company and its creditors. These proposals must, if they are to be put into effect under the Act, nominate a qualified insolvency practitioner to implement them. Where the nominee is not the liquidator or administrator, the person making the proposal (that is, the liquidator, administrator, or directors) must submit details of the proposals and of the company's creditors, debts, liabilities, and assets to the nominee. The nominee must then submit a report to the court stating whether or not he thinks that meetings of members and creditors should be called to consider the proposals.

26.3.2 Content of proposals

The proposals may be as simple or as complex as the situation of the company demands. In practical terms, the creditors are usually being offered something definite as an alternative to what they might obtain if the company was, for example, to be wound up. Examples of proposals which are commonly made may include one or more of the following:

(a) *Moratorium on repayment of debt*

Creditors are asked not to enforce debts for a specific period of time. The company may be unable to pay debts at present due to cash flow problems but may expect to be able to pay them in the near future.

(b) *Composition of debt*

Creditors are offered a percentage of their debt in settlement. For example, they might be offered '65 pence in the pound', that is, 65 pence for every pound which the company owes them.

(c) *Debt for equity swap*

Major creditors may be offered the chance to swap their debt for shares in the company. From the company's point of view, the removal of the debt should ease cash flow problems. The shares will usually give the creditors preferential rights which enable repayment through dividends as soon as profits are available. Such a proposal will often be combined with a fairly radical, general reorganisation of the company's affairs.

26.3.3 Meetings of members and creditors

Where the nominee recommends that meetings should be held, he may call the meetings unless the court orders otherwise. Notice must be given to every creditor of whose claim and address the person calling the meeting is aware.

The meetings of members and creditors then consider the scheme, which they may reject, approve, or approve with modifications. A simple majority is required at the members' meeting (members having the voting rights attached to their shares by the articles). The position is more complicated at the creditors' meeting but basically the net effect is that the resolution is only validly passed if approved by:

(a) at least three-quarters (by value) of the unsecured creditors; and
(b) a simple majority (by value) of the unsecured creditors who are not connected with the company.

In relation to (a) only, secured creditors may count in the vote, but only to the extent of the value of their claim which they estimate will *not* be recovered under their security.

The result of the meetings must be reported to the court. The court can reject the scheme on grounds of unfair prejudice or material irregularity.

26.3.4 Implementation of approved scheme by supervisor

Where both meetings approve a scheme, the scheme becomes binding on all persons who had notice of the shareholders' or creditors' meeting and were entitled to vote at that meeting, together with any creditors who would have been entitled to vote had they been given notice of the meeting. However, unless he agrees, the scheme cannot affect a secured creditor's right to enforce his security, nor a preferred creditor's preference.

Once approved, the scheme is implemented by the supervisor (who is the same person as the nominee unless the court or meetings decide otherwise).

26.3.5 Relationship between voluntary schemes and administration

The proposal that a voluntary scheme should be implemented does not create a moratorium so that, unless and until the scheme is approved, any creditor can seek payment of his own debt (by court action, petition for winding up, repossession, or any other lawful means available to him). Even when the scheme is approved it does not prevent secured creditors enforcing their security. A voluntary arrangement is, therefore, more likely to succeed if a company is first put into administration, thus giving rise to the moratorium. The administrator may then be able to put together a satisfactory voluntary scheme which he can supervise.

26.3.6 Moratorium for small companies

The directors of these companies may apply for a moratorium of up to 28 days to give them time to put their voluntary arrangement proposal to creditors. The moratorium is similar to that created on a petition for an administration order and will mean that creditors cannot take action against the company's assets during its term. The purpose behind the change in the legislation is to make the voluntary arrangement option more effective and thus attractive to companies in financial difficulties.

To obtain a moratorium, the directors must submit to the nominee the terms of their proposed voluntary arrangement together with a statement of the company's financial affairs. The nominee will then provide the directors with a statement indicating whether or not, in his opinion, the proposal has a reasonable prospect of approval. He will also indicate whether the company is likely to have sufficient funds available to it during the proposed moratorium to enable it to carry on its business, and whether meetings of the company and creditors should be summoned to consider the proposed voluntary arrangement. The directors must then file all the above documents, together with the nominee's consent to act and a statement that the company is eligible for a moratorium, with the court.

26.4 Receivership

26.4.1 Introduction

A receiver is a person who is appointed by or on behalf of a creditor to realise security, such as a charge or series of charges. His principal duty is owed to the party who appoints him, that is, the charge-holder. Whilst receivers may also be appointed by the court, in practice nearly all appointments are made by the charge-holder.

Since 1986, receivers have fallen into two broad categories: receivers appointed under charges over specific assets and administrative receivers, as defined by s. 29(2).

26.4.2 Receivers

A receiver appointed under charges over specific assets derives his powers from the charge under which he was appointed and from certain sections of the Law of Property Act 1925. The latter provides powers to manage, receive income from, and sell the property over which the receiver has been appointed. Sometimes this type of receiver will be referred to as a 'receiver and manager', 'fixed charge receiver', or 'LPA receiver'. His role is to deal with the property over which he is appointed in order to realise funds for the party which appointed him. A receiver need not necessarily be a qualified insolvency practitioner.

26.4.3 Administrative receivers

These are defined in s. 29(2) as:

(a) a receiver and manager of the whole (or substantially the whole) of a company's property appointed by or on behalf of the holders of any debentures of the company secured by a charge which, as created, was a floating charge, or by such a charge and one or more other securities; or

(b) a person who would be such a receiver or manager but for the appointment of some other person as the receiver of part of the company's property.

In practice, the person who holds such security will usually be a bank. The bank is also likely to have fixed charges over land owned by the company and certain other assets (e.g., book debts) but these would not prevent it from appointing an administrative receiver given the scope of s. 29(2)(a).

26.4.4 Impact of Enterprise Act 2002 on administrative receivership

The Enterprise Act 2002 effectively abolished administrative receiverships in respect of qualifying floating charges (as defined in para. 14, Sch. B1 IA 1986) created after the date the Enterprise Act came into force. The intention was to promote the out-of-court administration regime (see **26.2.4**). Administrative receivers may now only be appointed by the holders of floating charges created prior to implementation of the Enterprise Act and holders of charges created as part of specific transactions defined in ss. 72B–72G IA 1986. These include capital market arrangements, public–private projects, utility projects, and project finance arrangements. *Given these changes, the following paragraphs on the powers and duties of administrative receivers are only relevant to pre-15 September 2003 and 'specific transaction' floating charges.*

26.4.5 Administrative receivers—powers and duties

The administrative receiver, when appointed, effectively replaces the directors in the management of the company. His appointment is, therefore, a matter of great importance to the members, creditors, and employees of the company. The law recognises this and so grants powers to, and imposes obligations on, an administrative receiver which make his position very similar to the position of an administrator. The administrative receiver is chosen by the debenture holder, not by the court, but can only be removed by the court.

26.4.5.1 General powers

An administrative receiver has all the powers conferred on him by the debenture under which he is appointed and also specific powers listed in the Insolvency Act 1986. The statutory powers include power to deal with the assets of the company, take or defend proceedings in its name, and power to carry on the business of the company. These powers, listed in Sch. 1, are the same as those granted to an administrator.

26.4.5.2 Disposal of property subject to prior charge

Section 43 gives an administrative receiver power to go to court to obtain an order for the sale of assets free from any security with priority over the debenture under which he was appointed. The court may only authorise the administrative receiver to dispose of such property if it is likely to promote a more advantageous realisation of the company's assets. The court might, for example, authorise such a disposal so as to enable the receiver to sell the business of the company as a going concern. The proceeds of disposal (plus any difference between those proceeds and market value) must be paid to the person who was entitled to the security.

26.4.5.3 Legal position

The administrative receiver is deemed to be the agent of the company (s. 44). Any contract which he makes is, therefore, binding on the company. The agency, however, ends when the company goes into liquidation. Section 44 also makes the administrative receiver personally liable on any contract which he himself makes and on any contract of employment which he 'adopts'. Following the cases of *Paramount Airways* [1994] BCC 172, *Leyland DAF* [2004] UKHL 9, and *Ferranti* [1994] BCC 658, an employee's contract of employment is 'adopted' if he is continued in employment for more than 14 days after the appointment of the administrative receiver (or administrator in the case of administration). The administrative receiver is entitled to an indemnity against personal liability out of the assets of the company and, if the debenture so provides, will have an indemnity from his appointor.

26.4.5.4 Duty to pay preferential creditors

The primary duty of any receiver is to realise the security of the debenture holder who appointed him. A receiver appointed on behalf of a floating charge-holder (whether or not he is an administrative receiver as defined) is, however, under a duty to pay preferential creditors, (see **26.8.4**) in priority to the debt secured by the floating charge.

26.4.5.5 Investigation and report into company's affairs

An administrative receiver is entitled to a statement of affairs from the directors (or in certain cases other officials) of the company. Within three months of his appointment (or longer if the court so directs) he must make a report which he must send to the Registrar of Companies and to creditors.

The report must give details of the events leading to the appointment of the receiver, his dealings with the property of the company, his payments to the creditor who appointed him and to preferential creditors, and an assessment of what will be available (if anything) to ordinary creditors.

26.5 Liquidation or winding up

26.5.1 Types of winding up

There are two types of winding up: compulsory liquidation and voluntary liquidation. Compulsory liquidation is initiated by petition to the court. Voluntary liquidation is initiated by a decision of the members of the company. Both types of winding up are designed to bring the existence of the company to an end and to distribute its assets to those entitled to them.

26.5.2 Compulsory winding up

26.5.2.1 Grounds

Compulsory liquidation begins with a petition to the court (Chancery Division or, in some cases, county court—see **26.1.4** above). A petition can be presented on a number of grounds. By far the most common ground is that the company is unable to pay its debts (defined in s. 123). A company is treated as being unable to pay its debts if:

(a) a demand for payment, in the prescribed form (a 'statutory demand'), for more than £750 (this figure may be changed from time to time by regulations) has been left at the company's registered office and the company has neglected to pay the debt, or to secure or compound for it (that is, agree to a reasonable compromise) to the reasonable satisfaction of the creditor for three weeks; or

(b) execution or other process issued on a judgment, decree, or court order is returned unsatisfied; or

(c) it is proved that the company is actually unable to pay taking into account contingent and prospective liabilities; or

(d) it is proved that the value of the company's assets is less than the amount of its liabilities taking into account contingent and prospective liabilities.

Apart from inability to pay debts there are other grounds on which a company may be wound up. These are, however, seldom resorted to and are not considered in this book save that the 'just and equitable' ground is considered briefly in **Chapter 10**.

26.5.2.2 *Locus standi*

A petition for compulsory winding up may be presented by the company itself, any creditor or creditors (including contingent or prospective creditors), any contributory or contributories (the term 'contributory' includes the members of the company and certain former members) and, in very limited circumstances, by the Department for Business, Innovation and Skills. In practice, the overwhelming majority of petitions are presented by creditors.

26.5.2.3 Court's discretion to refuse order

Even where a creditor has proved grounds for winding up, the court has a discretion to refuse to make an order winding up the company. An order will normally be refused where:

(a) the petitioning creditor (together with any supporting creditors) is owed £750 or less. This is by analogy with the rule whereby a statutory demand for more than £750 can be used as proof of inability to pay debts;

(b) the majority by value of the creditors oppose the winding up of the company.

26.5.3 Voluntary winding up

26.5.3.1 Commencement

By s. 84 a company can be wound up voluntarily if:

(a) a special resolution to wind up is passed; or

(b) an extraordinary resolution is passed to the effect that the company should be wound up as it cannot continue in business because of its debts (that is, the company is, in effect, insolvent).

The winding up commences from the date of passing the appropriate resolution. A notice of the resolution must appear in the *London Gazette* within 14 days of its being passed.

26.5.3.2 Types of voluntary winding up

There are two types of voluntary liquidation: a members' voluntary winding up and a creditors' voluntary winding up.

Members' voluntary winding up

This form of liquidation is utilised if the company is solvent. Within the five weeks immediately preceding the date of the resolution (or on that date but before the resolution is actually passed) the directors (or the majority of them if more than two) make a statutory declaration setting out the company's assets and liabilities, and stating that they have made a full enquiry into the company's affairs and are of the opinion that the company will be able to pay its debts in full within 12 months of the commencement of the winding up. The declaration must be delivered to the Registrar within 15 days after the day the resolution was passed.

Creditors' voluntary winding up

If no such 'declaration of solvency' is filed, the winding up is a creditors' winding up. A meeting of the creditors must be called for a day not later than the 14th day after the day on which the meeting is held at which the members pass the winding-up resolution. Notice of the meeting must be posted to the creditors at least seven days before the creditors' meeting and the meeting must also be advertised in the *Gazette* and at least two newspapers.

Conversion from members' to creditors' voluntary winding up

During the course of a members' voluntary winding up, it may become clear that the company will be unable to pay its debts within 12 months of commencement of the winding up. If this happens the liquidator must report the fact to the creditors, call a creditors' meeting, and convert the liquidation into a creditors' voluntary winding up.

26.6 Liquidators

For all forms of liquidation, any liquidator appointed must be a qualified insolvency practitioner.

26.6.1 Compulsory liquidation

When a winding-up order is made, the official receiver of the court becomes the liquidator of the company and continues in office until someone else is appointed (s. 136(2)). The official receiver may summon meetings of creditors and contributories with a view to the appointment of a liquidator. He must either do so or give notice that he intends not to do so within 12 weeks of the winding-up order and may be required to call such meetings by one-quarter (by value) of the creditors.

Where meetings of creditors and contributories are held, each meeting may nominate a liquidator. If the same person is nominated by each meeting, he becomes the liquidator. If different people are nominated, the creditors' nominee takes office unless a creditor or contributory successfully applies to the court for the appointment of the contributories' nominee (either alone or jointly with the creditors' nominee) or of some other person.

26.6.2 Creditors' voluntary winding up

As we have already seen, in a creditors' winding up, a meeting of creditors must be held within 14 days of the meeting (of the members) at which the winding-up resolution was passed. The creditors may nominate a liquidator at their meeting. He will then become liquidator of the company but any director, member, or creditor may apply to the court for the appointment of the members' nominee (either alone or jointly with the creditors' nominee) or of some other person.

The members will often have appointed a liquidator at the meeting at which the resolution for creditors' winding up was passed. Such a liquidator is entitled to act until the creditors' meeting is held but during that period his powers are restricted to collecting the company's property, disposing of perishable goods or other goods which may decline in value, and taking other steps to protect the company's assets.

26.6.3 Members' voluntary winding up

The liquidator is appointed by the members in general meeting.

26.6.4 Functions of liquidators

The function of the liquidator of a company is to collect in the assets of the company and to pay their value to those creditors who are entitled according to the statutory order for payment (see **26.8**). If there is anything left after all creditors have been paid their debts and interest, the surplus goes to the members. If there are two or more classes of shares some members may have priority over others in claiming the surplus.

Sections 165 and 167 give liquidators extensive powers to assist them in performing their functions. These powers include:

(a) power to pay any class of creditors in full;

(b) power to enter into a compromise or arrangement with creditors (this can be made binding without the agreement of all the creditors in certain cases provided that the voluntary arrangements procedure (26.3) is used);

(c) power to compromise claims to which the company is entitled (the liquidator can only exercise the above powers with the sanction of an extraordinary resolution in the case of members' winding up, of the court, a committee of creditors or creditors' meeting in the case of creditors' winding up and of the court or committee in the case of compulsory winding up);

(d) power to bring or defend legal proceedings;

(e) power to carry on the company's business for the purpose of beneficial winding up (sanction is required in the case of compulsory winding up only;)

(f) power to sell the company's property;

(g) power to execute documents (including deeds);

(h) power to borrow on the security of the company's assets;

(i) power to act through agents;

(j) power to do 'all such other things as may be necessary for winding up the company's affairs and distributing its assets'.

(No sanction is required for items (f) to (j) in any type of winding up.)

26.6.5 Proceedings against the company

It would obviously be unfair if one creditor could start an action after the liquidation had begun and so obtain priority over the other creditors. Therefore, once an order for compulsory winding up has been made, no action can be started or proceeded with unless the leave of the court is obtained (s. 130). In addition, at any time between presentation of the petition and the making of the order, the company, or any creditor or contributory, can apply to have any action pending against the company stayed (s. 126). Furthermore, any execution, attachment, sequestration, or distress started after the commencement of a compulsory liquidation is void. However, if the attachment or execution was begun before presentation of the petition, it can only be avoided by the liquidator if it was completed after commencement of the liquidation. This last provision also applies to voluntary liquidations, the operative date being the date the resolution to wind up the company was passed.

With regard to voluntary liquidations, the liquidator, any creditor, or member may apply to the court to have actions stayed. Such a stay is not granted automatically although, if the action is begun after the date of passing the resolution to wind up an insolvent company, it will normally be granted.

26.7 Collection and distribution of assets in liquidation

26.7.1 Property of the company

26.7.1.1 Power to sell or charge

The liquidator has power to sell or mortgage the property and to satisfy the claims of the various people entitled in the company's liquidation (see **26.6.4**).

26.7.1.2 Power to disclaim

An important power of the liquidator in relation to the company's property is the right of disclaimer given by s. 178. The section gives the liquidator power to disclaim any of the company's property which consists of unprofitable contracts, or other property that is unsaleable or not readily saleable.

26.7.2 Assets in the hands of the company

26.7.2.1 Assets held on trust

The creditors of an insolvent company are entitled to payment from its assets. They are not entitled to any assets of which the company is the legal owner but which it holds on trust for a third party. This has been held to apply in certain cases where a company holds cash for its customers. In *Re Kayford Ltd* [1975] 1 All ER 604, the company put money received from mail order customers into a special trust account from which it only made withdrawals when goods were delivered to the customers. When the company went into liquidation it was held that the money in the account belonged to the customers whose orders had not been fulfilled and so was not available to the liquidator.

26.7.2.2 Assets subject to retention of title

Many suppliers of goods supply goods under contracts which contain retention of title clauses. These are clauses which state that the vendor retains title to the goods supplied until the purchaser pays for them. Such clauses have been considered in a number of reported cases (the leading case is *Aluminium Industrie Vaasen BV v Romalpa Aluminium* [1976] 2 All ER 552). Their effect varies depending on the exact wording which is used and on the circumstances of the case. A straightforward reservation of title clause is effective in ensuring that the vendor, not the liquidator, is entitled to the goods (or the proceeds of their further sale) if the company becomes insolvent. However, clauses which have tried to extend the unpaid vendor's rights (for example, by purportedly transferring them to newly manufactured goods only partly consisting of the goods which he originally supplied) have generally failed. (For the powers of an administrator to dispose of goods despite a retention of title clause see **26.2.8.3**.)

26.8 Entitlement to assets

26.8.1 Introduction

The principal duty of the liquidator of a company is to collect in and distribute the assets to those creditors entitled and to meet the costs of the procedure. In a large majority of cases there will be insufficient funds available to pay all the creditors in full. The question therefore arises as to how, to whom and in what order the company's assets (or monies realised from the sale of such assets) are to be paid.

In the majority of liquidations of any size, there is a high likelihood that there will be charged assets. Given that the standard form of floating charge will seek to cover all assets of a company, present and future, it will often be the case that the majority of assets available to a liquidator will fall into the class of charged assets. In such a case, the only free assets potentially available would be any amounts recovered through actions taken by the liquidator (see **Chapter 27**).

With this in mind, the best approach to understanding relevant entitlements is to look at those parties who have an interest in the assets of an insolvent company and, in each case, examine their legal entitlement.

26.8.2 Creditors with fixed charges

Creditors with fixed charges are entitled to payment out of the charged assets before those assets are used for any other purpose. As between creditors with fixed charges over the same assets, their priority to assets is governed by registration under s. 860 CA 2006. (It should be remembered that a fixed charge takes priority over any floating charge, even if the latter is created and registered first, unless the floating charge prohibited the creation of later fixed charges ranking in priority to it and the fixed chargee had notice of this prohibition when he took the charge.)

If the security of a fixed charge is inadequate (that is, the value of the charged assets is less than the amount of the debt), the chargee may claim the balance of its debt as an ordinary creditor (or under any valid floating charge in its favour). If the debt is oversecured (that is, the value of the charged assets is more than the amount of the debt), the chargee will be paid in full and the balance will be available for other creditors.

The costs of realising fixed charge assets should be paid out of the amounts realised from the sale of such assets.

26.8.3 Costs of winding up

The principal rules on how the expenses of a winding up are to be paid are set out in s. 176ZA of the Insolvency Act 1986, which came into force in April 2008. The Insolvency (Amendment) Rules 2008 provide additional detail. The expenses of a winding up should be paid out of the assets of the company available for the payment of general creditors. In so far as these are insufficient, the expenses will be paid out of assets subject to any floating charge created by the company. (The latter can include any amounts recovered through actions taken by the liquidator.) The effect of s. 176ZA is therefore to give priority to the expenses of a winding up over the claims of floating chargeholders.

In terms of the costs of any legal proceedings which a liquidator seeks to take to recover property—i.e., litigation expenses—the priority provided by s. 176ZA is not automatic: the liquidator must first obtain approval from the relevant floating charge-holder. If this is not forthcoming, the liquidator may seek approval from the court. Approval is not required if the litigation expenses are unlikely to exceed £5,000.

Finally, note that s. 176ZA IA 1986 does not affect the ring-fenced assets for unsecured creditors under s. 176A IA 1986 (see **26.8.5.2**).

26.8.4 Preferential creditors

After payment of costs and expenses, the next category of creditor is the preferred creditor. Categories of preferential debts are defined in Sch. 6 IA 1986. These categories were reduced in number by the Enterprise Act 2002, which abolished the Crown's preferential rights. Originally, the Crown had a claim to certain amounts due to HMRC and in respect of social security contributions. These funds will now be available for creditors further down the order. The remaining principal preferential debts are:

(a) A maximum total of £800 per employee for wages owed in respect of the four months before the relevant date (this figure may be varied from time to time by statutory instrument). If the employee is owed wages in excess of £800, the additional amount will be non-preferential. However, certain categories of holiday pay are preferential and a separate claim can be made for these.

(b) Money lent to an employer so as to enable it to pay debts in category (a) above and which was in fact used for that purpose. (Thus a bank is a preferential creditor if it allows an employer to overdraw a 'wages account' so as to keep on the workforce in the four months before the relevant date.)

The 'relevant date' is usually the date of the winding-up resolution or order (as applicable) or date of appointment of a receiver.

Preferential creditors (to the extent of their preference) are entitled to payment in full before ordinary creditors or holders of floating charges receive any payment—see s. 40(2) as regards receiverships and s. 175 as regards liquidations. If the assets are insufficient to pay the preferred creditors in full they rank equally *inter se* and so each is paid the same proportion of the preferred debt.

26.8.5 Creditors with floating charges

Creditors with floating charges will fall to be paid out of charged assets, following repayment of amounts owed to fixed charge-holders, costs, and expenses relating to any *receiver* appointed to realise the charged assets and preferential claims in any such receivership. (This assumes a receiver had been appointed prior to a subsequent liquidation.) In addition, as seen above in **26.8.4**, where there are insufficient free assets to pay preferential claims in a liquidation, charged assets can be applied to pay preferential claims.

The Enterprise Act 2002 changed the position of creditors who take floating charges over the assets of a company which enters into liquidation, administration, or receivership.

26.8.5.1 Pre-Enterprise Act 2002 floating charge-holders' position

For creditors who took floating charges over the assets of a company prior to 15 September 2003, they were (and continue to be) entitled, following payment of sums owed to preferential creditors, to sums realised from the assets the subject of their charge until their debts were fully satisfied. Any monies remaining following such payment would be available for unsecured creditors.

26.8.5.2 Current position

Following the Enterprise Act, s. 176A IA 1986 provides that, in relation to assets secured by floating charges created after 15 September 2003, a liquidator, administrator, or receiver is to make a prescribed part of the company's net property available for the satisfaction of unsecured debts. The way in which this prescribed part of the company's net property is to be calculated is set out in the Insolvency Act 1986 (Prescribed Part) Order 2003. The calculation is as follows:

(a) where the company's net property does not exceed £10,000 in value, 50% of that property;

(b) subject to the limit stated below, where the company's net property exceeds £10,000 in value the sum of—

   (i) 50% of the first £10,000 in value; and

   (ii) 20% of that part of the company's net property which exceeds £10,000 in value.

The value of the prescribed part of the company's net property to be made available for the satisfaction of unsecured debts of the company pursuant to s. 176A shall not exceed £600,000.

The prescribed part is not to be distributed to the holder of a floating charge except in so far as it exceeds the amount required for the satisfaction of unsecured debts. There is an exception to this rule where the relevant office-holder believes that the cost of making a distribution to unsecured creditors would be disproportionate to the benefits. *Re Hydroserve Ltd* [2008] BCC 175 was the first reported case where a court made an order to this effect, ruling that it was disproportionate to distribute a net £2,000 amongst 122 creditors at a cost of £3,000.

(Remember, following **26.8.2** above, that the costs of realising a fixed charge asset should be paid from the proceeds of such assets. Therefore, there will be an apportionment of costs between fixed and floating charge assets in those cases where both types of charge have been taken.)

26.8.6 Unsecured creditors

These creditors, sometimes referred to as ordinary creditors, rank behind preferred and secured creditors save to the extent of the provision made for them by s. 176A (see **26.8.5**). They rank equally *inter se*, that is, equally as between themselves in proportion to their respective debt. They would be paid out of free assets or any funds available from charged assets following payment of all prior claims (i.e., fixed charge-holders, preferential creditors, and floating charge-holders).

26.8.7 Interest on debts

Once all creditors have been paid in full any surplus is first used to pay interest on debts from the date of liquidation. This interest is paid to all creditors equally regardless of whether their debts ranked equally for payment.

26.8.8 Shareholders

Any surplus after payment of debts and interest goes to the members according to the rights attached to their shares. As with unsecured creditors, they would be paid out of free assets or any funds available from charged assets following payment of all prior claims (i.e., fixed charge-holders, preferential creditors, and floating charge-holders).

26.9 Dissolution

Once winding up is complete the company may be dissolved. This is achieved in the following ways:

(a) In compulsory liquidation the liquidator gives notice to the Registrar of Companies that he has completed the winding up. The company is then automatically dissolved three months later.

(b) In voluntary winding up the liquidator holds a final meeting and files certain returns with the Registrar of Companies. The company is then automatically dissolved after three months.

(c) The Registrar may dissolve a company by striking it off the register in certain circumstances where the company has ceased to trade.

26.10 Application to partnerships

26.10.1 Introduction

Care must be taken to define the precise nature of insolvency in relation to a partnership. It is possible for an individual partner to be bankrupt without the partnership being insolvent. Equally, it is possible for a partnership to be insolvent without any of the partners being bankrupt. Finally, a situation could exist where a partnership was insolvent *and* some or all of its partners bankrupt. A distinction must be maintained between an insolvent partnership and bankrupt partners since applicable procedures and the rights of the creditors of each will vary according to which you are dealing with. The provisions of the Insolvency Act 1986 relating to bankruptcy (see **Chapter 25**) will apply to individual bankrupt partners. In the case of an insolvent partnership, specific provisions of the Insolvency Act 1986 which apply to companies can also be applied to a partnership, as a result of the Insolvent Partnerships Order 1994.

26.10.2 Insolvent Partnerships Order 1994

26.10.2.1 Winding up as an unregistered company

The Insolvent Partnerships Order 1994 (the 'Order') provides that an insolvent partnership may be wound up as an unregistered company under the Insolvency Act. A petition may be brought by a partner or a creditor. If it is thought that debts will not be met from the assets of the firm, the Order allows bankruptcy petitions against individual partners to be brought in conjunction with the petition to wind up the partnership.

26.10.2.2 Priority of creditors on a winding up of a partnership

Under the Order, priorities operate as in the case of an insolvent company, with preferred and secured creditors having priority over ordinary creditors. However, the situation becomes more complex where a partnership is being wound up and bankruptcy petitions are being brought against individual partners. In this situation, there are effectively two sets of creditors, those of the partnership and those of the individual partners. The Order provides for the following priorities in such a situation:

(a) Partnership creditors must first seek to satisfy their claims from the partnership property.

(b) Creditors of individual partners must first look to the personal assets of those individuals.

(c) Should there be insufficient partnership assets, partnership creditors may seek to satisfy their claims from the personal assets of the individual partners. In such a situation, their claims are apportioned amongst the individual partners and *rank equally* with those of the creditors of those individual partners.

(d) Should creditors of individual partners find that those partners have insufficient assets to meet their claims, they may look to the partnership property. However, they can only do so *after* all the claims of partnership creditors have been met.

26.10.2.3 Disqualification

The Order applies certain provisions of the Company Directors Disqualification Act 1986 (see **9.8.2**) to partners of an insolvent partnership. A court may therefore, following a petition of the Secretary of State for Business, Innovation and Skills, find that a partner's conduct was such as to make him unfit to be concerned in the management of a company. If this is the case, the partner can be disqualified for a period of between 2 and 15 years from being involved in the management *of a company*. Such disqualification does *not* prevent him becoming involved in another partnership.

26.10.2.4 Administration and voluntary arrangements

The Order also provides that partnerships may be the subject of administration or enter into a voluntary arrangement with their creditors.

online resource centre

For further resources and online chapters please visit the Online Resource Centre at www.oxfordtextbooks.co.uk/orc/business13_14/.

27

Liabilities arising from insolvency

This chapter covers the following topics:

In this chapter we will look at a number of rules which enable insolvency practitioners to claim assets which are not held by the insolvent company itself. You should note that the ability to take action under some of these rules is limited only to a liquidator, or a liquidator or administrator.

27.1 Wrongful trading

Under s. 214, the directors of a company which is being wound up may be made liable, by the court, to contribute to the assets of the company if they are found to be guilty of wrongful trading.

27.1.1 Grounds

A person is guilty of wrongful trading where:

(a) the company goes into insolvent liquidation;

(b) that person knew or ought to have concluded (at some time before the commencement of winding up) that there was no reasonable prospect that the company would avoid going into insolvent liquidation; and

(c) that person was a director of the company at that time.

27.1.2 Defence

A defence is available to a director who shows that he took *every* step with a view to minimising the potential loss to the company's creditors as he ought to have taken. However, in judging whether this defence is available, the court applies a combined objective and subjective test in examining the knowledge and actions of the director. They are taken as being those of a reasonably diligent person having both:

(a) the general knowledge, skill, and experience that may reasonably be expected of a person carrying out the same functions as are carried out by the director in relation to the company; and

(b) the general knowledge, skill, and experience that that director has.

The steps which a director must take to avoid liability for wrongful trading will vary depending on the circumstances of the case.

27.2 Transactions at an undervalue and preferences

Certain transactions which a company has entered into may be set aside on the ground that they are transactions at an undervalue or preferences. An application to the court by the liquidator is required for such transactions to be set aside. The same rules apply in administration save that the application is then made by the administrator. (There are separate rules applicable to similar transactions in the context of personal bankruptcy—see **25.5.6.2** and **25.5.6.3**.)

27.2.1 Transactions at an undervalue

A transaction at an undervalue (s. 238) is a transaction where the company makes a gift to any person and receives either no consideration or consideration worth significantly less than the consideration provided by the company. However, a transaction cannot be set aside if it was entered into in good faith for the purpose of carrying on the company's business and at a time when there were reasonable grounds for believing that the transaction would benefit the company. For this reason a transaction cannot be set aside when the company sells stock or other assets at a reduced price so as to overcome cash flow problems.

27.2.2 Preferences

A preference (s. 239) is given if the company does anything or suffers anything to be done which puts a creditor, or a surety or guarantor of a debt of the company, into a better position on an insolvent liquidation than he would have been in if that thing had not been done. Examples of preferences include payment in full of a debt to a particular creditor who would only have received partial payment on winding up or the giving of security to a creditor. A transaction cannot be set aside as a preference unless the company was influenced in deciding to give the preference to a person by a desire to put that person into a better position on liquidation than he would have been in if it had not been done. Such a desire is presumed where the preference was given to a connected person (defined in s. 249), which includes any director of the company. (This presumption is rebuttable: *Re Fairway Magazines* [1993] BCLC 643.) Where payment was made or security was given to a creditor because he was threatening proceedings or otherwise insisting on payment he will usually be able to show that there was no desire to put him in a better position on liquidation. This will be on the grounds that the company was merely responding to genuine commercial pressure.

27.2.3 'Relevant time' requirement for transactions at an undervalue and preferences

Undervalue transactions and preferences can only be set aside if they were entered into at a 'relevant time'; that is, when both of the following requirements are satisfied:

(a) in the case of a transaction at an undervalue, the transaction takes place within two years before commencement of winding up or presentation of the petition for administration or, in the case of a preference, within six months before that date (unless the preference was made to a connected person in which case the period is extended to two years); and

(b) in the case of either an undervalue or preference, the company is insolvent at the time of the transaction or becomes insolvent as a result of the transaction. Where a transaction at an undervalue has been entered into with a connected person, insolvency is presumed unless it can be disproved.

27.2.4 Court can make order as it sees fit

Where it is shown that a transaction can be set aside as a transaction at an undervalue or preference the court can make such order as it sees fit for restoring the position to what it would have been if the transaction had not been entered into. This could include, for example, ordering the person who entered into the transaction or who received the preference to return property or its value to the company. The position of a bona fide purchaser for value is, however, protected.

27.3 Transactions defrauding creditors

Sections 423–425 contain further provisions by which transactions at an undervalue can be set aside. The application of these is not restricted to liquidation or administration and the undervalue transaction can be set aside whenever it was made. However, the person who applies to the court to have the transaction set aside must show that the company in entering into the transaction did so with the purpose of putting assets beyond the reach of that person.

27.4 Floating charges

Under s. 245, a floating charge is prima facie invalid if:

(a) it was made within 12 months before the presentation of a successful petition for winding up or for an administration order or before the passing of a winding-up resolution; and

(b) it was made at a time when the company was unable to pay its debts or became unable to do so as a result of the charge.

Where the company has created a floating charge in favour of a connected person the charge is prima facie invalid if it was made within *two* years before the petition or resolution. The charge is prima facie invalid in such a case even if the company was (and remained) solvent when the charge was created.

A floating charge created within the time limits (and so prima facie invalid) is, however, valid to the extent of:

(a) consideration for the charge consisting of money paid or goods and services supplied to the company at or after the creation of the charge; and

(b) consideration consisting of discharge or reduction of any debt of the company at or after the creation of the charge; and

(c) interest on (a) and (b) above.

EXAMPLE

Montrel Limited has a fully extended, unsecured overdraft with its bank, owing the latter £20,000. In September 2013, the bank agrees to extend the overdraft to £35,000 providing Montrel Limited grants the bank a floating charge to secure all sums due to it. Montrel does so, as it requires £15,000 to enable it to pay wages and money owing to HM Revenue and Customs. Two months later, Montrel, having drawn down the £15,000 but not repaid any money to the bank, becomes insolvent as a result of a winding-up petition.

The floating charge was given to the bank within 12 months of a successful petition for winding up and Montrel was unable to pay its debts at the time. As a result, it is prima facie invalid. This would have the result that the bank would rank as an unsecured creditor in Montrel's liquidation for the sum of £35,000. However, under the criteria above, the charge will be valid to the extent of the consideration for the charge supplied to the company consisting of money paid at or after the creation of the charge, namely the £15,000. The result of this is that the bank will, in Montrel's liquidation, rank as:

(a) a secured creditor (under the floating charge) for £15,000; and

(b) an unsecured creditor for £20,000.

Section 245 is designed to prevent a company benefiting a creditor by giving a charge for existing debt. The exceptions are designed to ensure that a company may still give security in order to obtain money or supplies even though in some difficulty. This should not in principle cause any harm to existing creditors.

online resource centre

For further resources and online chapters please visit the Online Resource Centre at www.oxfordtextbooks.co.uk/orc/business13_14/.

Additional topics

28 Choice of business medium

This chapter covers the following topics:

28.1 Introduction

The purpose of this chapter is to make a comparison between companies, on the one hand, and partnerships or sole traders on the other, with a view to explaining the various factors which ought to be taken into account when a choice is made between the two business media.

Once these comparisons are understood, **Chapter 29** should then be considered to understand how the further possible choice of a limited liability partnership should be assessed. As limited liability partnerships can effectively be treated as corporate entities, it is essential that either side of the spectrum of choice is considered first. As a general rule, once the possibility of a partnership has been rejected, the choice is then narrowed to that of a limited company or a limited liability partnership.

The choice will first be made when a new business is set up, but should be kept under review as circumstances (and the law) change. For the sake of clarity, the differences between companies and partnerships are considered under various headings. It is important to realise that in making a choice each factor should be taken into account. In particular cases one factor may outweigh all the others, but generally each medium has some advantages and some disadvantages so that often the choice will not be cut and dried.

28.2 Risk of capital

All business involves a risk of capital. The degree of risk obviously varies considerably depending on the nature of the business, the economic climate, and the skill of the people running the business. The amount of capital which is at risk also varies considerably—some types of business require a great deal of capital, others very little.

One advantage of a company over a partnership is that a company can be formed with limited liability. This means that the shareholders must contribute the amount unpaid on their shares, but no more, if the company goes into liquidation when it is insolvent. In the vast majority of cases the shares will be fully paid so that no contribution towards the company's debts has to be made. However, the shareholders will lose their shares when the company fails so that, realistically, the limit to their liability is what they have invested in the company. A shareholder who is also a director will also lose his employment with the company. A director (including a shadow director) may also become personally liable in certain circumstances when the company is wound up (see **Chapter 27**).

If a partnership becomes insolvent, each of the partners is jointly and severally liable for all the debts of the partnership. This means that they stand to lose not only what they have invested in the business but also any other property which they own. The liability of partners is, therefore, unlimited in amount. The partnership agreement may make provision as to how losses are to be shared between the partners but this does not prevent creditors claiming in full from a rich partner whose poor partners are unable to pay their share of the loss.

At first sight, limited liability would seem to be an enormous advantage to the proprietors of a business in every case. However, there are at least two circumstances where limited liability is not very significant:

(a) *Where there is little risk of substantial loss of capital*
The clearest example of this is a business involving the giving of advice, such as a consultancy. The proprietor expects to make profits by providing expertise in return for payment; comparatively little is required in the way of capital expenditure on equipment and the running costs of the business will be small. In many cases the biggest potential loss will be claims for damages if bad advice is given to clients and this can be covered by insurance.

(b) *Where the proprietor risks everything he owns in the business*
If the proprietor's only assets are what he has invested in the business, he will effectively lose everything when the business fails whether it is a company or partnership. (This is, of course, only true while all the capital remains in the business, so that limited liability will become relevant once the proprietor starts to take profits out of the business on a large scale.)

Limited liability afforded by incorporating a business can sometimes be made illusory by the directors of the company having to give guarantees. Many businesses rely on borrowed money. A bank lending to a small company will often require personal guarantees from the directors or shareholders, so that if the company cannot repay the loan, the bank has further security. Guarantees may also be required by the landlord of any premises which a company may lease. These will primarily be in respect of the company's obligations to pay rent but may also cover performance obligations, such as those requiring a tenant to keep the property in good repair.

Limited liability is most significant (and can realistically be achieved) where there is a substantial risk of loss of capital invested and the proprietor (or one of the proprietors) has private wealth not invested in the business. In such cases limited liability may be so desirable that it far outweighs any other consideration and, therefore, the business must be run as a company.

28.3 Expense

Certain expenses must inevitably be incurred when a company is formed. These include the Registrar's fee on incorporation and the cost of preparing the application for registration and articles. If a partnership is formed, these expenses need not be incurred, since there are no registration requirements. However, in most cases the partners will want a properly drawn up partnership agreement and will wish to instruct a solicitor to draw it up for them, thus incurring professional costs.

It is difficult to make any general comparison between costs of formation of either entity since they will depend largely on the complexity of the proposed articles or partnership agreement. However, the possibility of standard articles for companies and the ability to use a shelf company may mean that start-up costs for a company will be cheaper than those for a partnership with a comprehensive partnership agreement.

In addition to legal advice, the proprietors of a new business will often wish to seek advice from accountants. Again, the amount payable for the advice will depend on the complexity of the advice given rather than the business medium used. Similarly, common printing costs will be incurred for business stationery and promotional material.

After formation the major administrative costs of a business will again depend on the complexity of the business. However, in respect of accounts, a company is at a disadvantage when compared with a partnership. All types of business will wish to keep accounts, and prepare final accounts annually. Nearly all businesses will wish to pay a qualified accountant to draw up these accounts (if only to make sure that advantage is taken of tax reliefs and exemptions). A company, however, must draw up the accounts in a particular way. This means that the accounts must in some respects show more information than the accounts of a partnership and for a small business this may involve considerable extra cost. (It should be remembered that the partial exemption of 'small' companies from accounting requirements applies only to the published accounts—full accounts must be prepared for the members.) Furthermore, once the accounts have been produced they may have to be audited by an independent qualified accountant. This means that a company may incur higher accountants' fees annually than a partnership.

A company is also required to prepare an annual return and to pay a fee on its filing with the Registrar. (See appendix to **Chapter 8** for details.) The Companies Act also requires many other returns to be filed from time to time (e.g., particulars of directors, charges, and address of registered office). Although fees are not normally payable on the filing of these returns, their preparation will add to the running costs of the business. Many company directors will not feel able to deal with these matters themselves and so will have to seek professional assistance from their lawyers or other business advisers.

28.4 Management

The Companies Act lays down certain rules as to the management structure of companies. A company is, for example, required to have at least one director. Numerous statutory obligations are imposed on these officials. However, those obligations aside, a company is entitled to stipulate in its articles its own rules as to internal management. A partnership may also establish its own rules for management of the business. The Partnership Act 1890 lays down certain presumptions (e.g., that, in the absence of contrary agreement, decisions are taken by a majority vote of the partners except in a limited number of cases where unanimity is required). The partners are free to vary these presumptions by agreement or by a course of dealings. Both types of business medium are, therefore, entitled to choose a management structure which is suitable for the particular case.

28.4.1 Internal flexibility

It should be relatively straightforward to provide a suitable management structure for a company, by appropriate drafting of the articles. In turn, these should allow directors sufficient flexibility to run the company without the need for regular referrals to the shareholders. However, as a corollary to such flexibility, the articles may also restrict the powers of the board and require the approval of the members for particular designated decisions.

In the case of a partnership, the agreement between the partners can be altered. This normally requires the approval of all the partners so that the 'constitution' of a partnership is more rigid than that of a company. However, if, when the partnership agreement is drawn up, it is decided that a greater degree of flexibility is required, the agreement can provide for alteration by a majority (without unanimous agreement), either in general or in particular cases.

It is, therefore, possible for either business medium to have a very flexible or a very rigid management structure, as the proprietors wish.

28.4.2 Security of tenure

Just as the profits of a partnership are divided between the partners so, in the case of most small companies, the profits will be divided between the directors, either by way of enhanced salaries or bonus payments. Security of tenure as a partner or director is, therefore, of vital concern to the proprietors of a business.

A director is always subject to removal by an ordinary resolution of the members. However, a director who has the majority of votes at shareholder level (or a majority of votes on a shareholder resolution for his removal—see *Bushell v Faith* [1970] AC 1099, at **9.8.1.4**) is effectively irremovable. A director who does not have a majority of votes but who has a service agreement may be entitled to substantial compensation if removed from office, and so to that extent may be protected.

In the case of a partnership, removal of a partner will, subject to contrary agreement, involve the dissolution of the partnership. At first sight this would seem to put a partner in a stronger position than a director. However, in practice, this is not necessarily so. In some cases it will be possible for some of the partners to get rid of one of their colleagues and then set up a 'new' business after the dissolution, which will in effect be a continuation of the old business. This will be possible particularly if those who remain own the premises from which the business is carried on. The position of a junior partner is not, therefore, necessarily stronger than that of a director who is not in control of the company.

The practical reality of the situation is that if a director or partner is vital to the business, he cannot be removed without causing substantial upheaval to the business. However, where a director or partner is really no more than a senior employee, he can be removed on payment of any compensation provided for in his service contract or in the partnership agreement. A director, but not a partner, may also be entitled to compensation for unfair dismissal or to statutory redundancy pay. Note also that members of a limited liability partnership are unlikely to have any entitlement to employee rights due to the effect of s. 4(4) Limited Liability Partnership Act 2000. (See *Tiffin v Lester Aldridge* [2012] 1 WLR 1887 for the Court of Appeal's interpretation of the effect of s. 4(4).)

28.4.3 Succession to the business

The articles of a company may restrict the right to transfer shares, thus preventing a shareholder from selling out or giving away shares to anyone they please. Such restrictions may be coupled with pre-emption rights given to the other shareholders. Alternatively, shares may be freely transferable. It is, therefore, possible to make provision for succession in advance, provided that sufficient thought is given to the problem at the time when the articles are drafted. Similarly, a partnership agreement may make provision for bringing in new partners and for payment to the existing partners on leaving. If no other provision is made, unanimity is required for the admission of a new partner. Since the partners have to be able to work together in running the business, it is unlikely that they would be willing to allow admission of new partners without such agreement.

It is, therefore, possible to lay down rules for succession with either type of business medium. In practical terms the problem of succession is one which can only be solved if suitable purchasers can be found or if suitable donees willing to carry on the business are available. It is generally easier to achieve succession in the case of a company, since the sale of a majority shareholding passes control to the purchaser. The majority shareholder will usually be free to sell out since he has effective control of the board which will, therefore, be prepared to approve any transfer of his shares to an outsider.

28.5 Publicity

A company is required to make a considerable amount of information, including annual accounts, available to the public. A partnership is not required to make such information available. A desire to keep the affairs of the business secret may influence some people to prefer a partnership to a company, but it is not likely to be a major factor in most cases, especially since the partners will, in practice, be required to show their accounts to any prospective lender. Also, the fact that a great number of professional partnerships now operate as limited liability partnerships (which have approximately the same disclosure obligations as companies) is proof of the fact that confidentiality is not regarded as a major factor.

28.6 Taxation—trading profits

The reader is advised to have read **Chapters 17** to **24** before reading the rest of this section.

28.6.1 Companies

A company has a choice as to how to use its profits—they may be used to pay dividends, interest, or directors' fees, or they may be retained in the business. Each of these four possibilities has different tax consequences. Generally speaking, the payment of directors' fees is the most tax-efficient use of profits, and for a small, private company most of the profits will normally be used for this purpose for non-tax reasons anyway. This is because the directors must be compensated for the work that they do for the business and often little profit will be left over for other purposes.

Where profits are sufficiently large, however, a company can be used as a means of tax planning by deciding to retain profits or pay dividends. Retained profits are liable to corporation tax at between 20% and 23% (depending on the size of the profit). The rate can be kept down to 20% if sufficient is paid in directors' fees to keep the profits within the small companies' rate band. This rate of tax may be somewhat less than the director/shareholder's rate of income tax (which may be 40% or even 45%, if the additional rate applies). However, the future consequences of capital taxes must also be taken into account. The accumulated profits will be reflected in the value of the shares in the company so that, on a disposal of shares a higher CGT and/or IHT may be payable, thus reducing the effectiveness of the income tax saving resulting from retention of the profits.

As dividends are non-deductible for the paying company and will be made out of after-tax profits, their payment may be seen as inefficient from a tax perspective. However, such payments do not incur any National Insurance liability for either the company or a director, so there may be some important comparisons to be made between dividend payments and increased directors' salaries or bonuses. A decision to pay dividends may, of course, be taken for non-tax reasons, since it is the only way to provide a shareholder, who is not also a director, with a return on his investment.

28.6.2 Partnerships

A partnership offers less scope for tax planning in relation to income profits than a company. All the income profits are taxed as income of the partners whether they are actually paid to them or are retained in the business (unless a capital allowance is available). To the extent that profits are withdrawn from the business a partner is in the same position as a director receiving directors' fees—both pay income tax on the sums that are received. However, it should still be borne in mind that a payment of a salary to a director will suffer an immediate deduction for tax under the PAYE system, whereas drawings by a partner will not, being, instead, subject to the self-assessment regime.

To the extent that profits are retained in the business, a partner pays the same tax as if the profits had been withdrawn. This will be an advantage when compared with a company where the partner's rate of tax is less than the rate of corporation tax, and a disadvantage when it is more.

28.7 Interest relief

A payment of interest by an individual must generally be paid out of taxed income. However, in some cases, interest paid may be deducted from income before it is assessed to tax as a 'charge on income' (so that tax relief is available on the interest payment). This relief is available where money is borrowed to buy an interest in a partnership. Relief is also available where money is borrowed to buy shares in a close company provided that either:

(a) the shares give the borrower a 'material interest' (i.e., more than 5% of ordinary share capital or a right to more than 5% of the income); or

(b) the borrower owns some shares and, from the time when he used the loan until the time when the interest was paid, he was working for the greater part of his time in the management or conduct of the company.

28.8 Capital gains

A company pays corporation tax at an effective rate of between 20% and 23% on any capital gain which it makes. The disposal of assets by a partnership gives rise to tax at the appropriate rate for the individual partners, which is 18% and/or 28%. However, a company and its proprietors suffer two disadvantages in respect of capital gains. First, the profit made on the disposal of a capital asset (after payment of tax) will be reflected in the value of the shares in the company and further capital gains tax will be payable on disposal of those shares. For example, an asset is purchased by a company for £10,000 and sold for £20,000. Tax of (say) £2,000 will be paid, leaving a net profit after tax of £8,000. This profit will be reflected in the value of the shares so that if they are disposed of, a further gain of £8,000 will be taxed. Secondly, a company is not entitled to an annual exemption, whereas in the case of a partnership each partner is currently entitled to an annual exemption for the first £10,900 worth of gains.

However, an advantage for companies is that they may be able to use the indexation allowance in respect of capital gains to reduce the gain on which tax is charged.

28.9 Inheritance tax

28.9.1 Close companies and anti-avoidance

A company cannot normally be used as a means of avoiding IHT, since gifts by a close company are attributed to the shareholders in the company (s. 94 IHTA 1984). Nearly all small companies come within the definition of a close company. Similarly, gifts of partnership assets will be liable to tax as gifts of the individual partners. Inheritance tax is, therefore, generally a neutral factor in the choice of business medium.

28.9.2 Business property relief

Any shareholding in a private company will attract 100% business property relief, as will a partnership share, so the availability or otherwise of business property relief is not something which can be considered a deciding factor between the two business media (see **22.8.6** for further discussion on business property relief).

There is, however, still a difference in the relief given where an asset is owned by an individual partner or shareholder but used by the partnership or company. A partner whose private property is used by his partnership is entitled to relief of 50% when he gives the property away. Similar relief is available to a shareholder but only if he owns shares which give control of the company.

28.10 Pensions and social security

There are a number of ways in which people in business may provide for their retirement. The most favourable method from the tax point of view is an 'exempt approved occupational pension scheme'. Such a scheme affords generous tax relief on contributions by both employers and employees and further relief from capital taxes to the managers of the scheme. Its purpose is to provide a pension and, in some cases, a lump sum on retirement. Such schemes are not available to the self-employed (such as partners). Partners are able to get the relief by means of a personal pension. Contributions are deductible from taxable income up to a certain percentage of relevant earnings depending on the age of the contributor.

Social security also operates differently in respect of employees and the self-employed. Contributions (in the form of National Insurance) must be made by both employer and employee in respect of an employed person; a self-employed person must contribute at a rate higher than the employee's contribution but lower than the employer's and employee's contributions combined. This National Insurance saving can make a partnership (or a limited liability partnership, which would be taxed in the same way) preferable to a company (although the state benefits to which an employed person is entitled are correspondingly higher than those to which a self-employed person is entitled).

28.11 Raising finance

Whilst there are numerous partnerships which have bank borrowings, as a general rule companies are treated as a more attractive proposition as borrowers, because of their ability to grant floating charges, which in turn gives the lender greater security. (The same is true of limited liability partnerships.)

A corporate structure also makes the introduction of new investment capital easier. An investor in a partnership will ideally have to be made a partner, if he or she is to own a stake in the business. This can be disruptive for the existing management structure of the partners and also has the downside for the investor in that, henceforth, he or she will have unlimited liability for the debts of the partnership. Taking on a new shareholder in a company can have no disruptive influence on its management, since the roles of shareholder and director can be kept separate, and the investor only stands to lose the value of the investment and nothing further. Also, an equity investor in a company has greater flexibility in their exit from such an investment, in that they can sell all or part of their shareholding to existing shareholders, third parties (subject to any terms of pre-emption in the articles of association), or back to the company itself. With a partnership share the only truly feasible exit is to sell it in its entirety to existing partners.

An investor can, of course, simply lend money to a partnership. However, there will be no capital growth in such investment as there would be with becoming a partner and taking a partnership share. A shareholding, particularly if it has voting rights, will normally always have the possibility of capital growth.

28.12 Conclusion

It is not possible to lay down any hard and fast rule as to which business medium is the more beneficial since there are too many variables. In a significant number of cases the desirability of limited liability will mean that incorporation is the only viable option, although this can also be achieved by setting up a limited liability partnership. Where limited liability is not of great importance, the tax factors will be more significant and these would have to be examined from a number of perspectives, including the size of anticipated profits, the particular financial circumstances of the promoters of the business, and any particular expectations they had about their stake in the business.

online resource centre

For further resources and online chapters please visit the Online Resource Centre at www.oxfordtextbooks.co.uk/orc/business13_14/.

29

Limited liability partnerships

This chapter covers the following topics:

It is recommended that the concepts governing both partnerships and companies have been studied and understood before reading this chapter. In particular, as most of the regulation which governs companies also governs limited liability partnerships (LLPs), it is recommended that the reader has acquired a working knowledge of the regime which covers companies before considering LLPs.

29.1 Introduction

The popularity of private limited companies as business media can be attributed to one thing: the availability of limited liability for the owners and managers. However, the trade-off is public disclosure of much of what the company does, together with a complex regulatory regime. For this reason, the medium of a partnership can still be an attractive choice in certain circumstances, particularly for professional firms.

However, the major disincentive to setting up in business through the medium of a partnership is the exposure which each partner faces to liabilities of the partnership. Not only is each partner personally liable for all liabilities (either contractual or tortious) of the partnership, there is also no limit on such liability. This was a source of considerable concern to large professional partnerships, where the work undertaken could be advising on matters running into millions of pounds. With clients becoming increasingly litigious in relation to their advisers, the threat of a massive (and potentially ruinous) claim is ever present.

It was against this background that the concept of LLPs was introduced by the Limited Liability Partnerships Act (LLPA) 2000, which came into force on 6 April 2001. It is important to note that the Act merely provided a framework and that certain detail has been introduced by regulations made by the Secretary of State (ss. 14–17 LLPA 2000). Therefore, it is crucial that reference is made to such regulations. The key regulations in existence are the Limited Liability Partnerships Regulations 2001 (as amended) and the Limited Liability Partnerships (Application of the Companies Act 2006) Regulations 2009. In addition, there are regulations which impose the companies accounts regime onto LLPs.

It should be noted at the outset that the LLPA 2000 did not replace the regime for partnerships under the PA 1890. It is still possible, therefore, to operate a business as a 'traditional' partnership. In addition, LLPs are available to any type of business and not limited to professional partnerships. One restriction on their use, however, is the fact that the persons involved must be carrying on business with a view to profit. Non-profit making entities, therefore, cannot operate as LLPs.

The key rationale for the creation of LLPs is to allow entrepreneurs the protection of limited liability while preserving the flexibility of the partnership structure. As such, LLPs can best be described as a hybrid of both companies and partnerships. However, as will become apparent, they owe much more to the former than the latter. (This is reinforced by the fact that s. 1(5) LLPA 2000 states that the law of partnerships does not apply to LLPs.)

29.2 Key elements of LLPs

29.2.1 Limited liability

Third parties who deal with LLPs will contract and deal with the LLP as a distinct legal entity (s. 1(2) LLPA 2000). This is in contrast to partnerships, where the partners and the partnership are one and the same. This means that any recourse the third party has will be against the LLP entity and its assets rather than the members of the LLP themselves. That much is straightforward. What is more difficult is just how those members can limit their liability. Section 74 of the Insolvency Act 1986 (as it applies to LLPs) states that members of an LLP shall contribute to the assets of the LLP in the event of it being wound up as is provided for in the LLP agreement. Therefore, it is feasible that members' liability could be limited to as little as £1 or could be excluded altogether.

However, it is perhaps an over-simplification to imagine that those involved in LLPs will never incur any form of personal liability. Although the issue is not clear-cut, the view is that liability for negligent misstatement will still attach to the errors of a member. This is particularly germane in the instance of a professional LLP, such as a law or accountancy firm. As such, whilst the members as a whole may not bear the liability for negligent advice, the individual who gave that advice may be liable. One way to address this is by way of an indemnity for such a member. Regulation 7(2) of the LLP Regulations 2001 implies an indemnity in respect of payments made and liabilities incurred by a member in the ordinary and proper conduct of the business of the LLP. However, it is arguable that such an indemnity does not cover negligence. It may be preferable, therefore, to include a comprehensively drafted indemnity in an LLP agreement, although the inclusion of any such indemnity may be seen as erosion of some of the benefits of limited liability.

Furthermore, members of an LLP are subject to the provisions within the Insolvency Act regarding wrongful and fraudulent trading. In addition, s. 214A of the Insolvency Act 1986 applies specifically to LLPs. Any member who made withdrawals of any amounts in the two-year period prior to the insolvency of the LLP may find that those amounts are clawed back by the liquidator if it can be shown that the member in question knew or ought to have concluded that there was no reasonable prospect of the LLP avoiding insolvent liquidation.

29.2.2 Creation

An LLP is very much like a company in that it will have to be registered with the Registrar of Companies and a certificate of incorporation will be issued as proof of this fact (ss. 2 and 3 LLPA 2000). An LLP can be registered either in England and Wales, Wales, Scotland, or Northern Ireland.

To achieve incorporation, details of the LLP must be entered on form LL IN01 and submitted to the relevant Registrar of Companies with a fee. (Further details regarding fees are provided in an appendix to this chapter.)

The basic contents of the form are:

(a) the signatures of two or more persons associated with the business;

(b) name of the LLP (which must end with the words 'Limited Liability Partnership' or 'LLP');

(c) a statement about the intended location of the registered office and the actual address of the same;

(d) the names and addresses of those persons who are to be members of the LLP. (As with companies, both a service address and a residential address must be supplied, of which only the former will appear on the public record.)

This shares similarities with the procedure for registration of a company. However, one major difference is that there is no specimen constitution which an LLP can adopt (as the Model Articles for companies), nor must the LLP register its constitution with Companies House as a matter of public record. Perhaps the nearest approximation of a 'standard' constitution is the default provisions contained within regulation 7 of the LLP Regulations 2001, although, as their title suggests, they can be displaced by contrary agreement of the members. (Note that this regulation is influenced by s. 24 of the Partnership Act 1890.)

29.2.3 Unlimited capacity

Section 1(3) of the LLPA 2000 states that an LLP has unlimited capacity in the same way that companies formed under the CA 2006 now have unrestricted objects. However, a distinction seems to be that companies still have the option of restricting the scope of their objects in the constitution (s. 31 CA 2006). This possibility does not appear to be available to LLPs. One specific distinction to draw between LLPs and partnerships is that LLPs are capable of granting a floating charge, which may mean that there are greater financing opportunities than for a traditional partnership. (Note that most charges created by an LLP will be registrable at Companies House in the same way as for security granted by a company.)

29.2.4 Members and designated members

The initial members of the LLP are those who signed the incorporation document. Further members can join the LLP with the consent of the then current members. A properly drafted LLP agreement should make specific provision for the appointment (and removal) of members during the life of the LLP. (In the absence of any such provision, regulation 7(5) of the LLP Regulations 2001 will imply a prohibition on the admission of a new member unless agreed to by all members. Regulation 8, on the other hand, excludes any right of expulsion of a member by a majority of members, unless that right has been specifically reserved by agreement of the members.)

There must be a minimum of two members in an LLP. Should the number fall to one and remain so for at least six months, the benefit of limited liability will cease and the remaining member will be liable together with the LLP, for all debts and liabilities incurred during that period (s. 4A LLPA 2000). This requirement excludes the availability of LLPs for sole traders. It also puts LLPs at a disadvantage as compared to private limited companies, which can allow their membership to fall to one, should the situation ever arise.

There is a special class of members known as 'designated members', as specified by s. 8 LLPA 2000. The incorporation document will have to contain details of such members, although different persons can assume this role during the life of the LLP. There must always be a minimum of two designated members, but it is also possible to treat all members as designated members or a larger number than simply two members.

The LLPA imposes specific responsibilities on designated members, namely:

(a) to appoint an auditor, if it is necessary to do so;

(b) to sign off an LLP's accounts and file them with the registrar of companies;

(c) to ensure that an annual return for an LLP is filed with the registrar of companies;

(d) to ensure that an LLP complies with all statutory filing requirements (see **29.2.5** below).

29.2.5 Disclosure requirements

As with companies, the *quid pro quo* for limited liability is public disclosure. The key filing responsibilities of an LLP are:

(a) the filing of accounts;

(b) the filing of an annual return (on form LL AR01), together with the appropriate fee (see the appendix to this chapter);

(c) the notification of appointments to the membership (on form LL AP01);

(d) the notification of termination of membership (on form LL TM01);

(e) the notification of changes in members or designated members (on form LL CH01);

(f) the notification of a change to its registered office (on form LL AD01); and

(g) the notification of a change to its registered name (on form LL NM01), together with the appropriate fee (see the appendix to this chapter).

29.2.6 Relationship of members with the LLP, each other, and third parties

29.2.6.1 LLP

Every member is an agent of the LLP (s. 6(1) LLPA 2000). As such the common law fiduciary duties that an agent owes to a principal would appear to apply to members of an LLP. It is beyond the scope of this text to consider the relationship between an agent and its principal, but the basic parameters will be that the member:

(a) must act in good faith towards the LLP;

(b) must not put himself in a position of conflict with the LLP;

(c) must not profit personally from his position;

(d) must make full disclosure of information which is of legitimate interest to the LLP.

These implications would appear to be reinforced to an extent by certain provisions of the 2001 Regulations, namely:

(a) a duty to account to the LLP for any profits derived from a similar business which competes with the business of the LLP (regulation 7(9));

(b) a duty to account for any personal benefit derived from a transaction with the LLP or from the use of LLP property (regulation 7(10)).

Note, however, that whilst much of the Companies Act applies to LLPs, the statutory duties which apply to directors are not imposed on members of an LLP. The rationale for this is that members of an LLP cannot be equated with directors due to the absence of a distinction between the owners of an LLP and its management.

This agency relationship presumably also means that members acting with either actual or apparent authority have the power to bind the firm, although the Act does not make this point explicitly. What the Act does do, however, is provide an exception to this basic rule in s. 6(2), which is akin to the 'unless' exception in s. 5 PA 1890. Thus, if any member is acting without authority and the person he is dealing with either knows that he has no authority or does not know or believe him to be a member, the LLP will not be bound by the acts of the member.

Persons ceasing to be members of LLPs can still operate as their agents until either the third party is notified of the fact or notice is sent to the Registrar of Companies (s. 6(3)).

LLPs are also liable for the wrongful acts or omissions of individual members when acting in the course of the LLP's business (s. 6(4)) to the same extent as the member. The LLPA 2000 is silent on the meaning of 'wrongful acts or omissions'. This will likely include tortious acts, and it may also include criminal acts.

A somewhat problematic issue is that of ownership by the members of a stake in the LLP. Shareholders in a company can point to an asset which represents their holding in the company. Similarly, partners in a 'traditional' partnership have a direct proprietorial stake in the assets used by the partnership or at least a claim in their proceeds of sale (see *Popat v Schonchhatra* [1997] 3 All ER 800). However, with LLPs, the separation between the legal entity and its owners exists without any legal mechanism being in place to record ownership. Therefore, if an LLP uses its funds to buy an asset, that asset is owned by the LLP. However, in substance, the members will be of the view that it is their money which has been used and therefore the property is theirs. Furthermore, profits made by the LLP will be profits of that entity but must be available to the members.

Regulation 7, para. (1) of the LLP Regulations 2001 provides that members are entitled to share equally in the capital and profits of the LLP which borrows heavily from s. 24(1) PA 1890. Section 24(1) operates to allocate the entitlements of partners and does not act as a basis for determining ownership. There is no reason to assume that regulation 7, para. (1) should be treated differently. As such, it is arguable that in neither the LLPA 2000 nor the LLP Regulations 2001 is there an absolute statement about the rights of ownership which members enjoy in an LLP. Also, because of the effect of s. 1(5) LLPA 2000 it is not possible to treat members of an LLP as equivalent to partners in terms of their legal status.

That the law is silent on this issue is perhaps a strange oversight. Therefore, to ensure certainty, members will have to enter into arrangements with their LLPs to provide for these issues, namely, how a member's share in the LLP is determined, what a member may or may not do with that share, and any specific entitlement of a member when they leave the LLP.

29.2.6.2 Each other

As stated above, members of LLPs are free to organise their internal affairs as they wish. This is the flexibility of the existing partnership regime which the Government has wished to preserve. Should such an agreement not be in place, the default provisions in the Limited Liability Partnership Regulations 2001 can be relied upon. However, many of these will not be satisfactory for all but the simplest of LLP arrangements. For example, despite the duty to account for profits arising from a competing business implied by regulation 7(9), a well-drafted LLP agreement should probably contain a specific non-competition clause applicable both during and after cessation of membership. Furthermore, the specifics of an agreed decision-making process should also be set out, including, if thought necessary, the identification of any decisions which need to be passed either by a 'super majority', e.g., three-quarters of the members, or unanimously. (The default position under regulation 7(6) would be that 'ordinary matters' connected with the business of the LLP should be decided by simple majority but that no change could be made to the nature of the business without unanimous consent.)

29.2.6.3 Unfair prejudice

Of particular interest is the ability of members of an LLP to bring a claim for unfair prejudice under s. 994 CA 2006. However, this may be more of a theoretical possibility than real if an LLP agreement exists, for two reasons:

(a) The members can agree to exclude the possibility in the LLP agreement.

(b) In any event, the agreement may be comprehensive enough to deal with all internal disputes, excluding the need to assert unfair prejudice.

29.2.6.4 Third parties

Essentially there is no relationship between members of LLPs and third parties. Therefore, unlike in a partnership, issues of liabilities of a business following a member after retirement do not arise. However, as has been mentioned already, it is possible that, in certain circumstances, individual members may find themselves liable in tort to third parties, particularly when giving professional advice.

Also, there may be instances where due to the principal/agent relationship between an LLP and its members, a member may be held liable for breach of warranty of authority to an outsider.

29.2.7 Taxation

The principle of separate legal personality is not maintained as far as taxation is concerned, so an LLP is not a taxable person. Instead, as with partnerships, it is the members who are taxed as profit centres.

29.2.8 Execution of documents

LLPs execute documents in the same way as companies. As such, any member may execute a contract on behalf of an LLP. If, however, the document is to be executed by the LLP itself, the signatures of two members are required.

29.2.9 Impact of other Acts

Sections 14–16 LLPA 2000 allow for the Secretary of State to make provision for company and insolvency law to apply to LLPs. This has been done primarily through the regulations already mentioned. However, other regulations exist which deal with accounting and audit issues such as the Limited Liability Partnerships (Accounts and Audit) (Application of Companies Act 2006) Regulations 2008. As such, large tracts of the Companies Act 2006, the Company Directors Disqualification Act 1986, and the Insolvency Act 1986 apply to LLPs. As a general rule, it is safe to assume that much of the legislation which applies to companies and their directors applies equally to LLPs and their members, for example:

(a) The choice of an LLP's registered name is subject to the same controls and restrictions as a company's registered name. Furthermore, LLPs are subject to the same disclosure requirements about registered names as companies.

(b) LLPs' accounts have to be audited in accordance with the Companies Act 2006 to give a true and fair view of the business.

(c) Charges granted by LLPs over their assets have to be registered at Companies House, together with the appropriate fee (see the appendix to this chapter).

(d) Members of LLPs can face disqualification orders, such that they can be neither members of other LLPs nor company directors.

(e) Insolvent LLPs are subject to the same insolvency regime as companies and their members will find themselves subject to the same scrutiny as directors of insolvent companies, for example, they could commit wrongful trading.

(f) In the same way that company law recognises the concept and influence of a shadow director, so there exists the possibility of a 'shadow member'. In turn, shadow members can be both subject to disqualification proceedings and found liable for wrongful trading.

One material exception to this general principle is that LLPs are not subject to any capital maintenance obligations in the way that companies are.

29.3 Factors influencing choice

There will be two instances where the question of choosing an LLP arises: as part of a business start-up; or existing partnerships considering conversion. When considering LLPs, it should always be remembered that their resemblance to traditional partnerships is an exception rather than a rule and that it is better to think of them as corporate structures.

The authors consider that there is very little likelihood of the members of an existing company wishing to alter its status to that of an LLP as this will alter fundamentally their relationship with each other and their business medium with no corresponding benefit.

29.3.1 Business start-up

One easy decision can be made at the outset when advising on the appropriate business medium. If only one person is to be involved in the venture, neither a partnership nor an LLP is possible. Thereafter the basic rules about choice of business medium (as set out in **Chapter 28**) apply and, whilst there are three possible formats to choose from, the basic choice is between a corporate entity (company or LLP) or a partnership. In turn, this means a choice between limited liability, public disclosure, substantial regulations, and compliance and unlimited liability, absolute secrecy, and very limited compliance. This distinction is, however, blurred when taxation is considered because LLPs share the taxation regime of partnerships rather than companies. In addition, the internal management of an LLP is more akin to that of a partnership.

If a decision is made in favour of a corporate entity then some of the distinctions to be drawn are as follows:

(a) The decision-making regime within an LLP can be as simple or as complex as the members wish. There is no such choice with companies. However, the two-tier decision-making process within companies (that is, directors and shareholders) may allow for greater flexibility in power-sharing.

(b) Raising capital is still likely to be easier through a company because of the flexibility inherent in shares as an investment mechanism. If, however, the business is likely to remain close-knit and to rely primarily upon its initial members for finance, this may not be a disincentive to choosing an LLP.

(c) Within the framework of a company there is more scope for leaving profits within the company or paying them out. Within an LLP, profits earned are taxed in the hands of the members, irrespective of whether or not they are drawn out.

(d) The regime for companies is relatively clear and well understood, whereas the regime governing LLPs may throw up unforeseen problems as it matures.

(e) It is relatively inexpensive to set up a company and considerable precedents exist for many permutations of articles. Whilst an LLP members' agreement is not a requirement of law, clients would be ill-advised not to have one. The length and complexity of such documents may result in a considerable initial cost burden.

(f) The clawback provisions of s. 214A of the Insolvency Act 1986 are substantial, so it is arguable that members of an LLP face greater exposure to contribute to an insolvent LLP than directors in respect of their companies.

29.3.2 Conversion from partnership to LLP

Much of what has just been discussed will be relevant in this situation also. However, a number of other issues may have to be considered, such as:

(a) *The cost of conversion*. The re-draft of any existing partnership deed may be a lengthy and costly process. In addition, there is the practical issue that every existing partner should sign the incorporation document and it should contain their addresses. In a professional partnership of, say, more than 100 partners worldwide, this would pose logistical problems.

(b) *The cost/management of disclosure*. Notification must be made every time a member either joins or leaves and every time a member's address changes. Again, in large partnerships this is an extra burden of bureaucracy. Moreover, having such details on the public register may be regarded as undesirable by some.

(c) *Disclosure of financial information*. For professional partnerships, the disclosure of accounts is seen by many to be a major disincentive to adopting LLP status. Also, the accounts of a partnership are prepared for the purposes of internal consumption and those of HMRC, whereas the accounts of an LLP will have to conform to the standards and requirements set out in the Companies Act 2006 (and related regulations).

(d) *Borrowing*. When a bank lends to a partnership, it can take comfort from the fact that the individual estates of the partners will be available to meet any shortcomings in the assets of the firm. Such comfort would be removed if conversion to an LLP took place. To overcome this, banks may ask individual partners to act as guarantors of the LLP, thus partially eroding the benefits of limited liability.

(e) *Leasehold property*. Many of the same issues for banks also concern landlords in relation to any leases the partnership may hold.

(f) *Novation of key contracts*. Contracts with the existing firm will have to become contracts with the LLP.

(g) *Ownership of assets*. As mentioned in **29.2.6.1** it would appear that members of an LLP will own part of the LLP, rather than the LLP's assets direct. Conversion will, therefore, require the transfer of the business of the firm into the hands of the LLP. However, the LLP cannot offer shares in return, as would happen if a partnership were to convert to a company. It makes no sense for the LLP to pay the partners cash for the assets as this would involve the LLP borrowing money effectively to return every partner's capital contribution. Instead the consideration for the sale is best treated as the corresponding share which each member will enjoy in the LLP. Note that this transfer will be a tax-neutral event as the sale to the LLP will not be treated as a disposal for capital gains tax purposes. Moreover, in most circumstances, no stamp duty will be payable.

29.4 Conclusion

The rationale behind LLPs is admirable and they go some way to providing a middle ground between companies and partnerships. In many ways they owe more to companies than they do to partnerships and this lack of clear water between the two media may mean that the choice of a limited company is preferable, especially when the latter is a much more 'concrete' entity. Statistics do show a continuing upward trend in new registrations, however. For example, in the DTI report *Companies in 2002–2003*, the total number of LLPs registered as at 31 March 2003 was around 4,500. In the same report for the following year, this figure had increased substantially to nearly 7,500. Current statistics indicate that around 43,000 LLPs have been registered. There can be no doubt that, amongst the professions (and, in particular, the financial services industry), the LLP route is considered a valid option. However, average statistics for new incorporations of companies stand in excess of 350,000 per annum, so the limited company would appear to be still the main business medium for the time being.

APPENDIX
Companies House fees: limited liability partnerships

The following table sets out some of the more common fees which an LLP may have to pay in its lifetime. (They are, in fact, identical to the fees payable by companies.)

	Paper	Electronic Filing
Incorporation	£40.00	£14.00
Same-day Incorporation	£100.00	£30.00
Change of name	£10.00	£8.00
Same-day change of name	£50.00	£30.00
Annual Return	£40.00	£14.00
Registration of mortgage or charge	£13.00	£10.00

online resource centre

For further resources and online chapters please visit the Online Resource Centre at www.oxfordtextbooks.co.uk/orc/business13_14/.

30 Sale of a business to a company

This chapter covers the following topics:

30.1 Introduction

A sole trader or partnership may decide, for a variety of reasons, to incorporate the business. If this step is taken, although the business will remain unchanged, the incorporation will give rise to a number of tax and other problems. In this chapter, we will consider these problems and how they can be avoided, or at least mitigated. As we shall see, the tax rules are the most important in this area, since if they are not appreciated the payment of an unexpected tax bill can cause very serious cash flow problems. As an aid to understanding these problems, it is helpful to bear in mind that when the trader (which for these purposes includes partnerships) incorporates the business, it is transferred to a separate legal entity, the company. This means that the trader ceases to trade as an unincorporated business and disposes of the business and its assets to the company. The fact that the former proprietor or proprietors own the company and operate the business in exactly the same way as before is immaterial since the members and the company are distinct legal entities (*Salomon v A. Salomon & Co Ltd* [1897] AC 22).

It may therefore come as a surprise to many traders who incorporate their businesses to discover that incorporation can lead to the payment of income tax, capital gains tax, and stamp duty. In this chapter these tax liabilities will be considered in turn.

30.2 Income tax

30.2.1 The closing year rules

Of the possible tax liabilities which can arise, the one which may cause the most difficulties, if it is not provided for, is the liability to income tax. Transferring the business to the company means that the unincorporated trader has permanently stopped trading with the result that the closing year rules of assessment will apply. (See **17.3.2.3** for an explanation of the closing year rules.)

30.2.2 Loss relief

If a loss is made in the final 12 months' trading, it can be carried across against income from another source under s. 64 ITA 2007, and any unabsorbed loss carried back and set against the profits of the three tax years immediately preceding the year of incorporation, taking later years before earlier ones (s. 89 ITA 2007). If, having made use of both provisions, there is still an unabsorbed loss, it cannot be used by the company. However, s. 86 ITA 2007 permits the former proprietors, provided they sold the business in exchange wholly or mainly for shares in the new company, to set the remaining loss against income received from the company while they continue to own the shares. They must reduce earned income (such as directors' fees) before investment income (such as dividends).

Although it may appear strange that a loss-making business should be incorporated, there may be sound reasons for doing so. For example, the business may be entering a temporary period of recession and the trader may want to protect himself from personal liability for future debts, or the loss may have been deliberately created by claiming capital allowances in respect of items of plant and machinery bought shortly before incorporation.

30.2.3 Capital allowances

Whether or not the purchase of an item attracting capital allowances has created the final year loss, the trader's capital allowance position is the remaining income tax point which needs to be considered. The rules relating to capital allowances have already been considered (see **Chapter 21**). The important point to be considered in the context of incorporating a trader's business is that the transfer to the company, even if the purchase price is to be paid in shares, will be a disposal. If the capital allowances already claimed exceed the amount by which the assets have actually depreciated in value, HMRC has a right to levy a balancing charge. This means HMRC recovers the tax lost as a result of the over-deduction of allowances. Thus, there can be another additional income tax bill arising on the incorporation. However, it is possible to ensure that the transfer of plant and machinery is not to be regarded as a discontinuance of the trade for the purposes of capital allowances provided:

(a) the trader and persons connected with him (which includes partners) are the majority shareholders in the new company; and

(b) an election is made to the effect that if there is no discontinuance, there is no disposal and the balancing charge does not arise. The result is that the new company takes over the trader's capital allowance position and makes the appropriate claims for writing-down allowances in respect of the, as yet, unallowed expenditure.

30.3 Capital gains tax

30.3.1 The disposal

The incorporation of the old business not only means that there is a discontinuance for income tax purposes, but that there is also a disposal for CGT purposes. This disposal arises because the business, its assets, and connections (i.e., goodwill) are being *sold* to the company in exchange for shares. This is a chargeable disposal within the Taxation of Chargeable Gains Act (TCGA) 1992 and the trader will be liable for any gain that is realised.

This liability cannot be avoided by the company issuing shares of a purely nominal value in exchange for the assets, as HMRC has a right to substitute the market value of the assets in such circumstances. This gain could be considerable, especially if the business is successful and was set up several years previously. However, a number of reliefs operate in these circumstances which will be looked at in turn.

A business owner has essentially three options as to how his capital gains tax situation is managed on an incorporation:

(a) transfer the entire undertaking as a going concern in return for shares in the new company and claim roll-over relief;

(b) transfer certain business assets or all of them for full value and pay the tax on those, whilst ensuring that any beneficial reliefs, namely entrepreneurs' relief and the nil-rate band are used to reduce the overall tax liability. (Any retained assets can be leased to or licensed for use by the company);

(c) transfer certain assets either for nil consideration or at an undervalue and claim hold-over relief in respect of those and keep other assets and allow the company to use such retained assets.

Option (b) requires no explanation as the reliefs in question have already been considered in Chapter 22, but options (a) and (c) will be looked at in turn.

30.3.2 Relief under s. 162 TCGA 1992

30.3.2.1 The roll-over mechanism

Section 162 TCGA 1992 applies where a person (not being a company):

> transfers to a company a business as a going concern, together with the whole assets of the business, or together with the whole of those assets other than cash, and the business is transferred wholly or partly in exchange for shares issued by the company to the person transferring the business.

The effect of the relief is that the gain realised when the business and its assets are disposed of can be rolled over into the shares received as consideration. However, if not all the consideration is made up of shares, the section permits a reduction to be made in the gain benefiting from the relief. Section 162(4) provides that the amount of the gain which can be rolled over will be determined by the fraction A/B, where A is the 'cost of the new assets' (that is, the value of the shares issued to the former owner), and B is the whole of the consideration received by the former owner in exchange for the business. The effect of this is that, if the consideration received is made up entirely of shares in the transferee company, the former owner bears no CGT liability at the time.

EXAMPLE

If an owner transfers a business with assets worth £100,000 to a new company and receives £100,000 worth of shares in exchange, the gain to be rolled over will be determined by the fraction £100,000/£100,000, i.e., one hundred per cent. As such, if the gain on the transfer is £65,000, the owner's deductible base cost on any future disposal of the shares will be £35,000, not £100,000, to take into account the original rolled-over gain of £65,000.

However, if the consideration is made up of a mixture of shares and cash or debentures, there will be a corresponding reduction in the amount of gain which is rolled over.

EXAMPLE

If the former owner transfers a business with assets worth £100,000 to the new company and receives £90,000 worth of shares and £10,000 worth of debentures in exchange, the gain which can be rolled over will be determined by the fraction £90,000/£100,000, i.e., nine-tenths. As such, if the gain on the transfer is £65,000, the rolled-over gain will be nine-tenths of this, i.e., £58,500. The owner's deductible base cost on any future disposal of the shares will be £41,500 (£100,000 – £58,500), not £35,000, as in the above example. The balance of the gain which has not been rolled over, i.e., £6,500, will be chargeable at the time of the business transfer. (Note that the annual exemption, if not used elsewhere, would render the whole of the balance of the gain exempt in this instance.)

It should be noted that the relief only applies to the former owner(s) of the business. The company's acquisition price of the assets will be their full market value at the date of the disposal.

30.3.2.2 The assets transferred to the company

Although these rules may appear complex at first sight, two simple requirements can be extracted from them. First, to claim the relief at all, the whole of the assets of the business (other than cash) at the date of incorporation must be transferred to the company, and secondly, the relief may only be claimed in full if the consideration received was entirely in the form of shares. Provided these conditions are satisfied, the effect of s. 162 is that the former owner acquires the shares at a value equal to his original acquisition price of the assets that have just been transferred to the company, so tax is only paid when they are later sold or given away. Since s. 162 relief can be obtained so easily by following these rules, it may seem strange that a number of traders choose not to take advantage of the relief and actually retain ownership of certain assets which they subsequently allow the new company to use (whilst still transferring the bulk of the business assets to the new company). There is, however, a good reason for this, which is to avoid the 'double capital gains tax charge', which is a problem where companies own appreciating assets, such as land or buildings. If a company owns such an asset and disposes of it realising a gain, the company will pay corporation tax on that gain. The post-tax gain will then increase the value of the company's assets, which in turn has the effect of increasing the value of the shares. This will result in the shareholder making an increased gain, and so paying more capital gains tax, on a later disposal of the shares. Retaining the asset in the former owner's hands ensures that there is only one capital gains tax charge if the asset is disposed of. It may also produce a stamp duty saving (see **30.5**).

30.3.2.3 Method of payment for assets

Even if HMRC is convinced that all the assets comprised in the business have been transferred, the relief can only be claimed in full if the company 'pays' for the assets in shares. As has already been explained, if the consideration is wholly or partly in debentures and/or cash the roll-over relief is wholly or partly denied to the former owner.

It is much more common, however, for the former owner to be paid in shares and debentures (the reason being that, as a shell, the company will have no cash with which to make the purchase). Debentures have advantages for both the holder (in the form of security of both capital and income) and the company (in the form of a pre-tax deduction in respect of the interest payments), and these advantages may compensate the former owner for partial loss of capital gains tax relief. It should be remembered that receiving part of the consideration in debentures means a proportionate part of the gain is taxable, but this taxable gain could be reduced or wiped out by the annual exemption. This has the attraction of reducing any future taxable gain and also of ensuring that the owner does not lose the benefit of the annual exemption for the year of incorporation.

30.3.3 Relief for gifts of business assets (s. 165 TCGA 1992)

Section 165 gives 'hold-over' relief where an asset used by the trader in his trade, profession or vocation is transferred to a company, provided the transaction is not a bargain at arm's length. This means that if the asset is 'sold' at an undervalue, or even given to the company the trader and the company can elect that the company acquires the asset for a consideration equal to the trader's acquisition cost (if there is an outright gift) or the sale price (if there is a sale at an undervalue). The effect of the relief is to postpone the payment of tax until the asset is disposed of, when the *company* will be liable to pay the tax, not the trader

In contrast to the relief under s. 162 TCGA 1992, this relief operates even if not all assets are transferred simultaneously. It does, therefore, have the advantage of flexibility.

30.3.4 To retain or not to retain

It will be seen that there is no simple answer to the question of whether or not to retain assets. However, a number of matters can be borne in mind:

(a) The choice to retain an asset will result in the denial of relief under s. 162 TCGA 1992. The other possible relief under s. 165 TCGA 1992 will, however, still be available for other assets which are transferred. It should be remembered that this relief, in effect, puts the gain into the hands of the company.

(b) If the intention is that an appreciating asset is to be disposed of in the near future and replaced, then either the proprietor or the company may still be entitled to roll-over relief under s. 152 TCGA 1992.

(c) If the intention is that an appreciating asset is to be disposed of and *not* replaced, then which party is to realise the gain requires careful consideration. The proprietor, as an individual, is subject to CGT at 18% or 28% (see **22.2.5**). The company will pay at an effective rate of between 20% and 23%, depending on its profits, but may also claim indexation allowance. Therefore, the use of either s. 162 or s. 165 to first put the asset into the hands of the company may produce an immediate benefit. If, however, the proprietor has accumulated capital losses or is entitled to entrepreneurs' relief (see **22.2.15**), it may be sensible for him to realise the gain.

(d) The prospect of a double charge to tax may be more imagined than real, especially if the intention is that the proprietor will retain the shares for several years. Also, to substitute a single asset for a number of shares provides greater scope for tax planning as an asset will normally have to be sold *in toto*, whereas fractions of a shareholding can be disposed of over a period of time. Therefore, the use of s. 162 relief may produce a number of benefits in this regard.

(e) Stamp duty will play an important part in the decision. The retention of assets or their transfer for nil consideration, so as to claim s. 165 relief, will ease the stamp duty burden. However, a balance has to be struck between this and capital gains tax to ensure the best saving for the owner. Stamp duty is considered further at **30.5**.

30.4 VAT

If the trader is registered for VAT, VAT may be chargeable on the transfer of the assets unless the business is transferred as a going concern (s. 33 Value Added Tax Act 1983). Any decision to retain assets in the hands of the proprietor for reasons explained above may, of course, prejudice the availability of this exemption.

30.5 Stamp duty/stamp duty land tax

30.5.1 Introduction

The purchaser of certain assets, in this case, the newly formed company, should always consider whether or not such a purchase triggers a charge to stamp duty or stamp duty land tax. A limited number of transactions need to be considered as follows.

(a) *Stamp duty*

The transfer of shares and certain transactions involving partners and partnership property are subject to stamp duty.

(b) *Stamp duty land tax*

Transactions involving land and real property (both freehold and leasehold) are subject to stamp duty land tax.

As regards the incorporation of a business, *stamp duty* is, therefore, irrelevant. No existing shares in the newly-formed company are being transferred; there is simply an allotment of them to the proprietor. However, as most transactions are likely to involve a property element, *stamp duty land tax* will have to be looked at.

30.5.2 Stamp duty land tax

Stamp duty land tax (SDLT) applies to the acquisition of both freehold and leasehold interests in land. Therefore, the transfer of the property of the business to the new company may attract SDLT.

Unlike stamp duty, SDLT is not a charge on documents, but is a charge on transactions. As such, within 30 days of the completion of the relevant transaction, a land transaction return (form SDLT 1) must be completed and sent to HMRC together with any SDLT payable. In return, the company will receive a certificate of evidence of the same. Without this, title to the property cannot be registered.

30.5.3 The stamp duty land tax rates

The amount of stamp duty land tax payable is *ad valorem* that is, based on the value of the property interest transferred. In respect of the purchase of a freehold interest in business property, SDLT rates are as follows:

Purchase price	SDLT rate
Up to £150,000	0%
£150,001 to £250,000	1%
£250,001 to £500,000	3%
Over £500,000	4%

In respect of the grant or assignment of a leasehold interest in business property, SDLT has to be calculated both on the rent payable and any other consideration, most likely any premium. It is beyond the scope of this work to consider the detail of these complex calculations. However, by way of brief summation, the greater the rent payable and the longer the term of the lease, the larger the SDLT burden.

30.6 Subsidiary matters

The tax matters already dealt with will, of course, be important to the former owner but there are a number of other points that must not be overlooked.

30.6.1 The transfer and employment law

Historically, the general rule was that the transfer of the business terminated the contracts of employment of all the employees and, if common law and statutory claims against the business owner were to be avoided, the employees had to be notified of the transfer and offered employment with the new company on the same, or suitable, terms before the transfer took place. However, since the introduction of the Transfer of Undertakings (Protection of Employment) Regulations in 1981 (SI 1981/794) and their replacement in 2006 by the Transfer of Undertakings (Protection of Employment) Regulations 2006 (SI 2006/246), this has no longer been the case. Regulation 4(1) of the 2006 Regulations provides that a 'relevant transfer' shall not terminate a person's contract of employment and the contract shall have the effect after the transfer as if it had originally been made between the employee and the transferee. (A 'relevant transfer' is defined in regulation 3(1) as including 'a transfer of an undertaking, business or part of an undertaking or business situated immediately before the transfer in the United Kingdom where there is a transfer of an economic entity which retains its identity'.) Thus, if a business is transferred to a company, the employees are treated as if their contracts had originally been made with the new company, which takes over all the trader's rights, powers, duties, and liabilities under the employment contracts. Therefore, the employee's period of continuous employment is preserved, as are any pre-existing rights against the old employer for breach of contract or dismissal. As a result, the new company could be faced with liability for a dismissal arising from the previous proprietor's breach. Of course, in this context, the ultimate consequence for the proprietor/company is the same; it is a technical issue for the ex-employee's advisors to ensure that the correct person is proceeded against.

While these regulations do not prevent an employee bringing a claim against the trader if there is a substantial change made in his working conditions, no action can be brought simply because the identity of the employer has changed, unless the employee shows the change to be significant and to his detriment.

Regulation 5 does not enable the fact of the transfer to be kept from the employees. Regulation 10 imposes an obligation on the transferor to inform and consult with appointed employee representatives.

30.6.2 The transfer and company law

In addition to the matters that always arise on the formation of a new company, one special problem particularly relevant to this kind of transfer must be considered. On the assumption that the transferor of the business will also be a director of the new company, the consent of the members in general meeting will almost certainly be needed to the purchase by the company of the business. Section 190 CA 2006 requires such consent to be obtained if a director sells to (or buys from) the company a non-cash asset or assets of the 'requisite value', which means assets worth £100,000 or representing at least 10% of the company's assets (subject to a minimum value of £5,000). If the consent is not obtained, the transaction is voidable at the instance of the company and the director will have to account to the company for any profit made and indemnify it for any loss or damages arising. In order to obtain the necessary consent, a general meeting of the company will have to be held immediately after incorporation and before the transfer takes place.

Furthermore, the transferor must make sure that the new company's name is displayed in all relevant places, e.g., websites, registered office, place of business, stationery, and other publications and that its letters, order forms, and websites contain the required information, i.e., country of registration, registered office, and registered number.

30.6.3 The transfer and other miscellaneous matters

Further practical points to be dealt with include the following:

(a) The local inspector of taxes must be notified that there is a new employer for PAYE purposes as well as there being a new company liable to corporation tax.

(b) If the business's turnover exceeds the threshold for VAT registration (see **24.2**), its VAT registration must be cancelled and the company must apply to have itself registered. In order to ensure there is no gap in the VAT registration it is advisable to cancel the old one after the company's registration has been confirmed.

(c) The consent of a landlord to the assignment of a lease must be obtained. If the new company is also taking over responsibility for hire-purchase contracts, the consent of the finance house must be obtained.

(d) The former owner can bring his personal liability to existing creditors to an end by entering into a contract of 'novation'. However, the consent of the creditors is required. As a counterpoint to this, the owner may still be asked to guarantee liabilities which have been assumed by the new company, for example, indebtedness to a bank and those under a lease.

(e) The company must take out appropriate insurance cover.

online resource centre

For further resources and online chapters please visit the Online Resource Centre at www.oxfordtextbooks.co.uk/orc/business13_14/.

31

A debenture document

This chapter covers the following topics:

31.1 Introduction

In this chapter we will look briefly at some of the terms which might be found in a debenture document. Before reading this chapter you will find it useful to read **Chapter 11** again.

Debentures vary enormously. We will be looking at one type of debenture only; that is, a debenture which is given by a company in return for a loan by a bank. This type of debenture will contain different provisions from a debenture which is designed to secure a long-term loan from people who want to invest money in a company but who prefer a fixed return rather than the possibility of a variable dividend which would be produced by an issue of shares.

A debenture is likely to contain clauses dealing with the following matters:

(a) the amount of the loan (which may be fixed or variable);

(b) a promise by the company that it will repay the loan on a fixed date and/or on the happening of certain events;

(c) a promise by the company that it will pay interest at a fixed or variable rate;

(d) a charge or charges over some or all of the company's assets—this may include floating as well as fixed charges;

(e) clauses designed to protect the position of the lender (e.g., by giving the lender power to appoint a receiver).

In the rest of this chapter we have given examples of the sort of clauses which may be found in debentures of this type. They are not taken from the debenture of any particular bank. They are provided for the purposes of illustration only so that students may get an idea of what the different clauses in the debenture are for. In practice those who draft debentures for banks will (quite rightly) wish to cover every possible contingency in their debentures. The clauses which they draft are, therefore, usually much fuller than the illustrations given below.

31.2 Terms relating to repayment and interest

The debenture will include a promise by the company that it will repay to the bank the amount which is lent to it. Frequently the debenture will relate to any money which the company owes to the bank. In this case the debenture is mainly designed to secure the repayment of an overdraft by the company. The repayment clause will then refer to something along the lines of 'all monies or other liabilities actual or contingent now or in the future owed by the company to the bank on any account or for which the company may for any reason be or become liable to the bank now or in the future'. Usually provision is made for payment 'on demand', i.e., as soon as the bank asks for it.

If none of the money secured by the debenture consists of a long-term loan (so that the sums secured all relate to variable amounts such as overdraft, interest, and bank charges) there will often be a promise to pay a fixed small amount. The clause might, for example, include a term under which the company 'covenants to pay to the bank the sum of one pound (£1) on demand'. Such a provision ensures that the agreement between the company and the bank is not discharged if the company temporarily pays off its overdraft so that the bank temporarily is owed nothing.

There will be a promise to pay interest. In the case of the type of loan we are considering (i.e., a loan by a bank) this will usually be a promise to pay a variable rate of interest on any money outstanding from time to time. This clause could refer to a particular way in which interest is to be calculated (e.g., that it should be a certain number of percentage points above the bank's base rate from time to time). However, the more usual provision is to say that the interest is to be calculated 'in accordance with the bank's usual practice'. Provision may also be made for the rate to be agreed between the parties if possible. Such provisions might at first sight seem rather vague. However, the practice of banks in relation to various classes of loans can be determined objectively if it becomes necessary to do so. The bank is also protected by the fact that if the company does not pay the interest which it is asked to pay, the bank can always call in the whole loan. The company also has the right to redeem the loan by paying the bank, if it can afford to do so.

31.3 Terms relating to security

It is possible to have an unsecured debenture. However, the type of bank debenture which we are examining in this chapter is pointless unless security is given by the borrowing company to the bank. Before it will lend or allow an overdraft the bank will wish to be satisfied that the company is and is likely to remain solvent. Before it will lend or allow an overdraft the bank will also wish (in most cases) to be satisfied that the company's assets are sufficient security for the loan. This will require the bank to consider two matters:

(a) What is the value of the assets offered as security?

(b) Is the company free to give security over the assets?

Valuation is a question of fact. As far as security is concerned the bank will wish to know what other charges the company has already created over its assets. This information will be available from a company search (see the requirements as to registration in **Chapter 11** and as to searches in **Chapter 15**).

31.3.1 Mortgages and fixed charges

The first type of security which the bank will wish to consider is charges over the valuable assets of the company. A legal mortgage of any land which the company may own is likely to be viewed as the best security which the bank can take in most cases. This mortgage will be supplemented by a fixed charge over later acquired land (freehold and leasehold) which the company may acquire. This charge will be an equitable charge as a legal mortgage of land to be acquired in the future is not possible. The debenture will often also say that the bank can insist on the company executing a legal mortgage of any future acquired land once it is acquired and that the title deeds are to be deposited with the bank in the meantime. For most purposes a specific equitable charge is as good as a legal mortgage so this adds little to the bank's security.

The mortgage will require the company to insure the property and to keep it in a good state of repair.

The debenture will also usually provide for security by way of fixed charge over any shares which the company owns in other companies.

The debenture will also frequently contain a fixed charge over the company's goodwill. This is not necessarily a very valuable security as the goodwill is itself often of rather questionable value, especially as the security is only likely to be enforced if the company is in financial difficulties.

Modern debentures often contain a fixed charge over 'the book debts and other debts of the company'. Book debts are the sums owed to the company by, for example, its customers. In effect the fixed charge over book debts says that the bank is entitled to collect the money due to the company in order to discharge the company's own debt to the bank. The law recognises that such a charge is possible but there are technical problems regarding the charge as a fixed charge if the company is free to deal with its book debts as it wishes. The debenture will, therefore, provide that when payment of the debts is received by the company the money must be paid into the company's account at the bank and that the company is not to be free to assign or otherwise deal with its debts.

In light of the decisions of the Privy Council in *Agnew v IRC* [2001] 2 BCLC 188 and the House of Lords in *Re Spectrum Plus Ltd: National Westminster Bank plc v Spectrum Plus Ltd* [2005] 2 BCLC 269, it is highly questionable if a fixed charge over book debts can ever be achieved because of the level of restraint and monitoring required to be exercised by the chargeholder over the realisation of book debts.

Finally, the bank will also look to take a fixed charge over any other assets of the company which are permanent in nature, for example, large items of machinery. Because of the restrictions on the use and sale of assets owned by the borrower that mortgages and fixed charges impose, they are unsuitable security over assets of a transient nature, for example, vehicles and stock. The more suitable security in relation to these assets is a floating charge, which will be discussed next.

31.3.2 Floating charges

As we saw in **Chapter 11** a company can create a floating charge over any of its assets. This is a charge which allows the company to deal with the assets even though they are the subject of the charge. This has the benefit of giving the company flexibility while at the same time giving the bank some sort of security. The problem from the bank's point of view is that the charge is of uncertain value until the security crystallises. In order to reduce this problem it is usual to provide that the company is not free to sell the whole of its undertaking without the consent of the bank. There will also be provision stating that the bank can give notice of crystallisation. This is a clause which says that the bank may 'give notice to the company converting the floating security into a fixed charge in relation to any assets specified in the notice'.

The company will normally be prohibited from creating any later charge ranking in priority to the floating charge. Such a provision is necessary as without it the company is free to charge the floating charge assets by way of specific charge. This does not invalidate the floating charge but clearly if the assets are now subject to a fixed charge which will take priority, the value of the floating charge as a security is greatly reduced.

The company will usually also be required to insure the floating charge property.

31.4 Clauses designed to give the lender further protection

31.4.1 Personal guarantees

If the bank is not satisfied with the security which the company can provide, it may well require personal guarantees from the directors of the company, in addition to the security given by the company.

31.4.2 Appointment of a receiver

One of the clauses which will be contained in the debenture will allow the bank to appoint a receiver. (Note that in respect of most floating charges created on or after 15 September 2003, as a result of the Enterprise Act 2002, administrative receivers (see **Chapter 26**) may no longer be appointed.) The function of the receiver is to realise assets for the bank, pay it off, and then return the company to the directors. In practice the company may well be wound up after the receivership as the receiver will have withdrawn many of the assets of the company. The powers and duties of a receiver are dealt with in **Chapter 26**.

online resource centre

For further resources and online chapters please visit the Online Resource Centre at www.oxfordtextbooks.co.uk/orc/business13_14/.

32 Shareholders' agreements

This chapter covers the following topics:

32.1 Introduction

In this chapter we will look at shareholders' agreements. These are agreements between shareholders about how their company should be run. The company is also sometimes joined as a party in the agreement so that it too will be bound by the terms (the company cannot, however, override its statutory powers in this way). In particular they are likely to contain terms under which the shareholders agree how they will vote on various issues which may be raised at company meetings. For example, each shareholder might agree to support the re-election of the other shareholders as directors.

Shareholders' agreements are only likely to be effective in the case of companies with a small number of shareholders. If an agreement about how members will vote is to be effective it must usually be made by at least enough members of the company to ensure that a majority of the votes at any meeting will be cast in accordance with the agreement. If there are many members it will be difficult to get a large number of them to enter into a contract. Remember also that the contract (like any other contract) is only enforceable by and against those who are parties to it, so the effectiveness of the agreement is much reduced if a large number of members are not party to it.

32.2 Advantages of a shareholders' agreement

32.2.1 Secrecy

The agreement, unlike the articles, is not open to inspection by the public.

32.2.2 Protection of interests

A shareholders' agreement can protect the interests of some of the members in ways which cannot be easily achieved by the articles. In particular, unless the company provides for different classes of shares, all the shareholders have to be treated alike. If this is not what is desired then it may be much simpler to give one shareholder exceptional rights in a shareholders' agreement. For example, it may be intended that one person (perhaps the founder of the company) should remain a director throughout his life. This is quite difficult to achieve in the articles because the shareholders have a statutory right to remove a director from office. Added voting rights may effectively give a director an invulnerable position (see, for example, *Bushell v Faith* at **9.8.1.4**) but these rights will be attached to the shares and so will pass to the director's successors in title unless very cumbersome arrangements are made.

A shareholders' agreement can achieve this very simply if the shareholders agree to vote for X each time his re-election as a director is in issue and to vote against any resolution to remove him from office.

32.2.3 Difficulties of enforcing articles

Although the articles of a company are deemed to be a contract between the company and its members, many cases have decided that this does not mean that each individual member is entitled to enforce compliance with every term of the articles. Generally only those terms which relate to the membership rights of the shareholder can be enforced. If the terms are included in a shareholders' agreement then any party to the agreement can enforce it in full. Furthermore a shareholders' agreement can be enforced simply by means of an action by one shareholder against another. If a shareholder seeks to enforce a term in the articles he will normally have to sue in a representative capacity.

32.2.4 Veto

A shareholders' agreement may give each individual party to it a veto over any proposal which is contrary to the terms of the agreement. In this way a shareholder may be protected even though he only has a small number of shares. However, such agreements should not be lightly entered into. Each shareholder will wish to have a veto against any decisions which he thinks are inappropriate, but he should remember that the other parties will also have the same veto powers (unless he is able to negotiate them for himself alone).

32.3 Drafting a shareholders' agreement

The uses to which shareholders' agreements are put and consequently the clauses which are included in them vary greatly depending on the circumstances which lead to the particular agreement. In this paragraph we will examine some of the main types of provision which may be included.

32.3.1 Appointment of directors and service contracts

The agreement will frequently require all the parties to the agreement to vote in favour of any resolution which reappoints any of them to be a director of the company. It should then also include a term requiring each party to the agreement to vote against any resolution for the removal of any of the parties from the office of director. If it is decided to include such terms, then it may also be appropriate to consider whether there should be any time limit; for example, it might be for a fixed period of time, or it might only apply until each director reaches a specified age.

This clause might also provide for remuneration of the directors and approval of their service contracts for specified or indefinite periods exceeding five years.

32.3.2 Approval for policy decisions

The articles of almost all companies provide that business decisions are to be taken by the directors. It would usually be quite inappropriate for articles to provide that the shareholders are to have power to run the company's business. However, if there are particular issues which the shareholders have agreed to as matters of policy, these could be included in a shareholders' agreement. The agreement might, for example, require the agreement of the parties before any new ventures could be undertaken by the company, or before the company could expand the area of its operation. This would be reinforced by an agreement that the parties would vote against any attempt to circumvent such an agreement, and would take whatever steps they could to prevent these things from happening without such approval.

32.3.3 Issue of shares and protection of voting rights

One of the main purposes for which a shareholders' agreement may be used is to protect the shareholders from 'watering' of their interests. This occurs where new shares are issued and a shareholder does not get some of the shares. For example if a shareholder now has 40% of the 1,000 shares which have been issued, he has enough shares to block a special resolution. If a further 1,000 shares were issued and he got none of them then his interest would be reduced to 20% and so (unless the voting rights were changed) he would lose the power to block a special resolution. To prevent this from happening pre-emption rights may be included in the shareholders' agreement.

The considerations here are similar to those in relation to pre-emption rights contained in the articles of a company which we considered in **Chapter 14** (and remember that there are also statutory pre-emption rights in limited circumstances; see **11.2.4.3**). In some cases it may be more appropriate to include pre-emption rights in a shareholders' agreement. This would be so, for example, if the shareholders wished to keep the existence of the pre-emption rights secret or if they were to apply only to some of the shareholders.

An issue of debentures or other borrowing by the company will not affect the powers of the shareholders to vote in respect of their shares. However, the effect of borrowing will be to reduce the amount of profit available for potential dividend payments to the shareholders. It may, therefore, be appropriate for the clause to require the approval of the parties for borrowing above a certain figure.

A clause in a shareholders' agreement could be drafted so as to require approval of the parties to the agreement for any issue of shares or other reorganisation of capital. This would go further than a simple pre-emption right as it would effectively give the parties a right to veto issue of shares, not just a right to insist on taking some of the shares themselves. Alternatively the clause could provide that the existing shareholders would be bound to make further investment in certain circumstances specified in the clause. Obviously a shareholder should not undertake such an obligation lightly in case he does not have the resources to meet his obligation when it arises.

32.3.4 Withdrawal from the company

One of the principal features of company law is that a shareholder (unlike a partner in a partnership) is not normally allowed to withdraw his investment. This is the idea of maintenance of capital which we saw in **Chapter 11** (we also saw the limited exceptions in **Chapter 12** under which a company can redeem or buy back its own shares). A shareholders' agreement can be used to allow a shareholder an opportunity to leave the company and to take out his capital. For example, the agreement will often include a clause requiring a shareholder to offer his shares to the other members pro rata if he wishes to sell. As in the case of a pre-emption right on transfer contained in the articles (see **Chapter 14**), this clause will contain valuation provisions which will be designed to ensure fairness to both the selling member and the buying member.

A simple pre-emption right will not, however, ensure that the shareholder can sell his shares. He must offer them to the other members but they may not wish to buy. In this case the member is unlikely to be able to sell to an outsider, as there is likely to be a restriction on the right to transfer either in the articles or in the shareholders' agreement. It is possible to include a term whereby the shareholder who wishes to get out of the company has a right to insist that the other members of the company will buy his shares. Such a clause should only be entered into if the finances of the potential purchasers are likely to be strong enough to be able to comply with the agreement.

32.3.5 Payment of dividends

Although it is not likely to be one of the commonest clauses to be found in a shareholders' agreement, it is possible to include a term which will either require the payment of dividends or which will restrict the payment of dividends. A clause which purported to require payment of dividends other than out of accumulated realised profits (after deduction of accumulated realised losses) would be unenforceable as such payments would be illegal.

32.3.6 Restrictive covenants

Restrictive covenants may be included in a shareholders' agreement. This sort of term might be appropriate where a shareholder has brought particular expertise to the company and the other shareholders wish to preserve that expertise for the company. If such a clause is included it is likely also to appear in any service contract which the shareholder has with the company (for example where he is a director as well as a shareholder). Restrictive covenants are void on grounds of public policy unless they are reasonable in area and time.

32.3.7 An arbitration clause

Like many commercial agreements the shareholders' agreement will often include an arbitration clause so that any disputes which arise out of it can be resolved without the need for action in the courts.

32.4 Legal limits on the use of shareholders' agreements

32.4.1 Power to alter the articles

A company has a statutory power to alter its articles by special resolution. A shareholders' agreement cannot take this right away. However, it can provide that members are personally in breach of contract if they vote in favour of an alteration which is contrary to the terms of the agreement: see for example, *Russell v Northern Bank Development Corporation* [1992] 1 WLR 588.

32.4.2 Directors' duties

The directors of a company have a fiduciary duty to the company. A shareholders' agreement could not lawfully permit the directors to breach this fiduciary duty. Furthermore directors have a number of duties which are of a public nature (particularly in relation to insolvent companies). A shareholders' agreement could not authorise or direct the directors as to how they are to perform their functions. For example, a director would be liable for failure to make statutory returns to the Registrar of Companies even if his shareholders' agreement purported to require this. Similarly a director could not absolve himself from liability for wrongful trading on the basis of a shareholders' agreement.

32.5 Enforcing the agreement

A shareholders' agreement is a contract. Each party provides consideration by agreeing to abide by the terms of the agreement. It follows from this that if the agreement is broken, the other parties can claim damages. The agreement can also be enforced by an injunction which requires a shareholder who is a party to it not to vote in a way contrary to the terms of the agreement. It may also be enforced by a positive injunction requiring a shareholder who is a party to it to vote in accordance with its provisions.

online resource centre

For further resources and online chapters please visit the Online Resource Centre at www.oxfordtextbooks.co.uk/orc/business13_14/.

Index

J

L

T